Information Economics

Information is a magic commodity: easy to spread, hard to control but crucial to economic decisions. Important economic phenomena, like markets, rating agencies, banking or other forms of financial intermediation can be understood as the resourceful use of information. The failure of information transmission can cause severe problems such as market breakdowns or financial bubbles. This new text book by Urs Birchler and Monika Bütler is an introduction to the study of how information affects economic relations. The authors provide a narrative treatment of the more formal concepts of Information Economics, using easy to understand and lively illustrations from film and literature and nutshell examples.

Birchler and Bütler adopt three separate approaches for explaining the concepts. The book first covers the economics of information in a 'man versus nature' context, explaining basic concepts like rational updating or the value of information. Then in a 'man versus man' setting, Birchler and Bütler describe strategic issues in the use of information: the make-buy-or-copy decision, the working and failure of markets and the important role of outguessing each other in a macroeconomic context. The book also looks at the classical problems of asymmetrical information, optimal contracts, and incentives. It closes with a 'man versus himself' perspective, focusing on information management within the individual.

The concepts covered in this book cast light on many issues from genetic testing to life insurance and pensions to banking and finance and would be of great interest for both undergraduate and postgraduate students interested in information and its role in individual decision making, markets, financial disturbances, and macroeconomics. This is an ideal textbook for students seeking a way in to understanding the key concepts in this field.

Urs Birchler is a Director at the Swiss National Bank and a former member of the Basel Committee on Banking Supervision. He has taught at the universities of Zurich, Berne, St. Gallen and Leipzig.

Monika Bütler is Professor of Economics and Public Policy at St. Gallen University, CESifo Fellow and CEPR affiliate.

Routledge advanced texts in economics and finance

Financial Econometrics
Peijie Wang

Macroeconomics for Developing Countries (2nd edition)
Raghbendra Jha

Advanced Mathematical Economics
Rakesh Vohra

Advanced Econometric Theory
John S. Chipman

Understanding Macroeconomic Theory
John M. Barron, Bradley T. Ewing and Gerald J. Lynch

Regional Economics
Roberta Capello

Mathematical Finance
Core theory, problems and statistical algorithms
Nikolai Dokuchaev

Applied Health Economics
Andrew M. Jones, Nigel Rice, Teresa Bago d'Uva and Silvia Balia

Information Economics
Urs Birchler and Monika Bütler

Information Economics

Urs Birchler and Monika Bütler

Routledge
Taylor & Francis Group

LONDON AND NEW YORK

First published 2007
by Routledge
2 Park Square, Milton Park, Abingdon, Oxon, OX14 4RN

Simultaneously published in the USA and Canada
by Routledge
270 Madison Ave, New York NY 10016

*Routledge is an imprint of the Taylor & Francis Group,
an informa business*

Transferred to digital printing 2010

© 2007 Urs Birchler and Monika Bütler

Cover Design: Sarah Eva Birchler

Typeset in Times New Roman by
Newgen Imaging Systems (P) Ltd, Chennai, India

British Library Cataloguing in Publication Data
A catalogue record for this book is available
from the British Library

Library of Congress Cataloging in Publication Data
Birchler, Urs W.
    Information economics / Urs Birchler and Monika Bütler.
        p.cm. – (Routledge advanced texts in economics and finance)
    Includes bibliographical references and index.
        1. Economics–Decision making. 2. Information technology–Economic
aspects. 3. Information resources–Economic aspects. I. Bütler, Monika.
II. Title.

HB74.2.B57 2007
303.48′33–dc22   2006102041

ISBN: 978-0-415-37346-3 (hbk)
ISBN: 978-0-415-37345-6 (pbk)
ISBN: 978-0-203-94655-8 (ebk)

To Peter and Eugen

TROUBLED TIMES

War and Society

A series edited by S. P. Reyna and R. E. Downs

Volume 1
Feuding and Warfare: Selected Works of Keith F. Otterbein

Volume 2
Studying War: Anthropological Perspectives
Edited by S. P. Reyna and R. E. Downs

Volume 3
Troubled Times: Violence and Warfare in the Past
Edited by Debra L. Martin and David W. Frayer

Volume 4
Roots of Violence: A History of War in Chad
Mario J. Azevedo

This book is part of a series. The publisher will accept continuation orders which may be cancelled at any time and which provide for automatic billing and shipping of each title in the series upon publication. Please write for details.

TROUBLED TIMES

Violence and Warfare in the Past

Edited by

Debra L. Martin
*Hampshire College
Amherst, Massachusetts*

and

David W. Frayer
*University of Kansas
Lawrence, Kansas*

Routledge
Taylor & Francis Group
New York   London

Published in 1997 by
CRC Press
Taylor & Francis Group
6000 Broken Sound Parkway NW, Suite 300
Boca Raton, FL 33487-2742

© 1997 by Taylor & Francis Group, LLC
CRC Press is an imprint of Taylor & Francis Group

No claim to original U.S. Government works
Print

International Standard Book Number-10: 90-5699-534-0 (Softcover)
International Standard Book Number-13: 978-90-5699-534-8 (Softcover)

Cover: Healed nasal bone fractures in the cranium of a modern American in the collection of the Department of Anthropology, University of California, Santa Barbara.

Library of Congress Cataloging-in-Publication Data

Catalog record is available from the Library of Congress

Visit the Taylor & Francis Web site at
http://www.taylorandfrancis.com

and the CRC Press Web site at
http://www.crcpress.com

To all those who have suffered at the hands of others

CONTENTS

Introduction to the Series ix

Foreword xi

Introduction xiii

List of Contributors xxiii

ONE   Violence in the Ethnographic Record:
Results of Cross-Cultural Research
on War and Aggression
Carol R. Ember and Melvin Ember 1

TWO   Violence Against Women: Raiding and
Abduction in Prehistoric Michigan
Richard G. Wilkinson 21

THREE   Violence Against Women in the
La Plata River Valley (A.D. 1000–1300)
Debra L. Martin 45

FOUR   Patterns of Violence in Prehistoric
Hunter-gatherer Societies of Coastal
Southern California
Patricia M. Lambert 77

FIVE   Violence and Gender in Early Italy
John Robb 111

SIX   Wife Beating, Boxing, and Broken Noses:
Skeletal Evidence for the Cultural
Patterning of Violence
Phillip L. Walker 145

SEVEN   Ofnet: Evidence for a Mesolithic Massacre
David W. Frayer 181

EIGHT Evidence for Human Sacrifice, Bone
Modification and Cannibalism
in Ancient México
Carmen Ma. Pijoan and
Josefina Mansilla Lory 217

NINE Osteological Indications of Warfare in the
Archaic period of the Western
Tennessee Valley
Maria Ostendorf Smith 241

TEN The Evolution of Northwest Coast Warfare
Herbert D. G. Maschner 267

ELEVEN Frontier Warfare in the Early Neolithic
Lawrence H. Keeley 303

TWELVE Violence and War in Prehistory
R. Brian Ferguson 321

Index 357

INTRODUCTION TO THE SERIES

The *War and Society* book series fosters studies of organized violence and its consequences in all forms of society, from deep in the past until the present. It encourages different intellectual traditions from different disciplines. Its goal is to expand theoretical understanding of the causes and effects of war, thereby to provide intellectual tools for constructing a more peaceful world.

FOREWORD

Troubled Times: Violence and Warfare in the Past is a work of importance. For well over two millennia — from Herodotus to Hobbes and
Rousseau and on to Lorenz — humans have speculated about the
murders and mayhems of those who lived beyond history; and that
has been the problem. Discussion of prehistoric violence has been
largely in the realm of fantasy not evidence. The chapters that
comprise this volume offer the most complete compilation of evidence to date concerning various forms of violence in different
prehistoric societies.

The possibility of more rigorous conclusions exists now that there
is some evidence. Two issues, however, will need to be addressed to
further this rigor. The first concerns the representativeness of the
violences reported. Were they the common indignities of everyday
life or the rarities of exceptional circumstances? One suspects that
there will be different responses, and debates over the responses, to
this question. The second issue has to do with theory, and the *sine qua
non* of theory, conceptualization of observation. For example, do
theorists wish to include all violence for which there is some indication of organization within the rubric of "war"? One suspects that
here too there will be argument. But — and this is the crucial point
— thanks to the considerable labors of the editors of this book, such
controversy will be guided to a greater degree by evidence.

S. P. Reyna
University of New Hampshire
Durham

INTRODUCTION

Violence is an everyday occurrence in the modern world. In all forms of the media we are constantly reminded about the likelihood of being mugged, assaulted or murdered. Depending on where one is in the world at any given time, warfare is only a missile away, death is within a sniper's sights, and danger of all sorts is potentially around any corner. In short, at many different levels, people have come to expect violence as part of everyday "civilized" life. Yet, despite contemporary experiences/expectations about violence, many lay people and academics are surprised to learn that the troubled times of the present extend into the distant past, where it is often assumed the quality of life was better and interpersonal relations were more peaceful. As reviewed in the chapters of this volume, this romantic conception of the past does not accord well with osteological and archaeological data about ancient groups from the Americas and Europe. These articles[1] present and critically evaluate evidence for violence focusing on hunter-gatherer to state societies from the New and Old Worlds. Drawn from the perspective of cross-cultural analysis, archaeological data and skeletal remains, examples include evidence for domestic violence, homicide, ritualized combat, warfare, cannibalism and human sacrifice.

There are numerous theoretical models that seek to explain conflict and violence within preindustrial societies (e.g., Knauft 1987, 1991; Ross 1992), but much of the data for these models involve interferences from ethnographic sources rather than an evaluation or survey of the actual physical (archaeological or osteological) evidence. Most of the papers in this book take the opposite approach, steering away from model building and concentrating on osteological data in the form of identifiable trauma on human remains and archaeological data on fortifications and other defensive aspects of settlements. These form the core of the book which aims to show how violence and warfare are documented in skeletal and archaeological data. How these may relate to evolutionary patterns, environmental changes, subsistence and demographic stress, gender conflicts,

---

[1] These papers were first presented at the American Anthropology Association meetings in 1992 in Washington DC as part of an organized session on violence in ancient times.

changes in weapon systems, and political/ideological factors are considered. The diverse studies presented in the chapters indicate that violence, for whatever cause(s), was present in ancient times, and that in many respects, people lived in troubled times then as they do now.

Reconstruction of behavior in prehistoric societies is a challenging task, complicated by the fact that the only direct evidence for violence is encoded in the osteological and archaeological record, with the exception of art which is very unevenly represented and preserved. These studies will show that data recovered from the archaeological record can be used to infer actions of people collectively and individually, and physical evidence of trauma can be "read" from osteological analysis. While some inferences are more straightforward than others, it is difficult to unravel the reasons or motivations that inspired or led to specific acts of violence. Just as modern forensic investigations are complicated interpretations of prior events, interpretation of prehistoric data requires careful analysis to document the extent and patterning of evidence for conflict and violence. Similarly, data derived from the archaeological record require cautious interpretations from a number of different sources and observations. Whatever the shortcomings and problems with these bio-archaeological data, the preservation on the bones of indications of violence or in the ground of defensive structures or offensive artifacts constitutes material testimony of violence (and sometimes warfare) in past human groups.

While some studies on violence in past societies have focused on documentation of violence related to warfare (e.g., Bamforth, 1994; Blakely and Mathews 1990; Milner et al. 1991), most of the articles in this collection focus on non-war violence. The array of "crimes" encompasses a class of human behavior difficult to precisely define, in part because the acts are found in a number of contexts that could be interpreted in a variety of ways. In modern terms, such acts and behaviors include homicide, ritualized combat, hand-to-hand fighting, scalping, sacrifice, cannibalism, domestic abuse and any number of other violent acts that are part of conflict and strife, oppression and abuse. Further removed but also telling demonstrations about the level of violence in a prehistoric group can be seen in the defensive aspects of its settlement and changes over time in selecting locations for establishing villages. Clearly, these widely varying evidences for violence play out in a number of ways, all culturally mediated and tempered by personal and cultural perspective. Thus, attempting to provide a single definition of violence, particularly non-war violence, or to judge the meaning of these actions across temporally and culturally diverse human groups would be a task unsatisfying to many.

We have attempted to avoid these problems and included here studies on warfare and other kinds of non-war violence from varying time periods and geographic settings. Each is aimed at documenting violence rather than theorizing about its causes. On the whole, these studies are bioarchaeological in perspective in that each attempts, where possible, to integrate biological and archaeological data. We have also included two studies from the ethnographic perspective. In chapter one, Carol Ember and Melvin Ember focus on the prevalence of violence in a wide range of cultures with some inferences about its causes; in chapter twelve R. Brian Ferguson scrutinizes the kinds of archaeological data that can be used to infer warfare in the absence of osteological evidence. Overall, this collection of articles provides case studies for the identification of violent behavior in ancient populations, using examples from single episodes as well as examining trends and patterns over time.

The volume begins with a review of some aspects of violence and warfare in the ethnographic record by the Embers. This first essay sets the stage for many of the subsequent chapters in its demonstration that "war is almost ubiquitous in the ethnographic record," as is ethnographic testimony for interpersonal violence and homicide. As the Embers note, this magnitude of interpersonal violence and warfare is probably underestimated from ethnographic literature, given, most importantly, the forced pacification among native European colonizing groups on which the statistics are based. While some contributors to this collection would likely disagree with this statement, it seems probable that tabulations in the ethnographic record of violent behaviors, including war, in indigenous groups before the establishment of European colonization must be adjusted for forced pacification, which would have led to lowered rates in some colonial and postcolonial situations. The Embers show homicide and non-lethal interpersonal violence occur in moderate to high frequencies in 53% and 67%, respectively, of the groups in their sample. Equally important, the Embers note that warfare and violent behaviors occur across all subsistence categories, even if they are less common in foragers than food producers. Given the general propensity for violence divulged by the Embers' research and the time depth that the studies presented here review, it should come as no surprise that the evidence for violence is anything but rare in prehistory. None of this means that any authors in this book subscribe to a Hobbesian view of prehistory. Yet, it is intellectually and methodologically important to recognize that violence and warfare were important aspects in human prehistory and researchers should expect (rather than be surprised) to find indications of violence in osteological and archaeological situations.

In chapter two, Richard Wilkinson documents the osteological evidence for nonlethal, violent behavior in the Riviere aux Vase sample, a precontact horticultural group from southeastern Michigan. Contrary to expectations, he finds that females not males have a greater incidence of nonlethal violence represented by healed injuries of the forehead in frequencies four times that found in males. Based on accounts of early explorers and priests who lived among the likely descendants of these groups, Wilkinson effectively argues that the differential frequency between the sexes is not random, but is likely a manifestation of the abduction and forceful incorporation of women into the Riviere aux Vase group. Unfortunately, because of poor excavation techniques of the graveyard in the 1930s, he is unable to document differential burial patterns in the females to further support this hypothesis.

This is not the case in Debra Martin's review of data from the Four Corners region of the American Southwest (chapter three). Here, in sites more than 1000 miles away, but approximately the same time period (A.D. 1100) as Riviere aux Vase, she also finds greater frequency of nonlethal violence among adult females in the La Plata River Valley series. The women with trauma have about three times the cranial and postcranial injuries as males from the same sites and more cases of infection that likely resulted from nonlethal injuries. Because of better archaeological recovery, Martin is able to demonstrate that these injured females were interred differently from females and males with no signs of healed bodily trauma. Their haphazard placement in graves without grave good suggests they were members of an underclass, possibly foreign females who were incorporated into the La Plata River Valley pueblo societies. Martin is also able to make comparisons between two regions in the Southwest where lifestyles differed, and demonstrates that the more marginal groups of Black Mesa — who had poorer resources, more dispersed settlement, and generally lower health status — concomitantly had much lower telltale signs of nonlethal violence among women (and men).

In chapter four, Patricia Lambert's review of evidence for lethal (projectile wounds) and sublethal (healed blunt cranial fractures) injuries also finds ecological and demographic correlates to the frequency of violence. Studying skeletal material sampled over approximately 8000 years from the Santa Barbara Channel of Southern California, she shows that indications of physical violence increase to their highest levels during a period of ecological stress, brought about partly by greater population density and unstable (drought) environmental conditions. Her observations correlate well with the Embers' prediction from their Human Relations Area Files (HRAF) studies that violence and warfare increase in relationship to the occurrence (or likelihood) of unpredictable and uncontrollable natural calamities. The high frequencies of projectile and blunt force trauma in association with increased levels of nutritional stress are associated with increased population density, greater resource stress, and likely greater tension among the groups suffering through environmental degradation. Beyond these issues, Lambert shows that males are more likely to have nonlethal and lethal bone traumas spread over all adult age groups, while females are most susceptible to nonlethal blunt trauma during their reproductive years. These different frequency patterns along sex lines corroborate numerous other findings in this volume and underscore the importance of gender as a crucial variable in studies of prehistoric violence. Like others in this collection, Lambert also documents the occurrence of violence in American Indian populations in substantial frequencies well before European encroachment.

John Robb reviews his work with an Iron Age skeletal collection from Italy dating to about 300 B.C. in chapter five. He finds that sex is an important contributing variable to the likelihood of violence and trauma in this sample and that males have rates nearly five times those for females, especially in the later period of his sample. He suggests there are cultural attributes (as opposed to warfare) that explain this greater frequency of violence in male skeletons. Robb also extends his analysis to a diachronic evaluation of evidence for violence from the Italian Neolithic through the Iron Ages and develops methodological procedures for incorporating data on violence and trauma from a variety of sources. Based on this work, Robb concludes that physical evidence for violence is greatest in the Neolithic groups, which is at odds with the archaeological data indicating greater propensity of violence and warfare in the later periods. As skeletal samples become larger and data of the skeletal indicators of violence more refined in this long-range regional sample, resolution of this discrepancy between the archaeological and osteological data seems likely.

An analysis of the physical evidence for nonlethal violence in a variety of groups spanning a wide spectrum of economic systems is presented by Phillip Walker in chapter six. His study is unique in its cross-cultural approach and prodigious effort to personally collect these data on such dispersed collections from three continents. It is apparent from such a wide range of different cultures (and different samplings within specific groups, such as the Todd collection) that there is no single emergent cause for patterns of cranial and facial trauma he observes. However, certain distinct patterns, such as consistently located cranial vault injuries in the Santa Barbara Channel precontact groups or nasal bone fractures in eighteenth- to twentieth-century Yakuts from Siberia, have clear correlations to ethnographic and historical records of ritualized combat in the former or aggressive sports / foreign subjugation in the latter. Walker also demonstrates that distinctive patterns of violence crosscut economic barriers and social types, which has implications in models that attempt to find general explanations for nonlethal violence behaviors and their preservation in bone.

Unlike other studies, David Frayer's focuses on lethal, perimortem violence from a short segment of time as determined from two mass graves at a small cave known as Ofnet in Bavaria (chapter seven). This site dating to the Mesolithic (ca. 7000 B.P.) provides evidence of a prehistoric massacre (or possibly two separate ones) where only the heads and cervical (neck) vertebrae of mostly women, children and infants were buried in two common graves. Based on the perimortem nature of the cranial wounds, their consistent size/shape, and evidence indicating that the heads were placed into each grave in a single episode, Frayer concludes that Ofnet represents a prehistoric massacre(s). Moreover, since the demographic profile of the main pit does not represent a natural population, it is apparent that either many of the adult males were not present when the massacre occurred or males were not accorded the same burial treatment as the other unfortunate members of the groups. Finally, whether this is the result of hostilities between resident hunter-gatherers and invading agriculturalists or the lethal outcome of a dispute between hunter-gatherers or some other cause is presently unknowable; however, evidence from the site testifies to sporadic outbursts of lethal violence in these late European foragers. Just as in the cases drawn from North America, prehistoric Europe also provides evidence for deadly human interactions.

Carmen Ma. Pijoan and Josefina Mansilla Lory examine another aspect of violence (chapter eight), specifically sacrifice and cannibalism as these ritual events relate to the victims of warfare, conquest or subjugation. While some have questioned the existence of cannibalism among the Aztecs and their predecessors, using definitive procedures for identifying corpse manipulation, Pijoan and Mansilla Lory show that these 'practices extend fairly deep into the past of central Mexico. In the Formative/Preclassic site of Tlatelcomila they find unequivocal indications that human corpses were skinned and defleshed, the crania crushed to remove the brain, and postcranial remains pummeled into small fragments for fat and marrow extraction. These signs of processing and mutilation, coupled with the fact that bone remains were found in trash pits, strongly suggest cannibalistic practices by 500 B.C. The authors are also able to document human sacrifice associated with the construction of a large patio during the late Classic period at Electra and from Tlatelolco (during the Postclassic) very specific indications of cranial preparation for the skull racks recorded during the Aztec conquest. While no attempt is made to predict the region from where these sacrificial victims originated, it seems likely they were outsiders or war captives who paid the ultimate price. What is clear from their work, however, is that rituals involving human sacrifice and cannibalism have considerable antiquity in the region, leaving unmistakable signs in the remains of victims.

The final papers focus more on evidence for warfare in the prehistoric record. Maria Ostendorf Smith, in chapter nine, reviews very specific evidence in the Archaic period of the Tennessee River Valley indicative of lethal violence/homicide or mortal violence related to warfare or its spoils (such as nonhealed scalping and trophy taking). Unlike most of the other studies in this volume, Ostendorf Smith shows this period was remarkably peaceful, judging from lack of evidence of healed blunt trauma and low occurrence of skeletal indicators of lethal injuries. There is also a low frequency of cutmarks (indicating scalping) and little evidence of trophy taking. Yet, judging from an apparent massacre at the most peripherally located of seven sites, it is clear that lethal violence (whether inter- or intragroup) was not absent from this prehistoric period.

Shifting emphasis to archaeological data, Herbert D. G. Maschner concentrates on the Northwest Coast of North America, following a multifaceted, diachronic approach that evaluates indications of violence and warfare from skeletal evidence, site locations and their defensive aspects (including site positioning and fortifications), and evidence for weapons of war (chapter ten). For the latter, he finds an increase in the patterning of intergroup violence with the introduction of the bow and arrow between 100–500 A.D. and an overall trend for increase in violence and warfare through time, culminating in the historic period when warfare was an important part of life in most groups. As in most of the chapters in this book, evidence for violence and warfare are certainly not confined to the most recent periods. Rather, in the Northwest Coast cultural region, violence and warfare have deep roots in the precontact period.

In chapter eleven, Lawrence H. Keeley reviews patterning in the settlement of the earliest farmers of Belgium, noting the common concurrence of fortified villages with complex defensive structures. Based on his research, he also notes the lack of evidence for peaceful interactions between the resident hunter-gatherers and the Linienbandkeramik (LBK) agricultural invaders. Moreover, since hunting of wild game in these early agricultural groups was minimal, the high frequency of arrow points suggests these were weapons for the people inside the bulwarks used against others on the outside. Keeley argues that relations between natives and newcomers were hostile, which explains the aspects of vigilance recorded in the archaeological record. In contrast to this pattern for Belgium, Central and Eastern European LBK settlements show little evidence of fortifications and more indications of peaceful interactions (possibly through avoidance) with the native hunter-gatherer groups. In short, invading LBK groups had different social interactions with resident hunter-gatherer groups in the eastern and western parts of Europe, which seem likely to be closely related to patterns of occupation density and encroachment of either group onto contested lands.

The volume ends with R. Brian Ferguson's overview of early violence and warfare. In chapter twelve he situates violence and warfare in a broad perspective. He demonstrates the utility of understanding the complex realities that often end in conflict and war. Because of the more abundant theoretical models concerning warfare in past and present populations, Ferguson draws upon a number of frameworks for studying war. Non-war violence has not been considered to the extent that war has been focused on, and Ferguson suggests a number of ways that method, theory and data in studies of war in historic and contemporary non-industrialized societies can be used to provide more sophisticated analyses of past populations.

For some, documenting violence and war in past societies may only seem to bring out the negative side of human existence. While we do not intend to exploit or sensationalize the violence that occurred among precontact people, we think it is time for all anthropologists to recognize the abundant evidence indicating that violent interactions have long been part of human culture and society. We offer these studies with the intention that they will force a more thorough consideration of issues about nonlethal and lethal violence and warfare. None of the violence and warfare of the past justifies or legitimizes these far too common phenomena today, but it is hoped that these examples lead to insight about how and why violence and warfare persist in the present.

Debra L. Martin   *David W. Frayer*

References

Bamforth, D. G. (1994). "Indigenous People, Indigenous Violence: Precontact Warfare on the North American Plains." *Man*, **29**, 95–115.

Blakely, R. L. and Mathews, D. S. (1990). "Bioarchaeological Evidence for a Spanish-Native American Conflict in the Sixteenth-Century Southeast." *American Antiquity*, **55**, 718–744.

Knauft, B. M. (1987). "Reconsidering Violence in Simple Human Societies." *Current Anthropology*, **28**, 457–499.

(1991). "Violence and Sociality in Human Evolution." *Current Anthropology*, **32**, 391–428.

Milner, G. R., Anderson, E. and Smith, V. G. (1991). "Warfare in Late Prehistoric West-Central Illinois." *American Antiquity*, **56**, 581–603.

Ross, M. H. (1992). "Social Structure, Psychocultural Dispositions and Violent Conflict: Extensions from a Cross-Cultural Study." In *Aggression and Peacefulness in Human and Other Primates*, eds. J. Silverberg and J. Gray, pp. 271–292. Oxford: Oxford University Press.

CONTRIBUTORS

Carol R. Ember is a professor of anthropology at Hunter College of the City University of New York. Her cross-cultural research on war and peace (with Melvin Ember and Bruce Russett) has been supported by grants from the National Science Foundation, the United States Institute of Peace, and the Research Award Program of the City University of New York. Previous articles on that research have appeared in the *Journal of Conflict Resolution, World Politics*, and *Behavior Science Research* (now *Cross-Cultural Research*). She and Melvin Ember are also authors of the textbooks *Anthropology* and *Cultural Anthropology* (8th ed., 1996).

Melvin Ember is president of the Human Relations Areas Files, Inc., an international nonprofit research agency associated with Yale University. His cross-cultural research on war and peace (with Carol R. Ember and Bruce Russett) has been supported by grants from the National Science Foundation, the United States Institute of Peace, and the Research Award Program of the City University of New York. With Carol R. Ember, he has coauthored a number of cross-cultural studies relating war to social organization; see their *Marriage, Family, and Kinship: Comparative Studies of Social Organization* (1983).

R. Brian Ferguson is a cultural anthropologist who teaches at Rutgers University in Newark, New Jersey. His doctoral research analyzed social class transformations in Puerto Rico. He has published extensively on war, including *Warfare, Culture and Environment* (editor); *The Anthropology of War: A Bibliography* (with Leslie Farragher); *War in the Tribal Zone: Expanding States and Indigenous Warfare* (co-editor with Neil Whitehead); and *Yanomami Warfare: A Political History*. He is currently investigating "ethnic violence" and related conflicts in the contemporary world, and the history of policing in New York City.

David W. Frayer is professor of anthropology at the University of Kansas, Lawrence. His research studies concern human evolution in Europe, from the Mousterian to the Middle Ages. He is interested in exploring the interface between biology and culture, especially in the Upper Paleolithic and Mesolithic of Europe. He also raises chickens, against which he practices no violence.

Lawrence H. Keeley is professor of anthropology at the University of Illinois at Chicago. He has conducted laboratory research on the production and use of stone tools, cross-cultural research on economic complexity and plant cultivation among hunter-gatherers, and directed excavations at Final Mesolithic and Early Neolithic sites in Belgium. His collaborative work with Daniel Cahen on Early Neolithic fortifications led to his interest in prestate warfare. His book *War Before Civilization* was published by Oxford University Press in 1996.

Patricia M. Lambert is a visiting research instructor at the University of North Carolina at Chapel Hill. Her doctoral dissertation chronicles changing patterns of health and violence in prehistoric hunter-gatherer populations of the Santa Barbara Channel coast. Her most recent publications have appeared in the journals *Antiquity* and *American Antiquity*.

Josefina Mansilla Lory is a research physical anthropologist at the Dirección of Antropología Física at the Instituto Nacional de Antropología e Historia in México City. She specializes in stress markers in skeletons of prehispanic and colonial Méxicans. Her research has included work on skeletal remains of Mayas, Tlatelolcas, Cholultecas, Toltecas, Tlatliquences and postcontact groups. For the past eight years she has collaborated with Carmen Ma. Pijoan in studies involving bone modification, sacrifice, and cannibalism among the inhabitants of ancient México.

Debra L. Martin is an associate professor of biological anthropology at Hampshire College in the School of Natural Science. She has conducted fieldwork and laboratory analyses of human skeletal remains from the American Southwest, Sudanese Nubia, and the Arabian Peninsula. Her research has focused upon patterns of morbidity and mortality by age and sex, and these analyses have been published in the *American Journal of Physical Anthropology* and the *Journal of Human Evolution*. She is currently working on a book entitled *Health in America Before Columbus* (School of American Research Press).

Herbert D. G. Maschner is assistant professor of anthropology at the University of Wisconsin–Madison. For the last twelve years he has been conducting fieldwork throughout Alaska, but particularly in southeast Alaska, the homeland of the Tlingit. His major research interests include archaeological studies of the development of hereditary social inequality, the origins of sedentism, and prehistoric warfare. He has recently begun addressing these issues in the Aleutian Islands. His most recent articles on the archaeology of the North Pacific region have appeared in the journal *Antiquity*.

Carmen Ma. Pijoan is an investigator at the Dirección of Antropología Física at the Instituto Nacional de Antropología e Historia in México City. Her work has principally been in osteology and she has written several papers on a wide variety of topics. However, she mainly specializes in bone modification in prehispanic México as evidence for the presence of human sacrifice and cannibalism. Presently, she is working on a mass burial of about 200 individuals whose remains show a high number of cutmarks and blows.

John Robb is lecturer in archaeology at the University of Southampton. He received his MA and PhD in anthropology from the University of Michigan, and studies the development of complex societies in Italy between the Neolithic and Iron Age. He is especially interested in the skeletal signs of health, economy and social relations, in archaeological understandings of symbolic systems and gender, and in the areas of overlap among these topics.

Maria O. Smith is an assistant professor in the Anthropology Department of Northern Illinois University and a research associate at the Frank H. McClung Museum in Knoxville, Tennessee. She is a bioarchaeologist whose principal research interest is the paleopathology of the prehistoric populations of the Western Tennessee River Valley. Her current research has expanded to include paleopathological examination of precontact populations of the American Southwest.

Phillip L. Walker is professor of anthropology at the University of California, Santa Barbara. His research has focused on documenting the biological and cultural responses ancient human populations made during the shift from hunting and gathering to a more sedentary village life. His publications include papers on bioarchaeology, dental anthropology, demography, and faunal analysis. He is the author of *Chumash Healing: Changing Health and Medical Practices in a Native American Society* (1993). He is currently studying the health consequences of changes in socio-economic organization among ancient native Americans in Southern California and Iron Age pastoralists in Central Asia.

Richard G. Wilkinson is professor of anthropology at the University of Albany. He has done research on historic and prehistoric skeletal series from México and the United States' Midwest and Northeast; he has also researched historic demography in the Albany, New York area. His research on past peoples is directed at the elucidation of population processes, behaviors and interactions among groups for whom there is little, if any, written documentation.

Chapter ONE

Violence in the Ethnographic Record: Results of Cross-Cultural Research on War and Aggression

Carol R. Ember
Human Relations Area Files
New Haven, Connecticut

Melvin Ember
Human Relations Area Files
New Haven, Connecticut

What does the ethnographic record suggest about the prevalence and possible causes of violence in human societies? Did people in the societies described by anthropologists and others go to war less often than we do in the present, and did they have less

1

homicide and assault, as we might like to think? In this paper, we describe the results of our cross-cultural studies of war and aggression, and we discuss their implications for prehistory.

We begin with an important caveat. The ethnographic record *by itself* cannot imply anything about the prevalence of events in the past. The reason is that few if any societies described in the ethnographic record, even those described shortly after first contact with the West, were pristine in the sense of being completely unaffected by that contact (cf. Trigger 1981: 12–13). Whatever the earliest time of description, many societies had already been subject to a variety of forms of culture contact with a variety of effects, including serious depopulation due to introduced diseases (Ember and Ember 1972, Ember 1974), pacification (Ember and Ember 1992a, 1992b), depletion of resources by exploitative Western agents (Bodley 1990), and changes in subsistence patterns (Bradley *et al.* 1990).

Obviously, then, pacification has to be controlled in any statistical analysis that aims to provide an estimate of the prevalence of war. Societies that were pacified at the time of description, that had peace imposed upon them by external powers, are falsely low on the frequency of war. Thus, if we want to estimate the prevalence of war, and if we want to understand the causes of war, it is necessary to disregard societies that were completely or partly pacified at the time of first description. If we take this step, we would argue that an estimate of prevalence based on systematic, comparative studies is more reliable than an estimate derived from one or a few ethnographic cases, no matter how well those few cases are described.

Whatever we do, we should not generalize from one or a few classic cases, such as the !Kung San, as if they were typical of past (or even recent) hunter-gatherers. The fact is that the !Kung San were *not* typical in many respects. A systematic survey shows that, in contrast to the peaceful !Kung San of the 1950s and 1960s, 64% of the foraging societies in the ethnographic record had combat between communities or larger entities at least once every two years (Ember 1978). That percentage is undoubtedly an underestimate, since the survey did not discount pacified societies. In our studies of war and aggression (the !Kung San are one of our sample cases), we found that there was frequent armed combat between San bands in the 1920s, according to ethnographers on the scene. (See, for example, Source #3 [Lebzelter] in the file on the San in the HRAF database, page 30 of the HRAF translation from the German.) Subsequently (by the 1950s), after government patrols had apparently pacified the area, there was no warfare among San bands. Moreover, recent research (Schrire 1984; Wilmsen 1989) has revealed that the !Kung were not always foragers; they often relied on herding in the past. The lesson from this example is clear: we should not generalize from cases that may be untypical of their type. The only valid way to establish that a trait or correlation is typical for some set of societies in the ethnographic record is on the basis of systematic, statistical surveys of representative samples of that particular set (e.g., hunter-gatherers).

After describing the sample of societies used in our studies, we turn to the distribution of different kinds of violence in the sample and the variables that predict those types of violence. As we shall see, different forms of violence are related–that is, some societies appear to be more violent in general. More specifically, our results strongly suggest that more war is an important cause of more homicide and assault.

SAMPLE AND STRATEGY

Our project on warfare and aggression coded a number of warfare and aggression variables for a sample (Murdock and White 1969) of 186 largely preindustrial societies; one case had been chosen to represent each of 186 "distinctive world areas."[1] Each of these cases was coded by our assistants for a 25-year time period (15 years prior to 10 years after) around the particular focal year specified in Murdock and White (1969); the time focus varies from case to case, but usually is some time in the 19th or 20th centuries. The names of the sample societies and the coded data on war and aggression can be found in Ember and Ember (1992b). Frequency of warfare is judged on a five-point ordinal scale (5 is almost constant; 1 is absent or rare). War is defined as socially organized armed combat between members of different territorial units (communities or aggregates of communities). Overall frequency of war considers both internal and external war, if present. Internal war is between communities or larger aggregates *within* the society. External warfare is between the focal society and other societies. By "society" we mean a more or less continuously distributed population that speaks a common language. If coders could not tell that a named population was a society as here defined, they were instructed to consider it as such if the name for it was the name used by Murdock and White (1969).

We also rated individual aggression, by which we mean attempts to hurt or injure others *within* the community or local

group. We use a three-point ordinal scale (1 = low; 3 = high) to
measure homicide and assault. Homicide is defined as killing another person, exclusive of infanticide. (For why we exclude infanticide, see C. R. Ember and M. Ember 1993.) Assault is defined as
hurting or fighting with another person with the intent to do bodily harm. (A wrestling match is not assault.)

For all of our codes we had at least two coders (sometimes three)
make a rating after independently reading the ethnography for
that case (they used the Human Relations Area Files when possible; about 75 percent of the cases are found there). For all dis-
agreements, we asked for a resolved score. With regard to the
five-point warfare scales, we allowed averaging without discussion
if the initial scores were within one point of each other. If not, the
coders had to talk about their reasons for rating as they did. Sometimes one coder persuaded the other because of a piece of information not found by one of them initially. However, we did not force
a resolution; if they could not agree, a "zero" was recorded as the
resolved score. We also show a reliability score for each variable
(Ember and Ember 1992b) which indicates the degree to which the
independent coders had agreed or disagreed initially.

In analyzing the results, we discovered that they would improve
substantially when we omitted cases for which the original separate codings had been appreciably different (Ember and Ember
1992b: 172). Even though the coders had resolved many of those
cases, there clearly was more measurement error associated with
them, which was presumably why the results without them were
stronger. In the new results we present here (as in our previously
published results), we have omitted those war and aggression
scores for which reliability was poor (scores above 6 on the reliability scores presented in Ember and Ember [1992b]).

Because pacification by definition affects the frequency of war,
we also considered whether a society was forced to stop fighting
by external powers. Unless otherwise noted, when we refer to our
ratings of warfare frequency we are including only those cases in
which an external power had *not* tried to eliminate war (ratings of
1 or 2 on pacification–see Ember and Ember 1992b: 175).

THE PREVALENCE OF WARFARE
IN THE ETHNOGRAPHIC RECORD

We discovered that many societies had been pacified or forced to
stop fighting before the focal time period. This fact drastically

changes how we estimate the prevalence of war. Table 1.1 compares the distribution of warfare frequencies (in percentages) in our sample societies (ignoring whether or not they are pacified) and in the smaller set of nonpacified societies. If we look at all societies and ignore whether or not they had been pacified, we see a somewhat bimodal distribution: war is absent or rare (occurring less than once in 10 years) in 27.6% of the sample cases, and warfare is almost constant (occurring at any time of the year) in 38.06% of the sample cases. However, if we look only at those societies *not* pacified, very few societies (8.89%) had rare or no war and most societies are found at the highest scale score (warfare almost constant). Putting it a different way, war is almost ubiquitous in the ethnographic record, *in the absence of external powers that imposed pacification*, and the frequency distribution is skewed sharply toward the high end. It should also be mentioned that warfare is likely to be purely external (*only* with speakers of other languages) in small societies, unless the society is widely dispersed (Ember 1974).

Does war frequency vary with predominant subsistence type? More specifically, is war less frequent or even absent among hunter-gatherers (foragers), as is often assumed? The answer is yes and no. In the sample here, just as in a previous sample (Ember 1978), foragers are not particularly peaceful. As the reader will see below, foragers in the ethnographic record had warfare fairly often on average, but they do seem to have had less than nonforagers.

For the purposes of analysis, we classified our sample societies as follows in regard to predominant subsistence. Societies are classified as "intensive agriculturalists" and "horticulturalists" if they are rated by Murdock and Provost (1980: 148) as 4 and 3, respectively, on their Scale 3. Both 4 and 3 mean that the society depends mostly on cultivation for food; but 4 is intensive agriculture and 3 is nonintensive agriculture or "horticulture." For societies not dependent mostly on cultivation, the information in Murdock and

Table 1.1. Frequency of Warfare (Percentages)

	Absent or Rare	Once Every 3–10 years	Every two years or so	Every year in a season	Constant or any time
all societies (N = 134)	27.62%	13.43	8.96	11.94	38.06
nonpacified (N = 90)	8.98%	8.81	8.88	16.68	56.66

Provost (1980) was not sufficient to distinguish them otherwise, so we turned to the information on animal husbandry, hunting, fishing, and gathering in Murdock and Morrow (1980: columns 3–6). If animal husbandry was more important than anything else (P in column 3 of Murdock and Morrow), we classified the society as "pastoral." Societies are "foragers" if cultivation yields less than 10% of the food supply (0 or 1 on Scale 3 in Murdock and Provost) *and* there is little dependence on animal husbandry (O, N, or U) in column 3 of Murdock and Morrow. All other cases are classified as "Mixed." The mixed cases had agriculture and/or pastoralism yielding more than 10% of the food supply, but these activities were not dominant.

The median scale score for foragers on war frequency is 3 (i.e., war occurs once every two years). However, as is suggested by Figure 1.1, foragers do appear to have less warfare than other types of societies. Indeed, a nonparametric analysis of variance of frequency differences in the five groups shown in Figure 1 is statistically significant (Kruskal-Wallis test statistic = 12.597, p = .013), as is a comparison of foragers versus all other groups together (Mann-Whitney U test; Ns 20, 70; p = .001).[2]

Do these results for the ethnographic record suggest that prehistoric food-collectors (foragers) had less war than prehistoric food-producers? The answer is not necessarily. Most ethnographically described foraging societies had very small populations, were located in marginal environments, and many were surrounded by much more powerful societies. So it may be that the costs of war for foragers in the ethnographic record were much more prohibitive than they were for prehistoric foragers. It is possible that something about recent foragers worked against frequent fighting; we discuss that possibility later.

GETTING AT CAUSES: PREDICTING VARIATION IN WAR FREQUENCY

Let us turn now to what our cross-cultural results suggest about the causes of war in the ethnographic record. We turn first to predicting variation in overall warfare frequency. (Our results are reported in detail in Ember and Ember 1992a, 1992b; for their foreign policy implications in the modern world, see M. Ember and C. R. Ember 1993.)

To make a very long story short, we tested a large number of theories about what might predict more versus less war. Most of them failed to predict variation in war frequency. So, for example, we failed to find much support for two psychological theories, that frustrating socialization makes for more war and that conditions encouraging "protest" masculinity or "machismo" make for more war. Correlationally, we did find some support for the idea that aggression was learned, since socialization for fortitude and aggression in boys significantly predicts more war. However, we have considerable evidence that socialization for fortitude and aggression is more likely a *consequence* than a cause of war. To mention but one piece of evidence, pacified societies are less likely than nonpacified societies to socialize for aggression in boys, which suggests that parents are no longer interested in such socialization

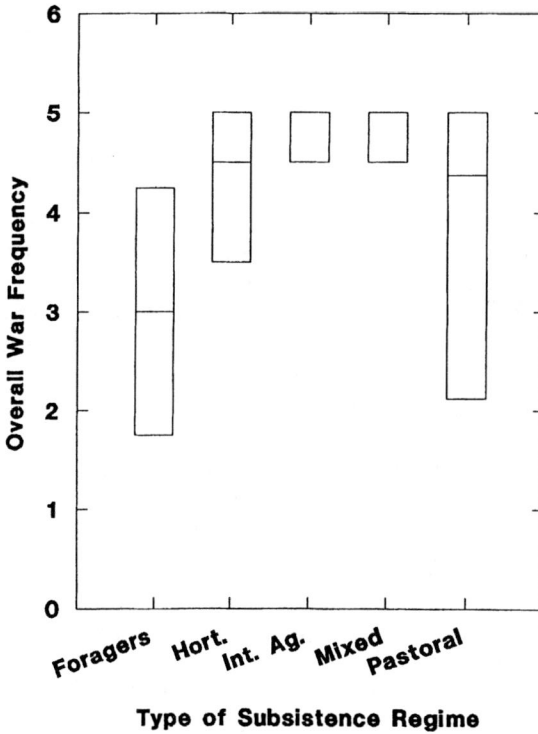

Figure 1.1. Box Plot of Overall Frequency of Warfare by Type of Subsistence Regime in Nonpacified Societies.*

*The median score on the ordinal warfare frequency scale is shown with a horizontal bar. The median for "intensive agricultural societies" is 5 as is the median for "mixed" subsistence regimes. The edges of the box split the remaining halves in half.

when they no longer need to produce unambivalent warriors (Ember and Ember 1994). We also found (unpublished data; see also Ember and Ember 1994) that hardly any measure of societal complexity predicts much of the variation in warfare frequency; and, in multiple regression analyses, indicators of complexity are not significant predictors. This result may seem contrary to our finding about foragers having less war than nonforagers; we discuss a possible explanation below.

When we began our research on war and aggression, we focused on ways to measure resource scarcity because many have postulated that population pressure is an important factor in understanding why people go to war. We also had empirical reasons to think that resource problems were important. Ember (1982) had analyzed data from Sillitoe (1977) on 26 New Guinea societies and found that warfare for land in those societies was strongly and significantly related to population density. He also analyzed data from Ember (1978) and found that severe food shortages were linked to more war.

While we did not see a way to measure whether a population might be approaching its carrying capacity, we did try to measure (following the reasoning of Ember [1978]) whether a society had exceeded its capacity by measuring the frequency of various kinds of food shortages. We constructed three measures of resource problems (Ember and Ember 1992b). Two of the measures tap serious but unpredictable fluctuations in the supply of food: threat of famines and threat of natural (weather or pest) disasters that destroy food supplies. Our third measure reflects the degree of chronic or regularly recurring scarcity. Our results suggest that one of these factors, threat of natural disasters, is a very strong predictor of warfare. In nonstate societies, the bivariate rank-order correlation (Spearman's) is .71, which means that this factor alone predicts about 50% of the variance in war frequency. Chronic scarcity is somewhat associated with more war, but in multiple regression analyses it drops out and has no independent effect. We found one other independent and significant predictor of more war, namely, socialization for mistrust. But threat of natural disasters is a much more powerful predictor (directly and indirectly) in multiple regression and path analyses.

Our results suggest to us that it is the *fear* of unpredictable disasters, rather than the actuality of shortages, that mainly motivates people to go to war (Ember and Ember 1992a). We say this because societies with only the threat of disasters in the focal 25-

year time period fight almost constantly, as do societies that had one or more disasters during the focal period. In addition, chronic or seasonal scarcity, which is predictable scarcity, does not independently predict more war. So, it would appear that people may mostly go to war in an attempt to cushion the impact of the disasters they expect to occur in the future, but cannot predict (nor control or prevent).

Consistent with the idea that warfare has economic consequences, if not motivations, the victors in those societies that fight at least once every two years almost always take land or other resources from the defeated. And this is true for simpler as well as more complex cases (Ember and Ember 1992a). In other words, it looks like even pre-capitalist societies may be motivated to go to war for economic reasons.

We should briefly note what our cross-cultural results suggest about whether warfare is internal (within the society) versus purely external. Although various cross-cultural researchers may disagree about the direction of the causality, they generally agree on the empirical findings: patrilocality is associated with feuding and internal war (Otterbein and Otterbein 1965; Otterbein 1968; Ember and Ember 1971; Divale 1974); matrilocal societies tend to have purely external war (Ember and Ember 1971; Divale 1974). Population size is linked to purely external war: relatively small societies (less than 21,000 in total population, which is true for most matrilocal societies) tend to fight purely externally (Ember 1974).

We recently conducted another study that is relevant to predicting internal war. With political scientist Bruce Russett, we cross-culturally tested the hypothesis (coming out of the cross-national literature) that democracies rarely if ever fight each other. We expected that if the "democracy" hypothesis is correct, it should be applicable to the ethnographic record, even if the biggest political entity in that record is often only the local group or community. Thus, we reformulated the hypothesis to fit the data from the ethnographic record and tested the following hypothesis: when adults participate more in the political process within the community and when they agree to disagree, communities or larger polities within the society should be less likely to fight with each other. (In measuring political participation, we followed the work of political scientist Marc H. Ross [1983] who had coded half the societies in our sample for local political participation; we coded the remainder. For this study we added an additional set of cases randomly chosen from the *Ethnographic Atlas* [Murdock 1967]. See our sample cases and codes in Ember, Russett, and Ember 1993.)

Our cross-cultural results are remarkably consistent with the cross-national findings (for details and discussion, see Ember, Ember, and Russett 1992). In a multiple regression analysis, three local political variables independently and significantly predicted less internal war in the society: 1) adults participate more in community decisions; 2) there are nonviolent ways to remove leaders; 3) and the community stays together after a political dispute. In addition, larger societies also were more likely to have internal war, as were societies located on an isolated island or group of islands. When we added patrilocal versus matrilocal residence as a possible predictor, that contrast did not significantly add to our ability to predict internal war, contrary to "fraternal interest group" theory (Otterbein and Otterbein 1965). This result, that patrilocal residence does *not* make internal war more likely, is consistent with the causal direction specified in our own theory about matrilocal versus patrilocal residence (Ember and Ember 1971; see also Chapter 1 in Ember and Ember 1983). Our theory is that internal war promotes patrilocality, that residence is a consequence rather than a cause of type of war. We suggest that parents would prefer to keep their sons at home after marriage to protect against attacks from close by, which is what internal warfare often involves.

FORAGERS AND WARFARE FREQUENCY

Earlier, in the section on the prevalence of war, we noted that foraging is associated with less warfare than other types of subsistence system in the ethnographic record. But that finding is not very informative; it does not by itself tell us why foragers may fight less. In other words, what is it about foragers that may explain their lower scores on war frequency? Is a foraging regime an independent predictor of less war? In the last section, we described two possibly causal predictors of more war, namely, threat of natural disasters and socialization for mistrust. And we noted that we found no independent effect of cultural complexity, although we did not look at foraging specifically. Other cross-cultural researchers have also found little relationship between war and complexity—see Loftin (1971) and Otterbein (1970).

Does foraging relate to the two predictors of more war? The answer is yes. Nonpacified foragers, as compared with nonpacified groups that get more than 10 percent of their food from food-producing activities, are significantly less likely to have unpredictable natural disasters. The data are not shown here but $p = .014$, by

Fisher's Exact Test; threat of disasters is dichotomized at scale score 1 versus scores 2–4 because its relationship with war frequency is not linear (Ember and Ember 1992a). And, nonpacified foragers are more likely (but not quite significantly) to be lower on socialization for mistrust. (All the results about foragers described in this paper have not been published previously.)

So foraging is not an independent predictor of less war; foragers may have somewhat less warfare than nonforagers for the same reasons already discussed. To test this conclusion further, we redid the multiple regression from our earlier study (Ember and Ember 1992a), adding the contrast between food-producers (score 1) versus foragers (score 0) as a dummy variable. Table 1.2 shows our original results (column 1) and the revised results adding food-production vs. foraging as a predictor. As we can see in column 2 of Table 1.2, the results are just about the same as before; food-production vs. foraging hardly adds anything to the variance explained and is not a significant predictor of war frequency. Foraging has no independent effect on war frequency in the ethnographic record; foragers have less war than food-producers because they have significantly less threat of natural disasters and less socialization for mistrust.

Still, the coefficient for food-production in column 2 of Table 1.2 is not close to zero, so something else about recent foragers (at least many of them) may help to explain why they have less war than food-producers. We have already noted that most ethnographically described foragers had very small populations and many were

Table 1.2. Multiple Regression Analysis Predicting Overall Warfare Frequency

	1 Original Analysis	2 Adding Food Prod.
Constant	0.000	0.000
Natural Disasters	0.591***	0.530***
Mistrust	0.296**	0.261**
Food Producing		0.209
N	30	30
R	0.71	0.73
R^2	0.50	0.54
p value	0.000	0.000

* $p < 0.05$, one tail
** $p < 0.025$, one tail
*** $p < 0.001$, one tail

surrounded by more powerful societies. We suggest now that going to war would not usually have been cost-effective nor feasible for many recent foragers. It would have been foolhardy to attack a neighboring, more numerous food-producing enemy, who was likely to have more warriors. Such an attack would be unlikely to result in victory for the foragers and the capture of resources. In short, foragers in the ethnographic record may have had less warfare than food-producers because the foragers had less chance of victory if they went to war.

Not only do recent foragers have significantly less war than food-producers overall; they also have significantly less internal war. Does this fact increase our ability to predict internal warfare over and above what we found before (Ember, Ember, and Russett 1992)? The answer is no. Table 1.3 compares the results we found previously with those adding the dummy variable of food-production versus foraging.[3] Not only are the results virtually unchanged (the R^2 or amount of variance explained increases by only one

Table 1.3. Multiple Regression Analysis Predicting Internal Warfare Frequency

	1 Original Analysis[a]	2 Adding Food Prod.
Constant	0.000	0.000
Population	0.477***	0.442**
Island	0.296**	0.466**
Checks on Power (6)	0.030	0.017
Removal of Leaders (7)	−0.474**	−0.432**
Consultation (8)	0.535**	0.516**
Extent of Participation (11)	−0.483**[b]	−0.448**
Absence of Fission (30)	−0.626***	−0.600***
Food Producing	–	0.139
N	37	37
R	0.77	0.78
R^2	0.59	0.60
p value	0.000	0.000

*$p < 0.05$, one tail
**$p < 0.025$, one tail
*** $p < 0.001$, one tail
[a] These results are slightly different from those reported in C.R. Ember, M. Ember, and Russett (1992) because of an error in one score discovered when we prepared the codes for publication in Ember, Russett, and Ember (1992).
[b] In the publication in which this table first appeared (Ember, Ember, and Russett 1992) the sign of this variable was reversed from that which appeared in Ross (1983). In our later codes paper (Ember, Russett, and Ember 1992), however, we used the same direction that Ross did.

percent); food-production is again far from significant as an independent predictor.[4] Thus, we think it is safe to conclude that foragers in the ethnographic record have less internal war for the same reasons any society in that record may have less internal war (i.e., more political participation, smaller total population). Consistent with this conclusion, our unpublished data show that foragers are significantly higher on some aspects of political participation and significantly smaller in total population than food-producers.

THE PREVALENCE OF OTHER KINDS OF VIOLENCE IN THE ETHNOGRAPHIC RECORD

In the ethnographic record, statistics on crime (i.e., rates per 100,000) are not usually available. So in our study of interpersonal violence, we opted to compare societies by rank-ordering them in terms of ethnographers' qualitative statements about the frequencies of homicide and assault. (For an extended discussion of how cross-cultural studies of interpersonal violence differ from cross-national studies, see Ember and Ember 1993.) With these rank orderings we could test to see what violence may be linked to, even if we do not have precise estimates of rates. Even though we cannot estimate quantitative rates of violence, our coders were able to make ordinal ratings of frequency (see Ember and Ember 1992b, 1994). Table 1.4 shows the distribution of the ordinal frequency scores grouped according to nearest integer (1 is low, 2 is moderate, and 3 is high in relative frequency). Interpersonal violence is certainly not uncommon in the ethnographic record. For example,

Table 1.4. Frequency of Homicide and Assault (Percentages)

	Low (1)	Moderate (2)	High (3)
Homicide all societies (N = 98)	46.94%	34.69	18.36
nonpacified (N = 64)	40.63%	35.93	23.44
Assault all societies (N = 95)	32.63%	37.89	29.48
nonpacified (N = 58)	32.76%	32.76	34.48

the frequency of homicide is moderate or high in about 53 percent of all the sample societies, and the frequency of assault is moderate or high in about 67 percent of all the cases. The percentages are slightly but not significantly different in the nonpacified cases.

Does type of subsistence regime make any difference in predicting the degree of interpersonal violence? The answer is no. A nonparametric analysis of variance (Kruskal-Wallis, not shown) comparing the different types of subsistence regime is not significant for either homicide or assault. Figure 1.2 shows a graphical comparison of homicide frequencies across the five types of subsistence regime.

WAR AND OTHER KINDS OF VIOLENCE

Cross national studies suggest that war is associated with other kinds of violence. Archer and Gartner (1984: 63–97) compared

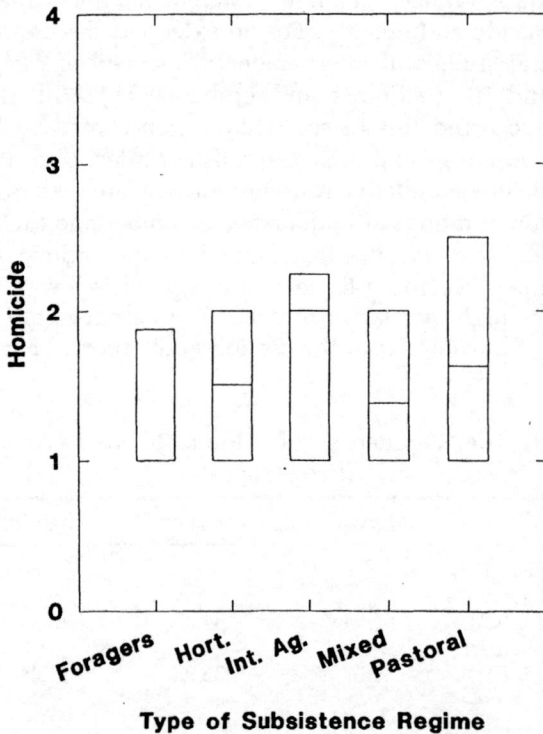

Figure 1.2. Box Plot of Homicide by Type of Subsistence Regime.*

* The median score on the ordinal homicide frequency scale is shown with a horizontal bar. The median for "foragers" is 1. The edges of the box split the remaining halves in half.

changes in homicide rates of various nations before versus after major wars. They found that homicide rates tend to increase following a war, whether the nation was defeated or victorious. This result is consistent with the idea that a society or nation legitimizes violence during wartime. After all, it is permissible to kill enemies during wartime; afterward, homicide rates may go up because inhibitions against killing have been relaxed.

In the ethnographic record too, war is associated with other kinds of violence. Societies with more war tend to have warlike sports (Sipes 1973), beliefs in malevolent magic (Sipes and Robertson 1975; Palmer 1970), and severe punishment for crimes (Sipes and Robertson 1975; Palmer 1965). Feuding is associated with war between polities (Otterbein and Otterbein 1965). Wife beating is associated with violent resolution of conflict (Levinson 1989) and with more war (Erchak and Rosenfeld 1994; Erchak 1994). And Ross's (1985) results suggest that some societies are generally more violent than others. In our own data, homicide and assault are significantly related to warfare in nonpacified societies (Ember and Ember 1994; cf. also Russell 1972 and Eckhardt 1973). Whether or not war is causally central to all forms of aggression and violence still needs further testing, but our own results (Ember and Ember 1994), reviewed below, strongly suggest that more homicide and assault is a consequence of socialization for aggression which in turn is a consequence of more war.

We first looked for bivariate correlations that significantly predicted variation in the relative frequency of violence, concentrating on homicide and assault. Since they are highly correlated with each other, we used a summary score for both together. We started with bivariate predictors which previous research had grouped into a few sets of related measures. The strongest predictor of each set in our data was then included in a multiple regression analysis. In addition to war frequency, those predictors included: socialization for aggression in late childhood for boys (as the indicator of socialization for aggression), low parental warmth (as the indicator of need-satisfaction in childhood), high parental hostility (as the indicator of punitive socialization), and mother sleeping closer to baby than to father (as the indicator of likely "protest" masculinity). Only one predictor emerged as significant in the multiple regression analysis, namely, socialization for aggression. We were not surprised that war was not significant by itself, since we think it has its effect mostly by increasing socialization for aggression. There may also be some effect because war legitimizes violence.

Just with war frequency and socialization for aggression as predictors, the multiple R is .68 (p < .001), which is almost as high as in the analysis using all of the predictors. And, when we limit the multiple regression analysis to nonstate societies, both war and socialization for aggression are significant predictors of homicide and assault (see Ember and Ember 1994 for details of these results).

Although we cannot go into those details here, we calculated some path analyses to try to discriminate among possible causal models linking socialization for aggression, homicide/assault, and war. The results are consistent with two path-analytic models. The first is that war causes socialization for aggression which causes more homicide and assault. The second model is that war causes socialization for aggression which causes more homicide and assault, and, in addition, war directly causes more homicide and assault by legitimizing violence. Since these two path-analytic models have the same total discrepancies, we cannot choose between them on the basis of existing results.

IMPLICATIONS FOR PREHISTORY

It is one thing to estimate the prevalence of war in the ethnographic record. It is another thing to do so in the archaeological record. Archaeologists are beginning to uncover unmistakable signs of war in prehistory (e.g., skeletal evidence of mass slaughter—see other papers in this volume). In the absence of such direct evidence, other kinds of inference are possible based on the cross-cultural (comparative ethnographic) evidence. As we discuss in Ember and Ember (1995), ethnographic analogy or distributional evidence in the ethnographic record are not sufficient to justify valid inferences about the archaeological record. Instead, in the absence of direct evidence, it is preferable to base inferences on what correlates with high versus low frequency warfare in the ethnographic record. But to do that we need archaeologically recoverable indicators of war frequency which we can apply to samples of archaeological sites. In short, the most helpful kind of indicator of war would be a material correlate of war which can be inferred easily from the archaeological record.

On the basis of cross-cultural research, Peregrine (1993) has identified one such correlate, a community layout variable (degree of permeability) that is strongly associated with variation in war frequency. Using "graph" theory, Peregrine counts the number of "steps" or "legs" it takes to enter the inner rooms of a dwelling from the outside. Cross-culturally, societies that have a permeability index of 3 or more almost always have war at least once every two years; those that have one step almost always have little or no war. Only the permeability ratings of 2 are somewhat ambiguous regarding warfare frequency.

Thus, given strong predictors (and probable causes) of variation in the frequency of war, and given archaeological indicators of war frequency and/or its predictors, we may soon be able to estimate the prevalence of war in the prehistoric past.

Moreover, if archaeologists could estimate the likelihood of unpredictable disasters that destroy food supplies for a sample of archaeological sites over time, and if one or more material correlates of war frequency could be estimated for the same sample of sites, we could have an archaeological test of the probable link between threat of disasters and war. Such an archaeological test could significantly increase scientific understanding of the causes of war, as well as the frequency of war in prehistory.

CONCLUSION

Our studies and those of other cross-cultural researchers have tested theories about why war occurs and what it is linked to. We are interested in such issues not only for scientific reasons. We are also concerned citizens. People in all segments of our society, not just researchers, are beginning to ask how we can rid our society of the rampant violence we see today. So far, no one we know of has said publically that our country's investment in war and our need to produce warriors might be a large part of the problem. War and violence appear to be causally related. If we want to rid the world of violence, we may first have to rid the world of war.

NOTES

[1] Although we would have preferred to use a random sample, we decided to use the Murdock/White sample because we wanted to use the extensive materials on childrearing already coded for that sample.

[2] Post-hoc Tukey t-tests indicate that there are significant differences between foragers and horticulturalists, between foragers and intensive agriculturalists, and between foragers and the "mixed" category.

[3] Since Ember, Ember, and Russett (1992) added a random sample of cases from the *Ethnographic Atlas* (Murdock 1967), we had to follow a somewhat different procedure for rating whether the case was a foraging or a

18 CAROL R. EMBER AND MELVIN EMBER

food-producing society. This time we used the ratings in column 7 of the
Atlas which gives approximate percentages of the diet from gathering,
hunting, fishing, animal husbandry, and agriculture (Murdock 1967). We
considered societies to be food-producers if more than 10 percent of the
diet came from other than foraging (as indicated by a score of 1 on
agriculture and/or animal husbandry).

[4] According to the Systat program, there is some evidence of multicol-
linearity between food-production vs. foraging and two of the political
variables (variable 6 and 11). Accordingly, we redid the analysis, omit-
ting each of the other predictors one at a time, to see if food-production
vs. foraging became more significant. It did not.

REFERENCES

Archer, Dane, and Rosemary Gartner (1984). Violence and Crime in Cross-
national Perspective. New Haven: Yale University Press.

Bodley, John H. (1990). Victims of Progress, 3rd ed. Mountainview, Calif.:
Mayfield.

Bradley, Candice, Carmella C. Moore, Michael L. Burton, and Douglas R.
White. (1990). "A Cross-Cultural Historical Analysis of Subsistence
Change." American Anthropologist, 92: 447–457.

Divale, William Tulio (1974). "Migration, External Warfare, and Matrilocal
Residence." Behavior Science Research, 9: 75–133.

Eckhardt, William (1973). "Anthropological Correlates of Primitive Militarism." Peace Research, 5: 5–10.

Ember, Carol R. (1974). "An Evaluation of Alternative Theories of Matrilocal versus Patrilocal Residence." Behavior Science Research, 9: 135–149.

(1978) Myths about Hunter-Gatherers. Ethnology, 17: 439–448.

Ember, Carol R. and Melvin Ember (1972). "The Conditions Favoring
Multilocal Residence." Southwestern Journal of Anthropology, 28: 382–400.

(1992a) Resource Unpredictability, Mistrust, and War: a Cross-Cultural
Study. Journal of Conflict Resolution, 36: 242–262.

(1992b) Warfare, Aggression and Resource Problems: Cross-Cultural
Codes. Behavior Science Research, 26: 169–226.

(1993) Issues in Cross-Cultural Studies of Interpersonal Violence. Violence
and Victims, 8: 217–233.

(1994) War, Socialization, and Interpersonal Violence: Cross-Cultural
Study. Journal of Conflict Resolution 38: 620–646.

Ember, Carol R., Melvin Ember, and Bruce Russett (1992). Peace between
Participatory Polities: A Cross-cultural Test of the "Democracies Rarely
Fight Each Other" Hypothesis. World Politics, 44: 573–599.

Ember, Carol R., Bruce Russett and Melvin Ember (1993). Political Participation and Peace: Cross-Cultural Codes. Cross-Cultural Research (former-
ly Behavior Science Research), 27: 97–145.

Ember, Melvin (1982). Statistical Evidence for an Ecological Explanation of Warfare. *American Anthropologist*, **84**: 645–649.

Ember, Melvin, and Carol R. Ember (1971). The Conditions Favoring Matrilocal versus Patrilocal Residence." *American Anthropologist*, **73**: 571–594.

(1983) Marriage, Family, and Kinship: Comparative Studies of Social Organization. New Haven, Conn.: HRAF Press.

(1994) Cross-Cultural Studies of War and Peace: Recent Achievements and Future Possibilities. In S. P. Reyna and R. E. Downs, eds. Studying War: Anthropological Perspectives, New York: Gordon & Breach, pp. 185–208.

(1995) Worldwide Cross-Cultural Studies and their Relevance for Archaeology. *Journal of Archaeological Research* **3**: 87–111.

Erchak, Gerald M. (1997). Family Violence. In Carol R. Ember and Melvin Ember, eds., Research Frontiers in Anthropology, Vol. 4. Englewood Cliffs, NJ: Prentice Hall.

Erchak, Gerald M. and Richard Rosenfeld (1994). Societal Isolation, Violent Norms, and Gender Relations: A Re-examination and Extension of Levinson's Model of Wife Beating. *Cross-Cultural Research* **28**: 111–113.

Levinson, David (1989). Family Violence in Cross-Cultural Perspective. Newbury Park, CA: Sage Publications.

Loftin, Colin Kim (1971). Warfare and Societal Complexity: a Cross-Cultural Study of Organized Fighting in Preindustrial Societies. Ann Arbor: University Microfilms, no. 71–30, 575.

Murdock, George Peter (1967). Ethnographic Atlas: A Summary. *Ethnology* **6**: 109–236.

Murdock, George P., and Diana O. Morrow (1980). Subsistence Economy and Supportive Practices: Cross-Cultural Codes 1. In Herbert Barry, III, and Alice Schlegel, eds. Cross-Cultural Samples and Codes. Pittsburgh: University of Pittsburgh Press, pp. 45–73. An earlier version appeared in *Ethnology* **9** (1970): 302–330.

Murdock, George P., and Caterina Provost (1980). Measurement of Cultural Complexity. In Herbert Barry, III, and Alice Schlegel, eds. Cross-Cultural Samples and Codes. Pittsburgh: University of Pittsburgh Press, pp. 147–160.

Murdock, George P., and Douglas R. White (1980). Standard Cross-Cultural Sample. In Herbert Barry, III, and Alice Schlegel, eds. Cross-Cultural Samples and Codes. Pittsburgh: University of Pittsburgh Press, pp. 3–43.

Otterbein, Keith F. (1968). Internal War: A Cross-Cultural Study. *American Anthropologist*, **70**: 277–289.

(1970) The Evolution of War: A Cross-Cultural Study. New Haven: HRAF Press.

Otterbein, Keith F., and Charlotte Swanson Otterbein (1965). "An Eye for an Eye, a Tooth for a Tooth: A Cross-Cultural Study of Feuding. *American Anthropologist*, **67**: 1470–1482.

Palmer, Stuart (1965). Murder and Suicide in Forty Non-literate Societies. *Journal of Criminal Law, Criminology and Police Science* **56**: 320–324.

(1970) Aggression in Fifty-eight Non-literate Societies: An Exploratory Analysis. *Annales Internationales de Criminologie*, **9**: 57–69.

Peregrine, Peter (1993). An Archaeological Correlate of War. *North American Archaeologist*, **14**: 139–151.

Ross, Marc H. (1983). Political Decision-Making and Conflict: Additional Cross-Cultural Codes and Scales. *Ethnology*, **22**: 169–192.

(1985) Internal and External Conflict and Violence: Cross-Cultural Evidence and a New Analysis. *Journal of Conflict Resolution*, **29**: 547–579.

Russell, Elbert W. (1972). Factors of Human Aggression: a Cross-Cultural Factor Analysis of Characteristics Related to Warfare and Crime. *Behavior Science Notes*, **7**: 275–312.

Schrire, Carmel (1984). Wild Surmises on Savage Thoughts. In Schrire, C. (ed.), Past and Present in Hunter Gatherer Studies, Orlando: Academic Press.

Sillitoe, Paul (1977). Land Shortage and War in New Guinea. *Ethnology*, **16**: 71–81.

Sipes, Richard G. (1973). War, Sports, and Aggression: An Empirical Test of Two Rival Theories. *American Anthropologist*, **75**: 64–86.

Sipes, Richard G. and B. A. Robertson (1975). Malevolent magic, mutilation, punishment, and aggression. Paper presented at the annual meeting of the American Anthropological Association, San Francisco.

Trigger, Bruce G. (1981) Archaeology and the Ethnographic Present. *Anthropologica*, **23**: 3–17.

Wilmsen, Edwin N. (1989). Land Filled with Flies: A Political Economy of the Kalahari. Chicago: University of Chicago Press.

Chapter
TWO

Violence Against Women: Raiding and Abduction in Prehistoric Michigan

Richard G. Wilkinson
University at Albany
Albany, New York

In 1916, the Seneca archaeologist Arthur C. Parker noted of his ancestors,

> Everywhere there was peril and everywhere mourning. Men were ragged with sacrifice and the women scarred with the flints, so everywhere there was misery. Feuds with outer nations, feuds with brother nations, feuds with sister nations and feuds of families and of clans made every warrior a stealthy man who liked to kill.

Parker's words have found empirical backing in countless studies of violence in ancestral human populations. These studies continue the documentation of the fact of human violence and aggression, and might be viewed as counterpoints to the conceptualization of the peaceful good old days of simpler societies, a conceptualization which represents a particular construction of reality born in the late 1960s. Perhaps viewing ancestral populations as pacific provided us with some hope for the future, as it suggested that current violence – then in Vietnam, now seemingly everywhere – is an aberration of the basic *blauplan* of humanity. Intergroup and interpersonal violence, hopes notwithstanding, is ubiquitous within our species, and in our closest evolutionary relatives (Wrangham 1987).

Excessive violence among non-Western peoples has often been seen as a result of contact with Europeans and other "advanced" cultures (see, for example, Ferguson and Whitehead 1992), and the inter-group violence among Native Americans graphically depicted in the ethnohistoric literature (the Jesuit Relations, for example) has been viewed as another example of contact-induced social pathology. In northeastern North America, it is axiomatic that European expansion and the development of the fur trade were crucial to Iroquoian militarism and to the diplomatic aspects of the Iroquois Confederacy (Abler 1992: 151). It seems unlikely, however, that such militancy appeared suddenly and without precedent in the 17th century. To use a biological metaphor, the behavioral variation that is aggressiveness must have been already present for "selection" to favor it. The social, psychological and biological ills which accompanied the European incursions in the Americas are, of course, real and certainly worthy of our concerns. But these related ills also may be used to mask the reality of populations which were engaged in occasional violence even without ideas from Western Europe.

The purpose of the present study is to describe evidence for interpersonal violence found within a prehistoric cemetery population. This evidence, in the form of cranial trauma, adds time depth to the types of interpersonal conflict related by Parker's quotation. Further, because of the unusual distribution of injuries by sex and age, the evidence from the Late Woodland site of Riviere aux Vase in Michigan is interpreted as demonstrating the role of women as frequent victims of this interpersonal violence. The present study is derived from a more detailed version which has been published elsewhere (Wilkinson and VanWagenen 1993).

MATERIALS AND METHODS

This study results from the continuing access to a valuable collection of prehistoric skeletal material. In examining the skeletal material from an archaeological site in Southeastern Michigan known as Riviere aux Vase, I noted that several of the individuals had cranial fractures. Over a period of time, it seemed to me that quite a few of these individuals were females, and that seemed unusual. A few years ago a graduate student, Karen VanWagenen, was looking for a research project, and I suggested that she inventory the collection for evidence of trauma, and especially among women. The result of the study is a compendium of bone-by-bone trauma in a skeletal collection (VanWagenen 1992), and I gratefully acknowledge Karen's diligence in searching through this complex collection. As is usually the case, once we knew what we were looking for, we started to find examples of cranial trauma, and gradually the magnitude of the evidence became obvious.

The Riviere au Vase site is a multicomponent occupation, most of which consists of a cemetery utilized during the period of A.D. 1000 to 1300 (Fitting 1965, Fitting and Zurel 1976, Krakker 1983). Chronologically, the site fits into the later part of the Late Woodland period, and the material culture and mortuary behaviors align the site with other contemporary occupations throughout southwestern Ontario, southeastern Michigan and northwestern Ohio (Stothers 1979, Murphy and Ferris 1990). The cemetery, excavated in the summers of 1936 and 1937, was located about a mile from the western shore of Lake St. Claire, north of Detroit, Michigan. The mortuary behaviors at the site are many and complex, and there remain many critically important questions to be answered about the site and the people who used it in prehistory. This study is another step in the direction of a more complete understanding of the Riviere aux Vase site and its place in the Late Woodland prehistory of the southern Great Lakes.

The skeletal sample from the site consists of the very incomplete remains of 220 to 350 people. A painstaking review of excavation records, site maps, photographs and skeletal material indicates that a maximum of about 370 individuals were interred in 145 burials (Wilkinson and Bender 1991); a variety of filters have removed significant parts of the original mortuary population. For example, this large site containing 145 burials was excavated over a period of weeks, not months, and many of the burials were superimposed, both factors contributing to some apparent confusion about burial and individual identity in the field. Post-excavational problems also resulted in the loss of provenience of some of the skeletal material; as many as three separate numbering systems were applied to the remains, with insufficient linkage among the systems.

A demographic reconstruction has been attempted elsewhere (Bender 1979) and, acknowledging all of the caveats about paleodemographic data and inferences, it can minimally be said that the Riviere aux Vase skeletal sample is concordant with many other paleodemographic reconstructions, showing a seeming under-representation of children and infants. It is otherwise "typical" with the possible exceptions of the presence of a fairly high frequency of older adults, and of young adults, especially females. The "over-representation" of young women in the mortality sample is of clear importance to the issue of violence in the Riviere aux Vase population, as is discussed below.

Age and sex determinations had been made on the sample in the recent past, and all individuals with trauma were subjected to additional sex and age related observations. Traumatic injuries are interesting and informative, but they take on additional significance when viewed through age- and sex-specific lenses. This significance becomes especially clear in the Riviere aux Vase sample, because of the unequal representation of sex, and to a lesser extent, age, in the injured subsample.

Determination of sex and age in this sample was accomplished using the usual battery of forensic techniques applicable to skeletal remains (see, for example, White 1991: 305–327), with emphasis on the bony pelvis when possible. Because of the mortuary behaviors in vogue at the site, however, the majority of the skulls did not have associated pelves; indeed, many did not have much in the area of postcranial material at all. In such cases, sex and age were estimated on the basis of skull morphology, dental attrition (Lovejoy 1985) and ectocranial suture closure (Meindl and Lovejoy 1985). While the aging methods are less precise than desired, the relatively strong degree of sexual dimorphism in the sample makes sex attribution quite comfortable. As is usual in osteological studies which utilize skeletal collections in relatively poor condition, broad age ranges are used to mitigate the effects of ambiguity in age at death determinations.

The assay which produced the cranial trauma observations consisted of a skull-by-skull examination of all represented individuals in the collection, including partial crania. Fractures were recorded as present when a depression or opening in the skull was observed, without evidence of infection, metabolic disease or other pathological condition, or of perimortem damage in the area of the fracture. To qualify as a fracture, the opening or depression must also show signs of healing, which eliminates post-mortem fractures

(Walker 1989). At least three individuals (two females, one male) did have "perimortem" fractures, and are excluded from the statistical data. Given the unambiguous evidence for cranial trauma in the series, however, I suspect that these individuals were additional victims of the violence within the society.

Data on the number of fractures per skull were recorded, as were the sizes of the injuries, their locations on the crania, and their severity, as measured by the presence or absence of endocranial damage. No accurate estimate of the frequency of cranial trauma can be made from the Riviere aux Vase sample, because of the incomplete nature of many of the crania. There are nearly equal numbers of adult male and female crania, and very unequal numbers of injured crania by sex, but meaningful frequencies are not obtainable.

AGE AND SEX

Nineteen skulls from Riviere aux Vase have depressions and/or openings which are consistent with a diagnosis of cranial fracture. Of these, fifteen are adult females, and four are adult males. The minimum age for "adults" in this study is 16 years. Of the crania in the total sample that could be assigned to a sex with a reasonable degree of certainty, 114 are female and 98 male. The female:male ratio in the injured sample is nearly 4:1, as compared to a 1:1 sex ratio (approximate) in the total sample. The difference is statistically significant ($X^2 = 4.819$; $.025 < P < .05$). In addition to the unequal distribution of injuries by sex, the age distribution also demonstrates some informative inequalities.

The age-at-death data for the cranial sample, by sex, are given in Table 2.1. Post-cranial remains are excluded from this study, as it cannot be determined how these data relate to the crania; some crania were "trophy skulls" and seemingly lacked postcranial remains, but the site also contains a relatively large number of individuals without crania. It is not currently possible to associate all of the crania with the postcranial remains. The inclusion of decimal data in the age columns of Table 2.1 reflects the distribution of individuals into the narrower age categories from previous, larger age categories (Buikstra and Mielke 1985:379, Wilkinson and Van-Wagenen 1993:194). The data in Table 2.1 form the basis of the mortality profiles represented in Figures 2.1 and 2.2.

Figure 2.1 illustrates the differences in the age-at-death distributions of the two sexes. Age categories are displayed along the

Table 2.1. Sex-specific mortality data for adults (crania only)

Age	Males	Females	Injured Males	Injured Females
16–20	3	21	0	1
21–25	7	14.25	0	3
26–30	4	4.75	0	0
31–35	10.71	8.25	0	1
36–40	8.29	7.75	1	1
41–45	11	12.18	0	2
46–50	8	5.82	0	2
51–60	14	9.43	2	3
61–70	4	13.57	1	2
71+	3	1	0	0
"Adult"	20	16	0	0
Totals	93	114	4	15

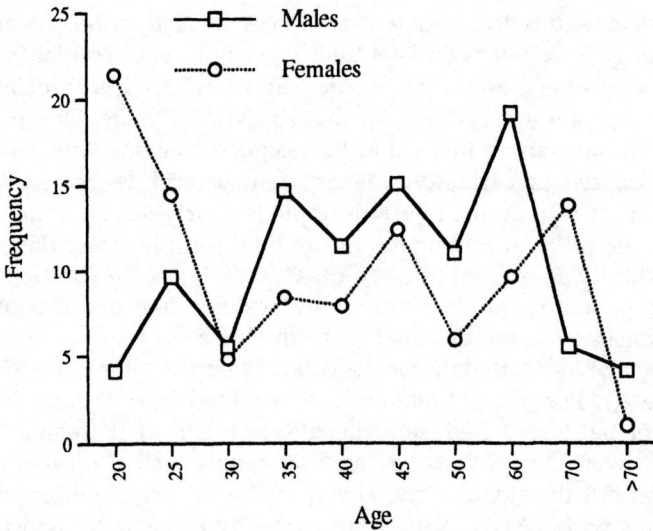

Figure 2.1. The distribution of ages at death, by sex.

horizontal axes of the mortality graphs depicted in Figures 2.1 and 2.2, with the number representing the last year in a five-year cohort, except for the 10 year intervals above age 50. The first interval depicted (20), therefore, represents ages at death from 16 to 20. Figure 2.1 demonstrates a general correspondence in the patterns

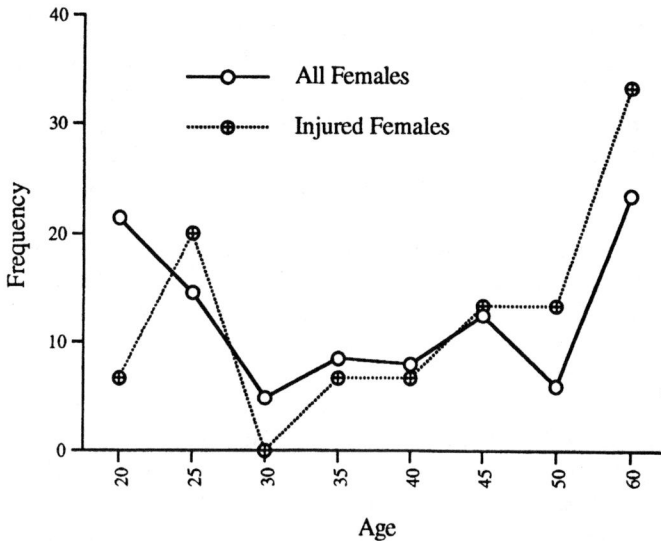

Figure 2.2. A comparison of all females with injured females, with aggregated older age groups.

of male and female mortality, with much of the difference between patterns most likely being due to small sample sizes within the age groups. There is an obvious difference, however in the young adult distributions, as females are in the clear majority. To the extent that the age-at-death data are actually representative of mortality patterns, young adult female mortality was very high within the Riviere aux Vase population. This female mortality pattern is presented in another form in Figure 2.2.

Starting with the 16–20 year age group, female mortality is high and declines precipitously to a plateau in the 26–40 year groups, then rises again in the older age groups. Mortality among the females with cranial injuries follows the same general pattern, but deviates from the overall female pattern substantially in the younger two age categories. Since only females with *healed* fractures are included in the fracture sample, it is not surprising that their numbers increase with age; to be included, a female must be a survivor of the injury. The high frequency of injured women who died in the 21–25 age range, combined with the large number of "uninjured" women who also died in young adulthood, is interpreted as evidence for substantial violence directed at this age group.

The older women in the injured sample ("older" being nervously set at 45 + years) constitute about half of the sample. With the exception of one female of about 60 years, all of these older women have "mild" injuries, consisting of relatively small, shallow depressions; the exception is a very serious fracture. It is possible that these "mild" injuries represent a form of unusual osteoporosis; typically, however, cranial indicators of post-menopausal osteoporosis are large shallow depressions in the superior parietals, and they are frequently bilateral. All of the depressions observable on these older females are consistent in their size, form, location and depth with injuries, but even if all were due instead to some improbable pathology or non-traumatic condition, there would remain an injured sample containing twice as many females as males, and all but one of reproductive age. And, all but one of the *severely* injured females are between the ages of 16 and 40.

The male cranial injury frequency estimate (4 of 93) is not unusual; indeed, it is sufficiently low to suggest that the people utilizing Riviere aux Vase as a cemetery were not experiencing generalized or random violence, *unless* males were being excluded from burial, or were being buried elsewhere. Males, of course, could have been dying on raiding parties, or may have been captured and not allowed to return, and there is ethnohistoric evidence for this pattern (the Jesuit Relations, for example). What we lack is positive evidence that it occurred in southeastern Michigan in A.D. 1300. While there are fewer male than female skulls in the Riviere aux Vase sample, the difference is not statistically significant.

The basic data, in terms of the age and sex of the injured sample by individual burial number are presented in Table 2.2, along with information on the size and severity of the injury, the number of individuals in the burial lot, the form of the burial and the number of injuries per person (Wilkinson and VanWagenen 1993: 209).

LOCATION AND SEVERITY OF INJURIES

The locational data provided in Table 2.2, combined with size of injury measurements are used to display graphically the distribution of injuries in the crania of females and males. Figure 2.3 displays the cumulative female injuries, and illustrates the fact that these injuries are numerous, widespread and of varying sizes. The fact that female skull fractures are found in the front, rear and both sides of the skulls made a flat projection of the skull necessary to illustrate the location and size of the injuries, and the facial bones

Table 2.2. Descriptive data on cranial injuries

Individual/ Burial	Age	No. injuries	Location of injuries	Size in mm.	Internal damage	No. in Burial	Burial form
FEMALES							
V6/B2	45–55	2	Lt. mid-frontal	17 × 15	no	2	Bundle
			Lt. anterior parietal	12 × 4	no		
V160/B23.2	20–25	1	Rt. posterior frontal	19 × 3	yes	2	Extended
V164/B23.1	20–25	1	Maxilla, lacrimal	na	yes	5	Skull
V177/B26	18–22	3	Rt. frontal	10 × 8	no	9	Bundle
			Center occipital	16 × 9	yes		
			Lt. parietal	53 × 25	yes		
V199/B28	40–50	1	Rt. posterior partietal	21	no	9	Skull
V201/B28	50 +	3	Lt. posterior parietal	12 × 9	no	9	Bundle
			Lt. posterior parietal	8	no		
			Lt. posterior parietal	9	no		
V204/B28	20–25	1	Rt. anterior parietal	50 × 15	yes	9	Bundle
V209/B28	50–60	1	Center occipital	39 × 12	no	9	Bundle
V212/B30	40 +	5	Center frontal	17 × 20	no	1	Extended
			Center frontal	13	no		
			Rt. frontal	11	no		
			Rt. posterior frontal	8	no		
			Rt. posterior frontal	9	no		

Table 2.2. (Continued)

Individual/ Burial	Age	No. injuries	Location of injuries	Size in mm.	Internal damage	No. in Burial	Burial form
V714/B66	50–60	1	Rt. posterior parietal	17 × 11	no	3	Bundle
V722/B70	60–70	1	Center frontal	13	no	2	Extended
V845/B76	30–35	3	Lt. spheno-parietal	70	yes	1	Extended
			Rt. posterior frontal	30 × 9	yes		
			Rt. occipital	33 × 19	yes		
V857/B83	35–40	1	Rt. posterior parietal	60	yes	6	Ossuary
V1027/vv25	40–50	1	Lt. superior parietal	21 × 14	no	3	n.a.
V1051/vv30	60 +	1	Center occipital	42 × 23	yes	2	Extended
MALES							
V328/B39	50 +	2	Center frontal	12	no	5	Extended
			Lt. frontal	14	no		
V555/B54	50–60	1	Rt. anterior parietal	17 × 6	no	9	Bundle
V736/B72	60 +	1	Rt. frontal	32 × 18	no	13	Skull
V863/B87	35–40	2	Center frontal	33 × 19	no	1	Extended
			Center frontal	10	no		

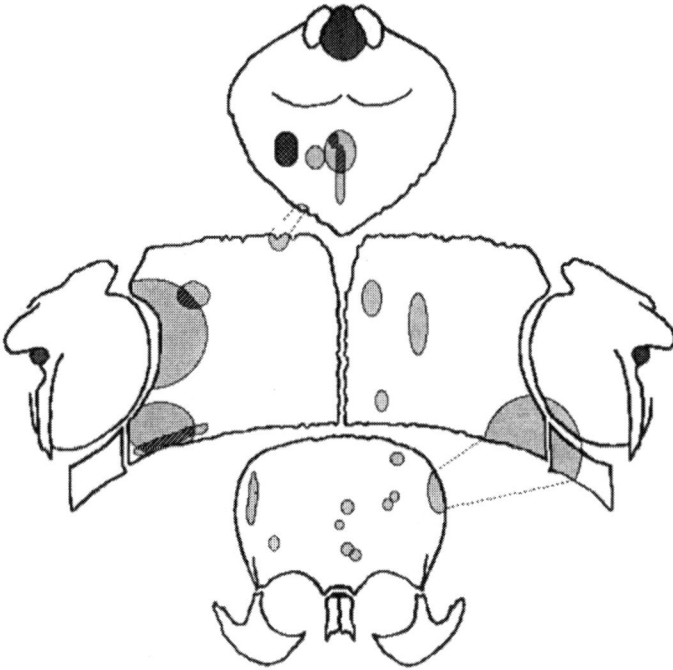

Figure 2.3. Location of injuries on the female crania from Riviere aux Vase.

were eliminated because only one individual has observable facial damage, and the damage is not depressive or penetrating. This female (V164) has injuries to the lacrimal bones and adjacent orbital section of the maxilla. Male injuries are illustrated in Figure 2.4; the relatively few, less severe injuries among males are restricted to the front portion of the skull. Modern data from northern Europe, in which the sample (300) was derived from emergency room cases of depressed fracture (Braakman and Jennett 1975), indicate a broadly similar locational distribution to the combined male and female samples from Riviere aux Vase. In the modern sample, the majority (53%) of the fractures were in the parietal bones, whereas the frontal bone is the more common site of the prehistoric fractures. The causes of the fractures in the two samples are, of course, radically dissimilar, as the modern sample is strongly influenced by vehicular accidents. If traumatic force was to be applied randomly or evenly across the skull, the parietals should show higher fracture frequencies because they

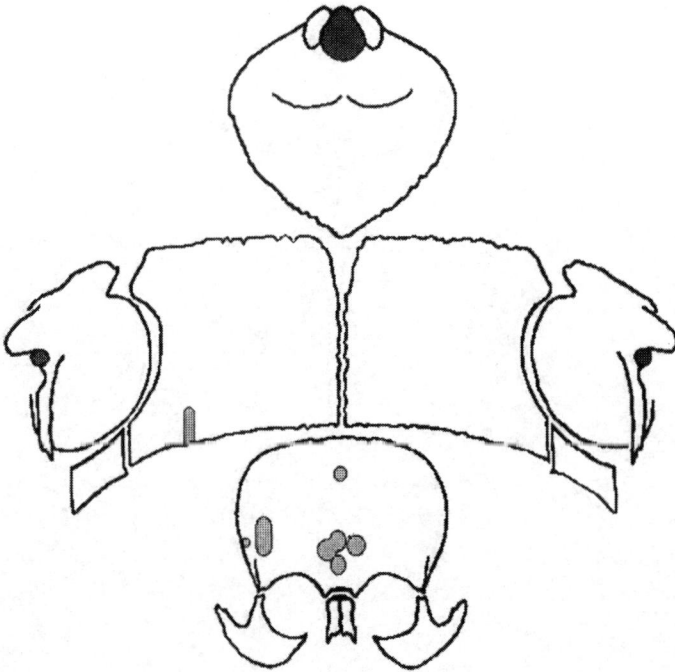

Figure 2.4. Location of injuries on the male crania from Riviere aux Vase.

constitute more area of the vault than does the frontal or occipital. Also, the frontal bone has twice the resistance strength of the parietals (DeGrood 1975), so the "preference" for frontal fractures in the Riviere aux Vase sample may be an indication of the (unknown) motivation for the attack. The severe injuries in the Riviere aux Vase sample, however, are in bones other than the frontal. The greater resistance strength of the frontal bone may explain some of the difference in the observed severity of the injuries, but it is also the case that the injuries in the frontal bones are smaller than those located elsewhere on the vault. Among the females, the frontal bone injuries (N = 10) have an average areal dimension of 148 mm^2, and the injuries to the parietals, occipitals and sphenoid/temporal areas (N = 14) are considerably larger in areal dimension (845 mm^2). Among the males, the average size of the frontal bone injuries (N = 5) is 310 mm^2. The one parietal injury among the males is a relatively small one, with an area of 102 mm^2.

Severity of injury is suggested by the presence or absence of endocranial damage. In the majority of the fractures, including those in the four males, there is no indication of internal injury; the inner table of the skull appears unaffected. In several of the females, however, the blow to the skull was forceful enough to depress the bone into the dura, and the bone did not resume its integrity after healing. In others the bone itself was apparently dislodged, leaving an opening in the skull, the borders of which are smoothed with remodeled bone. The evidence for cranial fracture, then, varies from small, shallow depressions which mimic those reported by Walker (1989) from the Channel Islands of southern California, to the most extreme case, V845, a 30–35 year old female with multiple, severe injuries. V845 has a large, healed "pond fracture" (cf. Merbs 1989) of the left temple, a deep vertical depression in the right temple, and a rectangular perforation in the occipital bone. All are healed, but the large, circular fracture in the left temple suggests that death occurred within weeks of this injury. Another female, V857, also has a large circular fracture which resulted in a permanent 10 mm displacement of the inferior parietal bone into the cranial cavity. This woman also survived this significant injury, as the circular crack which outlined the original break in the right parietal bone is about 90% obliterated. These two cases are illustrated in Figure 2.5.

Although this study concentrates on the cranial evidence for fractures, data are also available for the rest of the skeletal material from the site (VanWagenen 1992). Males and females experienced "normal" levels of postcranial fractures, and in "normal" locations: vertebrae, radii, clavicles and an occasional ulna and fibula. "Parry" fractures of the ulna occur, but infrequently. Unfortunately, the burial format and post-depositional disturbances make associating the ulnas with the skulls impossible in many cases. If the absence of forearm fractures is not simply an artifact of preservation, perhaps the women were bound or somehow restrained, and thereby prevented from deflecting the assault. Since most of the severe injuries are in the posterior 2/3 of the skulls, it is also possible that the usual mode of attack was from the rear. The most that can be said is that there are surprisingly few postcranial injuries, given the high frequency of cranial trauma. Violence, in the form of blunt weapon attack, was directed at the head, and it was directed at the women.

The severity, location and female predominance of the cranial injuries are clear indicators of intentional, interpersonal violence. Accidental injuries are too improbable, as one would have to assume significant sex differences in agility, and then posit that

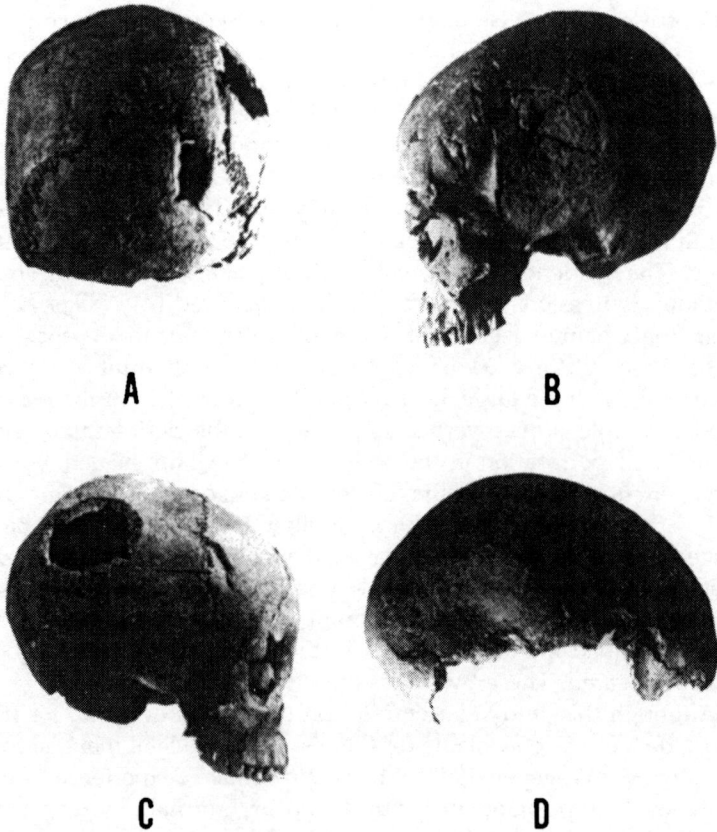

Figure 2.5. Examples of severe injuries in two Riviere aux Vase females, V845 (A,B,C) and V857 (D). See text for detailed information.

accident victims fell on or struck objects with their heads. The age distribution of the injured sample must also be considered, and far too many of the victims are young adults, and none are children, making accidental injury nearly impossible as an explanation. Self-infliction is just as unlikely, if not impossible, for the same reasons.

DISCUSSION

At this point it is necessary to place the Riviere aux Vase evidence into a broader, comparative framework, and then to deal with the question of the causes of the observed violence. Although we cannot determine the actual frequency or prevalence of cranial injury at Riviere aux Vase, the 19 identified individuals with cranial fractures are drawn from a total of 212 fragmentary and complete crania, and can be used to represent a minimum frequency estimate of 9%. The minimum frequency for the female subsample is 15/114, or 13%. Frequencies of fractures among the large Mississippian populations from Ft. Ancient (Cassidy 1984) and Moundville (Powell 1988) are less than 7%. At the Libben site in Northeastern Ohio, a site that is spatially, temporally and culturally very similar to Riviere aux Vase, none of the fractures have been attributed to violence, and the overall frequency is 7.1% (Lovejoy and Heiple 1981). Cranial fractures are especially uncommon among the Libben individuals. Evidence of violence is also lacking in the skeletal remains from six sites associated with the Caddoan cultural sequence (Rose *et al.* 1984).

Fractures were common among the Late Woodland and Middle Mississippian individuals from the Dickson Mound site in Illinois (Goodman *et al.* 1984), but specific data on cranial injuries are not provided, nor are causes assigned to the observed trauma. Direct skeletal evidence for substantial violence in the prehistoric record is available, however. At the prehistoric Norris Farms No. 36 cemetery in Illinois, for example, over 16% of the 264 individuals in the skeletal sample are interpreted as having been killed by others, and several have clear, weapon-fitting perforations in their skulls (Milner and Smith 1990, Milner *et al.* 1991). In what is one of the more compelling cases of prehistoric violence, the skeletal remains of more than 400 fourteenth century Indians from the Crow Creek site in South Dakota provide evidence of large-scale violence, complete with scalping and mutilation of all victims (Willey 1990). Of special interest is the relative scarcity of reproductive aged women in the Crow Creek sample. Since all individuals in the sample died violently, the scarcity of younger women may indicate that they were captured. As discussed below, this scenario may have relevance for understanding the *high* frequency of young women in the Riviere aux Vase skeletal sample.

Warfare and raiding were ubiquitous in Native American groups as first contacted and described by Europeans. Throughout the northeast and Great Lakes, and into the southeastern United States indigenous peoples participated in long-term, ongoing interactions punctuated by killing and abduction (Callender 1978; Day 1978; Eid 1979; Fenton 1978; Forbes 1970; Goddard 1978; Hadlock

1947; Heidenreich 1978; Hudson 191976; Knowles 1940; Otterbein 1979; Starna and Watkins 1991). The addition of prehistoric evidence from archaeology to the ethnohistoric and ethnographic descriptions of intergroup violence provides a powerful explanatory device for interpreting data such as those from Riviere aux Vase. Before dealing with the raiding and abduction model, however, some other scenarios need to be examined.

Inter- and intra-group violence is normally attributed to, and accomplished by, men (see Burbank 1992 for references and *caveats*). But it is also the case that women are responsible for aggressive acts, and we cannot dismiss women as perpetrators out-of-hand. Conflict among women, including physical assault, is more common in polygamous societies (Levinson 1989: 25, 32). Polygamy was not uncommon among Eastern Woodland groups after contact, although few women in these groups participated in this form of relationship.

Among the more comprehensive accounts of gender-based aggression is that provided by Burbank (1992), who documents interpersonal violence in an Australian Aborigine population. Aggression in this society is viewed as normal, and is brought under social control by members of the community. Both men and women are victims of violence, and both are perpetrators. Women are more often the victims of physical injury than are men, and women are injured twice as frequently by men as are men injured by women, but women are injured as frequently by other women as they are by men (Burbank 1992: 266). In this society, then, the existence of an injured woman does not provide evidence for determining the sex of the perpetrator. Burbank's study indicates a degree of variation in the participants of intra-group violence, variation which might otherwise be ignored as aberrant.

Assuming for now the more traditional view, that the perpetrators of the violence at Riviere aux Vase were males, the next choice is between males within the group, on the one hand, and those without, on the other. And from within, males can be unrelated or related, of the latter, by marriage or kinship. Attention in the latter case is most easily focused on spouses or their equivalents, as we are rather keenly aware of the high frequency of spousal abuse in certain societies, accounting for most of the cases of family violence in a world-wide sample (Levinson 1989). Spousal abuse would correlate with the unequal distribution of injuries in the two sexes, as it would explain both the higher frequencies of female injuries, and the low frequencies of male injuries. Spousal abuse would also correlate with the several cases of multiple injuries, as physically abused women tend to evince multiple injuries. The problems with this explanation include an absence of corroborating evidence in the ethnohistoric record, a probability of biasing the past with contemporary experience, and to a lesser extent the magnitude of the injuries in some cases.

The lack of contact-period observations of "domestic violence" may well be due to the lack of the observers' sensitivity to such violence. Perhaps the voyageurs did not deem the battering of women by their mates to be of sufficient importance to note. But the observers did notice, and reported on at length the existence of intergroup raiding, torturing and capturing of women. Such interactions occurred in the Great Lakes area within 200–300 years of the occupation of Riviere aux Vase. Bioarchaeological evidence from sites roughly contemporaneous with Riviere aux Vase – Norris Farms 36 in Illinois (Milner *et al.* 1991), Crow Creek in South Dakota (Willey 1990) – show prehistoric intergroup violence on a substantial scale. Interestingly, the age and sex data from the Crow Creek massacre show a deficit of reproductive age women. It is likely that these women escaped death at Crow Creek by being abducted.

The nearly universal occurrence of interpersonal violence within and among human populations, combined with observations of who participates in such violence, leads to the unhelpful conclusion that any group of people having the physical ability to cause harm to others may be responsible for causing such harm. Age and infirmity may be the only effective deterrents to the commission of violent acts, at least on a world-wide scale. In the face of such a ubiquitous penchant for aggression, can we make any reasonable or probabilistic statements about the Riviere aux Vase situation? Or are spousal abuse, intra-sex competition, and raiding and abduction all equally likely to have produced the observed injuries, or at least to have been responsible for some of the injuries?

Fortunately, we are not without evidence to implicate a more likely cause of the observed injuries at Riviere aux Vase. The injured women do not exist in a cultural vacuum, unassociated with a cultural history. Portions of this cultural history have been observed and recorded, in the form of the accounts of European explorers, and the archaeological documentation of the violence. I believe that we must place the people and behaviors of Riviere aux Vase within the framework of a broader historical context, a context which includes the various tribal groups which inhabited the

Great Lakes and Northeast several centuries after the occupation of Riviere aux Vase. The behaviors of these descendant groups are much more reasonable models of ancestral behaviors than are the contemporary accounts of violence among Australian Aborigines or middle class America.

If we look to the evidence at hand, and that which seems more relevant to the prehistoric occupants of Riviere aux Vase, abduction – or attempted abduction – seems the more likely explanation for the women's injuries. Abduction with or without subsequent slavery was relatively common among the Iroquois (Starna and Watkins 1991, Fenton 1978, Heidenreich 1978), the Western Abenaki (Day 1978), the Miami (Callender 1978b), the Illinois (Callender 1978a), the Delaware (Goddard 1978) and various tribal groups in the southeast (Hudson 1976:253). Abduction and/or "adoption" into a new group was commonly accompanied by physical violence.

The fact that abducted women were frequently incorporated into the social system of the capturing group, including European captives in historic times, makes the cultural identification of captives impossible, in terms of associating cultural materials, skeletal remains and extra-group affiliation. The injured women from Riviere aux Vase were not singled out for special burial rites, their bones were not subjected to special curation or alteration and they were, in general, treated as all other members of the burial sample (Wilkinson and VanWagenen 1993). If they were captives, they were integrated into the society well enough to be treated as natal members. If they were natal members, they may represent victims of attempted abduction; perhaps the severely injured women are those who failed to cooperate with their abductors.

At this point, clarification of the group memberships of the people interred at Riviere aux Vase is needed to deal with the questions surrounding natal vs. external affiliation of the women. The burial data can support conflicting interpretations: either the site was utilized by one group with widely varying and quickly changing mortuary rituals, or it was used by several groups with very different mortuary traditions. The site is characterized by extreme varibility in burial formats (Wilkinson and Bender 1991). Extended, primary inhumations are the more common form of burial, but also prevalent are ossuary-type burials, with apparent mixing of skeletal elements, group burials of one or more primary burials with accompanying secondary bundle burials, isolated skulls, isolated trunks (articulated thorax and pelvis), cremations, partial burials (selected parts of the skeleton are buried; some are articulated, some are re-articulated) and multiple-individual, primary burials. Given the high degree of cultural complexity implied by all of this mortuary diversity, it is hoped that biological evidence can be brought to bear on the question of group membership of the injured women, and this inquiry is currently being pursued by Carol Raemsch.

I am tempted to say that the relatively small number of injured females is an indication of occasional, sporadic violence. After all, 15 victims spread over 300 years of use of the cemetery may represent only one victim per generation. However, the evidence we now have represents only the *recovered cases*, and the cases where injuries affected bone and the victim survived. Also, most of the crania from Riviere aux Vase are fragmentary, and we therefore have a great deal of potentially missing data. To be included in our sample, the victim had not only to survive the injury, but she later had to die and be interred at Riviere aux Vase, and then her remains had to persist for the next 700 years. It is also the case that four of the victims were buried in the same grave, and whatever else this burial phenomenon may signify, it also indicates the relative contemporaneity of at least some of the victims of violence.

Bones relay only a partial story of a population's experiences, and a small amount of evidence may be indicative of a very common problem. What is needed now is a review of skeletal material from sites related to Riviere aux Vase in space and time. Riviere aux Vase is a site which has provided insight to lifeways of Native Americans, and continues to do so 60 years after its excavation. Now we must hurry before the information is lost forever in the process of reburial.

ACKNOWLEDGEMENTS

Early versions of this work were greatly improved with the assistance of George Milner, William Starna, Susan Bender, Karen Van-Wagenen and the ever-diligent anonymous reviewers; my thanks to all for your help, and my absolution from responsibility for the interpretations. The University at Albany Office for Research and Research Foundation provided funding for early research on the collections, and the University of Michigan Museum of Anthropology provided expertise, facilities and hospitality.

REFERENCES

Abler, T. (1992). "Beavers and Muskets. Iroquois Military Fortunes in the Face of European Colonization." In *War in the Tribal Zone; Expanding States and Indigenous Warfare*, eds. R. B. Ferguson and N. L. Whitehead, pp. 151–174. Santa Fe: School of American Research Press.

Bender, S. J. (1979). "Paleodemographic Analysis of a Late Woodland Site in Southeastern Michigan." *Mid-Continental Journal of Archaeology*, **4**: 183–208.

Braakman, R. and Jennett, B. (1975). "Depressed Skull Fracture (Non-missile)." In *Injuries of the Brain and Skull, Part I*, eds. P. J. Vinken and G. W. Bruyn, pp. 403–415. New York: American Elsevier.

Buikstra, J. E. and Mielke, J. H. (1985). "Demography, Diet and Health." In *The Analysis of Prehistoric Diets*, eds. R. I. Gilbert and J. H. Mielke, eds. pp. 359–422. New York: Academic Press.

Burbank, V. (1990). "Sex, Gender and Difference. Dimensions of Aggression in an Australian Aboriginal Community." *Human Nature*, **31**:251–278.

Callendar, C. (1978a). "Illinois." In *Northeast. Handbook of North American Indians, Vol. 15*, ed. B. C. Trigger, pp. 673–680. Washington, D. C.: Smithsonian Institution Press.

———— (1978b). "Miami." In *Northeast. Handbook of North American Indians*, **15**, ed. Bruce C. Trigger, pp. 681–689. Washington, D. C.: Smith- sonian Institution.

Cassidy, C. M. (1984). "Skeletal Evidence of Prehistoric Subsistence Adaptation in the Central Ohio River Valley." In *Paleopathology at the Origins of Agriculture*, Cohen, M. and Armelagos, G. J. eds. pp. 307–346, New York: Academic Press.

Day, G. M. (1978). "Western Abenaki." In *Northeast. Handbook of North American Indians*, ed. Bruce C. Trigger, **15**:148–159. Washington, D.C.: Smithsonian Institution Press.

DeGrood, M. P. A. M. (1975). "Skull Fractures." In *Injuries of the Brain and Skull, Part I*, eds. P. J. Vinken and G. W. Bruyn, pp. 387–402. New York: American Elsevier.

Eid, L. (1979). "The Ojibwa-Iroquois War: The War the Five Nations did not Win." *Ethnohistory* **26**:297–324.

Fenton, W. N. (1978). "Northern Iroquois Cultre Patterns." In *Northeast. Handbook of North American Indians*, Bruce C. Trigger, ed. **15**:296–321. Washington, D. C.: Smithsonian Institution Press.

Ferguson, R. B. and Whitehead, N. L. (Eds.) (1992). *War in the Tribal Zone: Expanding States and Indigenous Warfare*. Santa Fe: School of American Research Press.

Forbes, A. (1970). "Two and a Half Centuries of Conflict: The Iroquois and the Laurentian Wars." *Pennsylvania Archaeologist*, **40**:130–133.

Fitting, J. E. (1965). *Late Woodland Cultures of Southeastern Michigan*. Ann Arbor: University of Michigan Museum of Anthropology, Anthropological Papers, No. 24.

Fitting, J. E. and Zurel, R. L. (1976). "The Detroit and St. Clair River Area." In The *Late Prehistory of the Lake Erie Drainage Basin: A 1972 Symposium* Revised, ed. D. Brose, pp. 214–250, Cleveland: Cleveland Museum of Natural History.

Goddard, I. (1978). "Delaware." In *Northeast. Handbook of North American Indians*, ed. Bruce C. Trigger, **15**:213–239. Washington, D. C.: Smithsonian Institution Press.

Goodman, A. H., Martin, D. L. Armelagos, G. J. and Clark, G. (1984). "Indicators of Stress from Bone and Teeth." In *Paleopathology at the Origins of Agriculture*, eds. M. Cohen and G. J. Armelagos, pp. 13–49, New York: Academic Press.

Hadlock, W. S. (1947). "War Among the Northeastern Woodland Indians." *American Anthropologist*, **49**:204–221.

Heidenreich, C. E. (1978) "Huron." In *Northeast. Handbook of North American Indians*, ed. Bruce C. Trigger, **15**:368–388. Washington, D. C.: Smithsonian Institution Press.

Hudson, C. (1976). *The Southeastern Indians*. Knoxville: University of Tennessee Press.

Knowles, N. (1940). "The Torture of Captives by the Indians of Eastern North America." *Proceedings of the American Philosophical Society*, 82:151–225.

Krakker, J. J. (1983). *Changing Sociocultural Systems During the Late Prehistoric Period in Southeast Michigan*. Ph.D. dissertation, University of Michigan. Ann Arbor.

Levinson, D. (1989). *Family Violence in Cross-Cultural Perspective*. Newbury Park, CA: Sage Publications.

Lovejoy, C. O. (1985). "Dental Wear in the Libben Population: Its Functional Pattern and Role in the Determination of Adult Skeletal Age at Death." *American Journal of Physical Anthropology*, **68**:47–56.

Lovejoy, C. O. and Heiple, W.G. (1981). "The Analysis of Fractures in Skeletal Populations with an Example from the Libben Site, Ottawa County, Ohio." *American Journal of Physical Anthropology*, **55**:529–541.

Meindl, R. S. and C. O. Lovejoy (1985). "Ectocranial Suture Closure: A Revised Method for the Determination of Skeletal Age at Death Based on the Lateral-Anterior Sutures." *American Journal of Physical Anthropology*, **68**:57–66.

Merbs, C. F. (1989). "Trauma." In *Reconstruction of life from the Skeleton*, eds. M. Y. Iscan and K. A. R. Kennedy, eds. pp. 161–189, New York: Alan R Liss.

Milner, G. R. and Smith, V. G. (1990). "Oneota Human Skeletal Remains." In *Archaeological Investigations at the Morton Village and Norris Farms 36 Cemetery*, eds. S. K. Santure, A. D. Harn and D. Esarey, eds. pp. 111–148, Springfield IL: Illinois State Museum Reports of Investigations, No. 45.

Milner, G. R., Anderson, E. and Smith, V. G. (1991). "Warfare in Late Prehistoric West-central Illinois." *American Antiquity*, **56**:581–603.

Murphy, C. and Ferris, N. (1990). "The Late Woodland Western Basin Tradition of Southwestern Ontario." In *The Archaeology of Southern Ontario to A.D. 1650*, eds. C. J. Ellis and N. Ferris, pp. 189–278. London ONT: Occasional Publication of the London Chapter, Ontario Archaeological Society, Number 5.

Otterbein, K. (1979). "Huron or Iroquois: A Case Study in Intertribal Warfare." *Ethnohistory*, **26**:141–152.

Parker, A. C. (1916). *The Construction of the Five Nations, or the Iroquois Book of the Great Law*. Albany: New York State Museum Press.

Powell, M. L. (1988). *Status and Health in Prehistory: A Case Study of the Moundville Chiefdom*. Washington DC: Smithsonian Institution Press.

Rose, J. C., Burnett, B. A. Nassaney, M. S. and Blaeuer, M. W. (1984). "Paleopathology and the Origins of Maize Agriculture in the Lower Mississippi Valley and Caddoan Culture Areas." In *Paleopathology at the Origins of Agriculture*, eds M. Cohen and G. J. Armelagos, pp. 393–424, New York: Academic Press.

Starna, W. A. and Watkins, R. (1991). "Northern Iroquoian Slavery." *Ethnohistory*, **38**:34–57.

Stothers, D. M. (1979). "The Western Basin Tradition: Algonquin or Iroquoian?" *Pennsylvania Archaeologist*, **49**:13–30.

Van Wagenen, K. M. (1992). *Skeletal Fractures of the Late Woodland Riviere Aux Vase Skeletal Collection*. MA Thesis, University at Albany, Albany,

VanWagenen, K. M. and Wilkinson, R. G. (1990). "Skeletal Evidence of Sex-Specific Interpersonal Violence in a Great Lakes Prehistoric Population." *American Journal of Physical Anthropology*, **81**:311.

Walker, P. L. (1989). "Cranial Injuries as Evidence of Violence in Prehistoric Southern California." *American Journal of Physical Anthropology*, **80**: 313–324.

White, T. D. (1991). *Human Osteology*. San Diego: Academic Press.

Wilkinson, R. G. and S. J. Bender (1991). "Curation, Burial and Mortuary Ceremonialism at a Late Woodland Site in Michigan. Paper presented at the 56th annual meeting, Society for American Archaeology, New Orleans, LA.

Wilkinson, R. G. and VanWagenen, K. M. (1993). "Violence against Women: Prehistoric Skeletal Evidence from Michigan." *Midcontinental Journal of Archaeology*, **18**:190–216.

Willey, P. (1990). *Prehistoric Warfare on the Great Plains: Skeletal Analysis of the Crow Creek Massacre Victims*. New York: Garland Publishing.

Wrangham, R. (1987). "The Significance of African Apes for Reconstructing Human Social Evolution." In *The Evolution of Human Behavior: Primate Models*, ed. W. G. Kinsey, pp. 51–71, Albany: State University of New York Press.

Chapter

THREE

Violence Against Women in the La Plata River Valley (A.D. 1000–1300)

Debra L. Martin
School of Natural Science, Hampshire College
Amherst, Massachusetts

INTRODUCTION

Violence commonly occurs today and it most likely played an important role in the show of power, force and resolution of disputes in the precontact/precolonial world as well. The great majority of the work on violence as culled from osteological evidence of trauma has tended to focus on male activities related to warfare (e.g., Wells 1964; Brothwell and Sandison 1967; Blakely and Mathews 1990; Milner *et al.* 1991). Apart from these observations, there have been relatively few analyses of intentional injury and risk-group identification by gender within a framework that contextualizes violence within a broader biocultural perspective. Notable exceptions to this include the work of Wilkinson and Van Wagenen (1993) for a precontact site from Michigan, and Walker (1989) for precontact sites along the California coast. Both of these pioneering studies provide models for thinking about ritualized, institutionalized or sanctioned violence against women, as well as men, in the California case.

This study places osteological evidence of intentional injury within an economic and biocultural context that takes a number of factors into consideration. Using skeletal data on trauma from several sites in the precontact American Southwest, patterns of trauma are analyzed. An analysis of male and female differences in the number of sustained injuries is used to generate a series of hypotheses regarding local and regional economic influences.

STUDIES OF TRAUMA AND VIOLENCE IN THE SOUTHWEST

The Southwest provides a distinctive setting for study because of the long-term residence by ancestral Pueblo Indians. With thousands of years of habitation in the Southwest, the Pueblo groups offer insight into the mechanisms underlying adaptability and behavioral flexibility in the face of changes over time. An impressive wealth of data already exists for many aspects of Pueblo precontact history as reconstructed from the archaeological record (to name but a few, Cordell 1984; Crown and Judge 1991; Sebastian 1992; Gumerman 1994). The importance of the Southwest for archaeological research is summarized by Rouse thusly, "[t]he Southwest occupies a special place in American archaeology . . . it has become perhaps the most intensively excavated part of the New World. Much of the present generation of American archaeologists was trained in the Southwest, and many innovations in method and theory originated there" (1962:1). Since the 1930s, thousands of sites have been excavated, and the reconstruction of health, environment, climate, trade networks, population movement, settlement patterns, housing, subsistence activities, and other facets of prehistoric Pueblo existence continue to be documented and studied. Therefore, the Southwest as a multi-regional interactive area provides an unusually rich data base for exploring relationships among availability of resources, resource allocation, alliance formation, risk-sharing, population density, settlement, health and other factors likely to have a role in the creation or maintenance of violence.

Despite all the years of research, the osteological and archaeological literature on conflict, violence and warfare in precolonial times in the Southwest is relatively small. Only recently have larger reviews and synthetic research surfaced which focus on this. Haas and Creamer (1994) and Wilcox and Haas (1994) provide detailed overviews of archaeological data that demonstrate evidence of sustained inter-village conflict (e.g., fortifications, palisades, towers, burned structures) that likely increased over time. Although not everyone agrees with these interpretations (e.g., Cameron 1990), defensive architecture and strategic location of sites seems to have been important factors in the building of many Southwest villages.

Another feature of the precolonial Pueblo landscape is the occasional occurrence of human skeletal assemblages which are disarticulated, broken, chopped, sometimes burned, and that often show signs of dismembering. These collections (which include both children and adult males and females) have been variously interpreted to represent cannibalism (Turner 1993; White, 1992), witchcraft retribution (Darling 1993), warfare (Wilcox and Haas 1994) or ritualized dismemberment (Ogilvie and Hilton, 1993). Whatever the motivation behind presumed violent deaths and perimortem alterations of the victim's bodies, it does suggest some evidence for violent action directed against subgroups in most cases that seem to be conducted without regard to age or sex.

Collectively the archaeological data on fortification and strategic location and the osteological data on victims and mass graves suggest that fighting in the form of ambushes, raids, skirmishes, or attacks by a group of aggressors may have been the status quo in many parts of the precontact Southwest. Haas and Creamer (1993) suggest that these patterns of "chronic warfare" pushed previously egalitarian and loosely connected groups into larger, politically centralized units between A.D. 1100–1300.

The litany of injury and trauma on individual skeletal remains has been noted in the literature as well, but not always with much specificity and rarely linked to other aspects of local or regional dynamics. On the one hand there are places where virtually no intentional violence is apparent. For example, Miles analyzed 179 burials from Wetherill Mesa (A.D. 1200) and he states that "... the relative absence of fractures of major external force indicates that these people lived a rather quiet life without frequent warfare, and that they did not sustain many serious falls from the cliffs and mesas where they lived" (1975:20). He further states that "... there were no depressed skull fractures, and no arrowheads or other foreign bodies imbedded in bone" (1975:24).

Akins (1986) likewise found little evidence of trauma in the Chaco series she examined. Exceptions to this include a male (Number 14 from Room 33 at Pueblo Bonito) who has "... two holes and a gash in the frontal bone" suggesting that he died in a confrontation (1986:116–117). For skeletal remains from Chaco small sites, Akins notes a few cases of post-cranial fractures, and one female (age 30 +) who had four depression fractures on the parietal.

On the other hand, some sites have yielded evidence of strife. For the Transwestern Pipeline series (circa A.D. 1200), Hermann (1993) notes that several adult females have post-cranial fractures in the fibula, sacrum, radius, and tibia. Several women had multiple healed fractures on their lower body. One female had three depression fractures on the frontal (she also had post-cranial healed fractures), and one female had a perimortem fracture on the maxilla. At Carter Ranch (circa A.D. 1200) Danforth and colleagues summarize trauma in the following manner: "... One-quarter of 24 scorable adults had healed fractures. There are two nasal fractures, one associated with a broken mandible and the other with a bro-ken humerus, two radius fractures, a clavicle fracture and a femur fractures. Four of the six cases can be interpreted as the result of blows" (1994:96). Sex of the individuals is not specified.

Stewart and Quade (1969) present one of the more thorough accounts of bone lesions from North American precontact series. They provide information on frontal lesions from Pueblo Bonito and Hawikku (together) and derived a population frequency rate of 9% for males and 5.8% for female in the Southwest. The authors state that most of the lesions they saw from the Pueblo sites are due to trauma (1969:89).

For the Pecos collection, Hooton (1930) presents a detailed inven-tory of cranial trauma by sex. Out of a total sample size of 581, he found 20 cases of cranial trauma, representing a 3.4% frequency. Of these 20 cases, 5 (25%) are on females and the rest are on males (75%). The depression fractures are largely located on the frontal bones, although other areas of the crania are involved as well.

Stodder (1989:187) compiled a frequency chart for a number of archaeological populations from the Greater Southwest (New Mexico and adjacent parts of Texas and Colorado). These frequen-cies range from 2% to 22% with the highest percentages located at the Gallina sites. Regarding the frequency data, Stodder states

"... that the Gallina sample exhibits the highest reported frequencies of postcranial and cranial trauma is not surprising, as they are most often identified as warlike, with defensive architecture in relatively isolated locations" (1989:187). Moreover, the relatively high rates of cranial injury at San Cristobal (8%) is primarily in the males "... suggesting that they were engaged in warfare" (1989:187).

Allen and colleagues (1985) analyzed ten cases of scalping at Navakwewtaqa (A.D. 1200–1300) and Grasshopper Ruin (A.D. 1300). Some of the individuals who had been scalped exhibited depression fractures as well. For example, at Navakwewtaqa, there were four males ranging in age from 25 to 40 + who were scalped, and three females ranging in age from 25 to 35. One female had a depression fracture on the left frontal, and one female has a ovoid-shaped hole in the left parietal suggesting penetration by a weapon and the probable cause of death. At Grasshopper, two males (aged between 35 and 40 +) were scalped and a young female (age 15) exhibited a depression fracture above the left orbit as well. Interestingly, many of these individuals were buried with associated grave goods such as bowls, beads, bone awls, and quartz crystals. The authors suggest that this "indicates that it was members of these two communities themselves who were the victims of the practice [scalping]" (1985:30). However, the authors go on to state that "skeletal evidence for violence at the two sites is almost non-existent" and that it is "possible that the ten individuals described here were victims of isolated raids" (1985:30).

This cursory review of some of the pertinent literature on violence presents a rather complex view for the precontact past. The pattern regarding violent interaction seems to be that *there is no pattern*. Extreme variability exists in the ways that injurious actions sometimes occurred. Mass slayings, individual dismemberments, burning, possible cannibalism, scalping, intentional injury, and limited hand-to-hand combat do exist in the Southwest archaeological record, and these span the height of occupation (circa A.D. 800–1300). The extent to which these isolated incidences occur and their relationship to other political, economic and ideological currents is of interest. These cases of violence may represent relatively isolated examples, or they may be indicative of a more large-scale and integrated system of power dynamics, show of force, oppression, coercion, or conflict resolution. It is possible that in order to maintain unanimity and harmony across diverse (economically, linguistically and ideologically) Pueblo communities, some show

of force may have been necessary, but the degree to which this is
the case needs much more systematic study.

METHODS AND MATERIALS

Data on trauma are presented for two different regions, the La
Plata River Valley and Black Mesa in the Kayenta area (Fig. 3.1).
These represent two extremes on the Pueblo continuum in terms of
availability of resources (abundant versus poor), organizational
state (aggregated versus dispersed), position and location vis-a-vis
other spheres of influence (central versus marginal), health (low
morbidity versus high morbidity) and quantity of trade items
(abundant versus few).

Located near the borders of New Mexico and Colorado, the La
Plata River Valley was a permanently watered, productive agricultural area in which more than 900 sites have been reported (H.W.
Toll, 1993). The valley was continuously occupied from A.D. 200
until about A.D. 1300. Large communities were maintained
throughout the occupation. This area was lush by local and re-

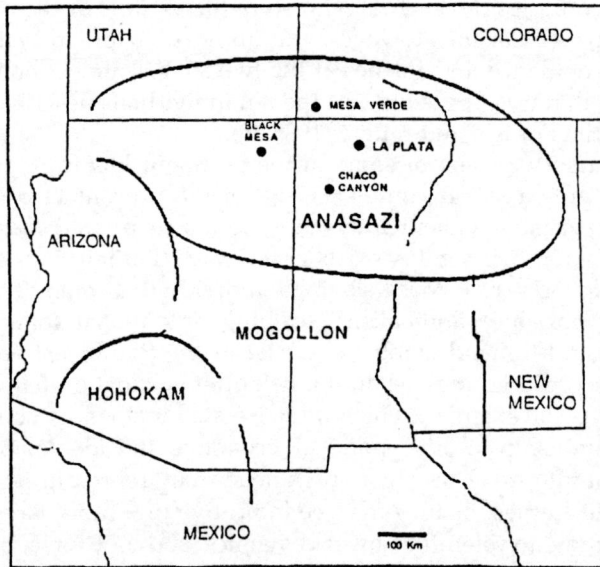

Figure 3.1. Four Corners region showing the cultural areas and
archaeological sites discussed in the text.

gional standards, and density of available resources was high. Agricultural potential was likewise very good; there is also ample evidence of wild game and domesticated turkey in the diet (M.S. Toll 1993). The burials came from sites that all date to approximately A.D. 900–1300. This area is located in the middle of a large and interactive political sphere of influence with Mesa Verde to the north and Chaco Canyon to the south. Trade items and non-utilitarian goods are present. Analysis of the skeletal remains for pathologies and nutritional stress revealed little evidence (Martin *et al.* in press).

In contrast, Black Mesa in northeastern Arizona represents a marginal and isolated environment that was abandoned during the height of Pueblo development in other areas (circa A.D. 1150). The analysis of diet for the Black Mesa Anasazi demonstrates a reliance on maize, although hydrological, palynological, and ethnobotanical data suggest that corn was never abundant (Ford 1984). However, there is evidence that maize was supplemented by a wide variety of non-domesticated plants and small game such as rodents and rabbits (Semé 1984). In eighteen years of excavation of over hundreds of sites, very little turquoise or shell was recovered suggesting little contact outside the immediate region (Gumerman, personal communication).

In contrast to the La Plata River Valley series, the pattern of disease confirms that nutritional stress and infectious disease was a chronic problem for most segments of the population on Black Mesa. Chronic and mild-to-moderate cases of nutritional anemia and systemic infections were a continuing problem, especially for children and women (Martin *et al.* 1991). Making a living on scarce and unpredictable resources posed challenges to the Black Mesa communities, and the result seems to have been frequent bouts of illness and, on occasion, death of the most vulnerable individuals. However, there is very little evidence of interpersonal violence.

Tracking violence in the osteological record is fairly straightforward (Merbs 1989). Applied force leaves a distinctive and permanent record on bone when the trauma occurs with enough power to cause tissue damage. Evidence of recovery from trauma is likewise among the more unambiguous types of bone changes that can be easily documented. Injuries to the head leave particularly characteristic lesions that last for many, many years after the original injury has long healed, thus providing a record of non-lethal blows to the head (Walker, 1989). Bhootra (1985:567) states that "... no injury of the head is too trivial to be ignored or so serious as to be despaired of ···" and for all deaths that result from violence, one fourth are attributed to head injuries in contemporary society. As background (taken from Gurdjian 1973:94–98), depression fractures begin with a traumatic event such as a blow to the head and this ruptures blood vessels in the bone marrow and periosteum. There is formation of a hematoma within 6 to 8 hours. This gradually is replaced by young connective tissue and it transforms into a fibrous callous. Through remodeling, this fibrous callous becomes gradually replaced with new bone. Depression fractures are produced by a force applied to just one side of the bone. The outer cortex of bone is clearly depressed inward while the underlying diploe space becomes compressed. There are three characteristics of depression fractures: (1) there are usually fine cracks that radiate from the depressed areas; (2) within the depressed area, the inner table of bone is beveled at the edges; and, (3) the surrounding areas of the depression are raised as it rebounds from the pressure build-up. With healing, these manifestations all but disappear but there is usually a diagnostic depression for long periods after the trauma. Thus, the depression fracture stays depressed long after healing because of bone necrosis.

For individuals who survive the initial effect of a blow to the head, one consequence of the process is that not enough oxygen may get to the brain (called hypoxia). Hypoxia further increases swelling and edema which in turn causes increased intracranial pressure. This can lead to brain herniation. In general, however, moderate increases in intracranial pressure can be survived, but there may be long-lasting neurological problems stemming from the healing process of the original injury.

Head injuries can produce neurological side-effects such as "amnesia, vertigo, epilepsy, poor concentration, reduced rate of information processing, fatigue, headache, irritability, emotional instability, attacks of emotional instability, and antisocial conduct" (Walker, 1989:322). Injury to the left frontal lobe of the brain can cause personality changes (such as loss of inhibition) or hallucination (Allen et al. 1985:31). These symptoms can be immediate or reveal themselves months or years after the original trauma.

The methods for assessment and analysis of trauma on cranial and post-cranial remains followed the recommendations of Merbs (1989), Ortner and Putschar (1981) and Walker (1989). The Black Mesa (A.D. 800–1150; n = 178) and La Plata (A.D. 900–1300; n = 65) burial collections were both analyzed by Martin and colleagues (see Martin et al. 1991 and Martin et al. in press). Both of these populations have been treated to systematic data collection of age, sex, pathologies, metrics and discrete traits using the Paleopathology Standards (Rose *et al.* 1991).

Data from individuals included the recording of burial location, strata, position, grave type, grave goods, and completeness and preservation. Pathological lesions were scored as osteoclastic/resorptive, osteoblastic/proliferative, or as trauma-related lesions. If trauma was present, it was further analyzed as to type, location, extent, and level of remodeling (healing). Cranial depression fractures were measured for width, height and depth. All fractures were X- rayed and differential diagnosis was aided by consultation with the late Dr. Gregory Gordon (Santa Fe, New Mexico) and Dr. Don Chrisman (Amherst, Massachusetts), both physicians.

OSTEOLOGICAL EVIDENCE OF INTENTIONAL VIOLENCE

La Plata

Evidence for trauma from the La Plata burial series includes healed fractures or traumatic injuries that are in the remodeling (healing) phase and are, therefore, injuries that were non-lethal. The cranial wounds at La Plata fit the description of depression fractures caused by blows to the head (e.g., Courville 1948; Stewart and Quade 1969; Merbs 1989; Walker 1989). For the individuals which could be analyzed for cranial and post-cranial healed traumatic injuries (n = 51), there were no unambiguous perimortem bone breaks or fractures and therefore, fractures and traumatic injury discussed here occurred sometime during the lifetime of individuals (Tab. 3.1). Young children were generally free of fractures; only one 15 year old (37592 B6) had a healed compression fracture on the left parietal.

A site-by-site description of individuals with cranial and/or post-cranial pathology related to trauma clearly shows different patterns between adult males and females (Tab. 3.2). The ages as-

Table 3.1. Frequency of healed trauma for La Plata population

	Children	Males	Females
Cranial	1/16[6.2%]	3/13 [23.1%]	6/10 [60.0%]
Post-cranial	0/16 [0.0%]	3/15 [20.0%]	6/12 [50.0%]

Table 3.2. Specifics of cranial and post-cranial trauma for La Plata adults

Site/ID	Age/Sex	Cranial	Post-cranial
37592 B6	15	left parietal: 7 × 12 mm depression fracture	
37593 B3	48 M		right sixth rib and left ninth rib: healed fractures; thoracic vertebrae (eighth and ninth): osteophytes and wedging
37594 B4	45 M		right first metacarpal; healed fracture
37599 B5	25 M	right parietal: 30 × 30 mm depression fracture (partly un-reunited)	
37599 B9	25 M	left frontal orbit: 6 × 9 mm depression fracture	
37600 B4	50 M		distal right radius & ulna: healed fractures
37601 B4	25 F	left parietal and frontal: six rounded depression fractures ranging in size from 9.25 mm	right scapula: depression near spine; right sixth and seventh ribs: healed fractures; left humerus: healed fracture; cervicle vertebrae (third through fifth): trauma induced osteophytes
37601 B5	35 M	left parietal: 20 × 15 mm depression fracture	
37601 B10	38 F	right frontal: 9 × 5 mm depression fracture	
37603 B2.1	30 F		
65030 B6	38 F	occipital: 24 × 24 mm depression fracture right and left nasals: healed broken nose	dista right radius: healed fracture
65030 B8	20 F		left innominate: trauma induced osteophytes cervicle vertebrae (first and second): healed fracture
65030 B9	33 F	frontal and parietals at bregma: 57 × 77 mm area with large raised area, sutures un-reunited	left innominate: fracture at pubic plate
65030 B16	28 F	right frontal: 17 × 17 mm depression fracture; occipital: 7 × 7 mm depression fracture	

signed represent the mid-point age based on the age-range assigned using a number of aging techniques (Bass 1971; White 1991).
For males, there are three cases of cranial trauma: One 25 year old
has a healed compression fracture of the right parietal (37599 B5),
another 25 year old has a healed fracture at the corner of the left
eye (37599 B9), and a 35 year old has a healed depression fracture
on the left parietal (37601 B5). Male post-cranial fractures include a
healed fracture of the right radius and ulna (the type one gets
when breaking a fall), a healed fractured right thumb, and an
individual with several healed rib and vertebrae fractures. All of
these post-cranial traumas are on males who are aged over 45
years and indicate trauma easily explained by occasional accident
or occupational hazard. These three post-cranial fractures did not
co-occur in any cases with the three cases of cranial trauma.

Six females (out of 10) demonstrate healed cranial trauma (largely in the form of depression fractures) and the ages of these women
range from 22 to 38. However, the inventory of healed non-lethal
cranial wounds for the females is longer and more extensive, with
three of the six cases involving multiple head wounds. The
youngest female (age 20) has a healed broken nose (65030 B8).
Another young female (age 22) with a cranial trauma demonstrates
two depression fractures, one on the forehead and one on the back
of the head (65030 B15). A 25 year old has multiple depression
fractures about the front and side of her head (37601 B4; Fig. 3.2). A
33 year old has a large un-reunited, but healed series of fractures at
the top of her head (65030 B9; Fig. 3.3). Of the two 38 year old
females, one has a healed fracture above her right eye (37601 B10),
and one has a depression fracture at the back of the head (65030
B6; Fig. 3.4).

In addition to these, six females demonstrate post-cranial
trauma. Two features of lower body trauma are distinctly different
from the male pattern: (1) In four out of six cases, the cranial and
post-cranial fractures co-occur, and (2) the post-cranial fractures in
the females occur in younger age categories, ranging from 20 to 38.
The youngest female (age 20) has fractures in the atlas and axis of
the neck vertebrae along with a broken nose.

A 25 year old (37601 B4) has several fractures (right shoulder,
left humerus, upper neck) along with multiple depression fractures
about the head. This female also had a severe case of osteomyelitis
that affected numerous bones. Parts of the sternum are thickened
with osteophytic reactive bone covering all surfaces. Some parts of
the bone surface appear smooth and rounded and these areas were

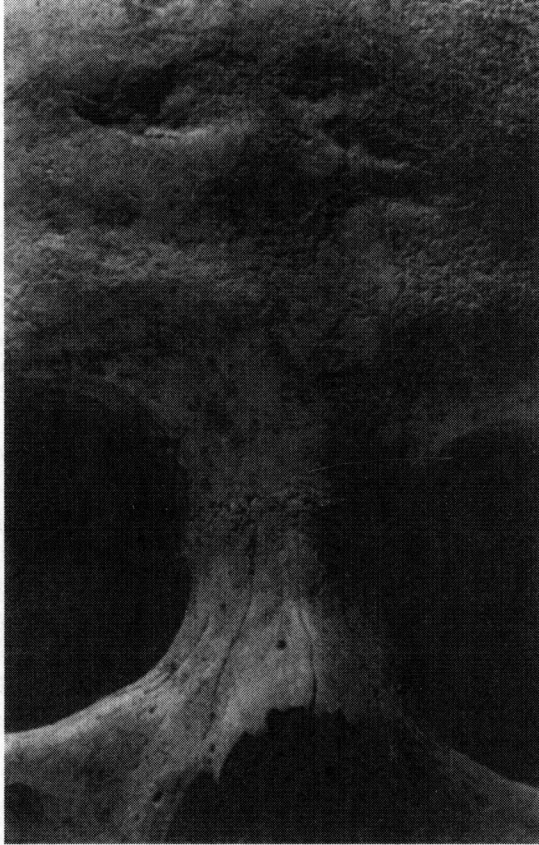

Figure 3.2. LA 37601 B4 female age 25 with multiple traumatic lesions on the frontal bone.

likely caused by lytic lesions and subsequent sclerotic processes (Ortner and Putschar 1986:111). The scapulae, clavicles and distal portion of one humerus are likewise massively remodeled and affected by the same process. Differential diagnosis relying primarily on X-ray examination suggests osteomyelitis, although the original cause of this massive infection confined to the shoulder and chest area can only be speculated upon. The right scapula near the spine and the sixth and seventh ribs show roughened depressed areas that appear to be healed fractures. There appears also to be localized, trauma-induced osteophytes on the third through fifth

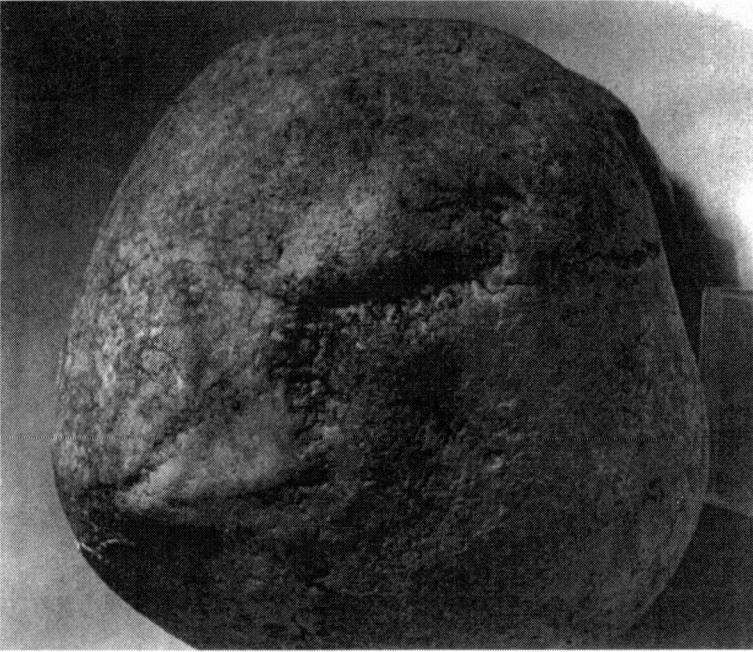

Figure 3.3. LA 65030 B9 female age 33 with cranial trauma on the parietal and occipital bones.

cervical vertebrae. It is possible that this woman was struck with an object hard enough to cause not only cranial fracturing, but also lacerated wounds on the shoulders and chest area.

Other post-cranial trauma on the females includes a 33 year old that demonstrates fractures of the left hip as well as on the top of her head. The oldest female (age 38) showed healed fractures on the left hip and also a depression fracture at the back of her head. A female with a post-cranial fracture may have died during childbirth based on the commingling of a term-fetus. She had a fracture of the right distal radius.

The frequencies of healed trauma for adults at La Plata reveal that females have an almost three-fold increase in the frequency of cranial trauma over males (23.1% versus 60.0%), and a two-fold increase in post-cranial trauma (20.0% versus 50.0%). Adult frequencies greatly outnumber those for subadults. The latter have an overall rate of 6.2% for cranial trauma and virtually no cases of post-cranial trauma.

Figure 3.4. LA 65030 B6 female age 38 with occipital depression fracture.

In reviewing other factors associated with health of adult males and females at La Plata, females have more cases of infection (38.5%) than males (6.7%) and some of these may be related to sequelae from the injury that produced the fractures (Martin *et al.* in press). Females demonstrated higher frequencies of childhood growth disruption for four out of six teeth, females had more hypoplastic lines and females with cranial trauma have more enamel defects than females without. For example, at Barker Arroyo site LA 65030, four females have cranial trauma and co-occurring severe or multiple hypoplastic defects, whereas the other two females from this site show no trauma and have few defects (Martin *et al.* in press). Other characteristics of the females with cranial trauma are that these women as a group generally have higher incidences of anemia and systemic infection. Additional observations regarding women with cranial trauma is that several exhibit more left/right asymmetry in long bone proportions (3 individuals in particular are asymmetrical, LA 65030 B6, B8 and B9) and more pronounced cases of post-cranial ossified ligaments, osteophytes at joint surfaces (unrelated to general osteoarthritis or degenerative joint disease) and localized periosteal reactions (enthesopathies). Whether these observations are the result of occupational stress (Kennedy 1989) or the sequelae of injuries which caused unusual and differential biomechanical problems is not clear.

An apparent association emerges when the mortuary contexts of the individuals with cranial trauma are examined. The majority of the burials from La Plata are flexed or semi-flexed, and placed within abandoned structures or in storage pits. Often burials contain associated objects, usually ceramic vessels or ground stone (as an example, Fig. 3.5a). Every female at La Plata with cranial trauma had a mortuary context that did not follow this pattern. All were found in positions that were loosely flexed, prostrate or sprawled. Particularly at two sites, both from Barker Arroyo (LA 37601 and LA 65030), the mortuary context of females with cranial trauma reveals that, unlike their age-matched counterparts without signs of trauma, they were generally haphazardly placed in abandoned pitstructures, and there were no associated grave goods (Figs. 3.5b–d; 3.6a–c).

At Barker Arroyo site LA 65030, three individuals found in the lower fill of Pitstructure 1 appear to have all died at approximately the same time and were interred together (Figs. 3.5b–d). These include two adult women aged at 20 and 33 and an 11 year old child. All are in a haphazard position as if thrown from a higher elevation. The cause of death could not be ascertained for any of these individuals, although, given the burial context, it is assumed that these individuals died at approximately the same time and were disposed of together. Also in Pitstructure 1, located in the middle fill on top of the roof fall, another female aged at 38 was placed facing downward in a semi-flexed position with no grave offerings (Fig. 3.6a). In the lower fill of Pitstructure 8, a 22 year old female was placed in semi-flexed position with no grave offerings (Fig. 3.6b). At another site, LA 37601, a 25 year old female with cranial and post-cranial trauma was located in a similar position with no grave goods (Fig. 3.6c). Of the three males with cranial trauma, at least one 25 year old from site LA 37599 was placed in Pitstructure 2 in a similar fashion with no grave goods (Fig. 3.6d). Unfortunately,

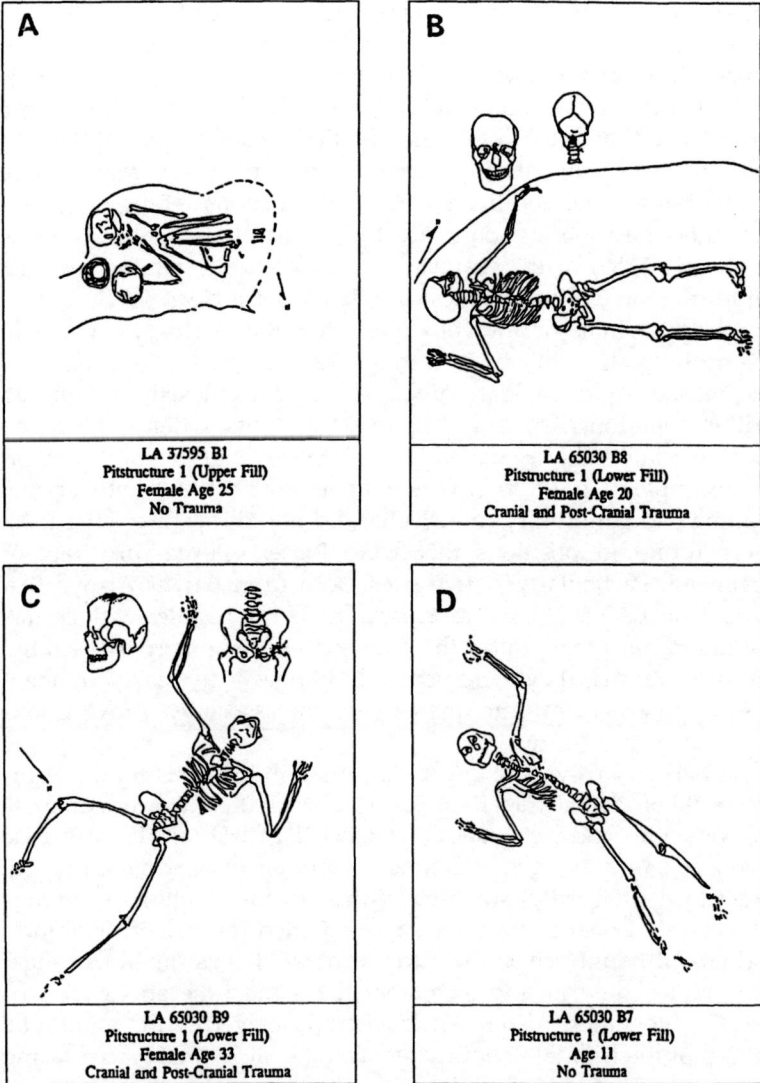

Figure 3.5. Diagrammatic representation of mortuary configurations. Figure 3.5a shows the common flexed position normally associated with Anasazi burial features with associated grave goods. Figures 3.5b, 3.5c and 3.5d show individuals with unusual mortuary contexts.

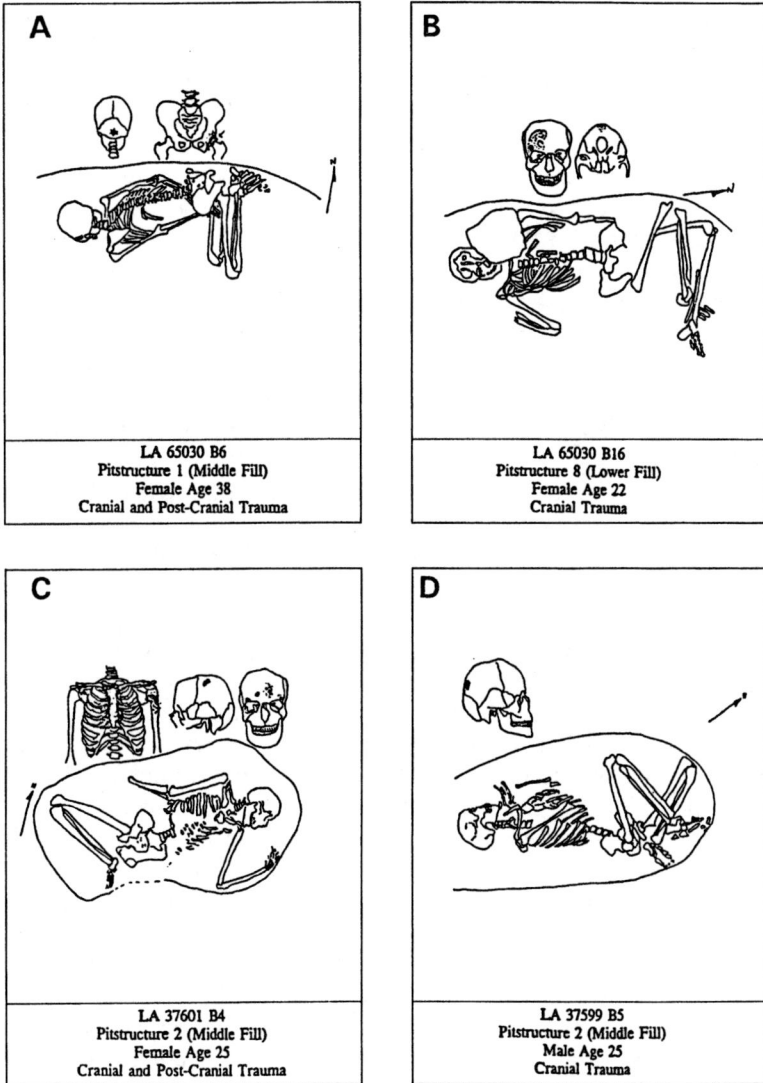

A

LA 65030 B6
Pitstructure 1 (Middle Fill)
Female Age 38
Cranial and Post-Cranial Trauma

B

LA 65030 B16
Pitstructure 8 (Lower Fill)
Female Age 22
Cranial Trauma

C

LA 37601 B4
Pitstructure 2 (Middle Fill)
Female Age 25
Cranial and Post-Cranial Trauma

D

LA 37599 B5
Pitstructure 2 (Middle Fill)
Male Age 25
Cranial Trauma

Figure 3.6. Diagrammatic representation of mortuary configurations demonstrating variability in mortuary contexts.

the mortuary context of the other 2 males with cranial trauma is unknown.

To summarize the association of healed cranial trauma and mortuary context, out of a total sample size of 14 adult females with crania, five show trauma and were buried with no grave goods and in either sprawled or semi-flexed positions (one female with cranial trauma could not be assigned to a mortuary condition), six females had no trauma and were in a flexed or semi-flexed positions with associated grave goods, one female had no cranial trauma, a semi-flexed burial but no grave goods, and one female with no cranial trauma had an unknown mortuary context.

For the 14 males that could be assessed for cranial trauma, six had no cranial trauma and were flexed burials with grave goods, five had no cranial trauma but also no grave goods (with a variety of positions ranging from extended to flexed). Of the three males with cranial trauma, one had grave goods, and two did not, although all were in a semi-flexed position. There is more variability in the relationship between cranial trauma and burial treatment for the males, with more males in general having less cranial trauma and no grave goods.

The variation in overall size and dimensions of the depressions suggest that any number of implements could have been used to cause these fractures. The location of two out of three of the male cranial fractures is on the parietals (one on the left and one on the right, both towards the back). For females, the lesions are largely located around the front of the head or on the far back (occipital) portion of the head. While it is difficult to identify the exact implement used in each case of cranial trauma at La Plata, modern forensic information suggests that fractures of the head can be made with any number of blunt or sharp implements (Petty 1980). In their review of artifacts associated with warfare and hand combat, Wilcox and Haas (1994:223–224) find little evidence for the manufacture of objects solely to be used as weapons. The strongest evidence that they could garner was of two bipointed axes found with a male burial at Aztec Ruin, and wooden sword-like implements found at Chaco Canyon.

While it is easy to envision a stone axe, hammerstone, core, chopper or projectile point causing damage, it is equally likely that bone, antler and wood objects could be used as well. For example, a forensic case involving cranial and post-cranial wounds similar to those at La Plata was caused when being struck repeatedly with a wooden yard broom handle (Bhootra 1985). This implement is similar to the size and shape of a Pueblo digging stick (Colton 1960:96). Digging sticks were most likely common in an agricultural community such as that of the Barker Arroyo sites at La Plata, and the use of such objects was primarily within the domain of men (at least in historic Pueblo societies) (Dozier 1970). Colton (1960:98) states that sometimes wooden digging sticks also had a hoe made of hafted stone, or with triangular pieces of basalt or sandstone. In addition, a variety of stone tools such as tchamahias and axes were found in the La Plata Valley, and any of these items could be used to cause injury.

Black Mesa

In comparison, skeletal material from Black Mesa presents a very different picture. Black Mesa is located within the desert plateau region of the Southwest it is a relatively isolated and marginal environment with an ephemeral water source. Although agriculture was practiced, many other local resources were exploited in order to exist year-around. In recent years, the archaeological data have been used to address organization of procurement systems, development of social networks and exchange systems, and explanations of behavioral and cultural variability (Gumerman 1988).

The burials on Black Mesa are from small, seasonally occupied, open-air sites. Black Mesa never was a major Anasazi population center, nor was it a "focal point for trade or Anasazi culture innovation" (Gumerman 1984:6). There is virtually no evidence of exotic trade items nor is there an abundance of non-utilitarian goods. It was populated largely by farmers living in dispersed small groups. Gumerman and colleagues (1972:198) characterized the archaeology of Black Mesa as "the archaeology of a provincial 'backwater' area. The people were simple farmers."

Recent archaeological interpretations suggest that the Black Mesa Anasazi had to by necessity be extremely versatile and innovative to remain in an area as harsh and ecologically unstable as Black Mesa (Martin et al. 1991). Powell and colleagues (1983:233) comment that "the Anasazi occupation of Black Mesa is a story of continual adaptive change in systems that probably never experienced periods of stasis."

An inventory of trauma on the remains from Black Mesa demonstrates negligible frequencies. Two males (out of 39, 5.1%) had unambiguous trauma. One male over the age of 40 had a healed broken rib, and one male (BM109 D:11:300), a very robust twenty year old, showed a healing traumatic injury to the left side of the mouth and cheek. Both were buried in common flexed positions with several accompanying grave goods.

For females, only one young sixteen year old (BM 081 D:72:17) (out of 52 females, 1.9%) demonstrated cranial lesions. In this female there are multiple depression fractures on the occipital and frontal bones, not unlike those found at La Plata. She also had lesions indicative of the most severe case of iron deficiency anemia encountered in this population. However, unlike the La Plata pattern, this young adult female was placed in a tightly flexed position with nine bowls, ladles, and pots.

Although Black Mesa individuals were relatively free of injuries with three exceptions, there was a morbidity burden unheralded in paleopathology studies in the Southwest. Virtually every individual from Black Mesa demonstrated signs of some chronic health problem, primarily either iron deficiency anemia or systemic infection. Eighty-seven percent of the Black Mesa individuals showed signs of iron deficiency anemia. For the combined population, 24% exhibit some type of infectious disease. Nutritional anemia and systemic infections co-occur in 61.9% of the children, and infection is particularly pronounced in infants under the age of 1. Children between the ages of 6 and 10 likewise show signs of infectious disease, which is unusual in this age grouping. Children were likely afflicted with repeated but non-lethal bouts of infection. Chronic, but relatively mild, transmissible diseases may have been endemic on Black Mesa. The infections were persistent enough to reinfect older children, but mild enough for them to show recovery. Finally, 85% of the individuals from Black Mesa have signs of growth disruption in the form of dental defects (hypoplasias). This is among the highest reported frequencies for precontact North American groups (Martin et al. 1991).

The health profile for Black Mesa is dominated by pervasive nutritional and infectious disease stress, but no subgroup is identified as being particularly at-risk for intentional violence. A picture emerges of endemic nutritional stress that had an impact on almost all age and sex groups. The generally mild nature of the iron deficiency, the pervasiveness of childhood growth disruption, and the clustering of pathologies around infancy and weaning, all point to a challenging existence.

The health indicators suggest a population that was stressed but other data show that the population was not dying out or in decline. In fact, Black Mesa experienced continual growth in population size throughout the occupation (Swedlund and Sessions 1976). The explanation for growth most consistent with the data is that it was from increased fertility and decreased mortality (Horowitz and Martin 1989). In short, the people living on Black Mesa appear to have been hardy group that survived (and indeed survived into old age) by being resourceful and responsive to local contingencies.

DISCUSSION

The frequencies of trauma and disease are distinctively different in the two regions. At La Plata, nutritional anemia and infections were relatively low in frequency, while on Black Mesa, virtually everyone suffered from some form of health problem. Although La Plata individuals did not suffer from nutritional problems and transmissible infections, numerous examples of multiple-traumata suggest that La Plata folk experienced a qualitatively different set of stressors emanating from different sources.

Violence and fear of injury may have played a significant role in oppressing some members of the La Plata community. Trauma is absent in children and generally infrequent and when present, minor in adult males (particularly the post-cranial trauma which occurred in elderly males). Females carry the unequal burden of traumatic injuries in this group. The location and size of the cranial injuries showed that by overall dimensions and size in area, female injuries covered a larger area, involved more bony elements, often occurred in multiples, and caused internal (endocranial) damage in some cases. Furthermore, the co-morbidity factors of cranial and post-cranial trauma, infections, and decreased life expectancy (there were very few females represented in the older age categories) suggest truly suboptimal conditions for some adult females. Females with these health problems are more likely to have been in mortuary contexts described as haphazardly thrown or discarded and with no associated grave offerings. As a group, they were younger when they died than females who had traditional prepared graves.

An examination of other attributes suggests that they were part of the Pueblo culture to the extent that most of these women have occipital or lambdoidal flattening consistent with the use of cradleboarding during infancy. Only one female with a compression fracture (37601 B10) did not show cranial flattening, but this is not unusual (Renaud 1927; Morris 1939). Cranial metrics and cranial and post-cranial discrete traits cannot be used to characterize the subgroups because of small sample size. This is very unfortunate because to understand the physical injury and differential mortuary treatment, it would be important to verify if the women with trauma were genetically related to the group as a whole.

The one physical characteristic that distinguishes at least several of the women with trauma is a pattern of non-pathological lesions and abnormalities associated with occupational stress or habitual use of select muscle groups. For example, both females in Pitstructure 1 from site LA 65030 demonstrate asymmetrical measurements for many of the width proportions of the long bones. Particularly, the humerus, radius and ulna are most affected. Trinkaus and colleagues (1994) examined modern, extant and extinct groups and found that humeral bilateral asymmetry related most often to activity-related functional changes.

Another attribute of some of these women is the occurrence of isolated osteophytes in places that correspond to muscle insertions. Because as a group these women are generally too young to have the osteoarthritic changes associated with aging, these morphological changes could be related to habitual use of certain muscles which can lead to the build-up of bone and changes at the site of the most biomechanical stress. Bridges (1990) examined the osteological correlates of weapon use in two precontact groups from Alabama and showed that the shift from hunting and gathering to agriculture can be correlated with non-pathological changes in morphology relating to different use of tools and weapons. Bridges noted that there were changes in porosity and osteophytic lipping at the shoulder joints and the elbow in particular. She also found bilateral asymmetry in the diameters of the radius and ulna between the groups. Although no statistically significant differences were found between women who demonstrate trauma and postcranial measurements, several of the La Plata females within the subgroup do demonstrate osteophytes and enthesopathies. These may indirectly relate to occupation or habitual performance of certain activities.

Although the subgroup sample sizes limit a detailed quantitative analysis of occupational stress markers, it is possible to speculate on a division of labor that was both by sex and possibly by "class" as well. Spencer and Jennings (1965), Titiev (1972), Dozier (1970) summarize sexual division of labor for Pueblo people documenting that in historic times, women ground corn, prepared food, gathered wood, built and mended houses, made pottery and clothing, gathered wild foods and made baskets. Men were responsible for farming, occasional hunting, and religious and ceremonial activities. The difficult task of grinding a season's crop of corn into meal to be stored for the year belonged to the women, who might spend as many as eight to nine hours a day at the grindstone for several weeks. Men were involved in no such strenuous activities.

In traditional subsistence societies with agricultural intensification, there is often a concomitant pressure on women to increase their productivity simultaneously with a decrease in birth spacing (Harris and Ross 1987:49). This places an enormous burden on women to partition their time, energy and activities between very different and competing tasks: economic labor and bearing/rearing children. Harris and Ross cite summary data (1987:50) on the number of hours that women work daily in agriculturally based villages and it ranges from 6.7 to 10.8 hours a day with the high end representing intensive agriculturalists.

It is possible that as the La Plata Valley population increased (through a combination of immigration and increased fertility), several conditions could arise. There would be a need to increase production of food to feed the increasing numbers of people, and therefore there would be a need for an increased labor pool. As more people moved into the La Plata Valley, it is possible that the more local or "native" populations maintained access and control of the resources. That is, individuals born into certain groups would have preferred access to food and other resources over non-related newcomers. This could effectively establish an underclass of people who were exploited in any number of ways. Reproductive-aged females would be the most advantageous group to exploit because they could aid in domestic tasks and food production, as well as in child rearing. This would not rule out the exploitation of males as well, although they would be less vulnerable to physical injury because of their ability to be more readily mobile (without children) and to fight and use weapons.

Although speculative, the pattern of violence against women at La Plata can be at least partially explained by increased population density and increased stratification, at least to the degree that subclasses were created. La Plata communities may have felt it necessary to construct rigid rules about resource allocation and they may have chosen a strategy that targeted a subgroup within the population. Reproductive-aged women migrating into the La Plata valley may have, in a sense, become indentured servants to others who had the power to enforce domination of this subgroup. How they may have come to be servant/laborers is less clear; it could have been through raiding and abduction of women from other villages, or through migration of women into the area and becoming part of an underclass.

The picture emerging from these scenario envisions an agricultural population that was doing relatively well given the circumstances of crowded living and subsistence farming. Anemia and infectious disease are expected outcomes of group living and agrarian lifeways, conditions not pronounced at La Plata. In comparison to nearby groups in the Mesa Verde and Chaco Canyon regions, La Plata individuals seem to be faring quite well, if not better than expected (Martin *et al.* in press). However, all of this is over-shadowed by the high frequencies of trauma found in the female subpopulation. The high frequencies of cranial trauma suggest signs of strife and troubled times for some living at La Plata even with abundant resources and low disease stress.

Walker (1989) demonstrates a pattern of non-lethal blows to the head for groups on the coast of California and nearby islands. Although there were no statistically significant gender differences in the patterning of lesions, males were more frequently involved. Cranial trauma was higher for the Islanders than for the coastal people and Walker attributes this to intense competition over resources on the circumscribed island. This economic explanation does not fit the data from the Southwest.

One hypothesis generated concerns the degree to which violence against women (versus men) corresponds to the relative availability of subsistence resources. It is generally assumed that where resources are high (as would be found near permanent water sources in the western deserts), people will "do better," there will be more food to share and to distribute, and there will be less "stress" and presumably less violence. Whereas, when resources are scarce and productivity is low, there will be an increased amount of "stress" and this will lead to poor health, conflict over scarce resources, and increased violence (Turner 1993; Haas and Creamer 1994). This is clearly not the case at La Plata and Black Mesa.

A series of hypotheses generated from a political-economic perspective however reveals some alternative possibilities. The La Plata communities are in the center of a highly interactive political and economic sphere of influence (H.W. Toll 1993). On the contrary, Black Mesa inhabitants resided outside this activity area and were relatively isolated from other groups. An area that provides a secure and high level of resources may attract people into the region. Population density increases and resources will be controlled and differentially allocated and distributed. Certain groups may control both production in the form of labor and differential distribution in the form of an underclass.

With this scenario in mind, settlements along the La Plata River may have grown increasingly dense, probably due to both in-migration and increased fertility. The La Plata communities were most likely not highly stratified, but there were conditions that could lead easily to status differentiation and power of some to control resources.

Why would this underclass be primarily women who were routinely battered? Spouse abuse or domestic violence can be ruled out because there are other adult females who demonstrate no trauma and were placed in prepared graves in a flexed position with grave goods. Also, the association of women with injuries and a young child in close association suggests that their children were also part of the underclass and when they died, the child was slain as well.

CONCLUSION

Standard economic models applied to precolonial groups that search for meaning within a local context will miss the complex and revealing patterns that exist. Violence against women in an area where there was an abundance of resources makes sense only if a regional model of shifting political and economic strategies are examined and considered. While the precontact Pueblo world in the Four Corners region was increasingly connected, it may not have been necessarily unified. The dynamics of social change at La Plata may have taken place in an arena of increasing domination and resistance. Health at La Plata, with its abundant agricultural and wild resources, cannot be understood without looking at the local and regional dynamics involving control of those resources.

Black Mesa, with few resources, followed a local and regional strategy that employed a more egalitarian distribution of resources, depended on strong reciprocal trade networks among extended families and communities, and relied on a diverse and flexible subsistence strategy through shared storage and redistribution of food. Ironically, archaeologists have written that La Plata was a "bread basket" and a favored place to live (H.W. Toll 1993); while Black Mesa has been referred to as a "backwater" region with the inhabitants as "poor cousins" to their more prosperous neighbors

(Gumerman 1988). In fact, Black Mesa inhabitants, although suffering from health problems, appear to have shared equal responsibility across members of the community for making a living on sparse resources. La Plata and the surrounding densely settled communities such as those at Mesa Verde, may have instead chosen a strategy of labor production and distribution that created classes of people and targeted groups. Economic security did not ensure equality for women; women may have been subject to increased violence either as captured or enslaved laborers, or as recipients of abuse caught in the struggle for control over labor, production and resources.

Black Mesa represents the ordinary folks living in small, remote farming villages. They were connected in a variety of economic, trade-related, and cultural ways to the larger centralized communities east and south of Black Mesa. The Black Mesa people were nutritionally stressed to some degree, and it is probable that infectious disease was common and significantly contributed to illness. Taken together, the data suggest that cultural systems operating on Black Mesa effectively buffered the group as a whole. Even though the later period (A.D. 1000–1150) signaled a change in settlement patterning that was potentially unstable (e.g., movement into the uplands with poorer agricultural land, increased sedentism, decreased ability for large game hunting), behavioral changes designed to minimize the negative effects on health and community viability seem to have worked on Black Mesa. The specific behaviors that help offset potential problems included flexibility in resource type and procurement, increased social integration within sites and between sites, and increased sharing and redistribution of resources (Plog and Powell 1984). These effectively enhance alliances and risk-sharing across groups. Furthermore, as procurement of food became increasingly difficult, Black Mesa inhabitants changed they way they processed food, increased the amount of storage of food, relied on a wide variety of pioneer annuals (amaranth and chenopodium), and exploited small rodents and insects in order to increase the diversity of the food base (Gumerman 1988). These kinds of strategies, deduced from the archaeological remains, suggest some of the ways that difficulties emanating from life in a marginal and unpredictable environment were handled.

The pattern of violence at La Plata has important implications for understanding the complex relationship between environment, resources, cultural systems, and morbidity and mortality. The social consequence of intentional violence goes well beyond the immediate physical trauma on individuals. Recent research suggests that "some of the worst and most degrading offenses work by sustaining a palpable threat of violence over a victim without ever having to produce much injury" (Moore *et al.* 1994:178). Violence diminishes the daily life of those who are threatened, afraid or hurt. Studies of violence in contemporary society demonstrate that fear and victimization is not randomly distributed in a population (Warr 1994:11). Thus, the study of violence in archaeological contexts must necessarily go beyond the proximate causes of individual cases of traumatic injury. To do so requires the use of a theoretical framework responsive to the historical and contextual factors that create and maintain violence.

ACKNOWLEDGMENTS

A deep gratitude is owed to Nancy Akins who was part of the team that analyzed the La Plata material. Alan Goodman and Shirley Powell provided insight and intelligent debate regarding interpretations of violence in precontact societies. Wolky Toll and Eric Blinman likewise offered thoughtful suggestions and criticisms. This research was supported by a School of American Research Weatherhead Fellowship and a Museum of New Mexico, Office of Cultural Affairs, Office of Archaeological Studies Grant (Contract No. 80-505-41-0053 CN - 41.493).

REFERENCES

Akins, N. J. (1986). *A Biocultural Approach to Human Burials from Chaco Canyon, New Mexico.* Reports of the Chaco Center No. 9. Santa Fe, New Mexico: National Park Service.

Allen, W. H., Merbs, C. F. and Birkby, W. H. (1985). "Evidence for Prehistoric Scalping at Nuvakwewtaqa (Chavez Pass) and Grasshopper Ruin, Arizona." In *Health and Disease in the Prehistoric Southwest*, eds. C. F. Merbs and R. J. Miller, pp. 23–42. Tempe Arizona: Arizona State University Press.

Blakely, R. L. and Matthews, D. S. (1990). "Bioarchaeological Evidence for a Spanish-Native American Conflict in the Sixteenth-Century Southeast." *American Antiquity* 55 (4):718–744.

Bass, W. M. (1971). *Human Osteology: A Laboratory and Field Manual of the Human Skeleton.* Columbia, Missouri: University of Missouri Archaeological Museum Society.

Bhootra, B. K. (1985). "An Unusual Penetrating Head Wound by a Yard Broom and its Medicolegal Aspects." *Journal of Forensic Sciences* **30**:567–571.

Bridges, P. S. (1990). "Osteological Correlates of Weapon Use." In *Life in Science: Papers in Honor of J. Lawrence Angel*, ed. J. Buikstra, pp. 87–98. Washington, D. C.: Center for American Archaeology.

Brothwell, D. and Sandison, A. T. (1967). *Disease in Antiquity*. Springfield, Massachusetts: C. C. Thomas.

Cameron, C. M. (1990). "Pit Structure Abandonment in the Four Corners Region of the American Southwest: Late Basketmaker III and Pueblo I." *Journal of Field Archaeology* **17**:27–37.

Colton, H. S. (1960). *Black Sand, Prehistory in Northern Arizona*. Albuquerque, New Mexico: University of New Mexico Press.

Cordell, L. S. (1984). *Prehistory of the Southwest*. Orlando, Florida: Academic Press.

Courville, C. (1948). "Cranial Injuries among the Indians of North America: A Preliminary Report." *Los Angeles Neurological Society* **13**:181–219.

Crown, P. L. and Judge, W. J. (1991). *Chaco and Hohokam: Prehistoric Regional Systems in the American Southwest*. Santa Fe, New Mexico: School of American Research Press.

Danforth, M. E. Cook, D. C. and Knick, S. G. III (1994). "The Human Remains from Carter Ranch Pueblo, Arizona: Health in Isolation." *American Antiquity* **59(1)**:88–101.

Darling, J. A. (1993). "Mass Inhumation and the Execution of Witches in the North American Southwest." Unpublished paper on file, Office of Archaeological Studies, Museum of New Mexico. Santa Fe, New Mexico.

Dozier, E. P. (1970). *The Pueblo Indians of North America*. New York: Holt, Reinhart and Winston.

Ford, R. I. (1984). "Ecological Consequences of Early Agriculture in the Southwest." In *Papers on the Archaeology of Black Mesa Arizona, Vol 2*, eds. S. Plog and S. Powell, pp. 127–138. Carbondale and Edwardsville: Southern Illinois Press.

Gumerman, G. J. (1984). *A View from Black Mesa: The Changing Face of Archaeology*. Tucson: University of Arizona.

_____ (1988). *The Anasazi in a Changing Environment*. Cambridge: Cambridge University Press.

_____ (1994). "Patterns and Perturbations in Southwest Prehistory." In *Themes in Southwest Prehistory*, ed, G. Gumerman, pp. 3–10. Santa Fe, New Mexico: School of American Research Press.

Gumerman, G. J., Westfall, D. and Reed, C. S. (1972). *Archaeological Investigations on Black Mesa, the 1969–1970 Seasons*. Prescott, Arizona: Prescott College Press.

Gurdjian, E. S. (1973). *Head Injury from Antiquity to the Present with Special Reference to Penetrating Head Wounds.* Springfield, Illinois: C. C. Thomas.

Haas, J. and Creamer, W. (1993). *Stress and Warfare Among the Kayenta Anasazi of the Thirteenth Century A.D.* Chicago: Field Museum of Natural History.

Harris, M. and Ross, E. B. (1987). *Death, Sex, and Fertility: Population Regulation in Preindustrial and Developing Societies.* New York: Columbia University Press.

Hermann, N. P. (1993). "Burial Interpretations." In *Across the Colorado Plateau: Anthropological Studies for the Transwestern Pipeline Expansion Project,* Volume XVIII, eds. C. Cohen, D. Bunds and N. Cella, pp. 77–95. Albuquerque: Maxwell Museum of Anthropology.

Hooton, E. A. (1930). *The Indians of Pecos Pueblo: A Study of Their Skeletal Remains.* (Papers of the Southwestern Expedition 4). New Haven: Yale University Press.

Horowitz, S. and Martin, D. L. (1989). *Life in a Prehistoric Marginal Environment: Effects on Reproduction, Health and Longevity.* Paper presented at the 88th Annual Meeting of the American Anthropological Association, Washington, D.C.

Kennedy, K. A. R. (1989). "Skeletal Markers of Occupational Stress." In *Reconstruction of Life From the Skeleton,* eds. M. Y. Iscan and K. A. R. Kennedy, pp. 129–160. New York: Liss.

Martin, D. L. Akins, N. J. Goodman, A. H. and Swedlund, A. C. (in press). *Harmony and Discord: Bioarchaeology of the La Plata Valley.* Santa Fe, New Mexico: Museum of New Mexico Press.

Martin, D. L. Goodman, A. H. Armelagos, G. J. and Magennis, A. L. (1991). *Black Mesa Anasazi Health: Reconstructing Life from Patterns of Death and Disease.* Carbondale, Illinois: Center for Archaeological Investigations, Occasional Paper No.14.

Merbs, C. F. (1989). "Trauma." In *Reconstruction of Life From the Skeleton,* eds. M. Y. Iscan and K. A. R. Kennedy, pp. 161–199. New York: Liss.

Miles J. S. (1975). *Orthopedic Problems of the Wetherill Mesa Populations.* National Park Service, Publications in Archaeology 7G, Wetherill Mesa Studies, Washington, D.C.

Milner G. R. Anderson, E. and Smith, V. G. (1991). "Warfare in Late Prehistoric West-Central Illinois." *American Antiquity* 56(4):581–603.

Moore, M. H. Prothrow-Stith, D. Guyer, B. and Spivak, H. (1994). "Violence and Intentional Injuries: Criminal Justice and Public Health Perspectives on an Urgent National Problem." In *Understanding and Preventing Violence. Volume 4 Consequences and Control,* eds. A. J. Reiss and J. A. Roth, pp. 167–216. Washington, D.C.: National Academy Press.

Morris, E. H. (1939). *Archaeological Studies In the La Plata District.* Carnegie Institution, Washington, D.C.

Nelson, B. A., Martin, D. L. Swedlund, A. C. Fish, P. R. and Armelagos, G. J. (1994). "Studies in Disruption: Demography and Health in the Prehistoric American Southwest." In *Understanding Complexity in the Prehistoric Southwest*, eds. G. Gumerman and M. Gell-Mann, pp. 59–112. Chicago: Addison-Wesley.

Ogilvie, M. D. and Hilton, C. E. (1993). "Analysis of Selected Human Skeletal Material From Sites 423–124 and 423–131." In *Across the Colorado Plateau: Anthropological Studies for the Transwestern Pipeline Expansion Project, Vol. XVIII.* eds., C. Cohen, D. Bunds and N. Cella, pp. 97–128. Albuquerque: Office of Contract Archaeology and Maxwell Museum of Anthropology.

Ortner, D. J. and Putschar, W. G. J. (1981). *Identification of Pathological Conditions in Human Skeletal Remains*. Washington D.C.: Smithsonian Institution Press.

Petty, C. S. (1980). "Death by Trauma: Blunt and Sharp Instruments and Firearms." In *Modern Legal Medicine, Psychiatry, and Forensic Science*, eds. W. J. Curran, A. L. McGarry and C. S. Petty, pp. 100–121. Philadelphia: Davis.

Powell, S., Andrews, P. P. Nichols, D. L. and Smiley, F. E. (1983). "Fifteen Years on the Rock: Archaeological Research, Administration, and Compliance on Black Mesa, Arizona." *American Antiquity* 28:228–252.

Renaud, E. B. (1927). "Undeformed Prehistoric Skulls from La Plata, Colorado, and Canon del Muerto, Arizona." *University of Colorado Studies* XVI(1):5–36.

Rose J. C., Anton, S. C. Aufderheide, A. C. Buikstra, J. E. Eisenberg, L. Gregg, J. B. Hunt, E. E. and Rothschild, B. (1991). *Paleopathology Association Skeletal Data Base Recommendations*. Detroit: Paleopathology Association Press.

Rouse, I. (1962). "Southwestern Archaeology Today." In *An Introduction to the Study of Southwestern Archaeology with a Preliminary Account of Excavations at Pecos*, ed. A. F. Kidder, pp. 1–53. New Haven: Yale University Press.

Sebastian, L. (1992). *The Chaco Anasazi*. Cambridge: Cambridge University.

Semé, M. (1984). "The Effects of Agricultural Fields on Faunal Assemblage Variation." In *Papers on the Archaeology of Black Mesa, Arizona, Vol 2*. eds. S. Plog and S. Powell, pp. 139–157. Carbondale: Southern Illinois University Press.

Spencer, R. F. and Jennings, J. D. (1965). *The Native Americans: Prehistory and Ethnology*. New York: Harper and Row.

Stewart, T. D. and Quade, L. G. (1969). "Lesions of the Frontal Bone in American Indians." *American Journal of Physical Anthropology* 30:89–110.

Stodder, A. L. (1989). "Bioarchaeological Research in the Basin and Range Region." In *Human Adaptation and Cultural Change in the Greater Southwest*, eds. A. Simmons, A. L. Stodder, A. L. Dykeman and P. A. Hicks, pp. 167–190. Wrightsville, Arkansas: Arkansas Archaeological Survey Research Series No. 32.

Swedlund, A. C. and Sessions, S. E. (1976). "A Developmental Model of Prehistoric Population Growth on Black Mesa, Northeastern Arizona." In *Papers on the Archaeology of Black Mesa, Arizona*, eds., G. Gumerman and R. C. Euler, pp. 136–148. Carbondale: Southern Illinois University Press.

Titiev, M. (1972). *The Hopi Indians of Old Oraibi.* Ann Arbor, University of Michigan.

Toll, H. W. (1993). *The Role of the Totah in Regions and Regional Definitions.* Unpublished paper presented at the 5th Occasional Anasazi Symposium, San Juan College, Farmington, New Mexico.

Toll, M. S. (1993). *The Archaeobotany of the La Plata Valley in Totah Perspective.* Unpublished paper presented at the 5th Occasional Anasazi Symposium, San Juan College, Farmington, New Mexico.

Turner, C. G., II (1993). "Cannibalism in Chaco Canyon: The Charnel Pit Excavated in 1926 at Small House Ruin by Frank H. H. Roberts, Jr." *American Journal of Physical Anthropology* 91:421–439.

Trinkaus, E., Churchill, S. E. and Ruff, C. B. (1994). "Postcranial Robusticity in *Homo*. II: Humeral Bilateral Asymmetry and Bone Plasticity." *American Journal of Physical Anthropology* 93:1–34.

Walker, P. L. (1989). "Cranial Injuries as Evidence of Violence in Prehistoric Southern California." *American Journal of Physical Anthropology* 80:313–323.

Warr, M. (1994). "Public Perceptions and Reactions to Violent Offending and Victimization." In *Understanding and Preventing Violence. Volume 4 Consequences and Control*, eds. A. J. Reiss and J. A. Roth, pp. 1–66. Washington, D. C.: National Academy Press.

Wells, C. (1964). *Bones, Bodies and Disease: Evidence of Disease and Abnormality in Early Man.* London: Thames and Hudson.

White, T. D. (1991). *Human Osteology.* Orlando: Academic Press.

White, T. D. (1992). *Prehistoric Cannibalism at Mancos 5MTUMR–2346.* Princeton, Princeton University.

Wilcox, D. R. and Haas, J. (1994). "Competition and Conflict in the Prehistoric Southwest." In *Themes in Southwest Prehistory*, ed. G. Gumerman, pp. 211–238. Santa Fe, New Mexico: School of American Research.

Wilkinson, R. G. and Van Wagenen, K. M. (1993). "Violence Against Women: Prehistoric Skeletal Evidence from Michigan." *Midcontinental Journal of Archaeology.* **18**:190–216.

Chapter
FOUR

Patterns of Violence
in Prehistoric
Hunter-gatherer Societies
of Coastal
Southern California

Patricia M. Lambert
*Department of Sociology, Social Work and
Anthropology, Utah State University
Logan, Utah*

ABSTRACT

Anthropologists have long debated the relative importance of cultural, biological, and historical factors in the origins and maintenance of different patterns of violence. Much of the evidence brought to bear on this issue has been generated by ethnographic research on modern non-industrial societies. While contributing significantly to our understanding of the proximate causes of violence, this avenue of inquiry lacks the time depth needed to identify and understand long-term trends in human interaction. Another complication with these studies is the difficulty of isolating 'indigenous'' patterns of behavior from those brought about by European contact. This chapter offers a broad temporal perspective in a pre-contact environment by reviewing the mortuary evidence for violent conflict in prehistoric hunter-gatherer societies of the Santa Barbara Channel Area, California. The evidence used to track temporal variations in violent conflict includes depressed cranial vault fractures and projectile wounds. Both types of injuries are relatively common in this area. Their frequency is not consistent across time, however, and there appears to be a strong correlation between violent conflict and periods of unfavorable climatic conditions. These data shed light on the causes of violent conflict in prehistoric societies and provide baseline data for understanding modern patterns of violence.

INTRODUCTION

For many years, the efforts of a diverse array of scholarly talent have been directed at elucidating the nature and causes of aggression and violence in modern human societies. Consequently, the literature pertaining to patterns of violence in modern groups is abundant and wide-ranging (e.g., Boehm 1984; Bohannan 1967; Chagnon 1974, 1988, 1990; Durham 1976; Ember 1982, Ember and Ember 1992; Fadiman 1982; Ferguson 1984, 1989, 1990; Fried *et al.* 1967; Gross 1975; Harris 1984; Koch 1974; Meggitt 1977; Nettleship *et al.* 1975; Otterbein 1970; Vayda 1976). The same cannot be said for that pertaining to violent conflict in prehistoric societies, although a few such studies have recently begun to appear (e.g., Haas 1990; Lambert 1994; Maschner 1991; Milner *et al.* 1991; Moss and Erlandson 1992; Owsley and Jantz 1994; Walker 1989; Willey 1990). This disparity is in large part due to the inherent difficulty of reconstructing patterns of behavior from the material remains of ancient peoples. As a result, we know surprisingly little about the nature of human conflict for most of the vast period of our existence. This chapter presents the results of one effort to bridge this tremendous gap in our knowledge of human behavior by examining the evidence for violent conflict in skeletal remains and associated burial objects of hunter-gatherers laid to rest hundreds and thousands of years ago in cemeteries along the coast of southern California.

The geographic focus of this study is the Santa Barbara Channel Area mainland coast and the large offshore islands of Santa Cruz and Santa Rosa (Fig. 4.1). At the time of European contact, this region was occupied by the Chumash, maritime hunter-gatherers who lived in large sedentary villages loosely organized into multi-village polities (Arnold 1991, 1992; Johnson 1988; King 1990). Avid traders and seafarers, the Chumash produced and used olive shell bead money in an exchange system that served to redistribute terrestrial and marine plant and animal foods, redwood plank canoes, otter skins, stone and shell beads, cooking and ceremonial vessels, and other commodities brokered by various southern California groups (Arnold 1991, 1992, 1993; Davis 1961; King 1971; Walker 1994). That all matters were not transacted peacefully is indicated by early historic accounts of inter-village hostilities (e.g., Bolton 1933; Brown 1967; Johnson 1988; Priestley 1937). For example, relations were so bad between the villages along the Goleta Slough, in the center of the Chumash territory, and their neighbors at Dos Pueblos to the west, that in 1782 the military

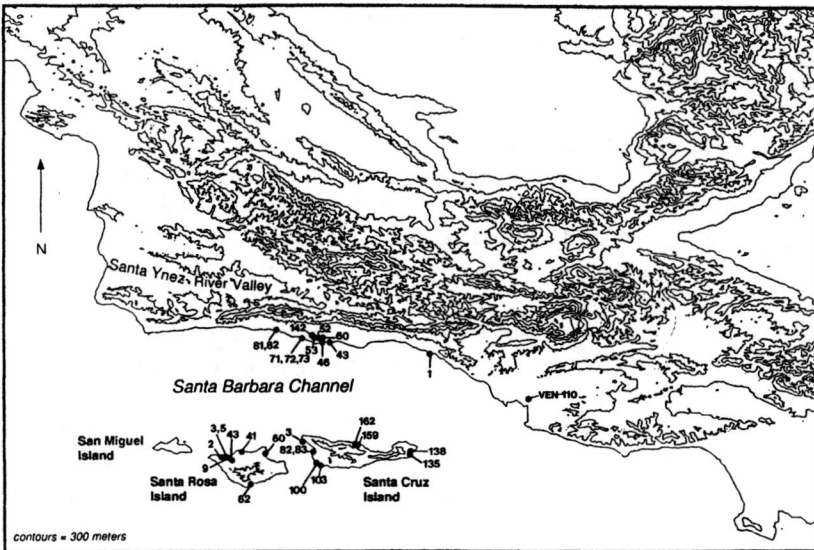

Figure 4.1. Map of Santa Barbara Channel area archaeological sites included in this analysis.

governor of California proposed that the Santa Barbara Presidio be located as a barrier between the two locales (Neve 1782, in Johnson 1988:124). Other accounts tell of burned or abandoned villages and lethal raids (Bolton 1927:164, 1933:262; Burrus 1967:135, in Johnson 1988:123), leaving little doubt that the Chumash heartland was not always a place of peaceful coexistence.

These historic accounts of the Chumash are fascinating and provide a gripping picture of life during the early Mission Period. The problem with using them to reconstruct indigenous patterns of amity and enmity is that they reflect a people fully embroiled in the effects of European contact (Walker *et al.* 1989). First contacted by Europeans some 240 years earlier when Spanish explorer Juan Rodriguez Cabrillo and his men sailed into the Channel waters (Hornbeck 1983), it is difficult to know the extent to which events in the late eighteenth century were shaped by the introduction of European ideology, technology, and disease.

Indeed, the almost universal nature of such contacts elsewhere in the world has led some researchers (e.g., Ferguson 1992; Ferguson and Whitehead 1992) to question the extent to which high levels of violent conflict in modern groups such as the Yanomamo, tribespeople long at the center of debates concerning the causes of human conflict (e.g., Chagnon 1988, 1990; Chagnon and Hames 1979; Ferguson 1984, 1989, 1990; Harris 1984), can be taken to reflect indigenous conditions. Less often questioned, but equally debatable, is the normalcy of the peaceful behavior (Dentan 1978) of contacted groups such as the Semai. Because ethnographic accounts at best pertain to a few generations, the lack of a broad temporal perspective makes it difficult to truly evaluate the importance of contact phenomena in bringing about a cessation of, or an increase in, levels of violent conflict. This is precisely the value of the archaeological record. Although the motivations of individuals cannot be studied in this way, the archaeological record offers the temporal depth necessary to identify and interpret changing patterns of peace and violence in the context of a changing physical and social landscape.

Most archaeological studies of violent conflict rely on site survey data and the identification of defensive sites and structures (e.g., Haas 1990; Larson 1972; Maschner 1991, 1992, this volume; Moss 1989; Moss and Erlandson 1992). Along the narrow coastal plains of the Santa Barbara Channel coast, where defensible locations are few and architectural features rarely preserved, the potential for such studies is more limited. Fortunately, the Santa Barbara

Channel area is unique to many areas in one important respect: the people of this region practiced burial as the primary means of disposing of the dead throughout the long period of prehistoric occupation (Kroeber 1922; Lambert 1994). For this reason, and because the area has been the focus of a number of archaeological reconnaissance and excavation projects (e.g., Harrison 1964; Olson 1930; Orr 1943, 1968; Rogers 1929; Yarrow 1879), extensive temporally and spatially discrete skeletal series spanning over 7000 years are available for analysis. Burial remains often preserve evidence of interpersonal conflict in the form of depressed cranial vault fractures and projectile wounds, so it is possible to reconstruct prehistoric patterns of violence through the analysis of these injuries.

Mortuary remains provide a particularly valuable source of information on prehistoric patterns of conflict because, unlike defensive sites and structures, which at best only suggest or imply the threat of violent intruders, injuries preserved in human burials document actual events and identify the victims. Since different types of conflict can result in distinct wounds (e.g., Chagnon 1992, Koch 1974), injuries can also aid in the identification of different processes of conflict resolution. When examined in the context of cultural and environmental variables, injury data can be used to test the explanatory power of theories proposed to explain violence and warfare in modern groups.

Recent anthropological debate concerning the causes of violence and warfare in non-industrial societies has primarily revolved around two theoretical arguments: 1) the extent to which violent conflict can be explained in terms of the battle for life-sustaining material resources (e.g., Chagnon 1988; Chagnon and Hames 1979; Ferguson 1989; Harris 1984), and 2) the effect of European contact on observed patterns of violence in recent and modern hunter-gatherer and horticultural societies (Ferguson 1992; Ferguson and Whitehead 1992). Much of the research pertaining to the first debate has focussed on the spatial distribution of people relative to protein resources or arable land (e.g., Ember 1982; Ferguson 1989; Gross 1975; Harris 1984; Meggitt 1977; Vayda 1976). The archaeological record of the Santa Barbara Channel area offers a different perspective. Through the use of skeletal indicators of health and violence, and paleoclimatic measures of resource productivity, it is possible to examine the nature of the relationship between violent conflict and major changes in the availability of food and water resources. Because the osteological record described here covers almost the entire prehistoric period, it is also possible to look at pre-European contact levels of violent conflict in order to assess the nature of violent conflict before and after the arrival of Europeans.

MORTUARY EVIDENCE FOR VIOLENT CONFLICT

The Sample

Mortuary remains from 30 Santa Barbara Channel area prehistoric and historic archaeological sites (Fig. 4.1) were examined for evidence of depressed cranial vault fractures and projectile injuries. To enable the assessment of temporal trends in injury frequencies, skeletal series were divided into five discrete time periods (Tab. 4.1). Temporal assignments of cemetery samples were based on artifact seriations and radiocarbon dates as described in King (1990) and Lambert (1994). Time periods were based on the chronological sequence devised by King for the Chumash region (King 1982, 1990). Recent revisions to King's chronological sequence suggested by Colten and Erlandson (1991) based on the calibration of dates used to construct King's chronology are included in Table 4.1.

Depressed Cranial Vault Fractures

Cranial injuries have proved to be a useful measure of violent conflict in archaeological contexts, as a number of recent studies can attest (e.g., Lambert 1994; Milner *et al.* 1991; Walker 1989; Webb 1989; Willey 1990). In the modern world, head injuries are a major cause of death in people under 45 years of age. Most of these are incurred in the context of industrial and motor vehicle accidents

Table 4.1. Santa Barbara Channel Area Chronology

Period	Estimated Dates (King 1982)	Calibrated Dates (Colten & Erlandson 1991)
Late (L)*	A.D. 1150–1804	A.D. 1380–1804
Late Middle (LM)	A.D. 300–1150	A.D. 580–1380
Early Middle (EM)	1400 B.C.–A.D. 300	1490 B.C.–A.D. 580
Late Early (LE)	3500–1400 B.C.	4050–1490 B.C.
Early Early (EE)	6000–3500 B.C.	6630–4050 B.C.

*Includes Historic/Mission Period (AD 1782–1804)

(Bagchi 1980; Bakay and Glasauer 1980; Shapiro 1983), but falls are another common cause of head trauma (Annegers 1983; Courville 1962a, 1962b). In all of these contexts, linear fractures of the cranial vault predominate (Courville 1962b; Zimmerman and Bilaniuk 1983). Prior to the age of industry, high-rise buildings, and modern forms of conveyance, most head injuries were probably sustained in the context of violent assaults, inflicted by weapons such as spears, rocks, and clubs (Bagchi 1980). According to modern medical research (e.g., Bagchi 1980; Courville 1962a, 1962b; Zimmerman and Bilaniuk 1983), such weapons are more likely to cause localized depressed fractures than linear cracks. It is therefore not surprising that depression fractures predominate in prehistoric skeletal samples (e.g., Cybulski 1990, 1993; Lambert 1994; Milner *et al.* 1991; Walker 1989; Webb 1989; Willey 1990).

Unfortunately, modern medical literature on depressed cranial vault fractures pertains almost exclusively to etiology, diagnosis, and treatment (e.g., Bagchi 1980; Bakay and Glasauer 1980; Hayward 1980; Shapiro 1983). The osteological manifestations of these injuries are rarely illustrated except in the form of radiographs, which are difficult to extrapolate to dry bone specimens. In a rare forensic treatise, Courville (1962b:310–312) provides a useful albeit somewhat theoretical discussion of the stages of depressed skull fracture that includes osteological descriptions. According to this scheme, depressed fractures can range from simple, non-penetrating indentations where the outer table is depressed against the inner table, to penetrating complex fractures where bone fragments are driven into the brain. The interim stage is an injury that affects the inner table without penetrating the fibrous connective tissue that surrounds and protects the brain. Differences in the severity of depression injuries relate to variations in the force of the blow, the shape and size of the traumatizing object, and the thickness of the cranial vault (Courville 1962b). Non-penetrating injuries to a stationary head result in minimal damage and are rarely fatal. Injuries penetrating the braincase, on the other hand, are cause for greater concern because they damage the brain and introduce infectious material (Courville 1962a, 1962b).

Researchers studying ancient skeletal remains have used basic diagnostic criteria such as the size, shape, and surface texture of cranial depressions to differentiate injuries attributable to assault from accidental fractures, post-mortem damage, and other cranial pathologies. Such criteria are important in modern forensic contexts for determining specific cause of death (Courville 1962b).

Clubbing instruments such as wooden clubs or stone celts are the agents most commonly implicated when blunt instrument trauma is observed in prehistoric contexts (e.g., Courville 1948, 1952; Lambert 1994; Milner *et al.* 1991; Tyson 1977; Walker 1989; Webb 1989). Cranial injuries attributed to clubs generally retain the round or elliptical shape, both in external and internal dimensions, of the instrument thought to have inflicted them (Fig. 4.2; see also Walker, this volume). Those attributed to weapons such as axes or ground stone celts tend to be elongated and somewhat v-shaped in cross-section (e.g., Milner *et al.* 1991; Willey 1990). Lesions fitting both descriptions have been observed in prehistoric North American skeletal remains (e.g., Courville 1948, 1952; Lambert 1994; Milner *et al.* 1991; Walker 1989).

Both healed and peri-mortem fractures have been identified in archaeological contexts (e.g., Lambert 1994; Milner *et al.* 1991; Tyson 1977; Walker 1989; Webb 1989; Willey 1990). Healed depression fractures are differentiated from other ante- mortem cranial lesions (such as the stellate scars of treponematosis) by the smooth texture of their rim and internal surface, well-defined rim margins, and in rare cases, remnant fracture lines along their periphery (Lambert 1994; Walker 1989). Scars from sub-lethal wounds may range from shallow (<1 mm) dents to deep (5 + mm) pools or depressions. Peri-mortem fractures are not likely to be confused with other cranial pathologies, but may be mistaken for post-mortem damage. However, penetrating wounds to fresh bone cause internal hinge fractures and spalling, and fracture lines that radiate away from a circumferential break (Courville 1962b). Post-mortem damage, on the other hand, is usually identifiable in dry bone specimens based on the lighter color, rougher texture, and perpendicular angle of fracture surfaces. In most cases, healed injuries are those that did not penetrate the braincase, whereas lethal, or peri-mortem, fractures are generally of the invasive type.

As noted previously by Walker (1989), lesions that exhibit characteristics of healed depression fractures (Fig. 4.2a) are common in Santa Barbara Channel area skeletal series, whereas peri-mortem depression fractures (Fig. 4.2b) are much less so. In the research described here, 105 crania with one or more obvious healed fractures, and 23 crania with lesions most reasonably interpreted as fracture scars, were observed in a total of 753 individuals with intact cranial vaults (Lambert 1994). The total number of individuals with healed cranial vault fractures is thus 128, or 17% of the total sample. Almost 90% of the 168 fractures identified in these

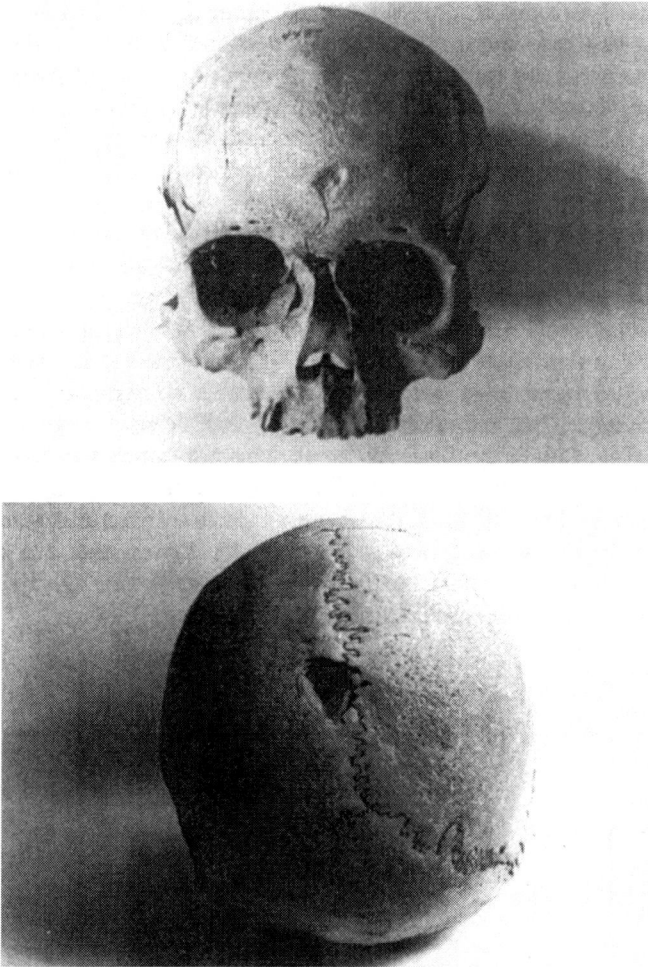

Figure 4.2. Depressed cranial vault fractures a) healed depression fracture (note: crack in forehead is a post-mortem fracture), b) peri-mortem compound fracture.

individuals are either circular or ellipsoidal in shape, implicating some type of rounded clubbing implement as the causal agent. Most are relatively small and shallow, however, with an average maximum diameter of 13mm and an average depth of 1.4 mm, and were not likely to have been seriously debilitating. Only 10 crania with peri-mortem fractures were observed in this sample, and in all but one case the inner table was perforated. Because peri-mortem fractures are infrequent in Santa Barbara Channel Area crania and apparently associated with a pattern of conflict distinct from that resulting in smaller, healed fractures (Lambert 1994), the following section focusses on the more common, sub-lethal form of cranial injury.

Both age and sex differences were observed in the frequency of healed cranial vault fractures. In a sample of 627 individuals of known age (Lambert 1994), the crania of children under ten years old were rarely affected, whereas the crania of adolescents were three times as likely to exhibit healed cranial vault injuries. Fracture scars were most frequent in the crania of mature adults, but surprisingly less common in those of individuals forty years or older (Fig. 4.3). Since these fractures are actually scars from old and in most cases relatively minor wounds rather than injuries that resulted in death, these data suggest that most fractures were sustained during adolescence and young adulthood, and that people who were not involved in the kinds of activities or lifestyles that resulted in fracture scars lived longer (Lambert 1994).

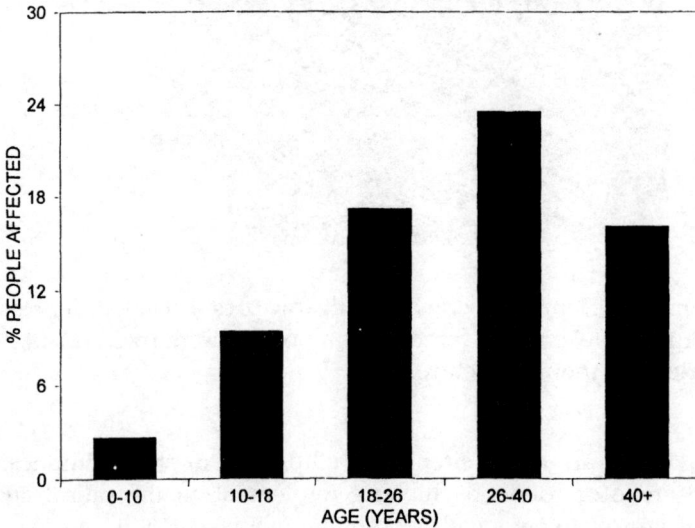

Figure 4.3. Age differences in the frequency of healed cranial vault fractures.

Sex differences in the frequency of these injuries are particularly illuminating with regard to the circumstances surrounding their origins. In a sample of 608 individuals of known sex (319 males, 289 females), healed fractures were more common in males than in females in all five time periods (Fig. 4.4). The cumulative difference in number of affected males and females is highly significant ($X^2 = 10.549$, $p = 0.001$). But whereas the frequency of fracture scars is about the same for young, mature, and old adult males, the frequency of injuries in mature adult females is approximately 50 percent greater than that observed in young or old adult females (Fig. 4.5). These data suggest that males primarily sustained cranial injuries as young men, retaining these scars into old age. Women, on the other hand, appear to have remained somewhat more susceptible to cranial vault injuries for a greater portion of their adult life, and, or, to have experienced differential mortality positively correlated with cranial trauma that resulted in a greater than average number of affected individuals dying in middle (26–40) rather than old age.

Differences between males and females in the location of these injuries provide insights into their causation (Fig. 4.6). In males,

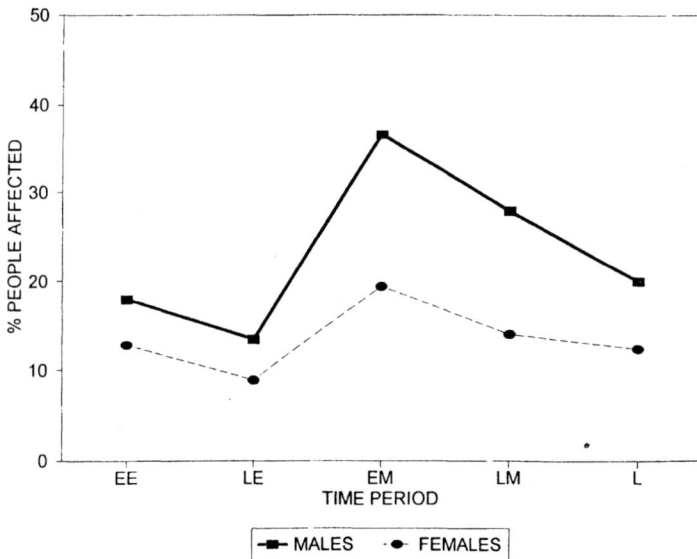

Figure 4.4. Sex differences in the frequency of healed cranial vault fractures.

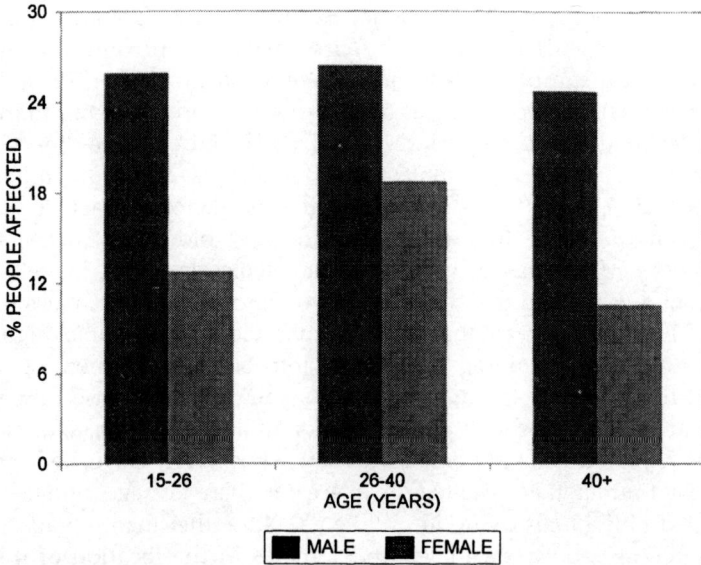

Figure 4.5. Age differences by sex in the frequency of healed cranial vault fractures

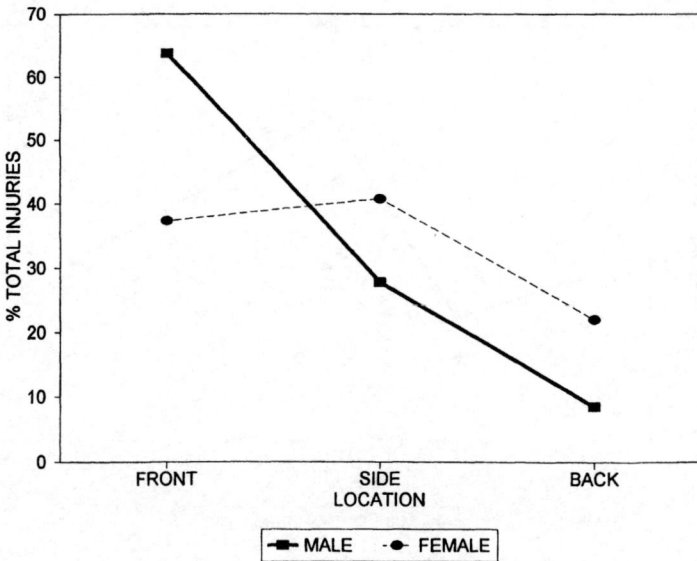

Figure 4.6. Sex differences in the location of depressed fractures on the cranial vault.

64% of all sub-lethal cranial vault fractures focus on the frontal bone. The frontal location of these injuries suggests a face-to-face form of conflict resolution, an interpretation supported by the greater frequency of injuries to the left side of the forehead, which would be expected if a right-handed aggressor hit out at a person facing them (Lambert 1994; but see also Walker 1989). It is possible that most of these injuries were sustained in the context of verbal disputes that escalated into physical standoffs such as the 'scuffles' seen among the Jalé of New Guinea (Koch 1974) and the chestpounding duels and clubfights of the Yanomamo of Venezuela (Chagnon 1992; Walker 1989). Such forms of regulated or ritualized dispute resolution serve to diffuse tensions without death, and are preferred over more lethal alternatives when important relationships are at stake (Chagnon 1992; Chagnon and Bugos 1979; Koch 1974). The low frequency of peri-mortem (i.e. penetrating) cranial vault fractures (<2% affected) observed in these populations overall supports the interpretation that the intention of those inflicting club blows was to injure rather than kill the victim (Lambert 1994).

Cranial vault injuries in females, on the other hand, show no such predilection for the frontal bone (37%), but are more diffuse across the vault (Fig. 4.6). This lack of patterning, coupled with the lower overall frequency of cranial injuries, suggests that women were not generally participating in the same activities that resulted in male frontal bone injuries. Rather, female injuries suggest a distinct causation. One possibility is that these fractures were sustained in the context of domestic disputes between women, such as has been documented in prehistoric and modern Australian Aborigine societies (Burbank 1994; Larsen 1997; Webb 1989). The focus of depressed fractures in the parietal regions of affected females from both groups (Lambert 1994; Webb 1989) would tend to support this hypothesis. This explanation seems unlikely, however, given that women in these Aborigine societies both inflict and receive the majority of sub-lethal cranial injuries (Burbank 1994; Webb 1989), a pattern distinct from that described above. A more likely possibility is spousal abuse, a form of violence that does not appear to have any strict rules of protocol and that follows the overall pattern of male-based physical, aggression evident in the Santa Barbara Channel Area data. It may be that the apparent correlation between healed cranial injuries and mortality in females reflects differences between injured and uninjured women in spousal relations that translated into differences in diet, workload, and general quality of life.

Sub-lethal cranial vault fractures are present in skeletal remains from all time periods, indicating that episodes of physical violence occurred throughout the prehistoric period. However, they appear to have peaked in frequency during the early (EM) and late (LM) Middle Period (Fig. 4.7), suggesting that these were years of rising internal tensions. This is consistent with our picture of life in the Middle period, a time of population growth, increasing sedentism, and increasing dependence on marine resources (Erlandson 1993; Lambert 1994). The decline in frequency of cranial vault fractures in the Late Period seems to indicate that tensions were either reduced or diffused through alternative strategies.

Projectile Injuries

Projectile injuries are wounds caused by stone, bone, wood, cane, or metal tipped projectiles. Since the weapons used to inflict these injuries are designed to kill (either directly or indirectly), and generally require careful aim in order to hit their mark, accident can be ruled out in most if not all cases. The very nature of this type of injury thus implies lethal intent. As such, projectile injuries provide a better measure of lethal violence. Although projectile violence in

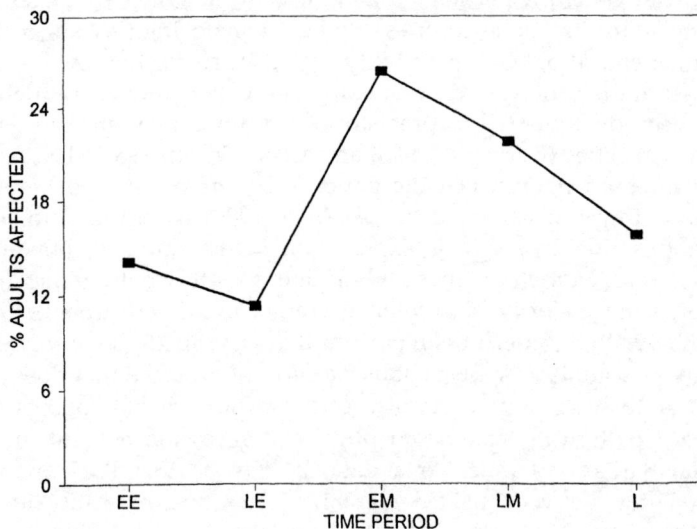

Figure 4.7. Temporal variation in the frequency of healed cranial vault fractures.

modern tribal groups sometimes involves close blood kin, it is more frequently observed in feuding, raiding, or open warfare between less closely related groups (Boehm 1984; Chagnon 1992; Fadiman 1982; Harner 1984; Koch 1974; Meggitt 1977).

There are several different types of projectile injuries that can be identified in archaeological remains. Stone points, point tips, or fragments from fractured points actually embedded in bone provide the best and most indisputable evidence for this type of injury

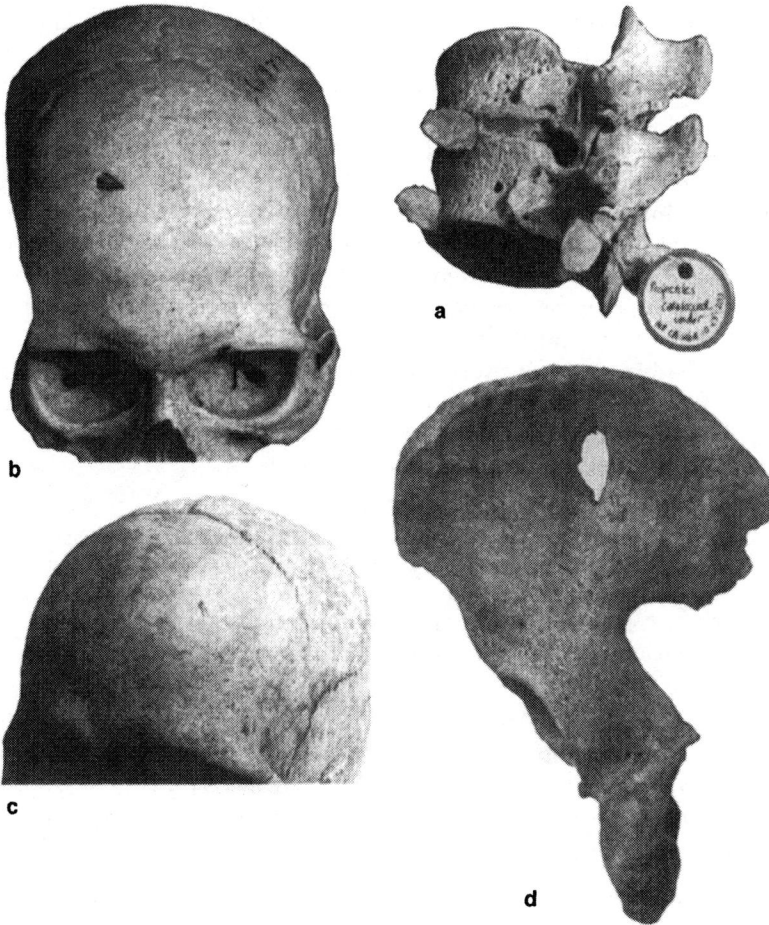

Figure 4.8. Projectile injuries a) chert arrow points embedded in thoracic vertebrae, b) chert point tip embedded in frontal bone, c) stone fragments embedded in frontal bone, d) piercing wound in left innominate.

(Figs. 4.8a–8c). Not surprisingly, most injuries reported for archaeological skeletal samples are of this variety. A second, more subtle
class of projectile wounds are scars in bone surfaces that appear to
have been caused by projectiles that either did not become embedded or were removed during life or after death (Fig. 4.8d). In other
words, these are holes or scars that by their surface appearance,
shape, and location are most reasonably interpreted as projectile
injuries. Both types of injuries involve bone, and are identified
through the analysis of skeletal remains.

Medical reports from the nineteenth century American Indian
wars (Bill 1862) and from modern Papua New Guinea (Meggitt
1977; vanGurp et al. 1990) indicate, however, that the most deadly
injuries are those to the thorax and abdomen, wounds that often do
not involve bone. Unless projectiles pass through the muscles and
internal organs of these cavities and lodge in the vertebral centra,
ribs, or innominates, such injuries can only be identified by the
discovery of projectiles within the body cavity during excavation.
Such evidence is most often contextual, and must be recognized
and recorded by the excavator at the time the burial is exhumed. It
is therefore only through the analysis of burial excavation records
that this third type of projectile wound – projectiles in wound-like
associations – can be identified. For example, Olson (n.d.) described this burial (D-11) from SCRI-100 in field notes made during
his 1928 excavations on Santa Cruz Island:

> 'At 3' & 7 1/2' from cliff, burial of a woman on face, head to right &
> down so that it lay on the forehead, flexed...One 3" obsidian arrow
> point & 1 small serrated gray obsidian point in thorax [probable
> wounds, counted as injuries]. 1 white flint point near throat & 1
> lying among bones of lower right leg. 1 butt of a spear point to left &
> 3" above middle of left femur...[suspicious associations, noted but
> not counted]'

None of these projectile associations clearly involved bone, although peri-mortem nicks were observed in several ribs. A burial
(AA) excavated by Orr (n.d., but see also Orr 1943) from SBA-46A
provides some idea of how many injuries might be expected to
involve the skeleton:

> "Adult in poor condition, all but ribs and scapulae saved. Contained
> 17 [16?] arrowheads, the majority definitely shot into him. One along
> side jaw – may have entered throat. Yellow jasper up against right
> clavicle [embedded in bone]. One in breast at 3rd right rib...Red
> jasper on right humerus. 2 in lower thorax near sternum. Large red
> one in 7th right rib back [embedded in bone]. One embedded in

centrum of 11th dorsal – driven from front [embedded in bone]. One embedded between centrum of 11th and 12th dorsal driven from front [embedded in bone]. One between 12 and 13th dorsal lumbar driven from front. One position uncertain, probably from vertebral column between 11–12. Small white point near sternum. Long greenish brown point between ribs 7–8 driven from low down in front.... appears as though the man had arrows driven into him as he lay on ground."

The analysis of burial records, skeletal remains, and catalogue records resulted in the following categorization of the 16 projectiles associated with this burial: four points embedded in bone, five probable wounds considered to be injuries, four suspicious point associations and three unclear point associations noted but not counted as wounds. As this example illustrates, not all projectile injuries involve bone.

In reconstructing patterns of projectile violence, it is important to consider all three types of projectile injuries described above. The exclusion of all but the most certain (i.e. points embedded in bones) is likely to result in a serious under-representation of the actual number of victims. The projectile wounds of Burial AA are useful in illustrating this point. The proportion of wounds actually involving bone in this individual with multiple injuries is at most 44% (4/9), but probably only 25% (4/16) of the total number of injuries. Thus, an analysis that included only projectile points embedded in bone would miss over half of the projectiles clearly described as embedded in Burial AA, and 75% of what was in all probability the actual number of projectile wounds. A conservative approach to the interpretation of projectile associations as injuries is thus still likely to underestimate rather than overestimate the total number of victims because wound associations are not always obvious and therefore not always scorable. For this reason, the cumulative figures presented here are more correctly viewed as relative estimates rather than absolute values.

Overall, projectile injuries are relatively common in Santa Barbara Channel area burials. Fifty-eight of the 1744 individuals (3.3%) for whom either skeletal material, and, or, burial records (describing a primary burial) were available for analysis had at least one projectile injury. Forty-three percent of these victims had more than one projectile injury, and a total of 118 wounds were observed in the sample. Of the 58 identified victims, 66% had at least one projectile embedded in bone; 24% of those remaining had at least one projectile association identified from burial records as an injury. Only 10% of the victims were identified exclusively by bone scars interpreted as projectile injuries. The most common site of bodily injury was the thorax, followed closely by the abdomen and head. Limb injuries were considerably less common (Fig. 4.9). At least 70% of the victims appear to have died as a consequence of their wounds, a much higher mortality rate for this type of injury than reported for modern tribal warfare (e.g., Meggitt 1977; van-Gurp *et al.* 1990). In all probability, this disparity has more to do with problems inherent in the archaeological record than it does with actual differences between prehistoric and modern projectile violence, because non-lethal wounds from which projectiles were removed during life are seldom visible in archaeological death assemblages. The high frequency of victims with multiple wounds, a frequency much greater than that reported for some modern groups (Meggitt 1977; vanGurp *et al.* 1990), may also reflect the bias inherent in death assemblages, because number of injuries and risk of death are likely to be positively correlated.

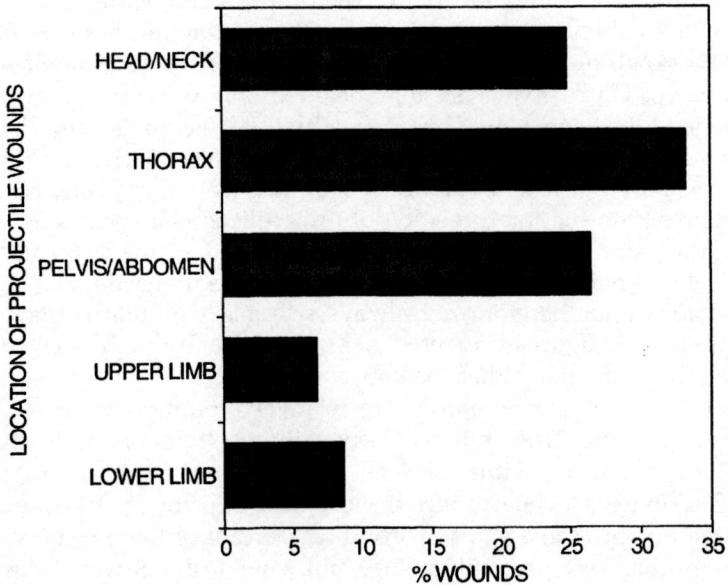

Figure 4.9. Distribution of projectile injuries within the body (Lambert 1994).

As with depressed cranial vault fractures, projectile injuries are not equally distributed between different age and sex classes. Such injuries are most common in the remains of young and mature adults, less common in the remains of adults over the age of forty, and absent in those of children under the age of ten (Fig. 4.10). These data suggest that old age, like childhood, afforded some socially-mediated protection from projectile violence. Males appear to have been much more likely than females to sustain projectile wounds throughout most of the prehistoric period (Fig. 4.11). As with cranial vault fractures, the cumulative difference in the frequency of projectile injuries to males and females is highly significant ($X^2 = 11.307$, $P = 0.001$). Given that most of the observed projectile injuries are unhealed, projectile violence appears to have been a more important cause of death among young and mature adult males than among females of any age or males over the age of 40 (Fig. 4.12), which probably reflects the greater participation of younger men relative to women and older men in violent activities such as feuding and raiding. This interpretation is consistent with violent interactions in modern non-industrial societies (e.g., Boehm 1984; Chagnon 1992; Fadiman 1982; Harner 1984; Koch 1974; Meggitt 1977).

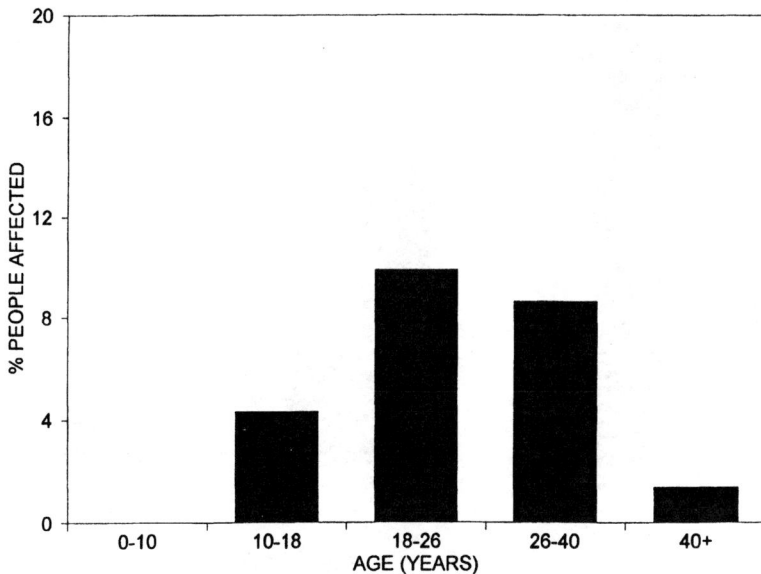

Figure 4.10. Frequency of projectile injuries by age group. Statistics pertain to age groups in the death assemblage rather than age groups in the living population.

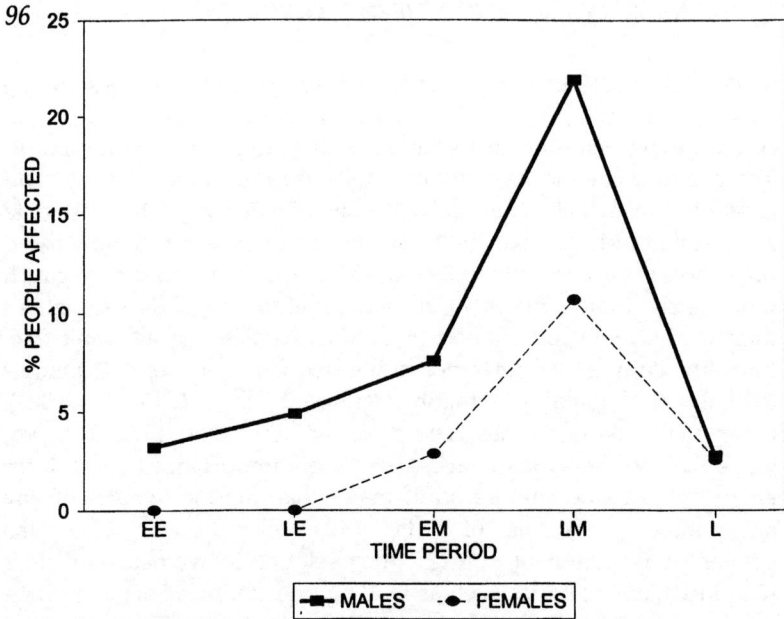

Figure 4.11. Sex differences in the frequency of projectile injuries.

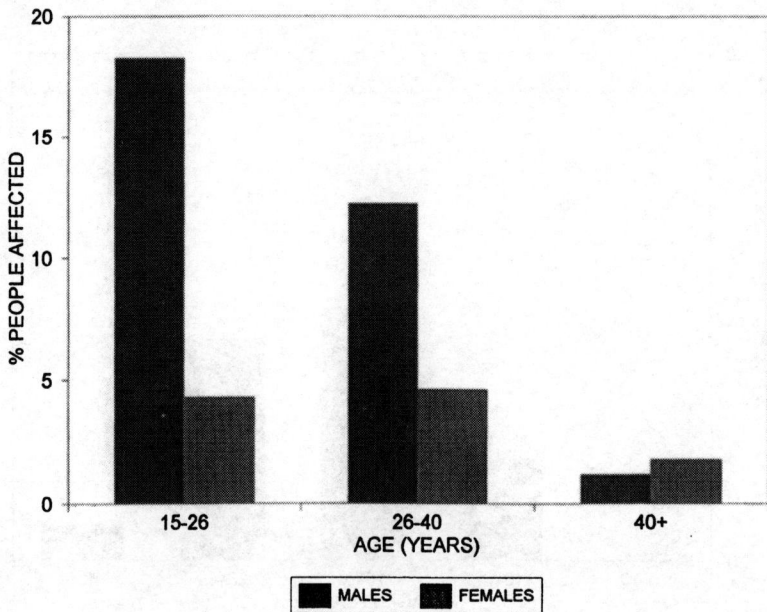

Figure 4.12. Frequency of projectile injuries by age and sex group. Statistics pertain to age groups in the death assemblage rather than age groups in the living population.

Projectile injuries can be found in individuals from all five time periods (early Early, late Early, early Middle, late Middle and Late) indicating that lethal forms of violence were also a part of life throughout the prehistoric sequence. However, they are much more common in late Middle Period samples than in those from any other time period, a pattern that is apparent no matter which way the data are analyzed (Fig. 4.13). These high injury rates can not be explained by the annihilation of a single village, such as occurred in the massacre at Crow Creek (Willey 1990). Rather, multiple victims were identified in six of seven late Middle Period cemetery samples (Lambert 1994). The presence of a few multiple graves or clusters of victims in these Santa Barbara Channel area cemeteries provide evidence that violent encounters sometimes

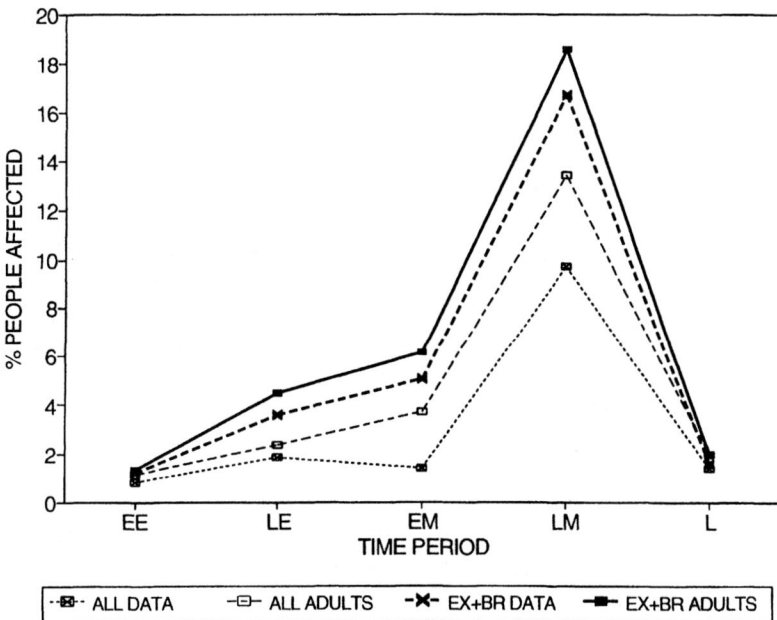

Figure 4.13. Temporal variation in the frequency of projectile injuries. Sample examined in four ways: all burials, and all known adult burials (18 +), for which burial records describing a primary burial, and, or, skeletal remains were available for analysis; all burials, and all known adult burials (18 +), for which both burial records and skeletal remains were available for analysis (Lambert 1994).

resulted in more than one casualty. However, most victims were scattered throughout cemeteries containing the remains of many individuals who do not appear to have died violently. Since multiple burials are known from this area, and because many cemeteries appear to have formed primarily by a process of accretion, this is evidence that lethal violence was constant but relatively small in scale (Lambert 1994). Overall, projectile injuries in late Middle Period population samples are similar in nature and distribution to those described for modern tribal groups such as the lowland Yanomamo (Chagnon 1992) and Mae Enga (Meggitt 1977), suggesting that levels and types of violence in the prehistoric maritime societies of this time period may have been similar to those observed in some modern groups.

DISCUSSION

Theoretically, the temporal trends in depressed cranial vault fractures and projectile injuries are intriguing for several reasons. First, it is clear from the data presented above that violent conflict did not originate in this region with the arrival of Europeans. The highest levels of violent conflict observed in the 7000 year sequence described in this chapter occurred during the Middle Period, a time period that ended at least 100 years before Columbus arrived on the east coast of North America, and over 150 years before the Spanish explorer Juan Rodriguez Cabrillo set eyes on the bustling townships of the Santa Barbara Channel shores. This is not to say that European contact did not play a role in escalating violence described in historic accounts, only that other causes of violence· are clearly implicated by the prehistoric data.

The temporal trends in projectile violence are particularly interesting in light of what it known about changes in the physical and social environment of the Santa Barbara Channel Area. Of particular interest is the evidence bearing on the question of resource stress as a cause of intergroup aggression. According to the resource stress model, violent conflict is a strategy consciously or unconsciously employed by individuals and groups to improve their chances of survival and successful reproduction through the forceful acquisition, reallocation, or protection of basic food resources (Ferguson 1990; Gross 1975; Harris 1984). It differs in this respect from other selectionist arguments, which emphasize the importance of reproductive resources (women) and kin selection (e.g., Chagnon 1988, 1990), although these two are not mutually exclusive. Battles over material resources, for example, are likely fought along the lines of kinship, just as mate selection, at least for males, is likely affected by ones ability to successfully protect or obtain food resources. The emphasis of the resource stress argument on materialist causation made it possible to investigate archaeologically, something that could not be done for more biologically oriented models.

The power of the resource stress model to explain patterns of conflict in the Santa Barbara Channel Area was evaluated through the use of two proxy measures of resource stress: paleoclimatic indicators of unfavorable climatic conditions, and skeletal evidence of ill-health. These were analyzed in the context of our present knowledge of changes in the demographic landscape of this region, since both the size and degree of sedentism of a population have important implications for susceptibility to malnutrition and infectious disease (Lambert 1993, 1994). Through the use of these measures time periods were identified when resource stress could be predicted by unfavorable climatic conditions and more directly implicated by declining health.

In analyzing the evidence for resource stress as a cause of violent conflict, the importance of population size as an independent variable had to be considered first. It is fairly evident from cemeteries and residential middens that the Santa Barbara Channel Area population gradually increased in size throughout the prehistoric sequence, and that villages came to be occupied by more people for longer periods, particularly after about 2000 B.C. (Erlandson 1993; Lambert 1994). It is therefore possible that escalating violence might have been related to organizational pressures such as scalar stress (see Johnson 1982) that had little to do with real resource deprivation, although population growth certainly must have affected the availability of at least some resources. Indeed, both sublethal cranial fractures and lethal projectile injuries appear to have gradually increased in frequency with the growth of the coastal population, at least up to the late Middle Period. These data suggest that population size, or density, did in fact influence the nature of human interactions. It is possible that as local populations increased in size, the need for one group to get along with any other particular group for the sake of marriage partners or subsistence relief declined, making it more likely that conflicts would arise and be allowed to escalate. This pattern of interaction characterizes lowland Yanomamo interactions today (Chagnon 1974, 1992). The exponential increase in lethal violence from the early

Middle Period to the late Middle Period, and the decline that appears to have occurred in both sub-lethal and lethal violence after the late Middle Period, however, cannot be explained by population increase alone, and there is good reason to believe that resource stress was an important ingredient in escalating violence at that time.

The study area is comprised of semi-arid stretches of narrow coastal plain flanked on the interior by mountainous terrain and bordering along its coastal margins one of the richest marine habitats on the California coast (Erlandson 1993). In this environment, fresh water is the single most important limiting resource. Wet conditions are associated with high seed and acorn yields, whereas dry years see a reduction in both terrestrial and estuarine resources (Larson *et al.* 1989). Similarly, cool oceanic temperatures are associated with a proliferation of nearshore kelpbed communities, while sea water warming has been shown to cause a die-off in these marine communities (Arnold 1991, 1992; Larson *et al.* 1989; Pisias 1978, 1979). Given our knowledge of these correlations, it is possible to use paleoclimatic data as a proxy measure of relative resource productivity, and thus to predict periods of resource stress.

This is precisely what was attempted by Larson *et al.* (1989) in their preliminary study of paleoclimatic conditions in the Santa Barbara Channel Area. Using tree ring and sea core data to reconstruct climatic conditions for the period between A.D. 400 and A.D. 1800, these researchers found that the late Middle Period was a time of unstable, drought-prone climatic conditions. At several times during this period, droughts appear to have coincided with sea water warming (Larson *et al.* 1989; Walker 1994). Other climatic reconstructions for central and southern California also document this late Middle Period warm/dry trend, a reversal that stands out in an otherwise cooler and wetter 4000 year sequence (Moratto *et al.* 1978; Stine 1994; Woodman *et al.* 1991). These data suggest that after a relatively productive 2000 + year period, during which the local population grew in size and came increasingly to live in large, permanent villages, the late Middle Period marked the onset of declining terrestrial productivity, including in particular sources of potable water. When drought co-occurred with periods of sea water warming, the marine food chain may likewise have been affected. In such times of deprivation, conflict over resources might be expected.

Skeletal evidence indicates that human health was indeed compromised during these years. Cribra orbitalia, or pitting of the orbital roof, is a skeletal lesion generally attributed to childhood iron-deficiency anemia (Stuart-Macadam 1985, 1987). Walker (1986) has documented a relationship in the Santa Barbara Channel Area between cribra orbitalia and the relative scarcity of potable water. In Late Period samples, lesions are most common in crania from the small island of San Miguel, where fresh water resources are minimal, and least common on the mainland coast, with its greater abundance of streams and springs. He attributes these patterns to the effects of childhood diarrheal disease caused by repeated or prolonged exposure to waterborne parasites. Not surprisingly, cribra orbitalia frequencies peak during the late Middle Period (Fig. 4.14), at least on the mainland coast and Santa Cruz Island, suggesting that the contamination of potable water sources was a particular problem at this time. These data further suggest that fresh water, and all of the plants and animals that depend on it, was not as readily available as in preceding and subsequent time periods. These findings are bolstered by other studies of Santa Barbara Channel area skeletal samples, which also indicate that the late Middle Period was a time of relatively poor health (Lambert 1993, 1994; Walker and Lambert 1989).

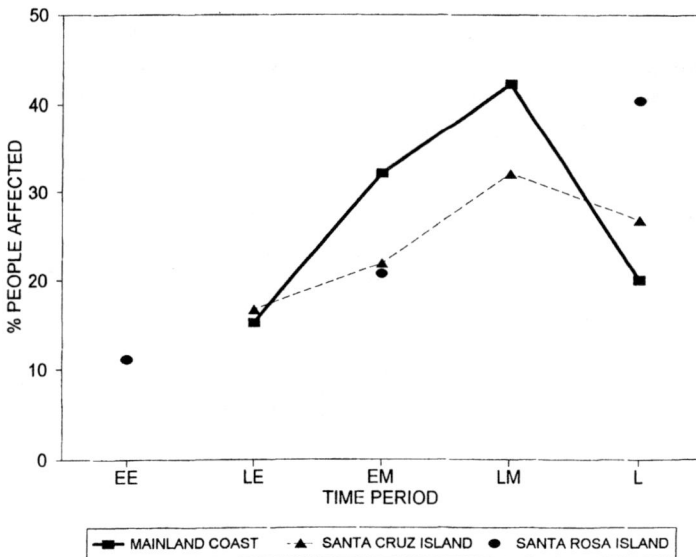

Figure 4.14. Temporal and geographic variations in the frequency of cribra orbitalia.

The correlation between unfavorable climatic conditions, declining health, and high frequencies of projectile injuries thus provides evidence for a positive correlation between resource stress and lethal violence in the late Middle Period. What specific processes caused the shift in focus from sub-lethal violence in the early Middle Period to an increasing emphasis on lethal forms of violence in the late Middle Period are debatable. Water and food shortages may have forced large numbers of unrelated people into closer proximity, resulting in an increase in levels of internal conflict. Competition over stored food supplies, fishing grounds, and, or well-watered habitable spaces may well have led to violent confrontations between unrelated kin groups. In addition, it is quite possible that, as systems of protocol broke down, physical violence replaced other, now ineffective pathways of goal achievement (Lambert 1994).

The extreme variability of terrestrial and oceanic conditions during the late Middle Period may also have affected human interactions. A worldwide survey of non-industrial societies indicates that people living in natural disaster-prone environments are more warlike than all others due to the distrust that the inhabitants feel towards real or potential bad-year competitors (Ember and Ember 1992). By all current accounts (Larson *et al.* 1989; Moratto *et al.* 1978; Pisias 1978, 1979; Stine 1994), the variable conditions of the late Middle Period would have provided ample inducement for war.

Extensive trade networks emphasizing the exchange of essential food resources that appear to have originated during the late Middle Period (Walker 1994) are further evidence that access to key resources was a problem during these years. Exchange is one of several very basic responses to risk (Minc and Smith 1989), and provides a viable alternative to open hostilities (Halstead 1989; Sahlins 1974). The stimulus for the development of this exchange system was likely population-resource imbalance, brought about or exacerbated by a growing population and a declining resource base. The success of this trade network in reducing the effects of local shortages, as well as the opportunities that it undoubtedly provided to a greater number of the local inhabitants, may also in part explain why levels of violence declined during the Late Period.

CONCLUDING REMARKS

The Late Period saw a coalescence of the traits we associate with chiefdoms-- economic and craft specialization, trade and exchange, ranking, and multi-village polities linking people in diverse resource zones (Arnold 1991, 1992, 1993; Johnson 1988; C. King 1971, 1990; L. King 1982; Lambert and Walker 1991; Martz 1992). Given the data described above, it is likely that this cultural coalescence can be viewed as an outgrowth of resource stress, poor health, and violent conflict in the late Middle Period. That conflict continued into the more productive, better organized Late Period may be more attributable to social stresses associated with high population densities, and to the legacy of blood revenge that had its origins in the harsh times of the late Middle Period. It may also in part reflect the effects of European contact, which had long since taken place when historic records of violence first began to be kept. For although it is clear that violent conflict did not originate with the arrival of Europeans in this area, it does appear from historic accounts that violence was once again on the rise during the early Mission Period (Johnson 1988; Lambert 1994; Walker *et al.* 1989).

REFERENCES

Annegers, J. F. (1983). "The Epidemiology of Head Trauma in Children." In *Pediatric Head Trauma*, ed. K. Shapiro, pp. 1-10. Mount Kisco, NY: Futura Publishing Company.

Arnold, J. (1991). "Transformation of a Regional Economy: Sociopolitical Evolution and the Production of Valuables in Southern California." *Antiquity* 65:953–62.

_____ (1992). "Complex Hunter-gatherer-fishers of Prehistoric California: Chiefs, Specialists, and Maritime Adaptations of the Channel Islands." *American Antiquity* 57:1:60–84.

_____ (1993). 'Labor and the Rise of Complex Hunter-gatherers.' *Journal of Anthropological Archaeology* 12:75–119.

Bagchi, A. K. (1980). *An Introduction to Head Injuries.* Calcutta: Oxford University Press.

Bakay, L., and F. E. Glasauer. (1980). *Head Injury.* Boston: Little, Brown and Company.

Bill, J. H. (1862). "Notes on Arrow Wounds." *American Journal of Medical Science* LXXXVIII. Oct: 365–387.

Boehm, C. (1984). *Blood Revenge: The Enactment and Management of Conflict in Montenegro and other Tribal Societies.* Philadelphia: University of Pennsylvania Press.

Bohannan, P. (1967). *Law and Warfare: Studies in the Anthropology of Conflict.* Austin: University of Texas Press.

Bolton, H. E. (1927). *Fray Juan Crespí. Missionary Explorer on the Pacific Coast 1769–1774.* Berkeley: University of California Press.

——— (1933). Font's Complete Diary. Berkeley: University of California Press.

Brown, A. K. (1967). "The Aboriginal Population of the Santa Barbara Channel." Berkeley: Reports of the University of California Archaeological Survey No. 69.

Burbank, V. K. (1994). *Fighting Women: Anger and Aggression in Aboriginal Australia*. Berkeley: University of California Press.

Burrus, E. J. (1967). *Diario del Capitn Comandante Fernando de Rivera y Moncada. Colleción Chimalistac de Libros y Documentos Acerca de la Nueva Espana*, Volumes 24 and 25. Madrid: Ediciones Jose Turanzas.

Chagnon, N. A. (1974). *Studying the Yanomamo*. New York: Holt, Rinehart & Winston.

——— (1988). "Life Histories, Blood Revenge, and Warfare in a Tribal Population." *Science* **239**:985–992.

——— (1990). "Reproductive and Somatic Conflicts of Interest in the Genesis of Violence and Warfare among Tribesmen." In *The Anthropology of War*, ed. J. Haas, pp. 77–104. Cambridge: Cambridge University Press.

——— (1992). Yanomamo. New York: Holt, Rinehart & Winston.

Chagnon, N. A. and P. Bugos, (1979). "Kin Selection and Conflict: An Analysis of a Yanomamo Ax Fight." In *Evolutionary Biology and Human Social Behavior: An Anthropological Perspective*, eds. N. Chagnon and W. Irons, pp. 213-238. North Scituate, MA: Duxbury Press.

Chagnon, N. A., and R. Hames, (1979). "Protein Deficiency and Tribal Warfare in Amazonia: New Data." *Science* **203**:910–913.

Colten, R. H. and Erlandson, J. M. (1991). "Perspectives on Early Hunter-gatherers of the California Coast." In *Hunter-gatherers of Early Holocene Coastal California*, eds. J.M. Erlandson and R. Colten, pp. 133–139. Institute of Archaeology, University of California, Los Angeles: *Perspectives in California Archaeology* 1.

Courville, C. B. (1948). "Cranial Injuries Among the Indians of North America: A Preliminary Report." *L os Angeles Neurological Society* **13**:4: 181–219.

——— (1952). "Cranial Injuries Among the Early Indians of California." *Los Angeles Neurological Society* **17**:4:137–162.

——— (1962a). "Forensic Neuropathology II: Mechanisms of Craniocerebral Injury and Their Medicolegal Significance." *Journal of Forensic Sciences* **7**:1–28.

——— (1962b). "Forensic Neuropathology IV: Significance of Traumatic Extracranial and Cranial Lesion." *Journal of Forensic Sciences* **7**:3:303–322.

Cybulski, J. S. (1990). "Human Biology." In *Handbook of North American Indians*, Vol. 7, ed. W. Suttles, pp. 52–59. Washington, D.C.: Smithsonian Institution Press.

_____ (1993). A Greenville Burial Ground: *Human Remains and Mortuary Elements in British Columbia Coast Prehistory.* Archaeological Survey of Canada Mercury Series Paper No. 146. Hull, Quebec: Canadian Museum of Civilization.

Davis, J. T. (1961). "Trade Routes and Economic Exchange." Berkeley: *University of California Archaeological Survey Reports* 54.

Dentan, R. K. (1978). "Notes on Childhood in a Nonviolent Context: the Semai Case (Malaysia)." In *Learning Non-Aggression*, ed. A. Montagu, pp. 94–143. New York: Oxford University Press.

Durham, W. (1976). "Resources, Competition and Human Aggression, Part I: A Review of Primitive War." *The Quarterly Review of Biology* **51**:385–415.

Ember, M. (1982). "Statistical Evidence for an Ecological Explanation of Warfare." *American Anthropologist* **84**:645–649.

Ember, C., and M. Ember (1992). "Resource Unpredictability, Mistrust, and War." *Journal of Conflict Resolution* **36**:242–262.

Erlandson, J. M. (1993). "The Evolution of Maritime Economies on the Southern California Coast." In *The Development of Hunting-Fishing-Gathering Societies Along the West Coast of North America*, ed. A.R. Blukis-Onat. Pullman: Washington State University Press.

Fadiman, J. A. (1982). *An Oral History of Tribal Warfare: The Meru of Mt. Kenya.* Athens: Ohio University Press.

Ferguson, R. B. (1984). "Introduction: Studying War." In *Warfare, Culture, and Environment*, ed. R. B. Ferguson, pp. 1-81. New York: Academic Press.

_____ (1989). "Ecological Consequences of Amazonian Warfare." *Ethnology* 28:3:249–264.

_____ (1990). "Explaining War." In *The Anthropology of War*, ed. J. Haas, pp. 26–55. Cambridge: Cambridge University Press.

_____ (1992). "Tribal Warfare." *Scientific American* **266**:1:108–113.

Ferguson, R. B. and Whitehead, N. (1992). *War in the Tribal Zone*. Santa Fe: School of American Research Press.

Fried, M., Harris, M. and Murphy, R. (1967). War: *The Anthropology of Armed Conflict and Aggression.* Garden City, NY: Natural History Press.

Gross, D. (1975). "Protein Capture and Cultural Development in the Amazon Basin." *American Anthropologist* **77**:536–549.

Haas, J. (1990). "Warfare and the Evolution of Tribal Polities in the Prehistoric Southwest." In *The Anthropology of War*, ed. J. Haas, pp. 171–189. Cambridge: Cambridge University Press.

Halstead, P. (1989). "The Economy has a Normal Surplus: Economic Stability and Social Change among Early Farming Communities of Thessaly, Greece." In *Bad Year Economics: Cultural Responses to Risk and*

Uncertainty, eds. P. Halstead and J. O'Shea, pp. 1–7. Cambridge: Cambridge University Press.

Harner, M. J. (1984). *The Jívaro*. Berkeley: University of California Press.

Harris, M. (1984). "A Cultural Materialist Theory of Band and Village Warfare: the Yanomamo Test." In *Warfare, Culture, and Environment*, ed. R.B. Ferguson, pp. 111–140. New York: Academic Press.

Harrison, W. A. (1964). Prehistory of the Santa Barbara Coast, California. Unpublished Ph.D. Dissertation, Department of Anthropology, University of Arizona, Tucson.

Hayward, R. (1980). *Management of Acute Head Injuries*. Oxford: Blackwell Scientific Publications.

Hornbeck, D. (1983). *California Patterns: A Geographical and Historical Atlas*. Palo Alto: Mayfield.

Johnson, G. A. (1982). "Organizational Structure and Scalar Stress." In *Theory and Explanation in Archaeology*, eds. C.A. Renfrew *et al.*, pp. 389–421. New York: Academic Press.

Johnson, J. R. (1988). Chumash Social Organization: an Ethnohistoric Perspective. Unpublished Ph.D. dissertation, University of California, Santa Barbara.

King, C. (1971). "Chumash Inter-Village Economic Exchange." *Indian Historian* 4:31–43.

_____ (1982). *The Evolution of Chumash Society*. Ph.D. dissertation, University of California, Davis. Ann Arbor: University Microfilms.

_____ (1990). *Evolution of Chumash Society*. Garland Publishing, Inc., New York.

King, L. B. (1982). The Medea Creek Cemetery (LAn-243): Late Inland Patterns of Social Organization, Exchange and Warfare. Unpublished Ph.D. Dissertation, University of California, Los Angeles.

Koch, K. (1974). *War and Peace in Jalémo*. Cambridge: Harvard University Press.

Kroeber, A. L. (1922). "Elements of Culture in Native California." *University of California Publications in American Archaeology and Ethnology* 13:8:259–328.

Lambert, P. M. (1993). "Health in Prehistoric Populations of the Santa Barbara Channel Islands." *American Antiquity* 58:509–521.

_____ (1994). War and Peace on the Western Front: A Study of Violent Conflict and Its Correlates in Prehistoric Hunter-gatherer Societies of Coastal Southern California. Unpublished Ph.D. dissertation, University of California, Santa Barbara.

Lambert, P. M. and Walker, P. L. (1991). "Physical Anthropological Evidence for the Evolution of Social Complexity in Coastal Southern California." *Antiquity* 65:963–973.

Larsen, C. L. (1997). *Bioarchaeology: Interpreting Behavior from the Human Skeleton*. Cambridge: *Cambridge Studies in Biological Anthropology*, Cambridge University Press (In press).

Larson, D. O., J. Michaelson, and P. L. Walker. (1989). "Climatic Variability: a Compounding Factor Causing Culture Change Among Prehistoric Coastal Populations." Paper presented at the 54th Annual Meeting of the Society for American Archaeology, Atlanta.

Larson, L. H. (1972). "Functional Considerations of Warfare in the Southeast During the Mississippi Period." *American Antiquity* 37: 383–392.

Martz, P. (1992). "Status Distinctions and the Political Economy in Channel Islands Prehistory." In *Essays of the Prehistory of Maritime California*, pp. 145–156. Davis: Center for Archaeological Research.

Maschner, H. D. G. (1991). "The Emergence of Cultural Complexity on the Northern Northwest Coast." *Antiquity* 65:924–34.

———— (1992). The Origins of Hunter and Gatherer Sedentism and Political Complexity: A Case Study from the Northern Northwest Coast. Unpublished Ph.D. dissertation, University of California, Santa Barbara.

Meggitt, M. (1977). *Blood is their Argument: Warfare among the Mae Enga Tribesman of the New Guinea Highlands*. Palo Alto: Mayfield.

Milner, G. R., Anderson, E. and Smith, V. G. (1991). "Warfare in Late Prehistoric West-Central Illinois." *American Antiquity* 56:581–603.

Minc, L. D. and Smith, K. P. (1989) "The Spirit of Survival: Cultural Responses to Resource Variability in North Alaska." In *Bad Year Economics: Cultural Responses to Risk and Uncertainty*, eds. P. Halstead and J. O'Shea, pp. 8–39. Cambridge: Cambridge University Press.

Moratto, M. J. King, T. F. and Woolfenden, W. B. (1978). "Archaeology and California's Climate." *Journal of California Anthropology* 5:2:147–161.

Moss, M. (1989). Archaeology and Cultural Ecology of the Prehistoric Angoon Tlingit. Unpublished Ph.D. dissertation, University of California, Santa Barbara.

Moss, M. and Erlandson, J. M. (1992). "Forts, Refuge Rocks, and Defensive Sites: the Antiquity of Warfare Along the North Pacific Coast of North America." *Arctic Anthropology* 29:2:73–90.

Nettleship, M. Givens, R. D. and Nettleship, A. eds. (1975). *War, Its Causes and Correlates*. The Hague: Mouton.

Neve, Felipe de. (1782). [Instructions for the *Comandante* of the Presidio of Santa Brbara and for the sergeants of the guards of missions to be established along the Channel, March 6, 1782, San Gabriel.] *Provincial State Papers* 3:85–89. Berkeley: California Archives (2:86–90), Bancroft Library.

Olson, R. (1930). "Chumash Prehistory." *University of California Publications in Archaeology and Ethnology* 23:1:1–21.

_____ (N.D.). Unpublished field notes on file. Berkeley: Phoebe Hearst Museum of Anthropology, University of California.

Orr, P. C. (1943). *Archaeology of Mescalitan Island and Customs of the Canalino.* Santa Barbara: Santa Barbara Museum of Natural History Occasional Paper 5.

_____ (1968). *Prehistory of Santa Rosa Island.* Santa Barbara: Santa Barbara Museum of Natural History.

_____ (n.d.). Unpublished field notes on file. Santa Barbara: Anthropology Department, Santa Barbara Museum of Natural History.

Otterbein, K. (1970). *The Evolution of War.* New Haven: HRAF Press.

Owsley, D. W. and Jantz, R. L. (1994). *Skeletal Biology in the Great Plains: Migration, Warfare, Health, and Subsistence.* Washington, D. C.: Smithsonian Institution Press.

Pisias, N. G. (1978). "Paleoceanography of the Santa Barbara Basin during the Last 8000 Years." *Quaternary Research* 10:366–384.

_____ (1979). "Model for Palaeoceanographic Reconstructions of the California Current During the Last 8,000 Years." *Quaternary Research* 11 (3):373–386.

Priestley, H. I. (1937). *A Historical, Political, and Natural Description of California by Pedro Fages.* Ramona: Ballena Press.

Rogers, D. B. (1929). *Prehistoric Man on the Santa Barbara Coast.* Santa Barbara: Santa Barbara Museum of Natural History.

Sahlins, M. (1974). *Stone Age Economics.* London: Tavistock Publications.

Shapiro, K. (1983). *Pediatric Head Trauma.* Mount Kisco, NY: Futura Publishing Company.

Stine, S. (1994). "Extreme and Persistent Drought in California and Patagonia During Mediaeval Time." *Nature* 369:546–549.

Stuart-Macadam, P. (1985). "Porotic Hyperostosis: Representative of a Childhood Condition." *Amer. Jour. Phys. Anthrop.* 66:391–398.

_____ (1987). "Porotic Hyperostosis: New evidence to Support the Anemia Theory." *Amer. Jour. Phys. Anthrop.* 74:521–526.

Tyson, R. A. (1977). "Historical Accounts as Aids to Physical Anthropology: Examples of Head Injury in Baja California." *Pacific Coast Archaeological Society Quarterly* 13:1:52–59.

vanGurp, G. Hutchison, T. J. and W. A. Alto, (1990). "Arrow Wound Management in Papua New Guinea." *Journal of Trauma* 30:2:183–188.

Vayda, A. P. (1976). *War in Ecological Perspective: Persistence, Change and Adaptive Processes in Three Oceanian Societies.* New York: Plenum.

Walker, P. L. (1986). "Porotic Hyperostosis in a Marine-dependent California Indian Population." *Am. Jour. Phys. Anthrop.* 69:345–354.

_____ (1989). "Cranial Injuries as Evidence of Violence in Prehistoric Southern California, Santa Barbara." *Am. Jour. Phys. Anthrop.* 80:313–323.

_____ (1994). "Animal Resources and the Evolution of Craft Specialization on Santa Cruz Island." Paper on file with the author. Santa Barbara: University of California.

Walker, P. L. and Lambert, P. M. (1989). "Skeletal Evidence for Stress During a Period of Cultural Change in Prehistoric California." In *Advances in Paleopathology, Journal of Paleopathology: Monographic Publication No. 1*, ed. L. Capasso, pp. 207–212. Marino Solfanelli, Chieti, Italy.

Walker, P. L., Lambert, P. M. and DeNiro, M. J. (1989). "The Effects of European Contact on the Health of Alta California Indians." In *Columbian Consequences I: Archaeological and Historical Perspectives on the Spanish Borderlands West*, ed. D. H. Thomas, pp. 349–364. Washington D.C.: Smithsonian Institution Press.

Webb, S. (1989). *Prehistoric Stress in Australian Aborigines: A Palaeopathological Study of a Hunter-Gatherer Population.* Oxford: BAR International Series 490.

Willey, P. (1990). *Prehistoric Warfare on the Great Plains: Skeletal Analysis of the Crow Creek Massacre Victims.* New York: Garland Publishing, Inc.

Woodman, C. F. Rudolph, J. L. and Rudolph, T. P. eds. (1991). *Western Chumash Prehistory: Resource Use and Settlement in the Santa Ynez River Valley.* Santa Barbara: Science Applications International Corporation.

Yarrow, H. C. (1879). "Report on the Operations of Special Party for Making Ethnological Researches in the Vicinity of Santa Barbara, Cal., with a Short Historical Account of the Region Explored. In *Archaeology. Reports Upon the Archaeological and Ethnological Collections from the Vicinity of Santa Barbara, California, etc. U.S. Geographical Surveys West of the 100th Meridian Vol. XII*, ed. F. Putnam, pp. 32–46. Washington, D.C.: Government Printing Office

Zimmerman, R. A., and L. T. Bilaniuk. (1983) "Radiology of Pediatric Craniocerebral Trauma." In *Pediatric Head Trauma*, ed. K. Shapiro, pp. 69–142.

Chapter
FIVE

Violence and Gender
in Early Italy

John Robb
Department of Archaeology
University of Southampton

INTRODUCTION

Violence straddles the boundary between the physical and the cultural world. Its effects are tangible enough to hurt, kill, and leave permanent traces on the skeleton; yet violent acts derive their meaning from their cultural context, and the semantics of violence are often an essential element in constituting power relationships (see articles in Riches 1986). In tracing the causes of violence, social theorists have laid the blame to innate human aggression (Lorenz 1966; Montagu 1973), to economic and political conflict over resources (Carneiro 1970) or political control (Haas 1990), to strategies for optimizing genetic fitness (Chagnon and Irons 1979; Daly and Wilson 1987), to social structures and

interaction (Knauft 1987, 1991), and to ethos or cultural style (Benedict 1934; Mead 1935). Students of inequality often view violence
as a form of social control; in a Marxist version (Bourdieu 1990),
"violence" includes all forms of the appropriation of labor and
encompasses a continuum ranging from symbolic co-optation to
physical repression.

Archaeologically, there are four basic sources on prehistoric violence: skeletal trauma, defensive architecture and settlement
patterns, weaponry and related artifacts, and iconographic representations of weaponry, violence, and related symbols. These indicators reflect different aspects of violence – its symbolization, its
effect on economy and settlement, and its actual occurrence – and
they are arguably most informative in those cases in which they do
not coincide. Such cases run counter to our common-sense view that
symbolism and social action tend to be consistent – the 'TV violence
makes violent kids" view. While we often do find such concordance,
we cannot assume it in advance, and when discrepancies between
symbolic life, political structure and actual behavior come to the
surface, investigating why they are discrepant almost always teaches
us more about ancient society than we expected to learn. Violence in
early Italy provides a good example of this (see below).

Of these four sources, skeletal remains are the only direct source
of information on the degree to which violence was actually practiced. Because skeletal remains are tied to individuals of determin-
able age, sex, and often social standing, they can reveal patterns of
violence in precisely the sort of groups among which violence is
often used to establish relations of dominance. Physical anthropology can thus make an especially valuable contribution to a broadly
anthropological view of the past.

Many osteologists have taken up this challenge, pioneering
methods for quantifying trauma (Burrell et al. 1986; Lovejoy and
Heiple 1981; Merbs 1989), and studying trauma and violence in
particular historical and prehistoric settings (for example, Jurmain
1991; Rose 1985). Particularly interesting for their consideration of
trauma in different sectors of society and over long time spans are
the studies of Powell (1988, 1991) and Walker and Lambert (Lambert and Walker 1991; Walker 1989). Violence has been linked not
only to social structures but to gender as well; both Shermis (1984)
and Wilkinson and Van Wagenen (1993) have documented violence against women in ancient populations skeletally.

This article follows the lead of these studies in studying violence
in its social and cultural context in early Italy. I first describe and

analyze traumas in 56 individuals from the Iron Age site of Pontecagnano, and then discuss what violence may have meant culturally in the Iron Age. Finally, I present data on trauma from a survey of skeletal material from the Neolithic through the Iron Age to discuss the prehistory of the particular configuration of gender and violence we observe at Pontecagnano on the threshold of Classical civilization.

SKELETAL TRAUMA AT PONTECAGNANO

Pontecagnano, called Picentia in ancient times, is located near Salerno in Campania, Italy (Fig. 5.1). Situated about five km from the Tyrrhenian Sea, it was the location of a sizable town and necropolis from Villanovan times (tenth century B.C.) until after the area was conquered by Rome in the third century B.C. This arc of time encompassed dramatic social changes. Greek colonization at nearby Ischia and later Naples began in the eighth century B.C., and Pontecagnano itself was colonized by Etruscans around the same time. Rich Orientalizing burials from this period attest the rise of a vigorous aristocracy. For several centuries, Greeks, Etruscans and native Italic peoples coexisted in Campania. In the fifth century, Greek and Etruscan power began to wane as a result of struggle with each other and the Carthaginians. Pontecagnano and other Campanian towns were conquered by Samnites invading from the mountainous interior. Warfare was common through the later fifth and fourth centuries as leagues of city-states fought each other and the Samnites, and the area was swallowed up by Rome after Rome's victory in the Samnite Wars of the late fourth century (D'Agostino 1974; Fredriksen 1974; Pallottino 1991).

Over 6000 tombs have been excavated at Pontecagnano's vast necropolis (D'Agostino 1974). While earlier burials are frequently cremations, later burials are usually single inhumations. Grave goods include fine ceramics, ornaments such as bronze fibulae, rings and earrings, and gender-specific items such as weapons and weaving tools (Vida Navarro 1993). Physical anthropologists have analyzed over 800 of these skeletons, focusing on demography, morphometric analysis, and dental anthropology and pathology (Fornaciari et al. 1984; Lombardi Pardini et al. 1984, 1992; Mallegni et al. 1984; Pardini et al. 1983, 1992; Sonego 1991). Aspects of nutrition, health and lifestyle have been studied by Sonego (1991) for 158 individuals from the seventh-fifth centuries B.C. The present analysis is based on a study of 56 adults, including 12 from the

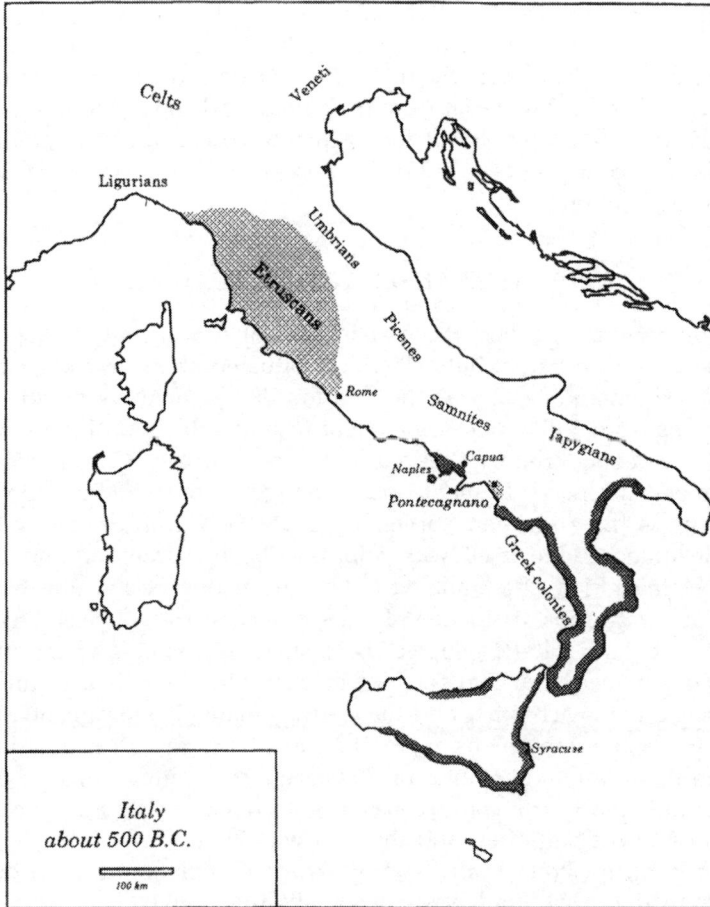

Figure 5.1. Italy around 500 B.C.

seventh-fifth centuries, 42 from the fifth-third centuries with the bulk from the end of the fourth century, and two which are cur-rently undated. These individuals were chosen at random from collections representing several 'neighborhoods' of the necropolis.

The biological background of trauma at Pontecagnano is known from a number of studies. Demographic studies of ca. 800 individuals show that infant mortality was high, with juveniles under five comprising a third to a half of samples for all periods, and average adult age at death was consistently higher for males (ca. 30–40) than for females (ca. 25–30) (Lombardi Pardini *et al* 1992; C. Scarsini, pers. comm.). The sex ratio of the burials are sometimes skewed by cultural factors, showing a slight preference for males over females in the fifth-fourth centuries (Pardini *et al*. 1983; Sonego 1991). In a subsample of ca. 150 skeletons, signs of generalized stress such as *cribra orbitalia* and enamel hypoplasia were found be common in both earlier (seventh-fifth century) and later (fifth-fourth century) burials (Sonego 1991). In the same study, generalized periostitis was evident on at least 20% of the skeletons in any given period and subgroup (Sonego 1991). Specific pathologies such as osteomyelitis, *hyperostosis frontalis interna*, and *humerus varus* are also known (Sonego 1991; Robb, original data). Dental health for different subgroups and periods always shows caries levels above 8% of observed teeth and ante-mortem loss above 6%, with total teeth decayed or missing ranging from 13.7% to 21.3%. Dental wear was rapid and severe (Fornaciari *et al* 1984; Sonego 1991; Robb, original data). A number of skeletal traits linked to specialized activities have been found at the site (Robb 1994b), and the distribution of muscle insertion markings evidences a complex, gender-differentiated pattern of occupational specialization (Robb 1994d).

Among societies studied by osteoarchaeologists, Pontecagnano strongly resembles New World urban slave populations in combination of its high rate of stress and disease and high variation in arthritis and heavy muscular activity (cf. Petrone (1993) for a similar case in a slave group from the nearby Phlegrean Fields). The latter particularly suggest a complex division of labor with significant occupational specialization within a working class group (Angel *et al*. 1987; Kelley, J. and Angel 1987; Owsley *et al*. 1987). This is a biological rather than a jural or social view of the group's status, however, as historical circumstances and grave goods from Pontecagnano suggest a free, sometimes prosperous group.

MANIFESTATIONS OF TRAUMA AT PONTECAGNANO

Five of the 56 adults studied showed healed cranial traumas (Tab. 5.1). Of these, three (Tombs 3499, 4016 and 4034) displayed small depressions in the left frontal squama. One individual (4029, Fig. 5.2a) displayed a smooth-edged depression in the right frontal above the eye, extending from the lateral edge of the orbit and interrupting a moderately marked browridge. This lesion probably resulted from an impact to the orbit with partial collapse of the

Table 5.1. Trauma cases at Pontecagnano

Tomb	Centuries B.C.	Sex	Age	Traumatic Lesions
3159		f?	18–22	
3413		f	40–49	
3499	6–5	f?	30–35	Left frontal squama
3520	7	f?	adult	
3533	3	m	50–60	Right metacarpals IV, V
3558	7–6	f?	25–29	
3574	7	f?	35–39	
3599	7	f	45–49	
3605	7–6	m	35–39	Right metacarpal II; right ribs (2 fractures)
3720	5–4	m	20–25	
3733	5	m	45–49	
3748	6–5	f	20–23	
3749	6	f	21–25	
3801	6	m	18–22	
3805	6	m	28–44	
3822	6	m	20–25	
3838	6	f?	20–25	
4012	4	m	40–45	
4013	4	f	30–40	
4015	4	m	40–49	Possible fracture, 10th thoracic vertebra
4016	4	m	20–30	Left frontal squama
4017	4	f	25–29	
4018	4	m	40–49	Left radius (Colles' fracture)
4019	4–3	f	20–25	
4020	4	f?	30–39	
4021	4	m	40–45	
4025	4	m	30–34	Left radius, distal shaft; left ulna, distal shaft
4026	4	f	40–50	
4027	4	m	20–25	Right ribs (5 fractures)
4028	4	m	40–49	
4029	4	m	18–22	Right frontal (orbit); right femur (midshaft)
4033	4	m	20–25	
4034	4	f	40–44	Left frontal squama; possible fractures, thoracic vertebrae
4035	4	f	40–45	
4037	4	m	35–39	
4038	4	m?	30–34	Left clavicle, midshaft; right parietal, perimortem depressed fracture

Table 5.1. (Continued)

Tomb	Centuries B.C.	Sex	Age	Traumatic Lesions
4039	4	m?	40–45	
4040	4	5	20–29	
4042	4	m?	45–49	
4043	4	m	40–44	Right radius, head
4045	4	f	20–25	
4046	4	m	40–45	Right zygomatic/maxilla
4047	4	m	50–60	Left metatarsal II, head
4051	4	m	30–35	Right ribs (3 fractures)
4058	4	m	40–50	
4059	4	f	18–22	
4065	4	f	50–60	
4083	4	f	25–29	
4084	4	f	40–44	
4085	4	m	22–24	L. humerus, traumatic ossification of deltoid, coracobrachialis tendons
4093	4	m	18–22	Right clavicle, midshaft; left clavicle, midshaft
4094	4	f?	18–22	
4100	4	m	40–49	
4102	5–4	m	23–45	
4105	4	f	18–22	
4106	4	f?	18–22	

frontal sinus cavity or spongy bone. The fifth individual (4046, Fig. 5.2b) had suffered a facial fracture on the right zygomatic arch at the zygomaxillary suture. Although the fracture was completely healed, a small chip of bone projected anteriorly about five mm from the cheek, and faint healed fracture lines were also visible on the adjacent maxilla.

In addition to healed cranial traumas, one individual (4038, Figs. 5.2c,d) displayed clear evidence of peri-mortem cranial trauma. This individual, probably a male about 30–35 years old, displayed a circular hole in the right parietal about three cm in diameter, clearly caused by a single impact rather than by diffuse forces such as soil pressure. Several features suggested a peri-mortem fracture rather than post-mortem damage. The margins of the hole were beveled inwards at about 45 degrees, creating an inside aperture considerably larger than the outside aperture, in the pattern of 'internal vault release' commonly found in forensic cases of blunt impact trauma (White 1992:134). Several long fracture lines

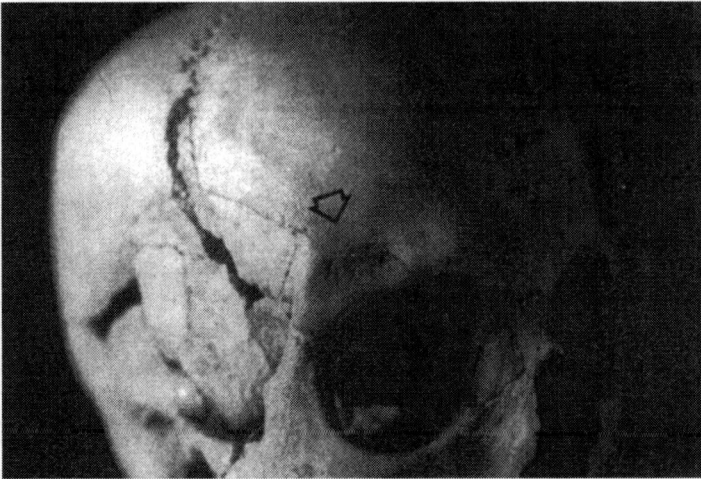

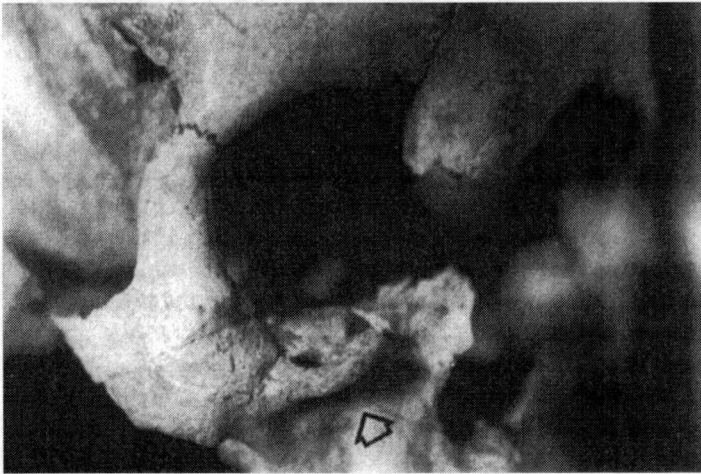

Figure 5.2. Cranial trauma at Pontecagnano. a. PC 4029, right orbit.
b. PC 4046, right zygomatic/maxilla. c. PC 4038, probable perimortem trauma, right parietal. d. Internal view of the same specimen.

radiated outward from the hole, also attesting a strong impact.
These extended medially and laterally, as well as anteriorly out to
the left frontal squama and posteriorly almost to asterion. In a
contrasting pattern, the vault areas between them were broken into

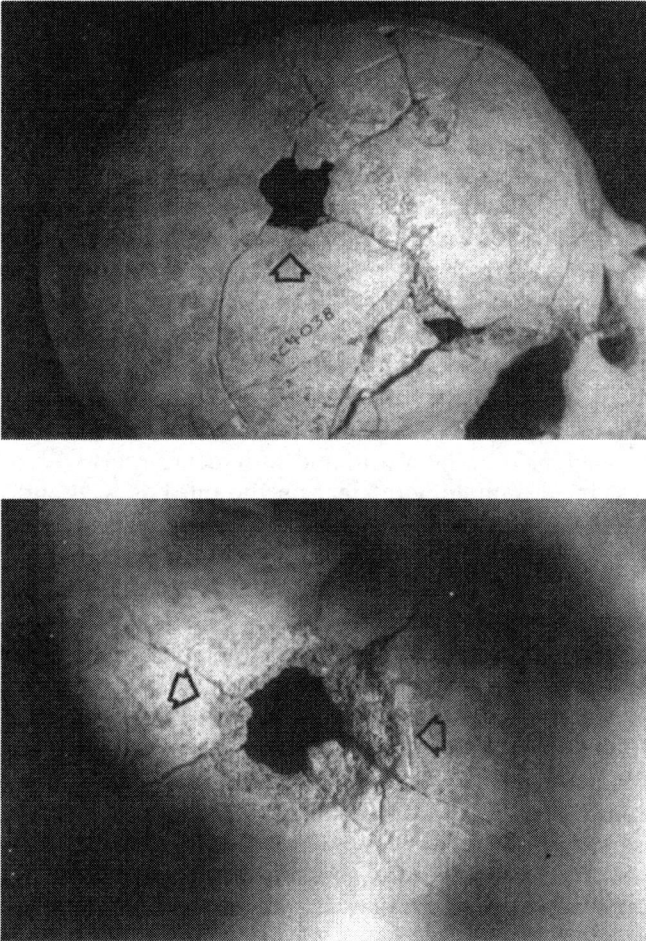

Figure 5.2. (Continued).

contained networks of small, subrectangular fragments with squared margins, the normal pattern in this collection for post-mortem breakage of dry bone. This implies that the heavy impact preceded *in situ* weathering and breakage. Weathering and archaeological concretions on the margins of the hole (White's "fracture antiquity" criteria (1992:133)) also imply that the hole did not result from recent causes such as excavation damage, and no major ancient taphonomic disturbance is evident elsewhere on the skeleton, which is in excellent condition and appears to have been an undisturbed burial. There is no sign of healing. The overall morphology thus suggests a blunt traumatic impact no earlier than a few days before death and preceding both *in situ* weathering and breakage and excavation.

While this is the only case of violent trauma at or before death evident in this sample, others are known from Pontecagnano, including one individual with a bronze arrowhead lodged and healed within the anterior proximal femur shaft (Tomb 4141, Fig. 5.3a).

Postcranial traumatic injury took less dramatic forms. Injuries to the upper limb included one healed Colles' fracture of the left radius (4018), one healed fracture of both the left distal radius and ulna (4025), and one healed fracture of the right radial head (4043). In the hand, two males displayed fractures of the right metacarpals, in one (3533) of the fourth and fifth metacarpals with a probably associated pathology evident on the third as well and in the other (3605) of the second metacarpal, possibly associated with eburnation of the right carpals. In both cases fractures occurred approximately at the midshaft and were healed with moderate volar angulation (Fig. 5.3b). These 'boxer's fractures' (Rogers 1992) often result from delivering a blow with the fist. Another individual (4065) displayed an unusual process extending anteriorly at the base of the left first metacarpal. This may have represented a healed Bennett's fracture (fracture of the base of the MCI), but was not sufficiently distinctive to diagnose without radiographs. Finally, one individual (4085) displayed ossification of the deltoid and coracobrachialis tendons on the upper lateral midshaft of the left humerus. The well-preserved skeleton displayed no signs of systemic infections or of generalized metabolic disorders such as fluorosis (Ortner and Putschar 1981:288) which might have resulted in systemic hyperostosis, and other muscle sites in the region gave no indication of heavy functional stresses. Ossification at these tendons seems likely to have resulted from localized trauma to the soft tissues of the arm and upper shoulder.

Only two individuals evinced trauma to the lower limbs. One (4029) had fractured the right femur at the midshaft, healing with slight (ca. 10–20 degrees) but noticeable posterior and medial angulation. Another individual (4047) displayed deformation and flattening of the right second metatarsal head which probably resulted from a crushing injury.

The most common loci for traumas in the trunk were the ribs and clavicles. Three individuals displayed healed rib fractures, in

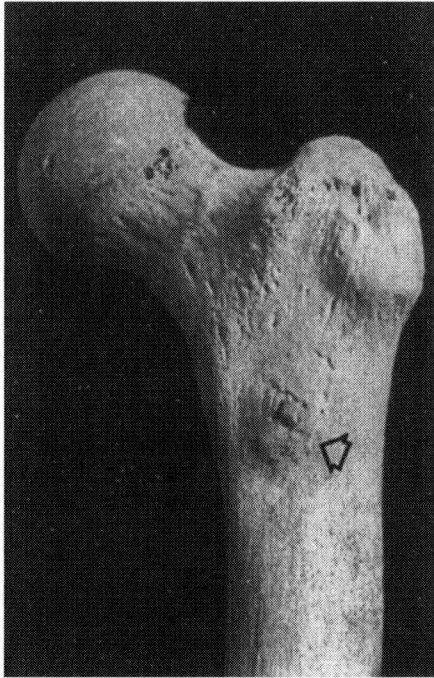

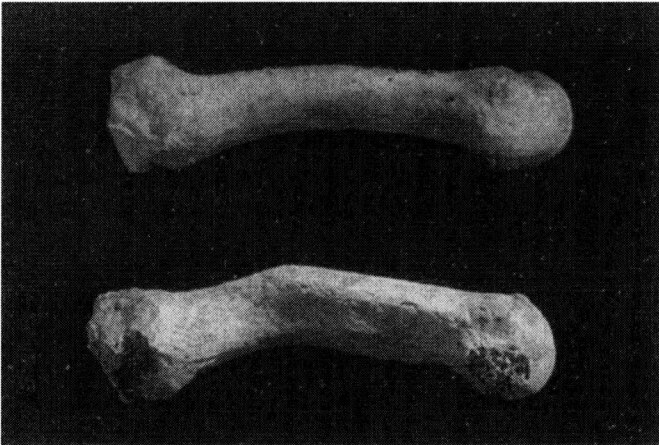

Figure 5.3. Postcranial trauma at Pontecagnano. a. PC 4141, bronze arrowhead lodged and healed in proximal right femur. b. PC 3065, healed 'boxer's fracture' of the right second metacarpal (upper specimen is normal metacarpal for comparison). c. PC 4027, healed fracture of five right ribs. d. PC 4093, healed fracture of the right clavicle.

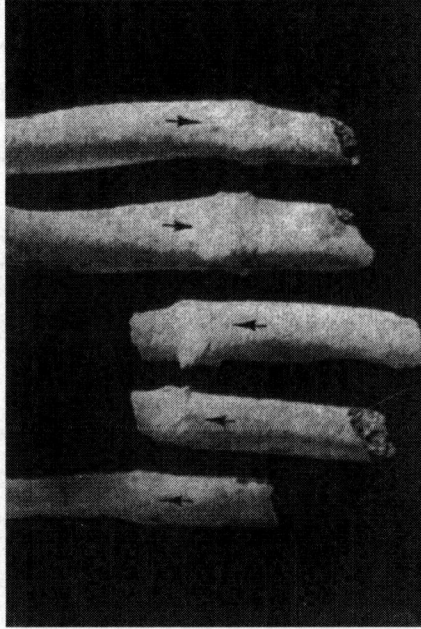

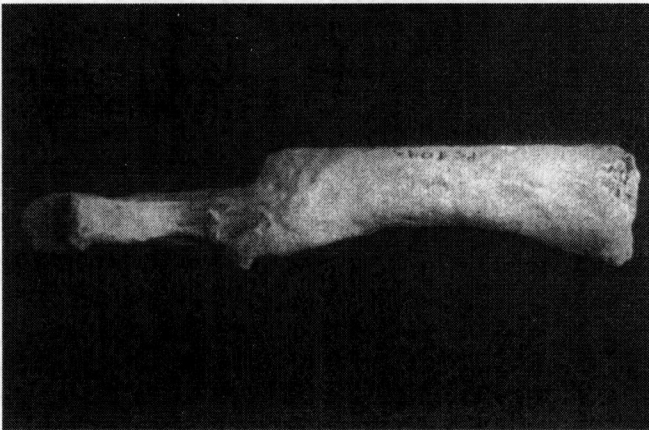

Figure 5.3. (Continued).

all cases involving multiple fractures to adjacent ribs on the right side (3605, two ribs; 4051, three ribs; 4027, five ribs) (Fig. 5.3c). One individual (4038) had fractured the left clavicle, and a second (4093) displayed healed fractures to both clavicles (Fig. 5.3d). Possible slight, healed vertebral fractures were evident in two individuals (4015, 4034), in both cases to lower thoracic vertebrae.

Few of these traumatic injuries may be ascribed to specific causes. Some appear to have resulted from direct interpersonal violence; these may include many of the cranial fractures and possibly the fractured metacarpals ("boxer's fractures") as well. Others such as fractured clavicles and Colles' fractures are typically produced by accidents such as falls. Others may represent industrial or work-related accidents, for instance the crushed metatarsal in the male from Tomb 4047; occupational specializations in early Classical Italy included a wide range of building, farming, transportation and manufacturing tasks (Joshel 1992), as well as the more exotic specializations like gladiators. Like broken ribs, most of the traumatic injuries could have resulted from several causes.

Regardless of cause, healing seems to have proceeded well. No individuals were found with active inflammations apparently resulting from infection or complications of traumas. Moreover, traumas generally healed with little deformity, as in the case of a fractured femur midshaft (4029). This contrasts with cases of marked deformation known both from historic sites such as Metaponto, where a similar femoral fracture resulted in dramatic angulation (Carter 1990; Henneberg et al. 1992) and from prehistoric sites such as the Grotta dello Scoglietto, where a Colles' fracture of the radius and ulna resulted in formation of a pseudarthrosis (Messeri 1962; Capasso and Piccardi 1980). The difference may reflect differences in access to medical care or its effectiveness; surgical intervention is evident in at least one skeleton (4046) in the form of small trepanations of the frontal squama.

SKELETAL TRAUMA AT PONTECAGNANO: PATTERNS OF DISTRIBUTION CHRONOLOGICAL

Chronological differences. Although evidence is slight, trauma seems to have become more common towards the later occupation of Pontecagnano. The 56 individuals studied included four males/probable males and eight females/probable females from the seventh-fifth centuries, 27 males/probable males and 15 females/probable females from the fifth-fourth centuries, and two females/probable females who were undated. Most of the later group dates to the end of the fourth century, the period of the Samnite Wars. Only 16.7% of the earlier group have traumatic lesions (25.0% of males, 14.2% of females); this is comparable to Sonego's (1991) trauma rates of 21.6% for males and 8.0% for females from a different sample from the earlier period. In contrast, of the later group, 35.5% display traumas (51.9% of males, 6.7% of females). What data are available thus suggests that trauma rates, at least for males, increased between the seventh-fifth centuries and the fifth-fourth centuries. Other eighth-sixth century Iron Age sites studied also had low trauma rates compared to fifth-fourth century Pontecagnano (Robb, original data).

Age-related differences. Traumatic lesions accumulate on the skeleton, and we might expect to see a relationship between age and traumas (Burrell *et al.* 1986). In the sample as a whole, this is obscured by different life expectancies for males and females. However, considering only males from the fifth-fourth centuries, eight of 12 (67%) males of 20-40 years were traumatized, compared with five of 14 (36%) males who died above this age. This runs counter to the expectation of more trauma in older individuals. While almost all of the trauma observed were healed and thus not directly related to the cause of death, this suggests that trauma resulted from an active lifestyle which may have been related to an earlier age at death through other episodes not recorded on the skeleton.

Trauma and sex. Trauma was very strongly linked to sex (Fig. 5.4, Tab. 5.2). In the earlier period, one of four males exhibits traumatic lesions, while only one of seven females does. While this sample is too small to mean much, Sonego (1991), studying a different sample from the earlier period at Pontecagnano, reports trauma rates of 21.6% for males and 8.1% for females. In the later period, males sharply exceed females with 14 of 27 males (51.9%) and one of 15 (6.7%) females displaying traumas (Tab. 5.2). The difference cannot be ascribed to a longer male lifespan, as a similar high trauma rate is evident in males dying at or below the average female age at death (see above). There is no clear single pattern of probable cause; both males and females have cranial trauma which may well have resulted from violence as well as postcranial fractures typically resulting from accidental causes. Instead, trauma of all sorts seems to have been a common consequence of adult male lifestyle.

The consequences of male lifestyle are clear in other biological markers of activity as well (Tab. 5.2). Schmorl's nodes are

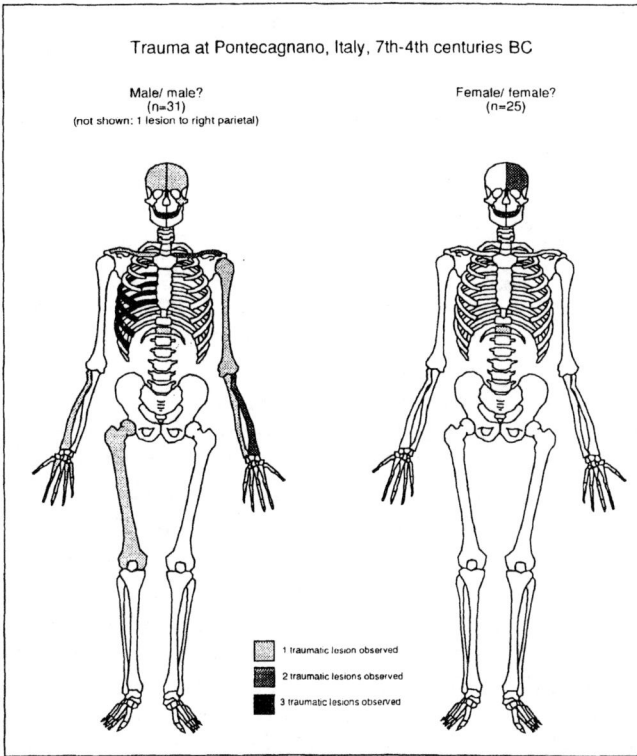

Figure 5.4. The distribution of traumas in males and females at Pontecagnano.

Table 5.2. Sex and biological indicators at Pontecagnano (fifth-fourth centuries B.C.).

	M/m?		F/f?		
	Present	Absent	Present	Absent	Chi-squared
Trauma	14	13	1	14	7.27, p = .007
Tibial periostitis	15	10	3	12	6.06, p = .014
Schmorl's nodes	17	7	4	5	1.97, p = .161
Enamel hypoplasia	17	8	8	4	.01, p = .935
Cribra orbitalia	4	19	5	7	2.43, p = .11

significantly more common among males than among females. These lesions represent herniations of the fibrous rings enclosing the intervertebral discs, and are consequences of aging and of traumatic injury to the lower thoracic and lumbar vertebrae (Ortner and Putschar 1981:421, 431). Similarly, tibial periostitis is far more common among males. Periostitis is a generalized reaction to a variety of causes (Kelley 1989; Stirland 1991). However, tibial periostitis occurs far more commonly among males than among females at Pontecagnano (it is evident in 55.1% of all males and 60% of fifth-fourth century males; see also Sonego 1991). It is highly localized along the anterior-medial midshaft, sometimes unilaterally, and appears to represent discrete episodes, as occasional cases show an active pathology overlying a completely healed one or different degrees of pathology on the right and left tibiae. For these reasons, and for its skewed sex distribution, in this case tibial periostitis probably resulted mostly from repeated low-grade traumas rather than from systemic conditions such as syphilis (Henneberg *et al.* 1992), other treponemal diseases or other systemic infections. It has been suggested that periostitis of the medial tibia may result from horseback riding (Alciati *et al* 1987; Sonego 1991). However, it seems unlikely that such a large proportion of an urban working-class group would have ridden much, as maintaining a horse and cavalry apparatus was expensive and sometimes considered a mark of the elite (cf. Alföldy 1988:7). One possible cause is stress fractures in the anterior tibia during locomotion (Keats 1990).

While these three indicators appear to represent the effects of a physically stressful life on Pontecagnano adult males, there is no statistical relationship among the three within males as a group (Table 5.3). Moreover, males with trauma did not differ significantly from individuals without trauma in frequencies of enamel hypoplasia, *cribra orbitalia*, or pathology. On the average, they had

Table 5.3. Trauma and biological indicators in Pontecagnano males (fifth-fourth centuries B.C.).

	With trauma		Without trauma		
	Present	Absent	Present	Absent	Chi-squared
Tibial periostitis	9	4	6	6	0.96, p = .33
Schmorl's nodes	6	4	11	3	0.97, p = .324
Enamel hypoplasia	8	5	8	3	0.34, p = .563
Cribra orbitalia	3	10	1	9	0.67, p = .412

slightly lower average muscle marking scores, but this probably reflects primarily a slightly earlier age at death rather than lifestyle differences. All of these suggest that the opportunity to suffer traumas was distributed among all males generally. A similar conclusion is suggested by patterns of multiple trauma. For fifth-fourth century males, 14/27 (51.9%) had suffered at least one trauma. However, only 4/14 (28%) of males who had suffered a first trauma went on to suffer a second one. This suggests that particular individuals were not especially "trauma-prone" and that the risk of trauma was not concentrated in a discrete sub-group isolated by activity or class.

CULTURE, GENDER AND TRAUMA

How can this gender distribution of trauma be explained? Warfare was a key symbolism for male gender in Iron Age Italy, as represented by hero mythologies, weapon images in tomb frescoes and statues, and grave goods. That this key symbolism was shared at Pontecagnano has been shown by Vida Navarro (1993). Some traumas at Pontecagnano do appear to represent the direct results of violence. However, warfare-related violence in itself cannot explain the dramatic gender differences in trauma, as most traumas in Pontecagnano males probably resulted from accidents rather than direct violence.

Instead, the causes of traumas probably lie deeper in the culture. From varied sources of evidence, it is clear that gender, sex and the capacity for violence were symbolically intertwined. Legendary stories such as the Rape of Lucretia (Livy I:59) make clear the link between male honor and the capacity to control access to womens' sexuality, by physical force when necessary, and informal evidence such as graffiti show that male sexuality was associated with aggression and physical dominance (Adams 1982). The resulting gender values probably closely resembled the 'honor and shame' ideology found ethnographically in many Mediterranean societies (Bourdieu 1990; Davis 1969; Peristiany 1966).

There were thus probably three routes through which culture influenced patterns of trauma. On the abstract level of key gender concepts, violence would have been associated with male honor, as representing the ability to protect one's dependents, rights, property and reputation. As a male *hexis*, or behavioral enactment of an ethos (Bourdieu 1990), this would have prescribed relatively aggressive behavior for males, resulting in informal, socially unorganized violence such as spontaneous fighting; the resulting traumas might include especially cranial, rib and hand fractures. Women may have had an opposite standard of reserved behavior, combined with an ideal of aristocratic, chaste seclusion, which may have reduced chances of trauma. Secondly, this symbolism would have segregated the formally organized practice of violence as warfare to males. Thirdly, such generative concepts typically provide symbolic grounding for the gender division of labor, particularly in prescribing appropriate tasks for different genders. In the case of Iron Age Italy, while women frequently performed arduous work in the fields and in many other occupations, recognized occupations considered to be "dangerous" or to require 'strength', such as in quarrying, mining, construction, and transportation, were often reserved for males (Joshel 1992). To the extent that these actually did involve the risk of accidents, males would have suffered more traumas.

VIOLENCE AND TRAUMA THROUGH ITALIAN PREHISTORY
A QUANTITATIVE APPROACH

Trauma is known throughout Italian prehistory. Upper Paleolithic cases include a complex fractured ankle in a young male from Vado all'Arancia (Minellono *et al.* 1980), and a Mesolithic individual from the Grotta dell'Uzzo displays post-traumatic *myositis ossificans* of the ilium (Borgognini Tarli *et al.* 1993). In the Neolithic, at least five cases are known in peninsular Italy, with others known from Liguria (Germanà and Fornaciari 1992; Germanà *et al.* 1990; Robb 1994c; Salvadei and Macchiarelli 1983). These include cranial traumas at Villa Badessa (female), Catignano (female), Massaria Valente (female), Ripa Tetta (male) and in a Ligurian male. Postcranial traumas include a broken clavicle from Massaria Valente and several fractures in Ligurian material. In the Copper Age, trauma is known at several locations in the Apuan Alps (Formicola 1980), at Ponte S. Pietro (Formicola and Garulli 1988), and in an example from Elba which appears to have a lesion caused by intentional violence with a polished stone ax (Germanà and Fornaciari 1992). Published examples from the Bronze Age include a number of traumas from the Grotta dello Scoglietto (Messeri 1962; Capasso and Piccardi 1980), Madonna di Loreto (Canci *et al.* 1993), and Toppo Daguzzo (Repetto *et al.* 1988), as well as an adult male from S. Benigno Canavese-Volpiano with a metal projectile embedded in the orbit (Germanà and Fornaciari

1992). Iron Age examples are relatively common (for instance, Macchiarelli *et al.* 1982), although few studies have attempted a serious survey of trauma incidences (Sonego 1991).

While these cases show trauma to be omnipresent in Italian prehistory, the published data do not allow meaningful comparisons among periods and regions. Without knowing the total number of pathological and non-pathological specimens examined or each period, it is impossible to convert the data into rates of trauma. Collections from different periods vary widely in skeletal preservation, and many traumas are reported incidentally in the course of other investigations rather than as part of a comprehensive paleopathological examination.

To put the Pontecagnano trauma into long-term perspective, trauma incidences from the Neolithic through the Iron Age are presented in Table 5.4. These data record trauma in adequate to

Table 5.4. The incidence of trauma in adults from the Neolithic through the Iron Age in pooled samples from prehistoric and early historic Italy (adults only, right and left sides combined, only regions half or more present included).

		Neolithic	Eneolithic	Bronze Age	Iron Age
Skull	maxilla	0/15	0/24	0/40	0/63
	zygomatic	0/19	0/24	0/35	1/78
	frontal orbit	1/26	0/41	0/71	1/105
	frontal squama	0/27	0/92	1/89	3/134
	parietal	1/36	1/97	3/91	1/142
	occipital squama	0/38	0/84	0/78	0/128
	occipital base	0/8	0/21	0/34	0/75
	temporal squama	0/23	0/36	0/48	0/103
	temporal mastoid	0/35	0/48	0/71	0/110
	temporal petrous	0/34	0/53	0/63	0/116
	sphenoid	0/8	0/17	0/29	0/49
Mandible		0/13	0/26	0/49	0/64
Clavicle	proximal epiphysis	0/8	0/12	0/51	0/75
	proximal shaft	0/24	0/25	0/80	0/105
	middle shaft	0/31	0/37	0/91	3/120
	distal shaft	0/31	0/35	0/92	0/117
	distal epiphysis	0/10	0/14	0/63	0/48
Scapula	glenoid	0/20	0/22	0/52	0/94
	base of spine	0/29	0/20	0/47	0/104
	coracoid	0/11	0/9	0/31	0/49
	spine/acromion	0/12	0/11	0/42	0/64
	body	0/10	0/9	0/32	0/35

Table 5.4. (Continued).

Humerus	proximal epiphysis	0/7	0/15	0/53	0/87
	proximal shaft	0/19	0/36	0/89	0/122
	middle shaft	0/24	0/57	1/95	1/138
	distal shaft	0/31	0/58	0/115	0/139
	distal epiphysis	0/24	0/32	0/68	0/97
Radius	proximal epiphysis	0/17	0/24	0/83	1/80
	proximal shaft	0/37	0/35	0/100	0/113
	middle shaft	0/34	1/35	1/97	0/114
	distal shaft	0/21	0/30	1/97	2/107
	distal epiphysis	0/12	0/32	0/68	0/97
Ulna	proximal epiphysis	0/18	0/31	0/86	0/81
	proximal shaft	0/30	0/44	0/92	0/116
	middle shaft	0/23	0/34	1/87	0/119
	distal shaft	0/18	1/19	1/66	2/103
	distal epiphysis	0/8	0/12	0/52	0/74
Sacrum		0/5	0/8	1/32	0/40
Innominate	ilium	0/23	0/17	0/37	0/83
	ischium	0/14	0/14	0/31	0/78
	pubis	0/10	0/5	0/16	0/22
Femur	proximal epiphysis	0/11	0/19	0/42	0/129
	proximal shaft	0/16	0/60	0/67	0/142
	middle shaft	0/13	0/60	0/73	1/145
	distal shaft	0/15	0/44	0/59	0/126
	distal epiphysis	0/9	0/15	0/38	0/106
Tibia	proximal epiphysis	0/6	0/21	0/30	0/75
	proximal shaft	0/16	0/47	0/55	0/121
	middle shaft	0/15	0/56	0/62	0/124
	distal shaft	0/16	0/44	0/56	0/111
	distal epiphysis	0/12	0/19	0/42	0/86
Fibula	proximal epiphysis	0/1	0/9	0/34	0/27
	proximal shaft	0/19	0/18	0/49	0/85
	middle shaft	0/26	0/25	0/57	0/96
	distal shaft	0/23	0/24	0/62	0/88
	distal epiphysis	0/8	0/13	0/53	0/55

well-preserved specimens observed during a detailed skeletal inventory (following methods recommended by the Palaeopathology Association (1991)).[1] A small number of traumas from skeletal regions not tabulated in Table 5.4 were also encountered, including mostly rib, vertebrae and metapodial fractures. These data come from over forty Central and Southern Italian sites; the earliest, Ripa Tetta, dates to the sixth millennium B.C., and Pontecagnano, a full-scale early Classical city, provides a fitting end to the skeletal series. This arc of time covers the Neolithic, the Eneolithic, the

Bronze Age and the Iron Age. The Neolithic (roughly 6000–3000 B.C.) encompasses the first farming societies in Italy, typically consisting of networks of small villages of 20–200 people practicing subsistence agriculture; hunting and gathering remained economically important in highland regions long after initial neolithization. The Eneolithic or Copper Age, occupying roughly the third millennium B.C., was a period of dispersed, archaeologically invisible settlements and prominent cemeteries or collective tombs often interpreted as evidence of an increasingly intensified pastoral economy. The Bronze Age (ca. 2000–900 B.C.) and Iron Age (after 900 B.C.) encompass increasingly complex, stratified and finally urban societies. Major social developments during this span included the rise of a prestige-goods economy centered on male gender ideology around the Neolithic/Eneolithic transition (Robb 1994a), and the accelerating growth of political centralization and economic stratification which began in the Middle Bronze Age and culminated in state formation in lowland regions in or shortly after the eighth century B.C.

Data analysis. Traumatic lesions at specific locations occur infrequently even in relatively large samples, and rates based on detailed raw data (Tab. 5.4) reveal more about statistical fluctuations than about general trends. I therefore tried to calculate an average trauma rate per skull for each period (Tab. 5.5a–c). However, this measure is biased strongly by bone preservation. Both burial practices and post-burial preservation vary wildly through Italian prehistory. Many Neolithic individuals are poorly preserved or known from scraps of isolated bone, and Copper and Bronze Age burials are typically disturbed, commingled multiple inhumations. Iron Age inhumations, which are typically single primary burials, vary dramatically in bone preservation from excellent at Pontecagnano to poor at cemeteries such as Osteria dell'Osa (Bietti Sestieri 1992). In this study, as the average number of skeletal regions per fragment examined (Tab. 5.5e,1) shows, most Neolithic specimens were small fragments, while Iron Age material was frequently virtually complete. Moreover, preliminary data screening showed clearly that trauma rates are biased by preservation when regions less than half present are included in tabulations. Consequently, comparing unstandardized trauma rates merely artificially inflates trauma rates in periods with better bone preservation.

Instead, a simple average was calculated based on skeletal regions the size of a cranial bone or a single section of long-bone shaft. For post-crania, the great majority of traumas occur in the

Table 5.5. Trauma in Italy from the Neolithic through the Iron Age: statistical summary. See text for explanation of calculations.

Cranial traumas	Neolithic	Eneolithic	Bronze Age	Iron Age
a. Total traumas, calotte	2	1	5	5
b. Total specimens examined	185	203	255	203
c. Trauma per specimen (%)	1.08	.49	1.56	3.14
d. Total regions examined, calotte (half or more present)	127	314	329	509
e. Regions present/specimen	0.69	1.55	1.29	2.51
f. Percentage of regions with trauma	1.57	0.32	1.22	0.98
g. Estimated trauma incidence for complete specimens (%)	11.9	2.5	9.3	7.6
Postcranial traumas				
h. Total traumas, long bones	0	2	5	9
i. Total specimens examined	357	446	984	1035
j. Trauma per specimen (%)	0	0.45	0.51	0.87
k. Total regions examined, long bones (half or more present)	546	824	1837	2417
l. Regions present/specimen	1.53	1.85	1.87	2.33
m. Percentage of regions with trauma	0	0.24	0.27	0.37
n. Estimated trauma incidence for complete skeletons (%)	0	9.7	10.8	14.5

proximal, middle and distal shaft sections of the seven long bones, rather than in the epiphyses. To obtain a composite average, the total number of trauma cases from these shaft regions was divided by the total number of regions examined (Tab. 5.5m). Epiphyses were left out to avoid artifically lowering trauma rates in well-preserved specimens. Likewise, most cranial traumas occur in the calotte (right and left frontal orbits, right and left frontal squamae, parietals, right and left occipital squamae). The composite incidence is thus the total number of trauma cases from these regions divided by the sum of regions examined (Tab 5.5f). The resulting figure represents the percentage of one-region units with traumas. This provides a lowest-common-denominator measure of trauma which is comparable among skeletons that vary in preservation and completeness (Fig. 5.5).

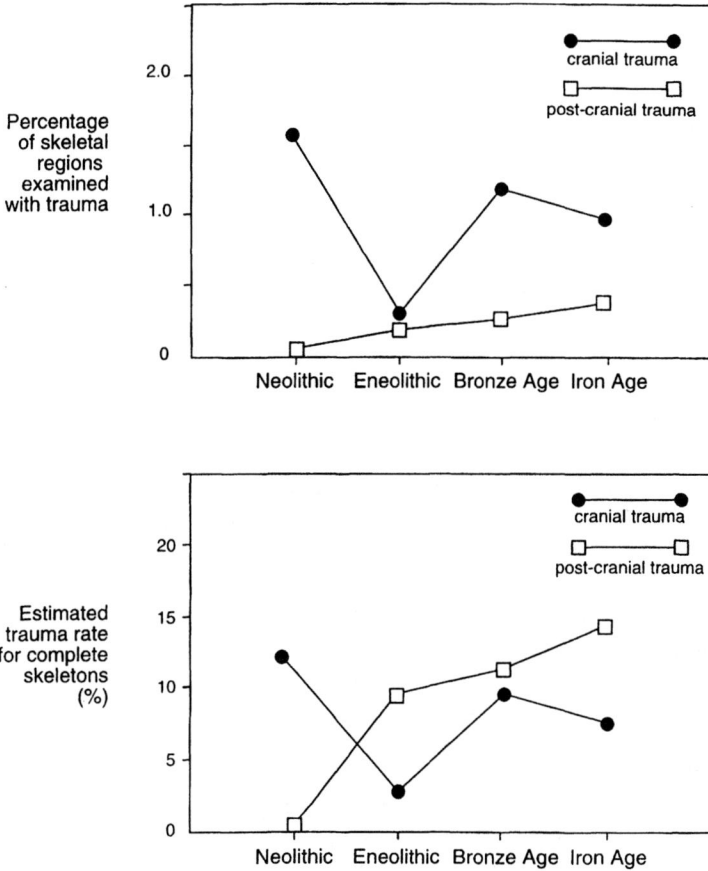

Figure 5.5. Trauma in Italy from the Neolithic through the Iron Age. a. Composite average incidences for individual skeletal regions. b. Estimated incidences in complete crania and postcranial skeletons.

This basal frequency can also be used to estimate the probability of traumas in complete specimens. If the probability that a given cranial vault region has a traumatic lesion is x, and a complete calotte has eight such regions, the probability of a complete calotte having at least one traumatic lesion is $1-(1-x)$.[8] Likewise, with 42 total regions of long bone shaft (right and left proximal, middle and distal shaft regions for the clavicles, humeri, radii, ulnae, femora, tibiae, and fibulae), the probability of a complete skeleton having at least one long bone shaft trauma is $1-(1-x)^{42}$. Using these, we can estimate a trauma incidence for complete skeletons or individuals even in cases where all archaeological remains are fragmented and commingled (Tab. 5.5g, n).[2]

Long-term trends. Between earlier and later periods, postcranial traumas increase (Fig. 5.5, Tab. 5.5). The absence of postcranial traumas in the Neolithic partially represents a sampling error, as examples are known anecdotally from Neolithic specimens not examined in this analysis (Messeri 1958; Robb 1994c; Salvadei and Macchiarelli 1983). Similarly, many Bronze Age cases come from a single site, the Grotta dello Scoglietto (Messeri 1962; Capasso and Piccardi 1980), which has an unusually high frequency of pathologies, and this may contribute to the Bronze Age "spike". Even so, postcranial trauma clearly rises after the Neolithic. The reason for this increase is not clear. Postcranial trauma such as the Colles' and parry fractures which make up most of the Eneolithic and Bronze Age long bone fractures reflect varied causes. Their increase with the Bronze and Iron Ages may reflect specific innovations such as the growth of horseback riding in the Bronze Age, as well as social developments such as economic intensification and rise of stratified societies in the Iron Age.

Cranial traumas are frequently caused by interpersonal violence, and changes in their frequency are especially interesting for understanding patterns of violence in the past. Surprisingly, although more actual cases are known from later periods, the rate of cranial traumas *per capita* turns out to be far higher in the Neolithic. Although the present analysis is based upon a relatively small Neolithic sample, published trauma cases (Germanà and Fornaciari 1992; Germanà et al. 1990; Messeri 1958; Robb 1994c; Salvadei and Macchiarelli 1983) in the small body of well-examined Neolithic data suggests that this is not a statistical fluke. Again, part of the high Bronze Age rate may represent a local variation at the Grotta dello Scoglietto, a site noted for numerous trepanations as well (Germanà and Fornaciari 1992; Messeri 1962). Overall, the data suggest tentatively that the level of cranial trauma, and probably interpersonal violence, was relatively high in the Neolithic, and declined in subsequent periods.

This result flatly contradicts the picture of violence in early Italian society drawn from archaeological evidence (Tab. 5.6). The Neolithic is typically seen as a relatively peaceful time; this view is based on its infrequent and casually made lithic weapons and the lack of weapons in grave goods and rock and cave art. At the same

Table 5.6. Archaeological signs of violence in prehistoric and early historic Italy.

	Neolithic	Eneolithic	Bronze Age	Iron Age
Iconography of violence	sporadic male hunting cults	weapons common in rock art, stelae; male-associated	weapons common in rock art, stelae; male-associated	weapons common in rock art, tomb art, statues, male-associated
Violence-related material culture	—	weapons central trade craft items, male grave goods	weapons central trade, craft items, male grave goods	weapons central trade, craft items, male grave goods
Defensive architecture	nucleated, ditched villages common	variable, dispersed, usually not defended	variable, dispersed, sometimes defended	fortified proto-urban, urban centers
Skeletal traumas	high cranial trauma, both sexes; low postcranial trauma	low cranial trauma, sexes?; low post-cranial trauma	moderate cranial trauma, mostly males; moderate postcranial trauma, both sexes	moderate cranial trauma, moderate post-crania; both predominantly in males

time, many Early and Middle Neolithic villages were surrounded by perimeter ditches, sometimes multiple, which were built with vast labor and which must have been at least partially defensive in purpose. In contrast, the Eneolithic is often viewed as a warlike period. Weapons became common grave goods, were traded and manufactured with fine craftsmanship of imported flint and metals, and became central themes in rock art. Weapons continued to be celebrated and archaeologically prominent through the Bronze Age. With the Iron Age, weapon symbolism was transferred to a full panoply of sword, spear and shield. These weapons continued to be common grave goods for males, and the vision of the aristocratic warrior hero formed one of the ideological pillars of early stratified societies (Robb 1994a).

What is striking is that actual violence, as far as cranial trauma reflects it, and the perceived threat of violence, as reflected in defensive architecture, appear to have declined precisely as the cultural celebration of violence increased[3]. This point has several implications. It contradicts concepts of physical violence as a simple reflex of a cultural style or propensity (*e.g.* Benedict 1934; Mead 1935) or of an innate "drive" (Lorenz 1966). The same is true for theories postulating some overriding economic need or political conflict which is effectively ameliorated by violence via the development of a warlike culture (Carneiro 1970; Haas 1990). It also suggests that violence *per se* is unlikely to result from direct repression associated with the existence of wealth, as there is little evidence for class stratification in earlier periods of Italian prehistory. The same observation may be made for ideological gender inequality as well. If violence against women helped maintain gender inequality from the Eneolithic through the Iron Age, as in several archeologically known societies (Shermis 1984; Wilkinson and Van Wagenen 1993), it did so either on an indirectly repressive symbolic level or in ways which left little distinguishable skeletal trace.

Cross-culturally, extremely high homicide rates are known from "peaceful" egalitarian societies such as the !Kung San, the Inuit and the Gebusi (Knauft 1987, 1991). In such societies, violence does not form part of the normal symbolic idiom of intra-group politics, and when it occurs, it often takes the form of sudden homicidal outbursts, socially sanctioned execution of witches or deviants, and endemic all-out hostility between neighboring villages (cf. Feil 1987). As Knauft points out, actual violence is often *less* frequent in societies with developed male status hierarchies, which channel conflict into the normal political process rather than excluding it until it reaches the threshold of violence. Moreover, prestige-oriented systems often depend economically on extended production systems requiring dispersed settlements and on complex systems of payments among exchange partners, kin and others involved in ritual obligations (Feil 1987). This provides both strong motivation for political actors to limit conflict rather than to let it spread and mechanisms for conflict resolution such as compensation payments.

This ethnographic point may help make sense of the trauma patterns in Italian prehistory. Neolithic societies appear to have been small-scale villages without developed political structures, and both their nucleated, defended settlement pattern and high cranial trauma rates suggest endemic conflict among them. Both cranial trauma and defended villages decline sharply with the rise of weapon iconography and material symbolism in the Copper Age. This florescence of weapon symbolism probably had as much to do with male prestige competition as with actual violence, and it was accompanied by settlement dispersal and greatly expanded trade, both probably signs of intensified production, exchange and alliance systems (Robb 1994a), economic features incompatible with unlimited actual conflict. It is likely that while the symbolic idiom of prestige competition was based on a culturally-constructed male capacity for violence, its practical effect was actually to *reduce* violence.

If this is so, it would also explain the sex distribution of traumas. The Neolithic and Eneolithic samples considered here are too small to analyze by sex, although known cases of Neolithic cranial traumas are distributed among males and females more or less equally (Robb 1994c). In contrast, in Bronze Age samples cranial traumas are concentrated in males (with 5 of 6 cases in this sample; sexed postcrania are too sparse to analyze), and both cranial and postcranial traumas in the Iron Age are more frequent among males. The increasing gender segregation of violence would be a logical development of the incorporation of violence within core symbolisms of gender ideology and political life.

CONCLUSIONS

This survey of trauma in Italian prehistory and at the protohistoric site of Pontecagnano (seventh-fourth centuries B.C.) suggests several conclusions.

1. Trauma at Pontecagnano was sharply divided by sex, with trauma of all kinds much more common among males. Most

traumas in males did not result from direct violence in warfare; instead, this common Iron Age pattern is explained primarily by reference to cultural structures prescribing violent behavior for males, both informally and in warfare, and underwriting a gender division of labor which allocated both organized violence in war and tasks considered heavy or dangerous to males. Inasmuch as any gender division of labor is culturally constructed rather than natural (Mukhopadhyay and Higgins 1988), this distribution of trauma reflects native gender concepts in the Italian Iron Age.

2. Through Italian prehistory, cranial and postcranial trauma appear to follow different trajectories. Cranial trauma seems relatively common in the Neolithic and diminishes in following periods, with a secondary increase in the Bronze Age. Postcranial trauma is relatively infrequent in the Neolithic and Eneolithic and rises in subsequent periods.

If cranial traumas reflects the level of interpersonal violence, this trajectory contradicts archaeological evidence, which suggests that weapons and violence were culturally glorified and socially important from the Copper Age on, culminating in the Iron Age ideal of the male warrior aristocrat. This apparent contradiction is explicable ethnographically, however. Rates of violence are often high in loosely-structured egalitarian societies and lower in societies with male status hierarchies (Feil 1987; Knauft 1987, 1991). In Italian prehistory, weapon symbolism was central to a male prestige system which linked violence and honor as an idiom for male interaction and at the same time incorporated political and economic mechanisms for reducing and containing actual conflict.

This analysis also suggests two theoretical conclusions. First, it suggests that variations in violence cannot be explained simply by reference to an innate aggressive drive, to a consistent cultural style, or as a straightforward reflex of political conflict or economic competition. Rather, violent acts, and the capacity to perform them, define and reinforce the identity of categories of people. The role of violence in a society depends at least partly on its place within the symbolic charter of relations between groups such as genders and classes. Secondly, incorporating violence into political symbolizations will also repattern its actual occurrence. In Italy, trauma rates among males and females dropped when the capacity for violence was integrated into the criteria for being a political actor. They began to rise again with the advent of formal social stratification, this time primarily among males. Hierarchical structures thus may neither uniformly increase or limit violence; instead, their effect may depend primarily on their symbolic context.

Finally, violence leaves diverse, often contradictory archaeological traces, and the contradictions often tell us more about prehistoric society than perfectly consistent data would. As the only direct evidence on the actual practice of violence, physical anthropology does not provide mere confirmation of other archaeological information. By affording independent testimony on violence in the past it can help render our picture of past societies ever more complex and accurate.

ACKNOWLEDGEMENTS

I am grateful to Marco Piccardi, Vitaliano Rossi, Caterina Scarsini, Fiorenza Sonego and Renzo Bigazzi for help, advice and discussion during research in the Museo Nazionale di Antropologia, Firenze, and to Professor B. Chiarelli for an opportunity to present a partial version of these results in a research seminar at the Università di Firenze. I also thank Prof. F. Mallegni and Prof. S. Borgognini Tarli (Università di Pisa), Dott.ssa M. Mazzei (Soprintendenza di Antichità di Foggia/Museo Nazionale di Manfredonia), Dott. R. Macchiarelli (Museo Pigorini, Roma) and Dott. G. Manzi (Università di Roma) for the opportunities to study skeletal material under their care, Russell Nelson for forensic advice on peri-mortem trauma, and Arthur Robb for advice on calculating probabilities. Research was supported by the Wenner-Gren Foundation for Anthropological Research and by the Department of Anthropology and Rackham School of Graduate Studies, University of Michigan.

NOTES

[1] Note that the skeletal element distributions in Table 4 include collections from a wide variety of excavation methods and thus cannot be used for taphonomic analysis.

[2] These formulae are derived as follows. The probability of having at least one traumatic lesion in the skull or skeleton is equal to one minus the probability of having no traumatic lesions in any region. If x represents the probability that a given region has a traumatic lesion, (1-x) represents the probability that it has none. The probability that neither of two regions has a traumatic lesion is $(1-x)^2$, and for n regions, the probability of no lesions is $(1-x)^n$. The probability of having at least one traumatic lesion is thus $1-(1-x)^n$.

Estimates calculated with these formulae generally fall within the same range as estimates directly from bone counts, but they are less biased by skeletal completeness and increase the information we can get from collections dominated by small commingled fragments.

[3] An alternate interpretation would read this as a shift in the kind or level of violence. Cranial traumas reflect short-range violence with a range of formal or *ad hoc* weapons, while long-range violence via projectiles is far less visible skeletally. A reduction in cranial traumas might thus imply a shift in patterns of violence from short-range to long-range. This would not be a technological shift (arrows were certainly available as lethal projectiles in the Neolithic, as the Porto Badisco cave paintings (Graziosi 1980) show); rather it would involve shifting the focus of conflict from within the group to among groups. However, defended villages in the Neolithic would suggest at least some perceived external threat, while Copper and Bronze Age dispersed and undefended settlements do not seem consistent with a model of endemic intergroup warfare.

REFERENCES

Adams, J. (1982). *The Latin sexual vocabulary*. London: Duckworth.

Alciati, G., Fedeli, M. and Pesce Delfino, V. (1987). *La mallatia dalla preistoria all'età antica*. Bari: Laterza.

Alfoldy, G. (1988). *The social history of Rome*. Baltimore: Johns Hopkins University Press.

Angel, J. L., J. Kelley, Parrington, M. and Pinter S. (1987). "Life stresses of the free black community as represented by the First African Baptist Church, Philadelphia, 1823-1841." *American Journal of Physical Anthropology* **74**:213–230.

Benedict, R. (1934). *Patterns of culture*. Boston: Houghton Mifflin.

Bietti Sestieri, A. (1992). *L a necropoli laziale di Osteria dell'Osa*. Rome: Quasar.

Borgognini Tarli, S., Canci, A. M. Piperno, and Repetto, E. (1993). "Dati archeologici e antropologici sulle sepolture mesolitiche della Grotta dell'Uzzo (Trapani)." *Bullettino di Paletnologia Italiana* **84**:85–179.

Bourdieu, P. (1990). *The Logic of Practice*. Stanford: Stanford University Press.

Burrell, L., M. Maas, and D. Van Gerven (1986). "Patterns of long-bone fracture in two Nubian cemeteries." *Journal of Human Evolution* **1**:495–506.

Canci, A., S. Minozzi, Borgognini Tarli, S. and Repetto, E. (1993). "I resti umani della media età del bronzo rinvenuti nell'ipogeo di Madonna di Loreto (Trinitapoli, Foggia)." *Antropologia Contemporanea* **16**:33–37.

Capasso, L., and Piccardi, M. (1980). "La grotta dello Scoglietto: un probabile centro nosocomiale dell'età del Bronzo in Toscana." *Rivista di Scienze Preistoriche* **35**:164–181.

Carneiro, R. (1970). "A theory of the origin of the state." *Science* **69**:733–738.

Carter, J. (Ed.) (1990). *The Pantanello necropolis*, 1982–1989: *an interim report*. Austin, TX: Institute of Classical Archaeology, University of Texas.

Chagnon, N. and Irons, W. (Eds.) (1979). *Evolutionary biology and human social behavior: an anthropological perspective*. North Scituate, MA: Duxbury Press.

D'Agostino, B. (1974). "Il mondo periferico della Magna Grecia." In *Popoli e civiltà dell'Italia antica*, eds. B. D'Agostino, P. E. Arias, and G. Colonna, pp. 177–272. Rome: Biblioteca di Storia Patria.

Daly, M. and Wilson, M. (1987). *Homicide*. Hawthorne NY: Aldine de Gruyter.

Davis, J. (1969). "Honor and politics in Pisticci." *Proceedings of the Royal Anthropological Institute* **5**: 69–81.

Feil, D. (1987). *The evolution of highland Papua New Guinea societies*. Cambridge: Cambridge University Press.

Formicola, V. (1980). "Gli uomini preistorici della regione apuana all'inizio dell'età dei metalli." *Annuario, Biblioteca Civica di Massa*, 1–71.

Formicola, V. and Garulli, A. (1988). "Il campione eneolitico di Ponte S. Pietro: indicatori di stress e condizioni di vita." Rivista di Antropologia **66**:77–88.

Fornaciari, G., Brogi, M. and Balducci, E. (1984). "Patologia dentaria degli inumati di Pontecagnano (Salerno), VII-IV sec. a.C." *Archivio per l'Antropologia e la Etnologia* **114**:73–93.

Fredericksen, M. (1974). *Campania*. Rome: British School at Rome.

Germanà, F. and Fornaciari, G. (1992). *Trapanazioni, craniotomie e traume cranici in Italia dalla preistoria all'età moderna*.Pisa: Giardini.

Germanà, F., Mallegni, F. de Pompeis, C. and Ronco, D. (1990). "Il villaggio neolitico di Villa Badessa (Pescara): aspetti paletnologici, antropologici e paleopatologici." *Atti, Società Italiana di Scienze Naturali* **97**:271–310.

Graziosi, P. (1980). *Le pitture preistoriche di Porto Badisco*. Firenze: Martelli.

Haas, J. (Ed.) (1990). *The anthropology of war*. Cambridge: Cambridge University Press.

Henneberg, M. Henneberg, R. and Carter, J. (1992). "Health in colonial Metaponto." *National Geographic Research and Exploration*, pp. 446–458.

Joshel, S. (1992). *Work, identity and legal status at Rome*. Norman, OK: University of Oklahoma Press.

Jurmain, R. (1991). "Paleoepidemiology of trauma in a prehistoric central Californian population." In *Human paleopathology: current syntheses and future options*, eds. D. Ortner and A. Aufderheide, pp. 241–250. Washington: Smithsonian Institution Press.

Keats, T. (1990). *Radiology of musculoskeletal stress injury*. Chicago: Year Book Medical Publishers.

Kelley, J. and Angel, J. L. (1987). "Life Stresses of Slavery." *American Journal of Physical Anthropology* 74:199–211.

Kelley, M. (1989). "Infectious disease." In *Reconstruction of life from the skeleton*, eds. K. Kennedy and M. Iscan, pp. 191-201. New York: Liss.

Knauft, B. (1987). "Reconsidering violence in simple human societies: homicide among the Gebusi of New Guinea." *Current Anthropology* 28:457–499.

_____ (1991). "Violence and sociality in human evolution." *Current Anthropology* 32:391–428.

Lambert, P. and Walker, P. (1991). "Physical anthropological evidence for the evolution of social complexity in coastal Southern California." *Antiquity* 65:963–973.

Livy (Titus Livius) (1960). *The Early History of Rome*. Translated by A. de Selincourt. Harmondsworth: Penguin.

Lombardi Pardini, E., Polosa, D. and Pardini, E. (1984). "Gli inumati di Pontecagnano (Salerno), VII-VI sec.a.C." *Archivio per l'Antropologia e la Etnologia* 114:3–62.

Lombardi Pardini, E., Fulciniti, G. and Pardini, E. (1992). "Somatologia, dimorfismo sessuale e struttura biologica di una popolazione campana del VII-IV secolo a.C." *Archivio per l'Antropologia e la Etnologia* 121:3–43.

Lorenz, K. (1966). *On aggression*. New York: Harcourt Brace.

Lovejoy, C. and Heiple, K. (1981). "The analysis of fractures in skeletal populations with an example from the Libben site, Ottawa County, Ohio." *American Journal of Physical Anthropology* 55:529–541.

Macchiarelli, R., Salvadei, and Dazzi, M. (1982). "Paleotraumatologia cranio-cerebrale nella comunità protostorica di Alfadena (VI-V sec. a.C., area medio-adriatica)." *Antropologia Contemporanea* 4:239–243.

Mallegni, F., Brogi, M. and Balducci, E. (1984). "Paleodontologia dei reperti umani di Pontecagnano (Salerno), VII-IV sec. a.C." *Archivio per l'Antropologia e la Etnologia* 114:63–93.

Mead, M. (1935). *Sex and temperament in three primitive societies*. London: Routledge.

Merbs, C. (1989). "Trauma." In *Reconstruction of life from the skeleton*, eds. Kennedy, K. and Iscan, M. pp. 161–190. New York: Liss.

Messeri, P. (1958). "Note di paleopatologia sui neolitici della Liguria." *Archivio per l'Antropologia e la Etnologia* 88:221–230.

_____ (1962). "Aspetti abnormi e patologici nel materiale scheletrico dello Scoglietto." *Archivio per l'Antropologia e la Etnologia* 20:129–159.

Minellono, F., Pardini, E. and Fornaciari, G. (1980). "Le sepolture epigravettiane di Vado all'Arancio (Grosseto)." *Rivista di Scienze Preistoriche* 35:3–44.

Montagu, A. (1973). *Man and Aggression*. New York: Oxford University Press.

Mukhopadhyay, C. and Higgins, P. (1988). "Anthropological studies of women's status revisited." *Annual Review of Anthropology* 17:461–495.

Ortner, D. and Putschar, W. (1981). *Identification of pathological conditions in human skeletal remains*. Washington: Smithsonian Institution Press.

Owsley, D., Orser, C. Mann, R. Moore-Jansen, P. and Montgomery, R. (1987). "Demography and pathology of an urban slave population from New Orleans." *American Journal of Physical Anthropology* 74:185–198.

Pallottino, M. (1991). *History of Earliest Italy*. Ann Arbor: University of Michigan Press.

Paleopathology Association (1991). *Skeletal Database Committee Recommendations*. Detroit: Paleopathology Association.

Pardini, E., Mannucci, P. and Lombardi Pardini, E. (1983). "Sex ratio, età media di vita, mortalità differenziale per età e per sesso in una popolazione campana vissuta a Pontecagnano, Salerno, nei secoli VII-IV a.C." *Archivio per l'Antropologia e la Etnologia* 113:268–285.

Pardini, E., Rossi, V. Innocenti, F. Stefanin, G. Fulgaro, A. and Patara S. (1992). "Gli inumati di Pontecagnano (Salerno), V-IV sec. a.C." *Archivio per l'Antropologia e la Etnologia* 112:281–333.

Peristiany, J. (Ed.)(1966). *Honor and shame: the values of Mediterranean society*. Chicago: University of Chicago Press.

Petrone, P. (1993). "Schiavitù, stress di attività lavoritiva, malnutrizione: condizioni socio-culturali quali principali causi di morbidità e mortalità in popolazioni d'età imperiale dell'area flegrea (Napoli, Campania)." Paper presented at the 10th Congress of Italian Anthropologists, Pisa.

Powell, M. (1988). *Status and health in prehistory: a case study of the Moundville chiefdom*. Washington, D.C.: Smithsonian Institution Press.

_____ (1991). "Ranked status and health in the Missisippian chiefdom at Moundville." In *What mean these bones? Studies in Southeastern Bioarchaeology*, eds. M. Powell, P. Bridges, and A. Mires, pp. 22–51. Tuscaloosa, AL: University of Alabama Press.

Repetto, E., A. Canci, and S. Borgognini Tarli (1988). "Indicatori scheletrici e dentari dello stato di salute nel campione dell'Età del Bronzo di Toppo Daguzzo, Basilicata." *Rivista di Antropologia* 66:89–112.

Riches, D. (Ed.) (1986). *The anthropology of violence*. New York: Blackwell.

Robb, J. (1994a). 'Gender contradictions: moral coalitions and inequality in prehistoric Italy." *Journal of European Archaeology* 2:20–49.

_____ (1994b). *Issues in the skeletal interpretation of muscle attachments*. Paper presented at the Annual Meeting of the Paleoanthropology Society, Anaheim, California.

_____ (1994c). "The neolithic of peninsular Italy: anthropological synthesis and critique." *Bullettino di Paletnologia Italiana*, 85:189–214.

(1994d). "Skeletal signs of activity in the Italian Metal Ages: methodological and interpretative notes." *Human Evolution*, 9:215–229.

Rogers, L. (1992). *Radiology of Skeletal Trauma*. 2nd ed., Vol. 2. New York: Churchill Livingston.

Rose, J. (1985). *Gone to a Better Land*. Research Series 25. Fayetteville AR: Arkansas Archaeological Survey.

Salvadei, L., and Macchiarelli, R. (1983). "Studi antropologici." In *Studi sul Neolitico del Tavoliere della Puglia*, eds. S. Cassano and A. Manfredini, pp. 253–264. International Series 160. Oxford: British Archaeological Reports.

Shermis, S. (1984). "Domestic Violence in two skeletal populations." *Ossa* 11:143–152.

Sonego, F. (1991). *Lo stato di salute a Pontecagnano in un periodo di 'crisi' (VII-1 meta V secolo a.C.): analisi di indicatori scheletrici e dentari*. Unpublished Tesi di Laurea, Università di Firenze.

Stirland, A. (1991). "Diagnosis of occupationally related paleopathology: can it be done?" In *Human Paleopathology: Current Syntheses and Modern Options*, eds. D. Ortner and A. Aufderheide, pp. 40–50. Washington: Smithsonian University Press.

Vida Navarro, M. (1993). "Warriors and weavers: sex and gender in Early Iron Age graves from Pontecagnano." *Journal of the Accordia Research Center* 3:67–100.

Walker, P. (1989). "Cranial injuries as evidence of violence in prehistoric southern California." *American Journal of Physical Anthropology* 80:313–323.

White, T. (1992). *Prehistoric Cannibalism at Mancos 5MTUMR-2346*. Princeton: Princeton University Press.

Wilkinson, R. and Van Wagenen, K. (1993). "Violence against women: prehistoric skeletal evidence from Michigan." *Midcontinental Journal of Archaeology* 18:190–216.

Chapter
SIX

Wife Beating, Boxing, and Broken Noses: Skeletal Evidence for the Cultural Patterning of Violence

Phillip L. Walker
Department of Anthropology University of California Santa Barbara, California

How have patterns of violence varied through time? This is a historical question that has important implications for understanding the interpersonal violence that afflicts many modern societies. Historical documents and ethnographic records provide data on the patterns of interpersonal violence in a few ancient groups and nonwestern cultures. The range of violent and nonviolent behavior documented, however, is minuscule in comparison to the diversity seen in the enormous number of prehistoric societies for which we have no written records. Even when historical documents are available, they are often difficult to interpret because the descriptions are colored by the cultural biases of the observer.

In contrast to historical records, human skeletal remains provide a direct source of evidence regarding patterns of violence in both prehistoric and historically documented societies. In certain respects, bones do not lie. If a person's skeleton is found with arrow points embedded in the bone, this says something indisputable about a physical interaction that took place between that person's skeleton and those arrow points. Such data are extremely valuable from a scientific standpoint. Unlike written records, they are physical facts and not culture dependent symbolic constructs.

Different types of violent behavior produce characteristic patterns of skeletal injuries. Analysis of these patterns in modern and ancient populations can thus provide information on the historical, cultural, and environmental factors associated with different types of aggressive behavior. Such studies are important because they help us place modern violence within an appropriate cultural-historical perspective. In doing so, they can provide answers to some basic questions about human aggression. For example, developmental trajectories and transitions in violent behavior over the life course have been identified in western societies (Laub and Lauritsen 1993). To what extent are such patterns present in earlier non-western societies? Are they universal or culture specific?

NONLETHAL CRANIAL INJURIES

Nonlethal cranial injuries are an especially interesting source of evidence concerning cultural differences in patterns of violence (Walker 1989). There is significant variation among groups in the extent to which various parts of the head are targeted during aggressive interactions. For example, the Yanomamö Indians engage in ritualized club fights in which the top of the head is the prime target (Chagnon 1992). Modern boxers, in contrast, focus their attention on producing a knockout with blows to the head and face (O'Reilly 1888, Blonstein 1965, Enzenauer 1989). As I will show, such cultural differences leave clear marks on the skull. The outer layer of the cranial vault, in particular, is a plastic medium that faithfully records the details of the objects that strike it. In the case of non-lethal injuries, these impressions provide a cumulative record of the person's history of cranial trauma.

A second advantage of studying non-lethal injuries is that their identification poses fewer technical problems than lethal injuries. Cranial remains from archaeological contexts are frequently highly fragmentary owing to the effects of ground pressure and other post-mortem processes. As a result, it is often difficult to decide if a fracture is due to this postmortem damage, or an injury sustained around the time of death. Since, by definition, non-lethal injuries show evidence of healing, they cannot be confused with post-mortem fractures and identifying them is thus comparatively easy.

COLLECTIONS STUDIED AND RESEARCH METHODS

To assess variability in patterns of violence I examined a worldwide sample of more than 2300 crania from archaeological excavations and museum collections (Tab. 6.1, Fig. 6.1). These people lived between 4000 B.C. and the first half of the twentieth century. They participated in a broad spectrum of economic systems including those based on hunting and gathering, fishing, pastoralism, subsistence agriculture, and modern industrial activities.

These skeletal remains come from a variety of sources. Some are from church crypts (St. Bride's and Christ Church), others are medical school collections (the Hamann-Todd and Terry collections). The rest are a result of cemetery excavations. Several collections have been reburied and are no longer available for study

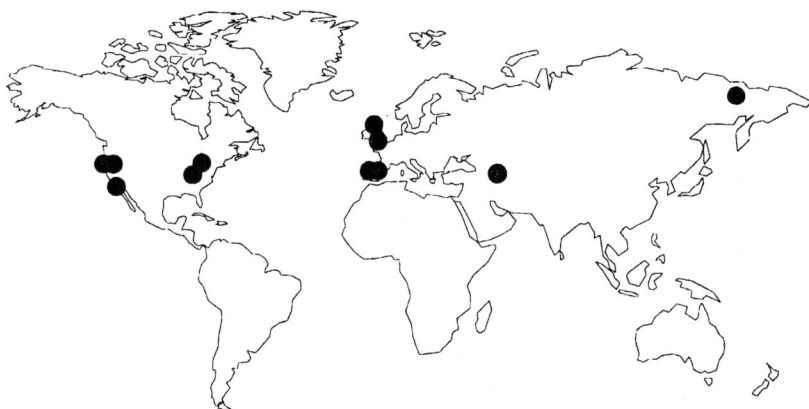

Figure 6.1. Map showing the geographic distribution of the populations studied.

Table 6.1. Collections Studied

Collection	Location	Economic System	Approximate Date
Asia			
South Aral Sea	Kazakhstan & Uzbekistan	Pastoralism	B.C. 700–400 A.D.
Yakuts	Eastern Siberia, Russia	Pastoralism	18th–Early 20th century
Europe			
La Olmeda	Castilla, Spain	Pastoralism	7th–11th Century A.D.
Wamba	Castilla, Spain	Agriculture, Pastoralism	16th–18th Century A.D.
Great Britain			
Poundbury	Dorset, England	Agriculture	4th–5th Century A.D.
Ensay	Outer Hebrides,Scotland	Agriculture	16th–19th Century A.D.
Christ Church, Spitalfield	London, England	Modern Industrial	17th–Mid 19th Century .
St Bride's Church	London,England	Modern Industrial	Mid 18th–19th Century
United States			
Palace of the Legion of Honor	San Francisco	Modern Industrial	Late 19th Century
Terry and Hamman-Todd	Cleveland & St. Louis	Modern Industrial	Early 20th Century
Native California			
Burton Estates	Northern California	Hunter-Gatherer	6th–12th Century A.D.
Santa Barbara Channel	Southern California	Hunter-Gatherer	B.C. 4000-1800 A.D.

(Palace of the Legion of Honor, Burton Estates, and some Santa Barbara Channel collections).

DETERMINING FREQUENCIES

The failure to systematically record the number of individuals examined for a condition is a serious problem in many studies of ancient trauma. Without such data, it is impossible to make meaningful population comparisons. The common practice of simply reporting the number of individuals examined, is inadequate in this regard. This is because the completeness of skeletons can vary markedly within and between archaeological collections owing to differences in soil conditions and archaeological technique (Walker 1994).

The problem of differential preservation is especially significant in the analysis of nasal fractures. These bones are thin and highly susceptible to damage and loss during archaeological recovery. The bones of the cranial vault are much more resistant to damage. Nevertheless, it is common to find highly fragmentary, partial crania in archaeological sites.

To deal with this problem, I recorded the completeness of the nasal bones and cranial vault completeness of each individual (Tab. 6.2). Fragmentary crania were recorded as fractional individuals. For example, if the left side of the nose was missing, that specimen contributed 0.5 to the total count of individuals examined for the presence of nasal fractures. If the cranial vault of the same specimen was complete, it contributed 1.0 to the total count of people examined for cranial vault injuries.

AGE AND SEX DETERMINATIONS

For the Hamann-Todd, Terry, St. Brides, and Christ Church collections, each person's sex and age at death is known from autopsy records or coffin plate inscriptions. For the remaining burials, age and sex determinations were made based on standard osteological criteria (e.g., Krogman 1962; Bass 1971; White 1991). Although they were often unavailable, pelvic remains were used for sex and age determinations whenever possible. Tooth wear was used to age many of the Santa Barbara Channel area collections (Walker *et al.* 1991).

Table 6.2. Number of people examined. The values for effective number of people account for the fact that some specimens were fragmentary. These specimens were counted as fractional individuals based on the amount of material preserved. The effective number of individuals is the sum of these values

Area/Group	Number of People			Effective Number of People					
				Nasal Area			Cranial Vault		
	Males	Females	Total	Males	Females	Total	Males	Females	Total
Asia									
South Aral Sea	93	121	319	64.0	83.5	218.0	86.5	106.0	288.0
Yakuts	9	9	18	9.0	9.0	18.0	9.0	9.0	18.0
Europe									
La Olmeda	50	56	106	29.5	25.5	55.0	50.0	53.0	103.0
Wamba	1	0	18	1.0		17.0	1.0		18.0
Great Britian									
Poundbury	62	71	162	18.3	22.3	45.2	46.0	50.0	120.0
Ensay	36	46	85	25.6	31.0	56.6	35.0	46.0	84.0
Christ Church, Spitalfield	17	27	67	12.9	21.4	34.3	17.0	25.5	64.5
St Bride's Church	51	38	89	35.0	26.0	61.0	51.0	38.0	89.0
United States									
Palace of the Legion of Honor	32	15	78	28.0	14.0	71.0	30.0	14.0	73.0
Terry and Hammon-Todd	120	105	227	119.0	104.0	223.0	120.0	105.0	225.0
Native California									
Burton Estates	49	54	113	17.5	13.0	31.0	39.5	40.8	88.3
Santa Barbara Channel	417	439	998	252.3	260.5	605.0	304.0	346.5	759.0
Total	937	981	2280	612.0	610.2	1435.1	789.0	833.8	1929.8

IDENTIFYING NONLETHAL INJURIES

Nonlethal cranial trauma results in several distinctive types of osseous lesions. An object that strikes the cranial vault with sufficient force can produce a depressed fracture or "dent" in the bone (Fig. 6.2). If the person survives the injury, the injury persists as a

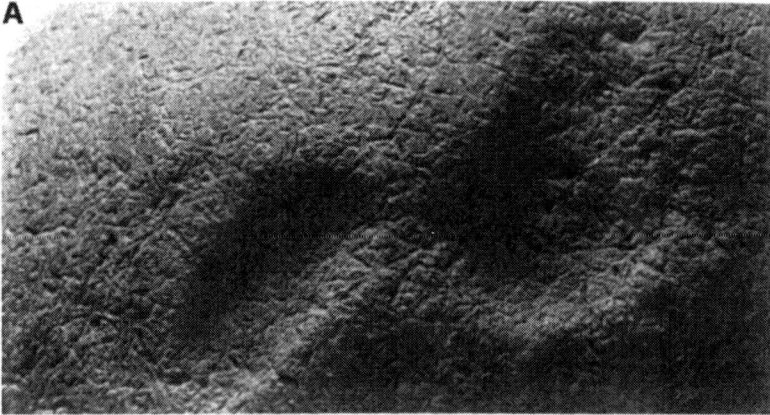

Figure 6.2. (Continued on page 152).

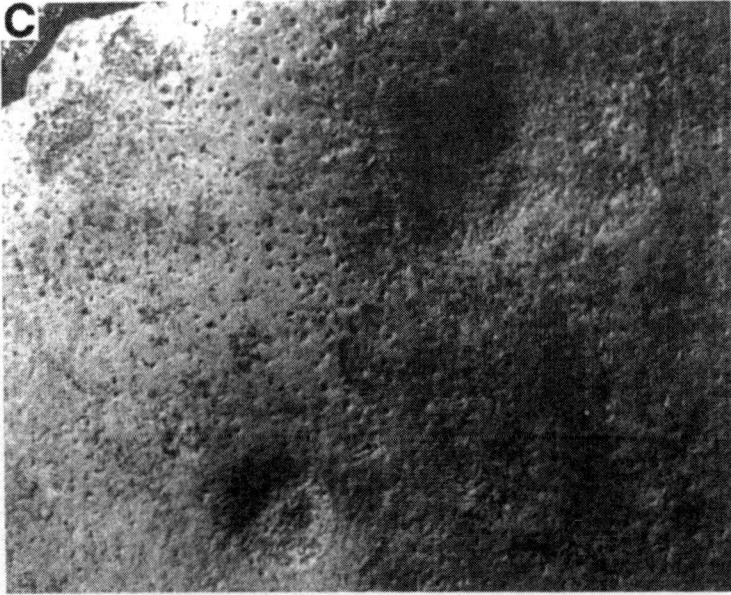

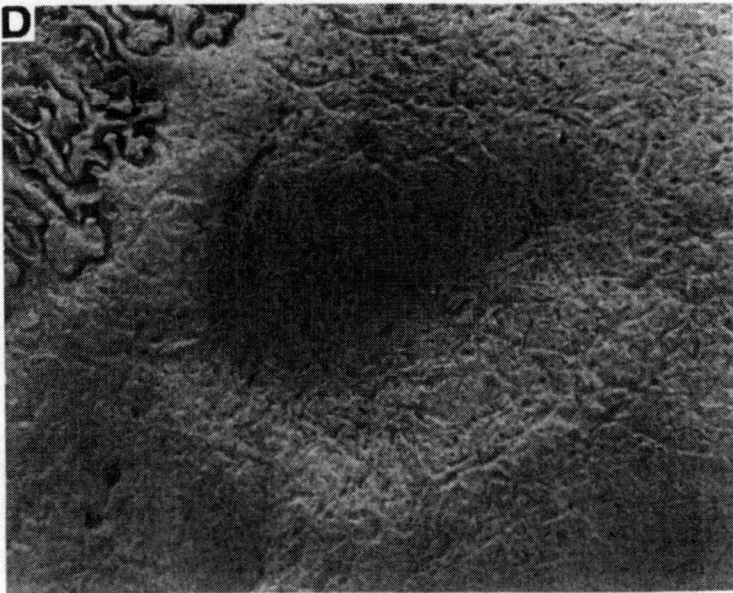

Figure 6.2. (Continued on page 153).

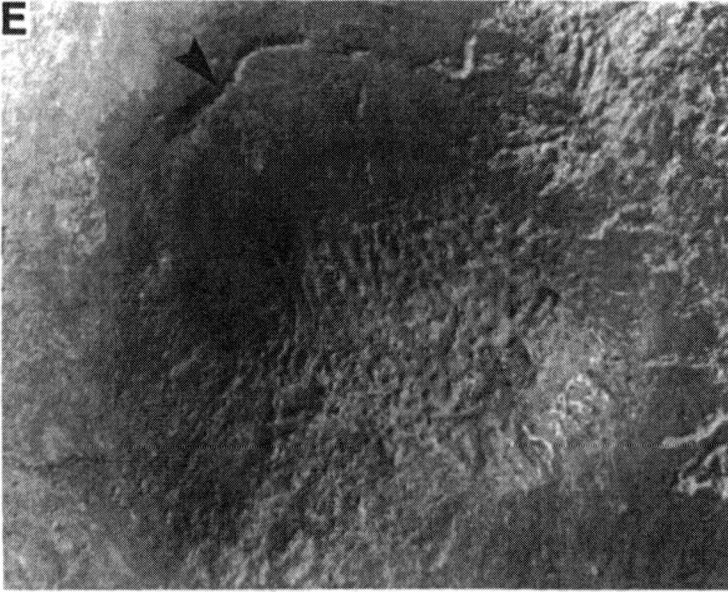

Figure 6.2. Photographs of cranial vault injuries. (a) Ellipsoidal parietal bone injuries in British Museum of Natural History cranium SK10068 from Santa Cruz Island, (b) Deep circular depressed parietal bone injury in male cranium SK10047, (c) Multiple circular frontal bone injuries in a female cranium from SBa-60, (d) Ellipsoidal occipital bone injury in female cranium SK10012, (e) Circular parietal bone injury in a female cranium from SBa-60 with arrow pointing to fracture line (from Walker 1989, copyright Wiley-Liss, Inc.).

depressed area in the surface of the skull. The shape of depression provides useful information on the shape of the object that produced it. In arrow wounds to the head, it is not uncommon to find fragments of stone points that failed to penetrate the brain-case embedded in the surface of the skull.

Sometimes, when the object striking the head has sufficient force, the external surface depression is accompanied by a raised area on the internal surface of the bone. Healed injuries of this sort are comparatively uncommon in archaeological collections, however, since they are likely to result in endocranial bleeding and death. Blunt trauma to the cranial vault can also produce linear fractures. These occur when the force of the blow is dissipated through an eggshell-like crack in the cranial vault. Again, because they are usually fatal, healed injuries of this kind are rare in skeletal collections.

Fractures of the nasal area are the most common skeletal manifestation of blows to the face. When the bridge of the nose is the point of impact, the result is usually a fracture that passes transversely across one or both of the nasal bones (Figs. 6.3 and 6.4). When the trauma is more severe and the force of the blow pushes the nose to one side, linear fractures are also sometimes seen in the lateral borders of the nasal aperture (i.e., the frontal processes of the maxillae).

I have taken a conservative approach to the identification of non-lethal cranial trauma. Fractures lacking clear evidence of healing (i.e., new bone formation) were not counted. I also was careful to exclude from consideration lesions of nontraumatic origin such as depressions left by dermoid cysts, and surface irregularities associated with either localized or systemic infection (see Walker 1989).

Identifying nasal fractures poses special problems. Often traces of old fracture lines are clearly visible on the bone surface. These are especially evident when dislocation occurs and the bones heal in an abnormal position. Sometimes, however, there is no dislocation and a callus of new bone forms on the surface that obliterates the fracture line. In such cases, evidence of the fracture frequently persists on the internal surface of the nasal bones. I found that examination with a bright transmitted light often helped me to identify old, well healed fractures of this type.

TRAUMA PATTERNS IN SKELETAL COLLECTIONS

Fractures of the nasal area are the most common injuries in the collections I examined (Tab. 6.3). Nasal fractures (including fractures of the frontal process of the maxilla) were found in 7% (n = 106) of the 1,506 individuals whose nasal areas were well enough preserved to examine for nasal injury. Out of a total of 2280 people whose cranial vaults were examined 4.6% (n = 104) had frontal bone injuries, and 3.9% (n = 90) had parietal injuries. A few additional injuries were observed on the occipital and zygomatic bones (n = 6).

The absolute frequency of injuries was significantly higher in males than in females for the nasal ($x^2 = 4.5$, p = 0.03), frontal ($x^2 = 21.2$ p < .0001), and parietal ($x^2 = 13.7$, p < .0001) areas. How-

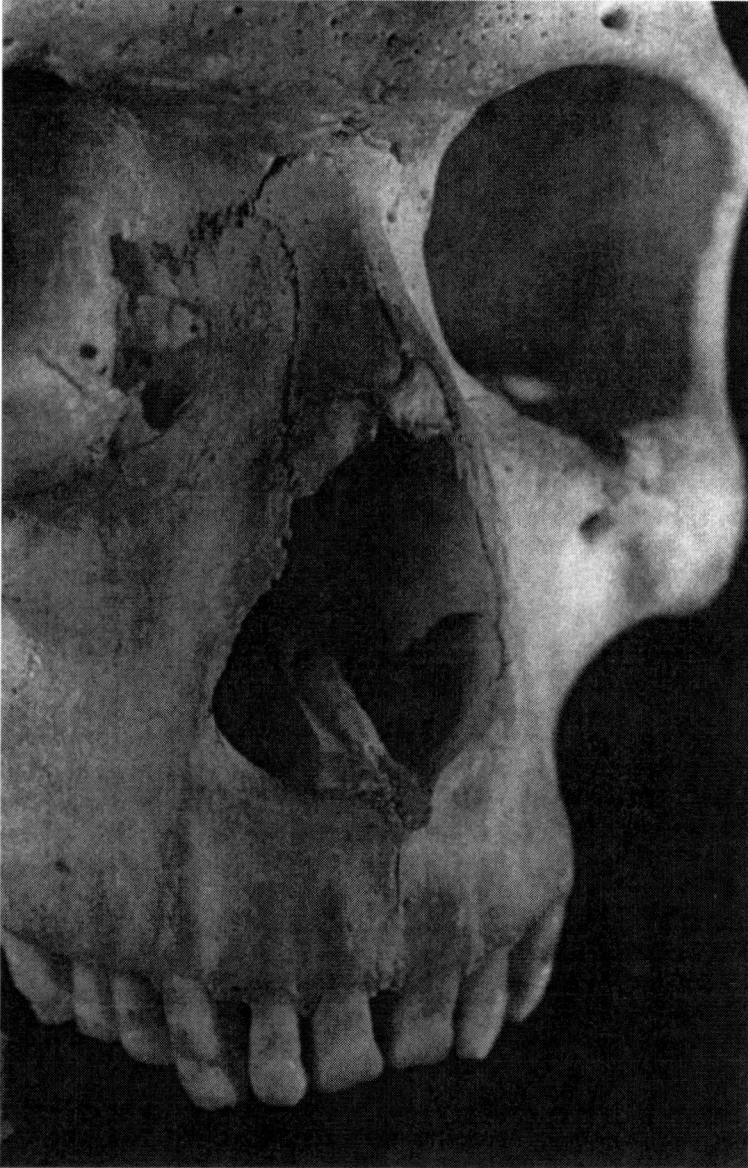

Figure 6.3. Healed nasal bone fractures in the cranium of a modern American in the collection of the Department of Anthropology, University of California, Santa Barbara.

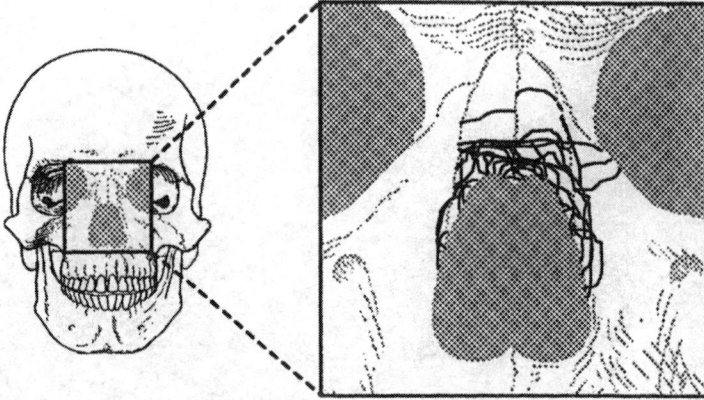

Figure 6.4. Diagram showing the superimposed distributions of healed nasal fractures of 25 modern Americans whose skulls are in the collections of the Cleveland Museum of Natural History and the Smithsonian Institution.

ever, the pattern of the injuries does not differ significantly between males and females; in both sexes, nasal injuries are more common than frontal injuries and frontal injuries are more common than parietal injuries ($x^2 = 2.9$, $p = 0.23$).

The left side of the head has many more injuries than the right side (Fig. 6.5, Tab. 6.3). Out of a total of 205 injuries clearly located on one side of the skull 63% were on the left side and 37% on the right. The deviation from a symmetrical distribution is statistically significant for the total sample of injuries ($x^2 = 3.84$, $p = .05$), but not when the injuries are subdivided by cranial area (nasal area: $x^2 = 1.07$, $p = 0.3$, parietal: $x^2 = 0.44$, $x^2 = 0.5$, frontal: $x^2 = 2.41$, $p = 0.12$). The ratio of left to right side injuries does not differ significantly ($x^2 = 2.3$, $p = 0.25$) between the nasal (58%) parietal (65%), and frontal (61%) areas. Men and women do not differ in the ratio injuries on the left and right sides of the skull (frontal, $x^2 = 1.47$, $p = 0.225$; parietal, $x^2 = 0.31$, $p = 0.58$; nasal, $x^2 = 0.006$, $p = 0.94$).

Although the mean age of people with cranial vault injuries is greater than that of people without injuries (37.4 vs. 36.4 years), this difference is not statistically significant ($t = 0.7$, $p = 0.48$). For injuries to the nasal area, in contrast, there is a highly significant relationship between increasing age and the presence of injuries

Table 6.3. Number of healed cranial injuries recorded in the bones of the face and cranial vault. Nasal Area = bones and frontal processes of the maxillae. L = left side injury, R = right side injury, ? = side of injury unclear.

Area/Group	Nasal Area				Parietal				Frontal				Occipital & Zygomatic			
	L	R	?	Total	L	R	?	Total	L	R	?	Total	L	R	?	Total
Asia																
South Aral Sea	3	4	1	8	0	0	1	1	5	3	0	8	0	0	0	0
Yakuts	2	1	3	6	1	0	0	1	1	1	0	2	0	0	0	0
Europe																
La Olmeda	0	1	2	3	1	3	1	5	2	0	1	3	0	0	0	0
Wamba	0	0	0	0	0	0	3	3	0	1	0	1	0	0	0	0
Great Britain																
Poundbury	1	2	4	7	3	2	0	5	2	1	0	3	0	0	0	0
Ensay	0	1	1	2	1	0	0	1	3	0	0	3	0	0	0	0
Christ Church, Spitalfield	1	0	0	1	0	0	0	0	0	0	0	0	0	0	0	0
St Bride's Church	0	0	5	5	0	0	3	3	0	0	1	1	0	0	0	0
United States																
Palace of the Legion of Honor	0	0	3	3	1	1	0	2	2	1	0	3	0	0	1	1
Terry and Hammon-Todd	16	9	37	62	7	6	2	15	11	4	0	15	1	2	0	0
Native California																
Burton Estates	2	0	0	2	0	0	0	0	1	0	0	1	0	0	0	0
Santa Barbara Channel	0	0	7	7	29	13	12	54	33	19	12	64	1	0	1	1
Total	25	18	63	106	43	25	22	90	60	30	14	104	2	2	2	2
Sex																
Males	14	10	36	60	25	15	12	52	36	18	10	64	1	0	2	3
Females	11	8	24	43	11	9	6	26	20	5	3	28	1	2	2	3

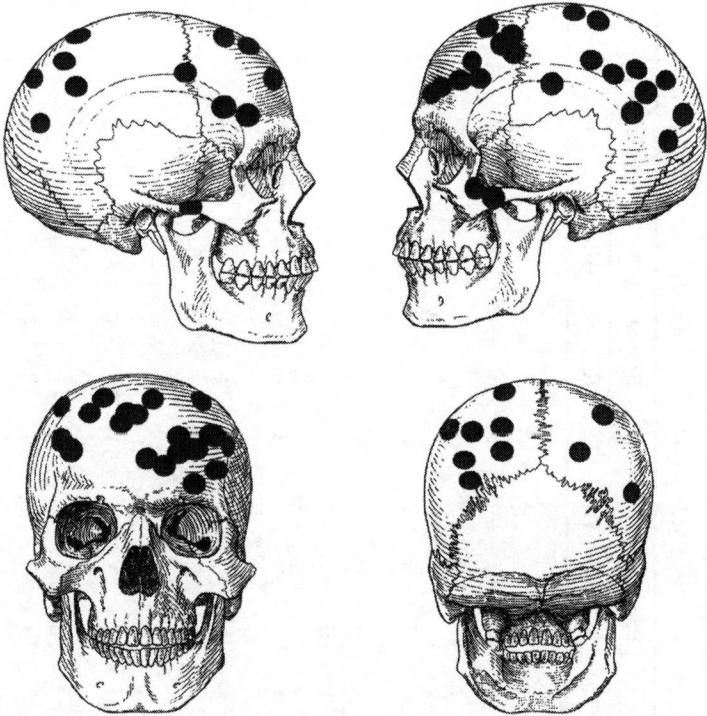

Figure 6.5. Diagram showing the distribution of healed cranial vault and zygomatic bone fractures in 31 modern Americans whose skulls are in the collections of the Cleveland Museum of Natural History and the Smithsonian Institution.

$(t = 7.15, p < 0.00001)$. People with nasal fractures, on the average, were 14 years older than those without them (51 vs. 37 years).

When the age-injuries relationship is analyzed separately for males and females, some interesting differences emerge (Fig. 6.6). For both sexes there is a more-or-less linear relationship between increasing age at death and the number of people with nasal injuries. Although sex differences are small for most ages, elderly males tend to have more nasal injuries than elderly females. Cranial vault injuries show a very different relationship to age at death (Fig 6.6). At all ages males have a substantially higher frequency of injuries than females. For females, there is no clear relationship between the presence of injuries and age at death. Women show a

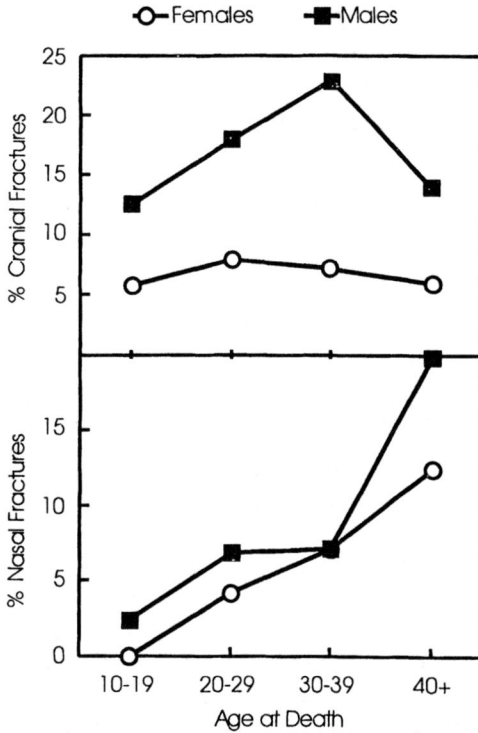

Figure 6.6. Age related changes in the percent of males and females in the collections studied with healed fractures of the nasal area and the cranial vault.

slight increase in injuries between the first and second decades of life. After that, there is a gradual decrease in their frequency. Men show a different pattern. There is a linear increase in cranial injuries until the age of forty when the trend is reversed. These males, who died at an elderly age, have a frequency of cranial vault injuries comparable to that of young adults (Fig. 6.6). From this it appears that living conditions associated with low fracture rates promote male longevity much more than that of females.

CAUSES OF MODERN TRAUMA

This cranial trauma clearly is a result of many different causes. Age and sex specific patterns of behavior, sociocultural, and historical factors are all likely to be involved. Before discussing some reasons for the age, sex, and population differences in these skeletal collections, it is worthwhile reviewing what is known from clinical studies about the cranial injuries of modern people. The causes of the cranial injuries in the ancient populations, of course, are likely to differ in many respects from those of modern people. Nevertheless, the clinical literature provides valuable comparative data and analogies for use in interpreting patterns of ancient trauma and it is directly relevant to the modern cranial injuries documented here. These clinical data show that modern cranial trauma results from three main causes: interpersonal violence, sports, and accidents.

INTERPERSONAL VIOLENCE

Assailants are not random in respect to the areas of the body they attack. Although there is considerable variation related to the sociocultural context in which the violence occurs, the head and neck clearly are favored (Kjaerulff *et al.* 1989, Shepherd *et al.* 1990, McDowell *et al.* 1992, Hussain *et al* 1994). The reasons for this are no doubt both strategic and symbolic. From a strategic standpoint, the head and especially the face are attractive targets because injuries of this area can be very painful. Well placed blows to the head are also likely to produce bleeding and conspicuous bruises that serve as a highly visible symbol of the aggressor's social dominance.

The idea that social or symbolic considerations relating to visibility of the injury influence the body part targeted is consistent with the kinds of injuries seen in cases of wife beating, assaults of people other than spouses, and assaults perpetrated by police officers. In modern western societies, men who beat their wives show a strong predilection for the face, especially the area around the eyes (Fig. 6.7; Fonseka 1974:400; McDowell *et al.* 1992). Black eyes are a common finding, and in one study 9% of the victimized wives sustained nasal fractures (Fonseka 1974:400). In assaults of non-spouses, injuries tend to be more widely distributed over the body (Fonseka 1974:400). Less emphasis on damaging the face is also seen in Chilean victims of police assaults (Aalund 1990). In these people the head-neck region and the trunk were affected with equal frequency.

A tendency for police officers to avoid the face may be explained by a desire to avoid social sanctions they might experience if they produced highly visible facial injuries in their victims. This may

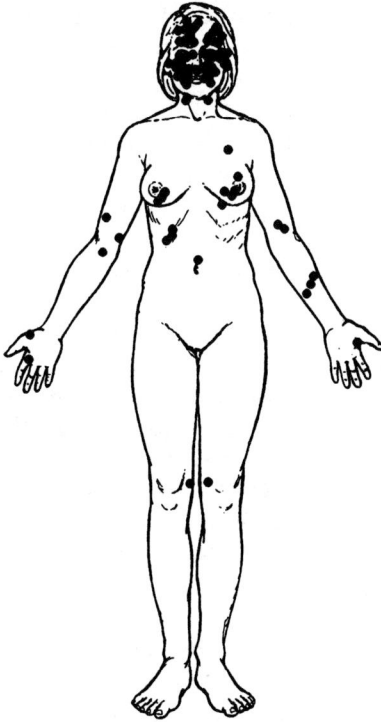

Figure 6.7. Pattern of soft tissue injury in cases of wife-beating. After Fonseka (1974).

not be an important consideration for husbands who beat their wives. On the contrary, one of their primary goals may be to stigmatize their wives with highly visible, symbolically salient signs of their physical dominance.

Cultural factors also influence the use of weapons by assailants. A study of assault victims in the United Kingdom found that injury most often resulted from punching (72% of assaults) or kicking (42% of assaults). Knife wounds were seen in 6% of victims and 11% were injured by broken drinking glasses (Shepherd *et al.* 1990). In another study of 788 patients at a large urban trauma center (Scherer *et al.* 1989), the most frequent causes of facial injuries were assault with a blunt object or fist (70.1%), followed by motor vehicle accidents (13.5%), falls (9.3%), and gunshot wounds (6.1%). The predilection for hitting, kicking and use of blunt objects

in these studies contrasts markedly with the results of a South
African study in which sharp weapons such as knives were used in
more than 50% of the attacks (Butchart and Brown 1991). Substantial differences in weapon use have also been identified in a comparative study of intentional violence in Denmark and Argentina.
In Argentina, clubs and firearms were used much more frequently
than Denmark, especially against male victims (Danielsen *et al.*
1989).

Considering the emphasis on the face as a target in interpersonal
violence, and the delicate construction of the nasal bones, it is not
surprising that most assault fractures are in the nasal area (Strom
et al. 1992, Husssain *et al* 1994, Paaske and Madsen 1987). In a
study of 950 consecutive patients at an urban, university hospital
(Hussain *et al* 1994), broken nasal bones were the most common
cranial fractures (45%), followed by cranial vault bones (24%),
mandible (13%), zygomatic (13%), orbital blow-out (3%), and maxilla (2%). In another study, 26% of the victims of violent crime
sustained at least one fracture. Nasal fractures were the most frequently observed skeletal injuries (27%) followed by zygomatic
(22%), mandibular body (12%), mandibular angle (12%), and mandibular condyle (9%) fractures (Shepherd *et al.* 1990).

A strong relationship exists between age and sex and the probability of being involved in a violent assault. Most assault victims
are young adult males (Kraus 1987, Aalund *et al.* 1990, Allan and
Daly 1990, Hussain *et al.* 1994). Modern urban craniofacial trauma
mostly involves young men. In the Johannesburg-Soweto area,
83.9% of all victims of nonfatal assaults are males. In a study of
1,162 mandibular fractures, many of which were due to assaults,
the male-female ratio was 4.4:1 and the highest incidence of trauma
was in the 20-29 year age group; these young males accounted for
nearly 40% of all patients (Allan and Daly 1990). A Chicago-area
cranial trauma study found that males were about 2.5 times more
likely than females to sustain a head injury (Whitman *et al.* 1984).

A clear contrast exists between urban areas where interpersonal
violence is the leading cause of injuries and rural areas where
automobile accidents are of greater significance. In a survey of 735
cases involving cranial injuries in Virginia during 1978 (Jagger *et al.*
1984), motor vehicles accidents accounted for most of the injuries
(55%), followed by falls (20%) and interpersonal violence (11%). In
the Chicago area, the causes of cranial injuries in the inner city
contrast markedly with those in the suburb Evanston. The leading
cause of head trauma and death from head trauma was interper-

sonal attacks for the inner city residents and vehicle accidents for the people in Evanston (Whitman *et al.* 1984). A comparable difference in the ratio of assault to accidental injuries has been documented between Bordeaux, France, and Bristol, England (Timoney *et al.* 1990). In Bordeaux, automobile accidents contribute to a high frequency of maxillary fractures. In Bristol, assault victims are a larger proportion of the people presenting with craniofacial injuries.

SPORTS INJURIES

Many sports are ritualized fights in which individuals or groups of individuals assault each other in socially sanctioned ways that reduce the likelihood of permanent injury or death. It is not surprising, therefore, that sports injuries show some similarities to those seen in assault victims. Boxing is the most obvious example; in "the manly art of self defense," the upper body and especially the head are explicitly targeted and blows below the belt prohibited (Blonstein 1965:107). As a result, about 40% of amateur boxing injures are to the head (Blonstein 1965, Enzenauer 1989). These injuries include facial cuts, especially in the eye region, and more serious injuries such as mandibular and nasal fractures.

Cranial injuries are common in team sports, particularly in stick games like hockey and lacrosse (Mayer *et al.* 1987). In hurling, an Irish game that resembles field hockey, 28% of the injuries are to the head (Crowley and Condon 1989). Almost one third of these were nasal fractures. Forehead and eyebrow lacerations, fractured zygomatic bones, and losses of teeth are also common. In soccer, nasal fractures often occur when players collide (Frenguelli *et al.* 1991).

ACCIDENTAL INJURIES

Injuries from falls and automobile collisions account for many modern cranial injuries (Gurdjian 1973:24). It is likely, therefore, that some injuries in the skeletal collections were from such accidents. Accidental injuries differ in several respects from those produced by interpersonal violence. For people between the ages of 15 and 50 years, violence is the main cause of cranial trauma. Among children and the elderly, in contrast, falls are often more important than violence as causes of cranial trauma (Hussain *et al.* 1994).

Nasal fractures from falls, in particular, are much more common in the elderly people over the age of 65 than they are in the general population (Paaske and Madsen 1987, Falcone *et al.* 1990).

Cranial injuries sustained by automobile occupants tend to concentrate in the midfacial area and in this respect are similar to those associated with interpersonal violence. Drivers are especially susceptible to nasal fractures owing to impact with the steering wheel (Rogers *et al.* 1992). Pedestrians, in contrast, show a propensity for cranial vault fractures, and bicyclists mandibular fractures (Hussain *et al.* 1994).

EXPLANATIONS OF POPULATION DIFFERENCES

The populations studied can be divided into several groups based on the frequency of cranial injuries and the distribution of these injuries on the skull (Fig. 6.8). Cranial injuries are common in some

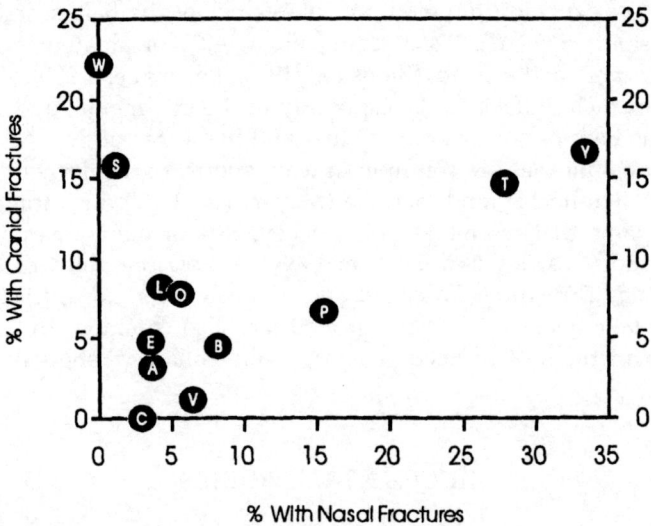

Figure 6.8. Plot of the percent of individuals with healed fractures of the nasal area against the percent of individuals with healed fractures of the cranial vault. South Aral Sea = A, Ensay = E, La Olmeda = O, Poundbury = P, Christ Church, Spitalfield = C, St Bride's Church = B, Palace of the Legion of Honor = L, Terry and Hamann-Todd = T, Burton Estates = V, Wamba = W, Santa Barbara Channel = S, Yakuts = Y.

groups and rare in others. Four of the samples had healed traumatic injuries of either the nasal area or the cranial vault in more than 10% of the crania examined (Fig. 6.8: Wamba, Santa Barbara Channel area, Terry and Hamann-Todd, and Yakuts).

The groups in which cranial injuries are common can be subdivided based on the relative frequency of nasal and cranial vault injuries. The Spaniards from Wamba and the Native Americans from the Santa Barbara Channel area are similar in that both groups have a high frequency (15–20%) of cranial vault injuries. Nasal injuries, in contrast, are almost nonexistent in these populations. These groups contrast markedly with the modern Americans in the Terry and Hamann-Todd collections and the Yakuts of eastern Siberia among whom nasal fractures are extremely common.

The lowest frequencies of cranial injuries are found in 17th–19th century Londoners buried at Christ Church and the Native Americans from the Burton Estates cemetery in Central California. Among the groups in which cranial vault injuries are rare, the Romano-British from Poundbury Camp stand out because of their comparatively high frequency of nasal injuries (Fig. 6.8).

CULTURAL AFFINITIES BETWEEN GROUPS

Cultural-historical factors clearly influence patterns of violence and this could account for some of the variation in the skeletal collections. For example, the U.S. South, and western regions of the U.S. initially settled by Southerners, are more violent than the rest of the country. Some attribute this to a traditional "culture of honor" among Southerners that endorses violence in response to insults (Nisbett 1993).

From the geographical distribution and cultural affiliations of the groups with high and low frequencies of cranial injuries, clearly this kind of cultural-historical explanation accounts for very little of the variation documented here in patterns of non-lethal violence. Groups with high and low frequencies of cranial injuries are present in Asia, Europe, and North America. Native Californians exhibit some of the highest and lowest frequencies of injuries as do the 19th and early 20th century American collections.

TEMPORAL VARIATION LEVELS OF VIOLENCE

Some differences in the frequency of injuries within the same geographical areas and cultural groups may be explained by temporal variation the frequency of interpersonal violence. For example, although the overall frequency of cranial injuries in the Santa Barbara Channel area is extremely high, there is a considerable amount of temporal variation (Walker 1989; Walker and Lambert 1989, Lambert and Walker 1991; Lambert 1994). The period around the end of the first millennium A.D. appears to have been especially violent. After that time, levels of violence decreased somewhat until the arrival of Spanish explorers (Lambert 1994). Ethnohistoric records show that there was another period of increased warfare and violence around the time of European contact (Walker and Hudson 1993, Walker and Johnson 1994).

TECHNOLOGICAL CHANGE

Differences in cranial injury frequency in culturally similar, spatially and temporally proximate groups can sometimes be explained by the introduction of new weapon technology. The introduction of the bow and arrow in the Santa Barbara Channel area, for instance, was associated with an increase in the level of lethal conflict, and a change in injury patterns (Lambert 1994). The historical and clinical literature is full of similar instances of the relationship between weapon technology and trauma patterns. Two examples are the rise of swords as dueling weapons between 1570–1620 (Cockburn 1991) and the recent increase in cranial trauma associated with the growing popularity of baseball bats as the weapon of choice for certain types of urban violence (Berlet et al. 1992, Groleau 1993).

THE RITUALIZATION OF VIOLENCE

The most remarkable feature of the cranial injury data I have collected is not that the frequency of injuries varies markedly between groups; large scale temporal and spatial variations in violence are well documented phenomena. Instead, it is the equally striking variation in the areas of the head that are injured. In the early 20th century American sample, injuries are concentrated on the face. In other groups, such as the Indians of the Santa Barbara Channel area, the nose is spared and the cranial vault is a site of frequent injury. It seems likely that cultural factors, at least in part, explain these differences in injury pattern.

THE SANTA BARBARA CHANNEL AREA

Elsewhere (Walker 1989) I have argued that the high frequency of non-lethal cranial injuries among the northern Channel Island Indians may be the result of a ritualized form of fighting in which opponents attempted to wound but not kill each other. Although there are no ethnographic descriptions of such a custom among the Channel Island Indians, the Spanish explorer Pedro Fages described fights of this sort among Indians living to the north of the Channel Islands in the Monterey area:

"If two of the natives quarrel with each other, they stand body to body, giving each other blows as best they can, using what might be called spatulas of bone, which they always carry for the purpose of scraping off their perspiration while in the bath and during the fatigue of their marches. But as soon as blood is drawn from either of the combatants, however little he may shed, the quarrel is forthwith stopped, and they become reconciled as friends even when redress of the greatest injury is sought" (Priestley 1937:67).

The development of a ritualized form of violence that facilitated non-lethal dispute resolution makes sense in view of the demographic constraints of island life. In small isolated populations such as those of the Channel Islands, resolving disputes through deadly conflict would have undesirable consequences easily comprehended by individual group members. People living in small groups can ill afford high rates of warfare related mortality. Such deaths can threaten everyone's survival. Not only is important technological information likely to be lost through the deaths of particularly knowledgeable people, but it is also possible that the size of the group will be reduced below that necessary for the performance of critical subsistence activities. The geographical circumscription of islands also greatly limits the options available for dealing with conflict. The common response of avoiding conflict by moving to a new area is not a viable option on small islands. Under such conditions the advantages of resolving disputes through non-lethal means would be obvious to everyone involved.

MODERN AMERICANS

Why are there so many broken noses in the skeletal sample of early 20th century Americans? Considerable circumstantial evidence suggests that this pattern, like that of the Channel Island Indians, is the product of a ritualized form of interpersonal violence.

An attempt to attribute some deeper cultural or symbolic significance to the concentration of injuries in the nasal area of these
modern Americans might be countered at the onset by a functional
argument. Many people assume that a fist in the face is the easiest
way to disable one's opponent. This is clearly untrue. According to
self defense books written for modern inner city dwellers, a kick to
the groin, a kick to the shin, or sharp blows to the solar plexus or
larynx are more likely to be disabling. These points are under-
scored by the modern rules of boxing which explicitly prohibit
"blows below the belt." The only blow to the face that self defense
books recommend is a specialized maneuver in which the heel of
the hand is thrust upward in a way that drives the nasal bones into
the brain.

Instead of being a longstanding functional solution to the problem of defending oneself, it seems more likely, based on the data I
have collected, that the interest of modern fighters in doing damage to their opponent's face is a recent product of cultural condi-
tioning.

Before pursuing this argument, it is important to consider the
possible contribution of accidental and sports injuries to the high
frequency of nasal fractures seen in the modern American skeletal
collections. Nasal fractures owing to impact with the steering
wheel are common in traffic accidents and may account for some of
these nasal fractures (Rogers and Mackay 1992). The proportion
that are due to this cause, however, is likely to be small. I say this
because the number of people in the population that break their
noses in automobile accidents is low in comparison to the large
number of people in these collections with nasal fractures.

Accidental falls are another common cause of modern nasal fractures, particularly in the elderly, and probably caused a number of
the modern American injuries. This explanation, however, fails to
consider the fact that in many of the other populations surveyed,
nasal fractures are virtually nonexistent. The large skeletal sample
from the Santa Barbara area, for example, contains its share of
elderly people. The hunting and gathering lifestyle and the rugged
local terrain, certainly provided ample opportunities for accidental
falls, yet healed nasal fractures are extremely rare in this group.
Likewise, nasal fractures are rare in people who lived in San Francisco and London during the 19th century (Tab. 6.2). In view of the
temporal and cultural similarities between these people and the
modern Americans, one would expect them to be similar in their
patterns of accidental injuries, yet they are not.

Sports are another common cause of nasal fractures and may be responsible for some of the excess nasal fractures in the modern American sample. Football, basketball, and baseball were popular sports in early 20th century America as they are today. Some male nasal fractures may have been sustained while playing these games. Sports injuries, however, cannot explain the fact that the women in the modern American collections have nearly as many nasal fractures as the men. This is because, until recently, American women were systematic excluded from sports involving vigorous physical activity likely to cause nasal trauma (Messner and Sabo 1990).

If accidents and sports injuries do not explain the high frequency of nasal fractures in the modern American sample, how can they be accounted for? Interpersonal violence seems a likely explanation for many of them. This is consistent with clinical data that show, in many areas of the United States, violence is the leading cause of cranial trauma. It also makes sense considering what is known about the socioeconomic status of the people involved. The Terry and Hamann-Todd collections are from medical schools. Some of these people donated their bodies to science. Many skeletons, however, are those of the indigent and homeless who were unable to provide for their own burial and whose bodies were unclaimed by relatives.

Public health surveys show that people living under such conditions are much more likely to have suffered from a history of interpersonal violence than the general public (Browne 1993, North et al. 1994). A study in St. Louis, the city the Terry Collection derives from, shows that homeless people there frequently had histories of physically aggressive behavior and violent trauma (North et al. 1994).

Attributing many nasal fractures in the crania of these early twentieth century Americans to high levels of violence in an environment of socioeconomic deprivation is not an adequate explanation of why they have so many of them. The lack of a comparable frequency of nasal injuries in the late nineteenth century burials from the Palace of the Legion of Honor cemetery in San Francisco is significant in this regard. Their socioeconomic status is likely to have been very similar to that of the people whose remains constitute the Hamann-Todd and Terry collections. Many of the people on the San Francisco cemetery appear to have been indigents who were buried in a pauper's field, yet nasal fractures are virtually absent in this sample.

PATTERNS OF VIOLENCE AND THE HISTORY OF BOXING

It is at least worth considering that the rise of the sport of boxing explains the nasal fractures of these modern Americans. Although my data are limited, this boxing hypothesis is consistent with the history of the sport and the relative frequencies of nasal and cranial vault fractures in the British, European, and American samples reviewed here.

Boxing was a favorite activity of the ancient Greeks and became a part of the Olympic Games in about 688 B.C. It continued to be popular until Roman times when it was developed into something akin to a gladiatorial sport in which the pugilists wore gloves studded with metal spikes and bloody, duel-to-death battles were common (Poliakoff 1987:68–88).

The popularity of boxing among Romans may explain the moderately high frequencies of nasal injuries in the Romano-British population of Poundbury (Fig. 6.8). The interpretation of these as boxing injuries, and not as the result of warfare, is consistent with the fact that cut marks and other evidence of lethal violence are remarkably rare in the Poundbury collection (Farwell and Molleson 1993:203).

Approval of violent combat sports was not universal in the ancient world. The Greek author Lucian points this out in an imaginary dialog between a Scythian and a Greek. The Scythian recoiled in horror as he watched Greek sports. He was especially appalled by a referee who praised a man for a well placed blow to the jaw that filled his opponent's mouth with blood (Poliakoff 1987:92). If this actually reflects the attitudes of the Scythians, it is directly relevant to explaining the low frequency of cranial injuries in collections I have studied from the south Aral Sea area (Tab. 6.3; Fig. 6.8). Many of these remains are from members of the Massagetae tribe (Yablonsky 1990), people closely allied with and culturally similar to the Scythians who may have shared their distaste for combat sports.

Boxing diminished after the fall of Rome. This may in part be due to its suppression by Christians as a pagan sport. Some authors link the decline of boxing to the rise of feudalism and a desire of the aristocracy to disarm the common people by denying them training in the skills of self defense (O'Reilly 1888). Whatever the causes of boxing's decline, it began to be replaced in Europe and Great Britain by other violent sports in which the combatants used cudgels (a short, thick stick), quarterstaffs (a pole 6 to 8 ft. long, tipped with iron), and backswords.

The rise of combat sports employing sticks after the fall of Rome perhaps explains the high frequency of cranial injuries, and the absence of nasal fractures in the 16th–18th century Spanish crania I examined from the Wamba cemetery in Castilla (Fig. 6.8). This injury pattern is very similar to that found in the Indians of the Santa Barbara Channel area and is consistent with the use of cudgel-like weapons.

The modern revival of boxing occurred in England at the beginning of the 18th century (Butler 1972: 6–7). At first, boxing matches appear to have been sideshows, staged by masters of stickfighting in conjunction with cudgel and backsword matches. Boxing rapidly gained popularity and by the 1720's well attended boxing matches were frequent events.

It is, I believe, not coincidental that the rise in the popularity of prizefighting coincides precisely with a change in English homicide patterns (Fig. 6.9, Cockburn 1991:81–82). Before 1720, coroner's records indicate that blunt objects such as clubs were frequently used as murder weapons. Although deaths attributed to "hitting and kicking" occurred, they were not especially common. This prevalence of blunt instrument deaths is consistent with the popu-

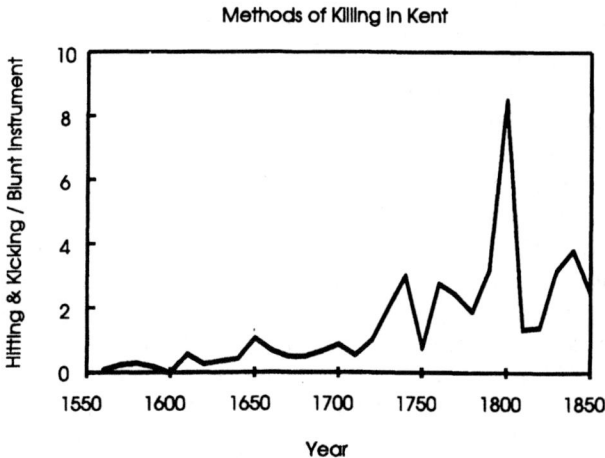

Figure 6.9. Ratio of deaths from hitting and kicking to deaths from blunt instruments. Methods of killing in the English county Kent were determined based on coroner's inquest records. These data are from Cockburn (1991 Table 2).

larity of stick fighting during this period. The birth of modern boxing is accompanied by a decrease in the number of blunt instrument homicides and a sharp increase in the number of hitting and kicking deaths. Hitting and kicking deaths peaked between 1780 and 1800 and then declined precipitously during the first two decades of the 19th century.

The trend toward an increase in hitting and kicking deaths, spans the formative period of English prizefighting (Ford 1971:26). Although it was declared illegal by an act of parliament in 1750, it continued to gain in popularity until the mid 1820's when it declined. Prizefights continued to be held throughout the 19th century but they seem never to have regained their former popularity.

Although boxing experienced periods of popularity in the United States throughout the nineteenth century, the end of the bare-knuckle era marked by the 1892 fight between Corbett and Sullivan was a clear turning point. At this time the sport became increasingly commercialized and, as a result, public interest in it increased (Gorn 1986).

It seems possible that the development of professional boxing at the beginning of the 20th century resulted in a change in fighting patterns used by people involved in violent domestic conflict. In this respect, the high frequency of nasal fractures in the early 20th century Americans may be similar to the changes in patterns of violence seen during the rise in the popularity of boxing in 18th century England.

If this hypothesis is true, then the strong propensity for modern men to assault their wives by beating them in the face (Fig. 7) owes more to lessons learned thorough the observation of and participation in the sport of boxing than it does to any innate tendency for humans to injure each other in this way.

The idea that beating people in the face with the fists during fights is a recent revitalization of an ancient behavior pattern is supported by the low frequency of nasal injuries in the skeletons of the people who were buried in San Francisco at the Palace of the Legion of Honor cemetery during the last half of the 19th century. In certain respects, these people fit the two-fisted, gun toting stereotype of the cowboys and miners who frequented San Francisco at this time. Many of them show skeletal changes in the bones of their hips associated with spending long hours on horseback, and several died of gunshot wounds to the head. The idea that fist fighting was a common cowboy activity, however, is belied by the low frequency of broken noses. This part of the "wild west" stereotype seems more a projection by cinematographers of the early twentieth American fascination with boxing than it is a reflection of historical reality.

THE YAKUTS

The Yakuts, of eastern Siberia are the only group comparable to the modern Americans in terms of the frequency of nasal fractures. Although the number of 18th-early 20th century Yakuts crania I was able to examine is small, clearly nasal injuries are exceedingly common among these people. In view of the cultural differences between these pastoralists and modern Americans, the cause of their injuries seems unlikely, at first, to be related to Western boxing. Fortunately, the culture-history of the Yakuts is well documented and provides some plausible explanations for their pattern of cranial trauma.

It is possible that some of the Yakuts nasal fractures are sports injuries. Czaplicka (1916) describes a popular Yakuts game called maasyuk that in many respects is similar to soccer. The ball is made of reindeer skin and is kicked and butted about with the head and "propelled by almost any means short of manslaughter" (Czaplicka 1916:117–118). Fouling is not penalized and if a kick is impossible, the ball may be picked up and thrown. In view of the clinical evidence that nasal fractures are a common result of collisions between soccer players (Frenguelli et al. 1991), this type of sports injury may well account for some of the nasal fractures, especially among Yakuts men.

There are other ethnographic data, however, that suggest another less attractive explanation for the prevalence of Yakuts cranial trauma. The subjugation of the Yakuts by the Russians was an extremely violent affair, reminiscent in many ways of the conquest of Native American cultures by European colonists. Beginning in the 17th century, Russians began to exert political control over the Yakuts and attempted to extract taxes. Resistance was met with such punishments as amputation of the ear, nose, or tongue, removing eyes, or burial in the ground up to the eyes. Yakuts were also quartered, impaled, boiled in cauldrons, and flayed alive (Shklovsky 1916:207–209).

During later times, Yakuts suffered terribly from their contacts with transported Russian criminals. It seems likely that the social disruption and Western patterns of violence introduced by these people accounts for many Yakuts cranial injuries. Weeks of drunkenness were apparently common among both natives and soldiers in Yakuts territory (Shklovsky 1916:199).

For Yakuts women, these problems of culture-shock were compounded by their low status in traditional Yakuts society. In comparison to boys, girls were considered of little value. Women had no inheritance rights and the sale of daughters was not unheard of during the 19th century (Kharuzin 1898: 43–44, 49–50, 53–54). According to Kharuzin (1898:42–43) if a woman's husband beat her "without good reason from the point of view of the Yakuts, then the wife had to right to complain to the clan government or to apply for protection from the tribal court."

The Yakuts practice of protecting their wives and daughters from the *haillak* (transported Russian criminals) by giving the Russians orphan Yakuts girls to cohabit with is directly relevant to explaining the high frequency of facial fractures in Yakuts women: "Pitiable indeed is the plight of this wretched girl: Her terrible tyrant rules her with fist and cudgel, and her face is never free from bruises. The *haillak* so despises the Yakuts, that he may live for years among them and the only word of their language which he will condescend to learn is "give!" (Shklovsky 1916: 72–73).

CONCLUSIONS

The systematic analysis of skeletal evidence for patterns of violence in earlier human populations is in its infancy. It seems clear that such research has enormous unrealized potential. There are several reasons for this. Until recently, most of the research on ancient violence has consisted of detailed descriptions and analyses of individual cases. This "case" approach has a long and distinguished history in the medical sciences and reflects the dominant role physicians have played in the field of paleopathology. The lack of a population perspective is a second reason for the unrealized potential of such studies and stems directly from this emphasis on the description of specific cases. For example, although we know that individual people throughout the world occasionally suffered from arrow wounds, almost nowhere are data available for making even a rough estimate of how frequent such injuries might have been. This is not surprising since to do so is a time consuming task. It requires the systematic examination not only of the small number of individuals with interesting injuries but also the large number of people whose remains lack any evidence of trauma. Although this kind of laborious research can at times be tedious, I hope that I have shown that it can be a rewarding scientific endeavor.

One thing is certain: as the amount of systematically collected data on collections from different locations and historical periods increases, so will the diversity of patterns of violence documented. This is good. Only through the identifying and analyzing the full range of human behavioral variation can we hope to understand the complex interactions between demographic variables, environmental change, and cultural-historical processes that shape our aggressive tendencies.

ACKNOWLEDGEMENTS

I thank Pat Lambert and Eric Ratliff for allowing me to use their unpublished data on Santa Barbara Channel area collections. Anne Haque's assistance greatly facilitated my work at the British Museum. I am grateful to the following people for allowing me to study collections under their care: Dave Hunt and Carol Butler (Smithsonian Institution), Lyman Jellema and Bruce Latimer (Cleveland Museum of Natural History), Leonid Yablonsky (Russian Academy of Sciences, Moscow), Juri Chistov and Sasha Kozinstev (Peter the Great Museum, St. Petersburg), Louise Scheuer, the Leverhulme Trust, and Canon John Oates (St. Bride's Church, London), Theya Mollison and A.E. Miles (British Museum (Natural History), London), Alejandro Perez-Perez, Carles Lalueza, and Daniel Turbon (University of Barcelona), Gonzalo Trancho (Universidad Compultense, Madrid), John Johnson (Santa Barbara Museum of Natural History), Charles Slaymaker and Suzanne Griset (Slaymaker and Associates), Mary Norten (Patwin Tribe), and Boyd Stephens (San Francisco Medical Examiners Office). Francine Drayer and Susan Siefkin collected the data on the Palace of the Legion of Honor burials. Cynthia Brock, Clark Larsen, and Don Symons provided valuable comments on the manuscript. My work in Spain was supported by a grant from the National Endowment for the Humanities. The analysis of the Santa Barbara Channel area collections was supported by NSF grant BNS 85-07836.

REFERENCES

Aalund, O. Danielsen, L. and Sanhueza, R. O., (1990). "Injuries Due to Deliberate Violence in Chile." *Forensic Science International* **46(3)**: 189–202.

Allan, B. P. and Daly, C.G. (1990). "Fractures of the Mandible. A 35-year Retrospective Study." *International Journal of Oral and Maxillofacial Surgery* **19(5)**:268–71.

Bass, W.M. (1971). *Human Osteology: Laboratory and Field Manual of the Human Skeleton.* Columbia Missouri: Missouri Archaeological Society and University of Missouri.

Berlet, A. C. Talenti, D. B. and Carroll, S. F. (1992). "The Baseball Bat: a Popular Mechanism of Urban Injury." *Journal of Trauma* **33(2)**:167–70.

Blonstein, J. L. (1965). *Boxing Doctor.* London: Stanley Paul.

Browne, A. (1993). "Family Violence and Homelessness: the Relevance of Trauma Histories in the Lives of Homeless Women." *American Journal of Orthopsychiatry* **63(3)**:370–84.

Butchart, A. and Brown, D. S. (1991). "Non-fatal injuries due to interpersonal violence in Johannesburg-Soweto: Incidence, Determinants and Consequences." *Forensic Science International* **52(1)**:35–51.

Butler, F. (1972). *A History of Boxing in Britain: A Survey of the Noble Art from its Origins to the Present-day.* London: Barker.

Chagnon, N. A. (1992). *Yanomamo.* 4th ed., Fort Worth: Harcourt Brace Jovanovich College Publishers.

Cockburn, J. S. (1991). "Patterns of Violence in English Society: Homicide in Kent 1560–1985. *Past and Present* **130**:70–106.

Crowley, P. J. and Condon, K. C. (1989). "Analysis of Hurling and Camogie Injuries." *British Journal of Sports Medicine* **23(3)**:183–5.

Czaplicka, M. A. (1916). *My Siberian Year.* London: Mills and Boom.

Danielsen, L. Aalund, O. Mazza, P. H. and Katz, A. (1989). "Injuries Due to Deliberate Violence in Areas of Argentina. II. Lesions. Copenhagen Study Group." *Forensic Science International* **42**:165–75.

Enzenauer, R. W. Montrey, J. S. Enzenauer, R. J. and Mauldin, W. M. (1989). "Boxing-Related Injuries in the US Army, 1980 Through 1985." *Journal of the American Medical Association* **261**:1463–6.

Falcone, P. A. Haedicke, G. J. Brooks, G. and Sullivan, P. K. (1990). "Maxillofacial Fractures in the Elderly: a Comparative study." *Plastic and Reconstructive Surgery* **86**:443–8.

Farwell, D. E. and Molleson, T. L. (1993). *Excavations at Poundbury 1966–80, Volume II: The Cemeteries.* Dorset Natural History and Archaeological Society. Monograph Series Number 11.

Fonseka, S. (1974). "A Study of Wife-beating in the Camberwell Area." *British Journal of Clinical Practice.* **28(12)**:400–402.

Ford, J. (1972). Prizefighting: *The Age of Regency Boximania.* South Brunswick: Great Albion Books.

Frenguelli, A., Ruscito, P., Bicciolo, G., Rizzo, S. and Massarelli M., (1991). "Head and Neck Trauma in Sporting Activities. Review of 208 Cases." *Journal of Cranio-Maxillo-Facial Surgery.* **19**:178–81.

Gorn, E. J. (1986). *The Manly Art: Bare-knuckle Prize Fighting in America.* Ithaca: Cornell University Press.

Groleau, G. A., Tso, E. L., Olshaker, J. S., Barish, R. A., and Lyston D. J., (1993). "Baseball Bat Assault Injuries." *Journal of Trauma* **34**:366–72.

Gurdjian, E. S. (1973). *Head Injury from Antiquity to the Present with Special Reference to Penetrating Head Wounds.* Springfield Illinois: Charles C. Thomas.

Hussain, K., Wijetunge, D. B., Grubnic, S. and Jackson, I. T., (1994). "A Comprehensive Analysis of Craniofacial Trauma." *Journal of Trauma* **36**:34–47.

Jagger, J., Levine, J. I., Jane, J. A., Rimel, R. W. (1984). "Epidemiologic Features of Head Injury in a Predominantly Rural Population." *Journal of Trauma.* **24**:40–4.

Kharuzin, A. N. (1898). "*Iuridicheskiia obichai IAkutov* (The Juridical Customs of the Yakut)." Ethnograficheskoe Obozrenie **10**:37–64.

Kjaerulff H., Jacobsen, J., Aalund, O., Albrektsen, S. B., Breiting, V. B., Danielsen, L., Helweg-Larsen, K., Staugaard, H. and Thomsen, J. L., (1989). "Injuries Due to Deliberate Violence in Areas of Denmark. III. Lesions. The Copenhagen Study Group." *Forensic Science International.* **1**:169–180.

Kraus, J. F. (1987). "Epidemiology of Head Injury." In: *Head Injury* (2nd Edition), ed. P.R. Cooper, Williams and Wilkins: New York. pp. 1–19.

Krogman, W. M. (1962). *The Human Skeleton in Forensic Medicine.* Springfield TL: Charles C. Thomas.

Lambert, P. M. (1994). *War and Peace on the Western Front: A Study of Violent Conflict and its Correlates in Prehistoric Hunter-gatherer Societies of Coastal Southern California.* Unpublished Ph.D. Dissertation, University of California, Santa Barbara.

Lambert P. M., and Walker, P. L. (1991). "Physical Anthropological Evidence for the Evolution of Social Complexity in Coastal Southern California." *Antiquity* **65**:963–973.

Laub, J. H. and J. L. Lauritsen (1993). "Violent Criminal Behavior Over the Life Course: a Review of the Longitudinal and Comparative Research." *Violence and Victims* **8**:235–52.

Mayer N. E., J. G. Kenney, R. C. Edlich, and R. F. Edlich (1987). "Fractures in Women Lacrosse Players: Preventable Injuries." *Journal of Emergency Medicine* **5**:177–80.

McDowell, J. D., Kassebaum, D. K. and Stromboe, S. E., (1992). "Recognizing and Reporting Victims of Domestic Violence." *Journal of the American Dental Association* **123**:44–50.

Messner, M. A., and Sabo D. F., (Eds.) (1990). *Sport, Men, and the Gender Order: Critical Feminist Perspectives.* Champaign, ITL.: Human Kinetics Books.

Nisbett, R. E. (1993). "Violence and U.S. Regional Culture." *American Psychologist* **48**:441–9.

North, C. S., Smith, E. M. and Spitznagel, E. L., (1994). "Violence and the Homeless: an Epidemiologic Study of Victimization and Aggression." *Journal of Trauma and Stress* **7**:95–110.

O'Reilly, J. B. (1888). *Ethics of Boxing and Manly Sport*. Boston: Ticknor and company.

Paaske, P. B. and Madsen, E. F. (1987) Naesefrakturer. Ugestrift Laeger **149**:1562–1563.

Poliakoff, M. B. (1987). *Combat Sports in the Ancient World, Competition, Violence and Culture*. New Haven: Yale University Press.

Priestley, HI (1937) *A Historical Political, and Natural Description of California by Pedro Fages, Soldier of Spain*. Berkeley: University of California.

Rogers, S., Hill, J. R. and Mackay, G. M., (1992). "Maxillofacial Injuries Following Steering Wheel Contact by Drivers Using Seat Belts." *British Journal of Oral and Maxillofacial Surgery* **30**:24–30.

Scherer, M., Sullivan, W. G., Smith, D. J. Jr., Phillips, L. G. and Robson, M. C., (1989). "An Analysis of 1,423 facial fractures in 788 Patients at an Urban Trauma Center." *Journal of Trauma* **29**:388–90.

Shepherd J. P., Shapland, M., Pearce, N. X., Scully, C., (1990). "Pattern, Severity and Aetiology of Injuries in Victims of Assault." *Journal of the Royal Society of Medicine* **83**:75–78.

Shklovsky, I. W. (1916). *In Far North-East Siberia*. London: Macmillan.

Strom, C., Johanson, G. and Nordenram, A., (1992). "Facial Injuries due to Criminal Violence: a Retrospective Study of Hospital Attenders." *Medicine, Science and the Law* **32**:345–53.

Timoney, N., Saiveau, M., Pinsolle, J. and Shepherd, J., (1990). "A Comparative Study of Maxillo-facial Trauma in Bristol and Bordeaux." *Journal of Craniomaxillofacial Surgery* **18**:154–7.

Walker, P. L. (1989). "Cranial Injuries as Evidence of Violence Prehistoric Southern California." *American Journal of Physical Anthropology*. 80(3):313–323.

———— (1994). "Problems of Preservation and Sexism in Sexing: Some Lessons from Historical Collections for Paleodemographers." In *Grave Reflections: Portraying the Past Through Skeletal Studies*, eds. A. Herring and S. Saunders, Canadian Scholars' Press Inc., pp 31–47.

Walker, P. L., and T. D. Hudson (1993). *Chumash Healing: Changing Health and Medical Practices in an American Indian Society*. Banning CA:Malki Museum Press.

Walker, P. L., and Johnson, J., (1994). The Decline of the Chumash Indian Population." In: C. Larsen and G. Milner (eds.), *In the Wake of Contact: Biological Responses to Conquest*. Wiley-Liss: New York. pp. 109–120.

Walker, P. L., and Lambert, P. M., (1989). "Skeletal Evidence for Stress During a Period of Cultural Change in Prehistoric California." In: Luigi Capasso (ed.), Advances in Paleopathology, *Journal of Paleopathology: Monographic* **1**, pp. 207–212,

Walker, P. L., Dean, G. and Shapiro, P., (1991). "Estimating Age from Dental Were in Archaeological Polulations." In *Advances in Dental Anthropology*, M. Kelley and C. S. Larsen, pp. 169–178. New York:Alan R. Liss.

White, T. D. (1991). Human Osteology. San Diego: Academic Press.

Whitman, S., Coonley-Hoganson, R. and Desai, B. T., (1984). "Comparative Head Trauma Experiences in Two Socioeconomically Different Chicago-area Communities: a Population Study." *American Journal of Epidemiology* **119**:570–80.

Yablonsky, L. T. (1990). "Burial Place of a Massagetan Warrior." *Antiquity* **64(243)**.

Chapter
SEVEN

Ofnet: Evidence for a Mesolithic Massacre

David W. Frayer
Department of Anthropology
University of Kansas

With the discovery of cutmarks on the Bodo cranium (White 1986) and the recognition of others on numerous fossil and subfossil specimens (Ullrich and White 1988), there has been an heightened interest in evidence for violence in the Old World prehistoric record. It is clear that considerable evidence exists for burial preparation and ritualism in ancient populations, part of which would seem to relate to violence and homicide. Some of the research has led to a resurgence of interpretations for cannibalism in the fossil record, bolstered by the discovery at La Baume Fontebregoua of sound evidence in the French Neolithic for the mutilation and food preparatory techniques involving human bones (Villa 1992; Villa *et al.* 1986). Since no one assumes that the victims were scavenged, this must mean that homicide preceded the cannibalism. Besides paleontological concerns, with the re-analysis of hunter-gatherer and horticultural population dynamics, it has become apparent that many pre-state societies do not fit their peaceful, "harmless people" stereotype. Clearly, violence leading to homicide is an ordinary occurrence in most ethnographic-present hunter-gatherer and horticultural groups (e.g, Chagnon 1988; Knauft 1987). As Ember observed some years ago,

> [I]f we exclude equestrian hunters... and those with 50 percent or more dependence on fishing... warfare is rare for only 12 percent of the remaining hunter-gatherers. In sum, hunter-gatherers could hardly be described as peaceful (1978:443).

It is evident that one reason for the underestimation of levels of violence and homicide in pre-state societies relates to past theoretical expectations about the harmonious nature of hunter-gatherer societies. This is especially true when the Dobe !Kung were used to typify hunter-gatherers (Lewin 1988). With further research on violence and homicide in pre-state groups, it is clear that both were common occurrences in many pre-state groups. While many ethnologists have underestimated (or under-recorded) lethal violence in the groups they study or in the ethnographic record in general, paleoanthropologists have probably overestimated the incidence of violence and homicide in the fossil record. Beginning with Dart's ideas about bloodbaths among the earliest hominids (Ardrey 1961; Dart 1953) and continuing to European Upper Pleistocene samples where cannibalism has often been postulated (e.g., Malez 1985), a substantial number of fossils have been interpreted as having met some kind of violent end. More than 25 years ago, Roper (1969) catalogued cases of prehistoric violence from australopithecines to early moderns. Given the difficulty in determining the cause of healed wounds in absence of a weapon buried in the bone, as Roper noted, very few of the specimens she tabulated can be confirmed as resulting from interpersonal violence or a homicide. In a later study of traumatic injuries in the Western European Mesolithic, Constandse–Westermann and Newell (1982:75) suggest that, except where a projectile point is present, it is difficult to separate "inflicted" from "accidental" trauma. With cautious interpretation, the injuries on many fossils are not especially telling about the specific incident of trauma responsible for the injury. For example, the healed head wounds on the Zhoukoudian skulls (Weidenreich 1939, 1943) or many of the Shanidar Neanderthal skeletons (Trinkaus 1983) may indicate violence, but just as likely could be the result of human-animal interactions, hunting accidents, accidental falls, or a myraid of other "natural" etiologies.

Obviously, evidence for perimortem trauma or indications of violence leading to a suspicion of homicide are difficult to demonstrate in the fossil record. Perhaps, the earliest recorded case is Skhul IX which possesses multiple evidence for perimortem injuries (McCown and Keith 1939). Following their analysis, the individual was speared one or two times in the left leg, with one spear thrust immobilizing the hip and penetrating the pelvic cavity, undoubtedly leading to the death of the individual. The same specimen shows indications of perimortem head wounds, although McCown and Keith were less certain of these. Much later in time, in the European Mesolithic, numerous cases of mortal injuries are known which must have been homicides. One case, an adult male (# 16) from Téviec (France), has two arrow tips buried in thoracic vertebrae 6 and 11 (Boule and Vallois 1939). Neither wounds show signs of healing and provide evidence for a prehistoric murder, unless one postulates that the victim fell backward on his spears. There is also homicidal evidence in skeletons from other Mesolithic sites, such as Henriksholm/Bøgebakken (Denmark) where an adult male (# 19A) in a triple grave was found with a bone point piercing the ventral intervertebral space between the 6 and 7 cervicals (Albrethsen and Brinch Petersen 1976). If found in a modern context, there would be little doubt for suspecting a homicide in such cases.

Finally, in the Upper Paleolithic and Mesolithic, there are a number of double and multiple interments of complete skeletons which are likely the result of homicides. While none preserve evidence of perimortem trauma, the fact that the corpses were buried simultaneously is suspicious since it is unlikely that two or three people would die of natural causes at the same time. Examples of these cases include the early Gravettian burial at Dolní Věstonice of three young males, the triple burial at Barma Grande of a male and two females, numerous double burials (e.g., Parabita, Grotte des Enfants, Romito), and multiple individual interments at numerous Mesolithic sites (e.g., Henriksholm/Bøgebakken, Skateholm, Téviec).

In addition to these cases, the late Mesolithic site of Ofnet in Bavaria, provides a relatively unique example of prehistoric violence: a massacre in which a large number of men, women and children were slaughtered with selected parts buried in two mass graves. This site represents the first clear evidence for a mass murder in prehistory, yet is seldom mentioned in the literature. As proposed here, Ofnet represents one of the earliest and most convincing sites for interpersonal violence in prehistory.

BACKGROUND ON THE SITE

Human sketetal remains from Ofnet were excavated by Schmidt in 1908. Prior attempts to excavate the sediments were foiled by a large ceiling rock which covered most of the exposed floor. But, after this slab was blasted apart, excavations proceeded in 1908. The cave is a small, low chamber with a single opening which faces southwest. The limited space in the cave precluded its use as a habitation site and, except for the "skull nests" described below, archaeological discoveries in the cave are meager. All human material derived from two pits dug into a late Magdalenian deposit (level VI), located about 0.9 meters below the original cave floor (Schmidt 1913). The pits were overlain by Neolithic and later deposits, and the two mass graves were at approximately the same depth, separated from each other by about one meter (Fig. 7.1). The larger of the two pits measured .76 meters in diameter, the smaller pit was .45 meters across. As initially described by Schmidt (1913), the heads were placed in the shallow pits like "eggs in a basket" with the most of the faces pointing west. In both pits, only skulls along with cervical vertabrae were found, so that the only post-cranial remains associated with the skulls are cervical vertebrae. All the human material was heavily stained with red ochre and a

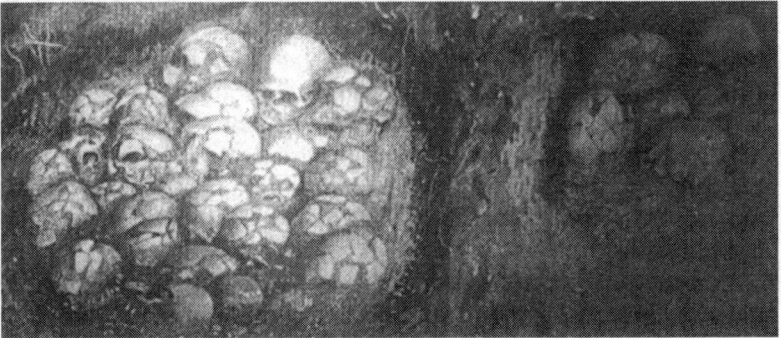

Figure 7.1. The two skull nests at Ofnet as depicted by Schmidt (1913).

number of pierced red deer teeth and shells were found associated exclusively with heads of adult females and unsexed subadults.

All reports on this material list 33 individuals (27 from the main pit; six from the smaller one), but most previous investigators considered this a minimum count (e.g., Gieseler 1951:292). In my work with the material, an effort was made to compile a complete inventory of the individuals from both pits. This was not an easy task, since the collection has been studied numerous times by different people and a certain amount of mixing of the bones must have occurred. While making the inventory it was apparent that several of the individual specimen boxes included isolated teeth or bones which could not belong to the main specimen in the box either because the age did not match or because an isolated bone duplicated a bone present on the more complete specimen. After attempts to crossmatch isolated bones (or teeth) with other specimens found in the grave near the main specimen in the box, I arrived at four individuals above the original estimates. Each of these came from the main pit. The inventoried specimens are listed in Table 7.1 and those with an "a" following the Anthropologische Staatssammulung catalog number (e.g., 2476.3a) represent the additional specimens. Another specimen from Ofnet was discovered in the collections of the Institut für Anthropologie und Humangenetik, Tübingen. This fragmentary, young adult female (with no information about provenience other than noted as deriving from "Grosse Ofnethöhle") is listed in Table 7.1 as number 900. Thus, my inventory of Ofnet amounts to 38 individuals, 31 from the large pit (2474.1–2499.27), six from the small one (2500.28–2505.33), and an additional individual (900) which cannot be assigned to either pit. Technically, this is a minimum number of individuals from the two pits, but it is difficult to imagine that the estimate does not also represent a maximum number of individuals.

Except where noted below, sex was determined by traditional osteological techniques. After initial sexing, all the adult skulls were laid out on a table and seriated from the most robust to the most gracile. Generally speaking there was a clear differentiation between male and female skulls, with little overlap in levels of robusticity and gracility, although this does not assure sexing is 100% accurate. Sexing reported here is similar to results obtained by Scheidt (1923). Aging of subadults was accomplished by tooth eruption, using standards published by Ubelaker (1978). Once the third molar was erupted, individuals were aged by tooth wear as

Table 7.1. Ofnet: Specimen Inventory

Specimen#	Sex	Age	Specimen #	Sex	Age
2474.1	?	5–6	2488.16	?	2
2475.2	Male	Adult	2489.17	?	2–3
2476.3	Female	Y.Adult	2490.18*	Female	Adult
2476.3a	?	5	2491.19	?	3–4
2477.4*	Female	Adult	2492.20	?	9–10
2478.5	?	7–8	2493.21*	Male	Y.Adult
2479.6	?	1–2	2494.22	?	3–4
2479.6a	?	1–2	2495.23	?	6–7
2480.7	?	7–8	2496.24*	Male	O.Adult
2481.8	Female	Y. Adult	2497.25	Female	15–16
2482.9	?	4–5	2498.26*	?	7
2482.9a	?	0–1	2499.27	?	2–3
2483.10	?	11	2500.28	?	5–6
2484.11	Male	Y. Adult	2501.29	Female	17–18
2484.11a	?	4–5	2502.30	?	8–9
2485.12	?	7–8	2503.31	?	6–7
2486.13*	Female	Y. Adult	2504.32	Male	Y. Adult
1812.14	Female	15	2505.33	?	3
2487.15	Female	Adult	900	Female	Y. Adult

*specimen with ancient cutmarks on the vault (see text)

Young Adult, Adult, and Old Adult. Table 7.1 summarizes the results of aging and sexing.

Since the discovery of these two skull pits, the cultural affiliation and age of the skeletal material from Ofnet has been much debated. Schmidt (1913) described and illustrated two geometric microliths, which he attributed to the "Azilian-Tardenoisian." Subsequent analysis of these triangles indicates they are typical of post-Upper Paleolithic times (Naber 1974; Schulte im Walde *et al.* 1986), and, given their diagnostic usefulness, it is fortunate that one was found in both the large and the small pit. From these details it seems that the two pits are probably contemporaneous with each other, at least culturally. Despite what appear to be diagnostic tools of the Mesolithic, their presence at the site did not convince everyone of a Mesolithic cultural affiliation, since some argued for a late Upper Paleolithic or Neolithic date. For example, before the application of absolute dating techniques, Breuil (1909), Boule and Vallois (1957), Gieseler (1938, 1949, 1951), and Saller (1962) were comfortable with a Mesolithic attribution, while Birkner (1915), Mollison (1936), and Scheidt (1923) considered the site as either Azilian or late Magdalenian. At least one scholar has suggested a Neolithic affiliation (Schwidetzky 1970). For some the radiocarbon determinations of 13,100 ± 100 B.P. and the seemingly confirmatory amino racemization dates of 13,000 B.P. by Glowatzki and Protsch (1973) clinched the late Upper Paleolithic date of these remains (e.g., Newell *et al.* 1979:157). However, both Naber (1974) and Frayer (1978) contested the dates and discounted the Upper Paleolithic attribution based on suspicions about the reliability of the dating techniques and inconsistencies with the archaeological information. A more recent C^{14} determination suggests the site is better attributed to the Mesolithic. This date run at Köln on cranial pieces indicates the site clearly belongs in the late Mesolithic, with an age of 7720 ± 80 B.P. (Schulte im Walde *et al.* 1986; Schwabedissen 1983). A second date for the Ofnet material has been published later (Hedges *et al.* 1989) using the Oxford accelerator. This run, based on five separate skull fragments from both pits, has a narrow time span and low associated error (7360 ± 80 − 7560 ± 110 B.P.). With these new dates there can be little doubt that the Ofnet material is solidly dated to the late Mesolithic and that the two pits are roughly contemporaneous.

Work by paleoanthropologists on the skeletal remains has mainly centered on two issues: (1) the variation in cranio-facial form, particularly as it related to the identification of racial types (Heberer *et al.* 1959; Merkenschlager and Saller 1934; Saller 1962; Scheidt 1923) and (2) the analysis and interpretation of evidence for violence in the cranial and limited infracranial remains (Gieseler 1949, 1951; Mollison 1936; Saller 1962). This paper focuses on evidence for the grisly end of the remains preserved in the two pits at Ofnet.

Before reviewing the evidence for perimortem trauma, it is important to consider the original state of the collection and some of the history of the work performed on it, since these definitely have an impact on interpretations about the evidence for violence at the site. Today, preservation is excellent for most of the Ofnet material. But the current condition of the cranial remains belies the state of most of the remains until about 1962. According to Scheidt (1923, quoted in Saller 1962:4–5)

> The majority of the pieces found at Ofnet are very fragile and consist of numerous fragments. The reconstruction... presented difficulties, because most of the skulls were compressed and heavily deformed by the layers of overburden. Therefore, a complete and indisputable reconstruction was not possible in most cases [translated from German].

The first round of reconstructions was accomplished by the preparator Witscher in Stuttgart, but only the most intact skulls were
reconstituted (Saller 1962:4). Apparently, during the initial reconstructions a considerable amount of plaster was used, since when
Mollison (and Saller's wife) made a second attempt at reconstitut-
ing the skulls in the early 1930s, their job was made difficult by the
removal of plaster (Saller 1962:8). During this second attempt at
reconstruction under Mollison's direction, after the plaster was removed, the skulls were disassembled and hardened with "Zaponlack" (Saller 1962:8). After the reconstructions were completed, it
is apparent that the skulls were covered with a heavy coat of
lacquer. These conservation procedures were obviously important
for the preservation of the fragile bone, but they probably eliminated forever the chance to conduct SEM analysis on the crania.
Further work in München was done by the preparator Hirschuber,
who filled the missing areas with plaster and stained the filler to
match the red stained bone in a few specimens (Schröter pers.
comm.).

Following the discovery of the skull nests, five of the adults were
very crudely molded. These copies still exist in the Institut für
Anthropologie und Humangenetik, Tübingen, and, as far as I am
aware, there is no published account of the origin of these rough
casts. At least one specimen (Ofnet 2493.21) was molded a second
time in München in the 1930s (Schröter pers. comm.). As discussed
below, production of these casts is relevant to the appearance of
cutmarks on some of the cranial vaults.

Thus, what started as a crushed, deformed mishmash of fragile
skulls became the well-reconstructed collection now housed in
München. Obviously this work has been of great benefit to those
interested in the metric and morphological description of the material. Yet, the repeated reconstructions and restorations have complicated interpretations about the origin of the holes and the many
cutmarks which occur on the vaults.

EVIDENCE FOR PERIMORTEM VIOLENCE: BLUDGEON MARKS

The first person to study the collection for evidence of violence was
Mollison (1936). Previous workers had discounted any indications
of violence (except for the possibility of cutmarks on the vertebrae),
but upon undertaking a new round a reconstructions, Mollison
convincingly demonstrated that some of the skulls showed

evidence of bludgeon marks. Mollison provided a description of 33 skulls and conducted a forensic analysis for each specimen. According to him, violence was signalled by elliptical holes found on the vault and face. Mollison (1936:79) noted that

> A large number of skulls show... injuries caused by blows with stone hatchets, carried out with so much force that they destroyed the wall of the skull when the hatchet penetrated deep into the skull. Many of the injuries are obvious to anyone who the worked with skull injuries. [translated from German]

He based this evaluation on the common shape of the holes and the fact that the edges of these holes were beveled, with the broken angle widening from the ecto- to the endocranial surface. Mollison also noted evidence for bone scars flaked from the endocranial surface. In a later review of the material, Saller (1962) found no reason to dispute Mollison's interpretations.

With the discovery of the three isolated skulls at Hohlenstein (some 40km SW of Ofnet) the year after Mollison's report was published, further evidence surfaced for corroborating the evidence for violence at Ofnet. These three specimens (a young adult male, young adult female and two-year old infant) were buried in a shallow, funnel-shaped depression, aligned with the male in front and the female and infant in the rear (Gieseler 1951). Like Ofnet the specimens were heavily stained with red ochre and the only postcranial remains were cervical vertebrae. Except for some "frauenfisch" (carp) vertebrae, no other cultural materials were associated with the triple head burial. Gieseler described unmistakable evidence for perimortem violence on the adult crania and concluded that "[v]iolent death of the people of Hohlenstein seems to be the only possible conclusion" (1951:296). He drew parallels to the situation at Ofnet, noting similarity in burial treatment, skull orientation, and cutmarks on the cervical vertebrae. The only major difference was the shape of the cranial holes which at Hohlenstein did not take the lozenge form found at Ofnet.

Based on these previous analyses, the Ofnet remains were studied to verify the presence of perimortem trauma. All work was done on the original specimens housed at München and Tübingen. Each specimen was studied on two different occasions, once in 1986 and again in 1988. The skulls were inspected by eye and with a hand lens, cutmarks were recorded, and the bludgeon holes were measured in their two major axes, as well as drawn on standardized cranial outlines. Since numerous skulls are missing parts of the vault and face, four main criteria were used to distinguish perimortem from postmortem holes. These included

(1) beveling of the fractured wall of the holes. Only cases where the angle of the level increased from the ecto- to the endocranial surface were identified as perimortem injuries.
(2) hinge fractures and spalling on the endocranial surface.
(3) compression fractures radiating from the hole located on the ectocranial surface.
(4) color of the fractured vault wall. Since the specimens were reconstructed several times, soaked in "Zaponlack," and possibly re-stained for aesthetic purposes, this criterion was not especially useful, except in identifying recent breaks.

The first three of these features correspond to criteria used for the identification of blunt weapon injuries (and fatalities) in forensic medicine. For example, in describing depressed skull fractures related to massive blunt forces Courville (1962:310) states

> Radiating away from the circumferential break may be short lines of fracture caused by the original modification of the surrounding area of bone. ... The first stage [of the fracture] consists of a depression of the outer table of the skull against the inner table. With a continuation of the traumatizing force, the inner table is fractured, resulting in a greater degree of shelving of this inner table. The outer table, continuing along its line of force, drives the inner table through the dura and into the underlying brain. In other words, the fragments of the bone from the outer table also act as a traumatizing agent as far as the inner table is concerned, thus resulting in further fragmentation of this table.

Similar observations have been obtained in experimental studies on cadavers. Producing depression fractures with a hammer, Spitz (1973: Figs. 25–26) illustrates hinge fractures across the diplöic and internal cranial faces, and Gurdjian and Webster (1958: Fig. 13) show radiating fractures on the ectocranial surface and fragmentation of the endocranial table. Thus, bony consequences of powerful blunt injuries to the head leave distinct attributes which relate to the transmission of forces acting on the external and internal tables. Of particular relevance to the Ofnet material is the disintegration of the bony tables. The external table may break up on impact and as the force continues through the diplöe, the internal table implodes into the vault as energy is released from the weapon (Courville 1962). This aspect of blunt weapon injuries may explain why so few of the perimortem holes in the Ofnet skulls have the missing fragment(s) replaced into the opening (Fig. 7.2). It seems likely that head blows splintered the bone at the injury site into many small fragments, and, as the weapon drove through the bone, the diplöe broke into separate ecto- and endocranial pieces. Further fragmentation would have occurred perpendicular to the external and internal tables as the weapon penetrated the bone surfaces (see Courville 1962: Fig. 6). Assuming this degree of bone disintegration occurred, the pulverized pieces could have easily been missed during excavation or reconstruction.

In addition to the fragmentation of the bone surfaces, it is often possible to reconstruct the type of weapon (or object) which produced a cranial injury from the nature of the bony remains. Courville notes the weapon (or object) producing the cranial wound can often be identified by the size and shape of the hole, an observation confirmed by other reports in the forensic and osteological literature (Bhootra 1985; Gurdjian 1973; Ortner and Putschar 1981; Spitz 1973; Takizawa et al. 1989; Wahl and König 1987).

Figure 7.2. A lozenge-shaped wound running nearly horizontally over the left orbit of Ofnet 26. There may be another perimortem wound perpendicular to it, but this was not scored as one in the analysis.

Of the 38 individuals of Ofnet, the majority are represented by some vault piece. In the following analysis, a specimen was included in the comparisons when it was represented by at least one complete (or virtually complete) vault bone. Using this selection criterion, in six cases the cranial pieces were either too fragmentary for reliable analysis or the individual consisted only of teeth, leaving a cranial sample of 32 individuals. Finally, given that a number of individuals are represented by an isolated cranial part, the following figures certainly under-estimate the number of perimortem wounds in the sample, since missing parts likely possessed evidence of bludgeon wounds.

SEX/AGE DISTRIBUTION OF THE BLUDGEON WOUNDS

Distributed among 32 individuals, 37 holes were identified as perimortem bludgeon wounds. These are found in 18 of 32 skulls, so just over 50% of the specimens show some indication of perimortem trauma. Broken down by sex, these are made up of five males, three females and ten unsexed subadults. As shown in Table 7.2 males have between two and seven bludgeon wounds, while females and unsexed individuals consistently show a smaller number of wounds per skull (0–3). Thus, while all males show evidence of two or more perimortem bludgeon wounds, only 23% of the females and 59% of the subadults have similar wounds. Gender differences in frequency are reflected in the mean number of bludgeon marks per skull, which in males is ten times the female mean and five times the subadult mean when the total sample

Table 7.2. Bludgeon Wound Frequencies at Ofnet

	Males			Females			Subadults		
	mean	(n)	range	mean	(n)	range	mean	(n)	range
Total Sample	4.0	(5)	2–7	0.4	(10)	0–2	0.8	(17)	0–3
Percent with Wound	100%[2]			23%[3]			58%		
Bludgeoned Sample	4.0[1]	(5)	2–7	1.3	(3)	1–2	1.3	(10)	1–3

[1]significantly different from females and subadults with Mann-Whitney U at p < 0.002
[2]significantly different from females and subadults with Chi-square at p < 0.0001
[3]significantly different from subadults with Chi-square at p < 0.0001

is considered (Tab. 7.2). When only specimens which possess at least one bludgeon wound are considered, males show a mean frequency in number of wounds (4.0) three times higher than females (1.3) and subadults (1.3). These mean differences reach statistical significance between males and both of the remaining groups, whether measured by the number of holes per skull (with Mann-Whitney U; $p < .002$) or for the presence/absence of a bludgeon wound (using Chi-square; $p < .0001$). For the latter comparison, subadult specimens (compared to females) also have significantly more individuals with at least one bludgeon mark (Chi-square; $p < .0001$). In sum, statistics according to sex, illustrate clear differences in the number of the wounds per skull and in prevalence of skulls with bludgeon wounds.

As shown in Table 7.3, all the age categories possess at least one specimen with a bludgeon wound and, while some variation exists among the age classes, none of this variation is significantly different using Kruskal-Wallis ($p < .30$). Furthermore, when the sample was separated into only subadult and adult categories and tested for the presence (or absence) of bludgeon wounds by Chi-square, no significant differences occur ($p > .60$). Thus, the number of bludgeon wounds does not differ significantly across age classes nor between adults and subadults.

The dimensions of the bludgeon wounds on the Ofnet skulls are relatively consistent in shape and size. As noted by Mollison (1936) virtually all of the wounds are lozenge-shaped with an identifiable long and short axis (Fig. 7.3). These were quantified by measuring the maximum length and breadth of the opening on the ectocranial surface. Dimensions of the bludgeon wounds show a long axis averaging 35.3 mm and a short axis of 17.9 mm and no statistically significant differences in either axes are found among males, females and the unsexed individuals (Tab. 7.4.). In general the long

Table 7.3. Frequency of Bludgeon Wounds by Age Category

Age Category	Number of Holes								% with at least one hole
	0	1	2	3	4	5	6	7	
infant (0–2)	1	1	0	0	0	0	0	0	50.0
child (> 2–12)	6	6	1	1	0	0	0	0	57.1
adolescent (> 12–16)	2	1	0	0	0	0	0	0	33.3
young adult	3	1	2	0	1	0	0	0	62.5
adult	2	1	0	0	0	1	0	0	50.0
old adult	0	0	1	0	0	0	0	0	100.0

Figure 7.3. One of (at least) seven wounds on Ofnet 21. This one is centered on the right parietal near the sagittal suture which it roughly parallels. Unlike many others, this elliptical wound has the impact fracture fragment glued back into the opening. The sagittal suture is barely visible to the left of the wound.

and short axis dimensions decrease from young to old individuals, but the size changes over age classes do not reach statistical significance. When grouped into subadult and adult categories, the means are not significantly different, so despite the variation across

Table 7.4. Bludgeon Wound Dimensions by Sex and Age (in mm.)

Sex	Long Axis			Short Axis		
	mean	(n)	range	mean	(n)	range
Male	34.4	(5)	30.0–38.0	14.3	(4)	11.3–16.0
Female	33.2	(3)	28.0–37.5	19.2	(1)	
Subadult	37.4	(8)	29.0–43.0	19.8	(7)	16.0–31.0
Age Class						
Age 0–2	–			18.0	(1)	
Age 2–12	38.6	(7)	35.0–43.0	20.7	(5)	16.0–31.0
Age 12–15	29.0	(1)		17.0	(1)	
Young Adult	35.2	(5)	30.0–38.0	13.5	(2)	11.3–15.7
Adult	31.9	(2)	28.0–35.8	16.7	(2)	14.2–19.2
Old Adult	32.0	(1)		16.0	(1)	
Subadult Average	37.4[1]	(8)	29.0–43.0	19.8[1]	(7)	16.0–31.0
Adult Average	33.9	(8)	28.0–38.0	15.3	(5)	11.3–19.2
Total Average	35.3	(16)	28.0–43.0	17.9	(12)	11.3–31.0

[1] not significantly different from adult average $p > 0.10$ with student's t.

age categories in long and short axis dimensions, none of this variation is statistically significant. Finally, the ratio of the two axes dimensions was calculated for all wounds. The long axis is generally about twice the dimension of the short axis and, although not given in the tables, no statistically significant differences occur in this ratio across age or sex classes. Consequently, for both age and sex there are no significant differences in the dimensions nor the form of the perimortem wounds, which show an overall consistency in size and shape.

LOCATION AND ORIENTATION OF WOUNDS

The bludgeon wounds are not distributed equally over the bones of the vault. Figure 7.4 illustrates the cumulative positioning of bludgeon marks in left/right lateral, posterior, and facial views for the skulls for the entire sample. In the lateral views which plot all the wounds, 14 wounds are located on the left side and 23 on the right, indicating that almost two-thirds of the blows were directed to the right side of the skulls. Most of these are positioned below the skull's crown, concentrated mainly in the supraorbital and parietal/occipital regions. In the posterior view, eight wounds occur on the left, eleven on the right, and one is located on the sagittal midline. It is obvious that the most heavily affected areas

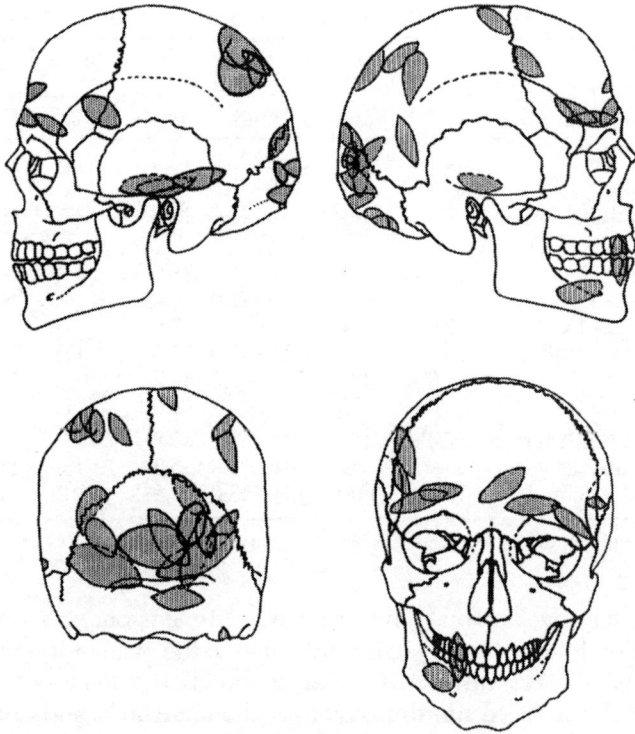

Figure 7.4. Cumulative frequency of all the perimortem wounds for all specimens.

are the parietal boss and occipital above the superior nuchal line. In frontal view, four perimortem wounds are situated over the right orbit and three over the left orbit, with two wounds located in the right lower face. No evidence for bludgeoning occurs above the middle of the forehead (above *metopion*) nor on the parietals along the sagittal suture.

The location of these wounds provides some further support that these holes are not the result of postmortem factors, especially ground pressure, removal of the rock overburden by blasting, pre-excavation trampling, or excavation/reconstruction procedures. These phenomena would surely not have caused the consistently shaped, elliptical openings. Moreover, if diagenetic factors were important in producing the holes (especially blasting and trampling), the breaks should occur more commonly on the crown of the skull, rather than in the more protected areas of the browridges and posterior vault. Furthermore, the orientation of the holes is not random, but generally aligned along either the sagittal or coronal plane. For example, on the frontal view five of the eight lozenge wounds are located in the paracoronal plane, while on the occipital most of the holes are oriented in either the parasagittal or para-coronal planes. Thus, in addition to the common shape of the holes, their distribution on the skulls suggests a prehistoric origin of the wounds.

CUTMARKS: CRANIA

Many of the skull vaults show what appear to be cutmarks, but numerous factors impinge on the reliability of identifying these marks and incisions as ancient. Not the least of the ambiguity relates to the successive reconstructions of many specimens. During these procedures, the bones were initially cleaned of the remaining matrix or soil and, much later, plaster from previous reconstructions was removed from some of the vault bones. These cleaning/reconstructive episodes could easily have left what now appear to be ancient marks, since it is likely that sharp instruments were used and the bones were initially described as "soft." In addition, soaking the skulls in harderner (Zaponlack) and covering the cranial bones with preservative has added to the difficulty in interpreting the marks, especially since recent marks now covered with lacquer may now appear to be "ancient" ones.

No less impacting on the nature of these cranial cutmarks was the production of casts of some of the specimens between 1910–1930. Of the six specimens possessing ancient cutmarks (Tab. 7.1), four of these were casted at least once. Yet, inspecting the mold marks on the original casts in Tübingen and comparing these mold lines to the cranial cutmarks shows little correlation between the two. For example, Ofnet 2485.13 was molded in Tübingen. The cast was limited to the production of a calotte and mold lines circle the skull from *glabella* across the temporal above *porion* to *inion* and back, following the same line across the opposite side of the skull. The cutmarks on the original specimen do not have this orientation, but rather occur only on both posterior parietals, running nearly perpendicular to the mold lines on the cast. In Ofnet 2493.21 the preparator (Hirschhuber) at München made a composite replica, casting the individual bones (or major skull pieces), then re-assembled the parts (Schröter pers. comm.). Mold lines appear along the diplöic surface of the casts, but there is no evidence of cutmarks, related to cutting the mold, on the original diplöic edges. Thus, the cutmarks on the posterior parietals of this specimen do not appear to be related to mold production. Consequently, while some specimens which were molded possess cutmarks, others do not and, in general, there is little correspondence between the observable mold lines on the casts and cutmarks on the original specimens. Nevertheless, it is not possible to irrefutably exclude casting techniques as the origin of some of the cranial cutmarks.

Finally, over the years the Ofnet skulls have been studied by numerous researchers and there can be no doubt that some of the scratches are related to damage by sharp-pointed calipers or craniographic instruments. For example, Ofnet 2477.4 and 2493.21 have scratches along the mid-sagittal plane which closely resemble those attributed to the use of craniophore in the Neanderthal child, Engis 2 (White and Toth 1989). These mid-sagittal incisions on Ofnet 2477.4 run from *nasion* to *opisthion* and are definitely recent, based on the fact that they penetrate the lacquer coating the vault and expose the underlying white bone. Scheidt (1923) illustrates sagittal and transverse craniograms of nine skulls, and, while not all possess remnants of mid-sagittal or transverse incisions, at least for the two specimens discussed above, the mid-sagittal cutmarks seem almost certainly to have been produced by the craniographic techniques.

In short, while the following text documents the presence of suspicious marks on a few of the specimens, not every one of these may correspond to marks made prior to burial. The presumably ancient cutmarks were characterized by their deep incision into the bone with the entire mark resembling the same red stained color as the surrounding, intact bone. The edges of these cutmarks were generally steep walled and perpendicular to the ectocranial surface. In most cases, two or more lines were grouped together and almost never crossed over each other, but rather ran in sets as parallel (or nearly parallel) cutmarks across the bone surface. As much as they are comparable, the macroscopic features of the marks resemble the microscopic descriptions of cutmarks or butchering marks on other fossil material (Cook 1986; Shipman and Rose 1983; White 1986). Despite this conservative approach in identifying these marks as ancient, it seems certain that the cranial cutmarks will continue to be problematic with respect to their origin.

Thirty-two specimens are represented by at least one cranial piece. Of these only six individuals (17%) bear what seem certain ancient cutmarks. Two males, three females, and one seven-year old child possess marks under lacquer and in regions unrelated to measuring or casting. For the most part, these cutmarks are limited to the upper portion of the vault, located primarily on the parietals and occipital. Specimens 2477.4 and 2496.24 provide the most extensive evidence for cutmarks (Fig. 7.5 a,b). On 2477.4, four parallel incisions traverse both parietals from the lambdoidal to nearly the coronal suture. Cutmarks on the right side are deeper, but distinct on both sides. Across the back of the skull, overlapping and intersecting at right angles to these are six distinct cutmarks. These cross the parietal beginning some 50 mm above *lambda* and extend to (and intersect with) the sagittally directed incisions. While other recent scoring appears on the vault, the lines identified here as ancient cutmarks are more deeply etched into the bone and evenly stained with no part of the marks showing the white underlying bone. In addition, several breaks in the individual bones on 2477.4 occur and glue holds these portions together. The cutmarks do not penetrate this glue, indicating that the marks were made before the fragmentary parts were cemented together. While these observations do not prove the marks are ancient, they do suggest the

Figure 7.5a. Cranial cutmarks on the posterior parietals of Ofnet 4.

Figure 7.5b. Cranial cutmarks on the posterior parietals of Ofnet 24.

marks were made before the pieces were cemented together in the current reconstruction. There appears to be some chance these cutmarks are associated with burial preparation.

On Ofnet 2496.24, cutmarks occur in virtually the same positions as in Ofnet 2477.4 (Fig. 7.5b). They appear bilaterally on each parietal, beginning just anterior to the coronal suture, stretching posteriorly over the parietal boss. On the posterior parietals two main incisions run in the coronal plane from boss to boss and overlap the sagittally directed cutmarks. These are under the lacquer and appear old. There are some additional cutmarks on the right temporal above the zygomatic root and a fairly deep, single incision running in a superior-inferior direction on the mastoid. The deepest of these cutmarks have a double channelled cross-section while the more shallow ones are single channelled. All are covered by lacquer and stained red. There is no record of Ofnet 2496.24 having been casted, so the marks on this specimen are either related to cleaning/reconstruction events or to perimortem burial practices.

The remaining specimens exhibiting cranial cutmarks at Ofnet include 2483.13, 2490.18, 2493.21, and 2470.26. None of these have as many cutmarks, but most show a similar location to Ofnet 2477.4 and 2496.24 in the placement of the marks along the lateral walls and posterior aspect of the parietals. For example, Ofnet 2483.13 has a series of parallel lines under the lacquer on both posterior parietals. Ofnet 2493.21 also has a series of sagittally oriented cutmarks on the right parietal (only) and a few short lines on both parietals just superior to *lambda*.

During the various times I studied the material, I was first convinced that many of the marks were ancient, then considered all of them the result of cleaning, skull reconstruction, or molding, then finally returned to the conclusion that at least some were probably related to perimortem circumstances. One thing is clear: the marks were not made during the lifetime of the individuals, since there is no evidence of infection or healing associated with any of the marks. Yet, only six of the 35 specimens exhibit cutmarks which indicates that defleshing the vaults was not widely practiced by those who buried the Ofnet heads. Neither is there evidence in cutmarks (or in skull breakage) that would indicate removal of the brain or cannibalism. For the cutmarks along the lateral and posterior skull walls, these may be marks left from making a flap, for carrying the skull, but this is difficult to prove.

Finally, specimens with cutmarks were found only in the large pit and, except for Ofnet 2477.4, all were found in the northern half of the pit. It seems reasonable to tentatively conclude that these skulls were accorded some kind of special treatment, perhaps scalping, and then were ceremonially buried as a group. The distribution of skulls with indications of bludgeon wounds shows no similar segregation apart from the other skulls. Finally, it perhaps noteworthy that the two specimens with the greatest number of cutmarks (2477.4 and 2496.24) are the oldest female and male, respectively, at the site.

In summary, while perimortem cutmarks on the vaults of the Ofnet specimens are not numerous, the facts are that (1) they often occur in a common location across the sides and back of the parietals, (2) are under the lacquer, (3), cross bone breaks, (4) are present in highest frequency on the oldest individuals, and (5) in five of the six cases individuals with cutmarks are buried in one area of the large pit. These observations provide some support for the contention that cutmarks are related to the perimortem circumstances affecting a few individuals and/or desecration of some of the heads.

CUTMARKS: CERVICAL VERTEBRAE

While cutmarks on the vaults may be somewhat difficult to interpret, those on the cervical vertebrae provide convincing evidence
of being prior to burial. Unlike the vaults, the cervicals have never
undergone extensive (or any) reconstruction nor been casted. They
have not been repeatedly measured by researchers over the past 80
years and the location of the cutmarks makes it impossible to interpret them as the result of trampling or other nonmortuary influences. Consequently, the marks on the bones cannot be due to
postmortem factors. In a few cases (e.g., the atlas of Ofnet 2), a
chalky matrix still adheres to the bone and incisions are distinct,
but these clearly are "fresh" marks determined by the exposure of
underlying white bone against the red ochre stained matrix. Such
cases are readily distinguished from perimortem cutmarks which
were primarily identified by their deep scoring of the bone surface
with the entire channel stained with red ochre. Finally, all the
heads were placed into the two pits shortly after death, since the
mandibles and, in many cases, the cervical vertebrae were still in
articulation with the crania when they were excavated. Since the
heads must have been severed from the vertebral column, the presence of cutmarks on the cervicals is not unexpected.

One hundred cervical vertebrae were identified in the collections
at München. This inventory is about twice the number reported by
Scheidt (1923) and repeated by Saller (1962). It is unclear why these
authors found fewer cervicals, but it is possible they only counted
complete (or reasonably complete) specimens. In my inventory all
fragmentary parts were included in the count when they did not
match any of the fragmentary or whole vertebrae. In this sample,
all five males have at least two cervical vertebrae, while females
and subadults have a more sporadic representation. A few of the
latter have nearly complete cervical columns, others no vertebrae
at all.

As shown in Table 7.5, males are represented by 19 cervicals,
females by 30, and subadults by 51. These are distributed among
33 individuals, so most (87%) of the skulls have at least one associated vertebrae. Overall only 13 of the 100 cervical vertebrae possess at least one cutmark, accounting for one-third of the
individuals. No substantial differences occur with respect to age
or sex and, except for two females, never more than one vertebra
is cut per individual. However, multiple cutmarks on a single
vertebral centrum are common (as shown in Figure 7.6a) and when

Table 7.5. Cutmarks on Cervical Vertebrae

	Males	Females	Subadults	Totals
Number of cervical vertebrae	19	30	51	100
Individuals with cervical vertebrae	5	10	18	33
Number of vertebrae with cutmarks	2	6	5	13
Percent vertebrae with cutmarks	11%	20%	10%	13%
Individuals with cut cervicals	2	4	5	11
Percent individuals with cutmarks	40%	40%	28%	34%

they occur, they more often involve adults than subadults. Cervical 4 is the most common site for a cutmark with more than half the individuals showing a cut ventral surface. This suggests that the decapitations were initiated above the hyoid and thyroid cartilage. Cutmarks occur on the ventral surface exclusively in 62% of the cases, on the dorsal surface exclusively in 15% of the cases, and on both the ventral and dorsal surfaces in 23% of the cases. There is a consistent pattern in the placement of these cutmarks, so that when they appear ventrally, the marks are only on the centrum;

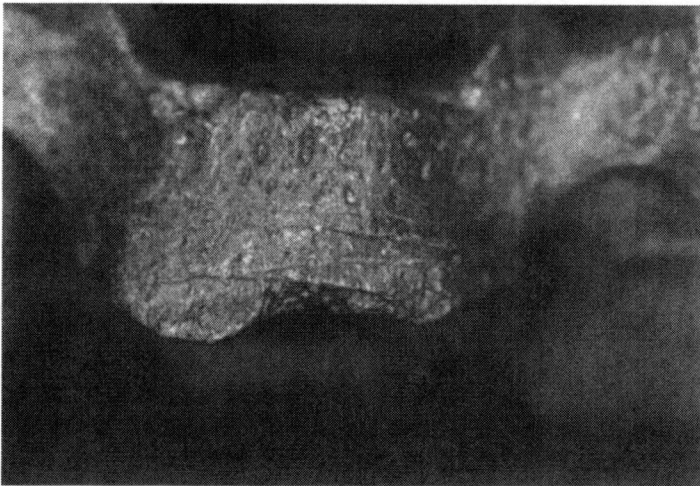

Figure 7.6a. Cutmarks on the ventral face of the cervical vertebra on a young adult, Ofnet 21.

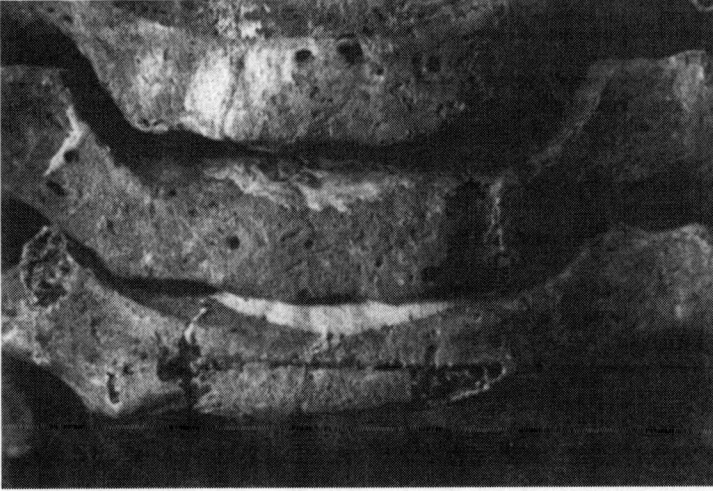

Figure 7.6b. Cutmarks on the ventral face of the cervical vertebrae on a 7–8 year old, Ofnet 5. The lower left border is broken (cut) away on Ofnet 21 (Fig. 7.6a), but is intact (except for a small, recent break) in the lower left margin of Ofnet 5 (Fig. 7.6b). The vertebrae are not at the same scale.

when they appear dorsally, they are only on the pedicles or the laminae. While no depth measurements of the cutmarks were taken, those on the ventral surface were always much deeper than the dorsal ones, which consisted mainly of superficial scratches. Ventral cuts often penetrated the thin cortical surface and extended into the cancellous bone. These cuts often resulted in bone spalling superior (or inferior) to the line of the cut. For example, on cervical 4 of Ofnet 21, four fairly deep incisions run across the ventral face of the centrum. The most inferior one perforates the cancellous bone and has spalled off the left half of the lower border of the centrum (Fig 7.6a). Figure 7.6b shows a close-up of the ventral surface of the fifth cervical vertebra of Ofnet 5. Here, there is a single cutmark which runs across nearly the whole ventral surface. The mark pentrates through the cortical wall, is evenly stained with red ochre, and extends into the cancellous bone. The depth of the cut surface is probably related to the relatively young age of the victim and his/her thinner cortical bone.

As proposed by Schmidt (1913), Scheidt (1923), Mollison (1936) and Gieseler (1951), cutmarks on the cervical vertebrae must relate ot the final disposition of the corpses in preparation for burial. The cutmarks are located in regions where the deep vertebral muscles and ligaments would need to be severed to disarticulate the head from the spinal column. Since the most frequent and deepest cutmarks occur on the ventral surface, it is clear that the decapitation began by cutting the throat, then was completed by separating the cervical column always above the first thoracic.

EVIDENCE FOR PREMORTEM INJURIES

In addition to perimortem trauma, four specimens provide indications of healed wounds which occurred well before death. These injuries differ from the perimortem wounds in that they all show signs of healing, are never crescent-shaped, never penetrate through the endocranial table, and tend to be more on the crown of the skull. None appear to be related to the demise of any individual and all are unspecific traumatic lesions. The most curious appears on Ofnet 2505.33, a 2–4 year old child. This specimen shows an extensive pair of healed wounds on the left frontal. Two wounds occur above the orbit in the middle portion of the frontal squama and deeply penetrate the external table, extending into the diplöe, but do not show any evidence of endocranial penetration. The smaller of the two wounds is located in a more inferior, lateral position and is roughly circular in shape (10 mm in diameter). Its inferior-lateral surface is interrupted by a postmortem break, but the bone below the break shows no continuation of the wound in the inferior direction. On the superior margin of this wound, a low ridge of the original cortical surface remains, which, unlike the healed wound, shows no indication of a periosteal reaction. Above this small wound, in a location just lateral to *metopion*, is squared-off area measuring 24 by 28 mm, oriented obliquely to the mid-sagittal plane (Fig. 7.7). A postmortem break interrupts the corner of the wound closest to the midline, but the other margins are intact. The wound is extremely well-defined and remarkable in its square shape. While the margins are framed by the intact, non-inflamed external surface, the interior of the wound is depressed some 2 mm through the external bone surface. In this depressed region, the outer table is mostly absent, replaced by a fine mesh-work of reactive bone, some of which appears to be healed diplöic bone. This region shows very minor evidence of infection and

Figure 7.7. Ofnet 33 showing a rectangular, healed premortem wound on the left frontal squama.

seems to be nearly completely healed. Almost certainly these two healed wounds are interrelated; in fact, it seems likely the smaller one occurred first. I suspect (but cannot prove) the individual received a blow to the left frontal which produced the small wound, then some attempt was made to treat the trauma. The squared-off area appears as if the cortical bone was scraped away, similar to skulls occurring much later in time where trepanation was performed (Bennike 1985). On the intact cortical bone around the margins are some short, shallow cutmarks, but these are not completely convincing as being ancient. More important are the three intact corners of the wound, forming almost perfect right angles, which would not be expected in the normal healing processes of a traumatic injury.

Another square-shaped healed wound occurs on the left parietal of an adult male (2475:2). While the margins are not as clearly defined as in the child, there is a remnant of right-angled corners. Both these cases seem to be examples of some kind of prehistoric surgical intervention for treating a head wound. But, it is impossible to determine whether these premortem wounds were accidental or intentional. Since none conform to a crescent shape, it seems unlikely they were made by the same weapons which left their impression on many of the other skulls.

DEMOGRAPHIC ASPECTS OF OFNET

One of the most striking demographic features of the Ofnet sample is the great number of subadults compared to adults. Based on tooth eruption and wear, more than two-thirds of the sample is below the age of 20 and nearly 60% of the sample is below the age of 15. Compared to other Mesolithic cemeteries, such as Téviec/Hoëdic (France) and Skateholm (Sweden) where subadults make up less than 25% of the buried individuals (Frayer unpublished), the age structure at Ofnet is clearly different in its high frequency of subadults. In general, infants, children, and subadults may not be accorded the same burial treatment as adults which, in part, accounts for their under-representation in most burial grounds (Weiss 1973). But, Ofnet clearly deviates from this pattern with its high number of subadults.

Table 7.6 reviews demographic aspects of Ofnet, compared to three other groups. The first sample derives from the Talheim burial pit, a Bandkeramik site in Baden-Württemberg (Germany), which is dated some 500 years after the Ofnet burials and interpreted as a massacre (Wahl and König 1987). Crow Creek in central South Dakota (USA) is a late prehistoric mass gave attributed to a massacre (Willey 1990). For a living pre-state population,

Table 7.6. Comparative Demographics for Ofnet, Talheim, Crow Creek, and Dobe !Kung (Percent of sample in various age grades)

Age	Ofnet	Talheim[1]	Crow Creek[2]	Dobe !Kung[3]
0– < 5	29.8%	8.8%	–	11.3%
5– < 10	27.0%	23.5%	–	6.9%
10– < 15	2.7%	11.8%	–	8.8%
15– < 20	8.1%	2.9%	–	7.8%
20– < 34	21.6%	20.6%	–	25.5%
34– < 60	8.1%	17.6%	–	29.4%
60–	2.7%	14.7%	–	10.3%
Subadults[4]	59.5%	44.1%	46.3%	27.0%
Adults	40.5%	55.9%	53.7%	73.0%
Sex				
Male	33.3%	56.3%	56.3%	54.7%
Female	66.7%	43.7%	45.3%	48.6%

[1]from Wahl and König, 1987
[2]from Willey, 1990, p. 47
[3]from Howell, 1979
[4]individuals < 15, except Crow Creek (< 14).

demographic data were abstracted from Howell's (1979) study of the Dobe !Kung. As shown in comparative table, the age and sex profiles at Ofnet are substantially different from each of the three examples. Compared to Talheim, Ofnet has a greater representation of individuals aged 0–10 and a correspondingly smaller number of mature and old adults. Whereas Talheim has a greater number of adults (55.9%) than subadults (44.1%), the opposite is true for Ofnet where adults account for only 40.5% of the individuals in the two pits. Frequencies for subadults and adults are similar between Talheim and Crow Creek, further highlighting the elevated number of subadults of Ofnet. Compared with the Dobe !Kung population, the Ofnet pits contain nearly three times the number of individuals aged $0 - <5$ and about four times the number of individuals aged between 5 and 10. At the opposite end of the age categories, compared to the Dobe !Kung, Ofnet has a substantial under-representation of adults, notably those in the middle and old age categories.

In addition to the atypical age profiles at Ofnet, there is also an over-representation of adult females. In the Mesolithic cemeteries mentioned earlier, females constitute 48.4% of the adult sample in the Téviec/Hoëdic and Skateholm cemeteries (Frayer, unpublished). These cemetery data are identical to the Dobe !Kung figures for females (48.6%) and not a major deviation from the sex ratio at Talheim (43.7%) or Crow Creek (45.3%). However, each of these sex ratios contrasts markedly with Ofnet where females make up 66.7% of the adult sample.

These comparisons demonstrate that the demographics at Ofnet are unlike either a Mesolithic cemetery where individuals were interred over an undetermined time interval (Téviec/Hoëdic and Skateholm) or a living population (Dobe !Kung). The demographics at Ofnet also do not resemble a massacre when presumably all individuals were interred in a mass pit. While it not possible to determine if the two Ofnet pits were loaded with skulls during the same burial event, it seems extremely likely that each pit was filled with skulls on a single occasion. For example, there is no evidence to support the contention that the pits were open for any length of time after the heads were deposited. If this were the case, evidence for rodent/scavenger activity would be expected, but none of the skulls show tooth marks or any other evidence of animal disturbance. Furthermore, during the excavation, the mandibles and in many cases cervical vertebrae were still articulated with the crania, so very little jumbling of the skulls characterized the head arrangement in the pits. If the pits served as periodic repositories for deceased individuals, one would have expected more anatomical confusion in the funeral pits. Finally, given the fact that the skulls were laid into the pits in close proximity (like "eggs in a basket"), it seems very likely that the individuals in each pit represent a mass burial resulting from a single incident. The interesting implication from the skewed sex ratios and the high incidence of sub-adults is that a number of adults (especially males) were either not included in the graves or somehow escaped the fate of the others. The burial conditions and demographic pecularities at Ofnet, then, suggest that only a segment of the total population is represented in the two graves.

Forensic details and demographic characteristics of the individuals found in the two pits at Ofnet indicate that the site does not represent a "natural" burial ground or a collection of trophy skulls. Rather, it was special event where part of the original population was pummeled and killed with blunt weapons, then decapitated with only the heads and the necks buried in the two pits. None of the weapons which produced the head wounds were found in the pits (or embedded in the vaults), but the shape of the holes in the skulls suggests they were made by a weapon with a crescent cross-section. Mollison (1936) speculated that these holes were produced by limestone maces which might not have been recognized as tools during the excavations, while Gieseler (1951) felt that either hardened antler or ground stone hatchets were responsible for the wounds. Whatever the specific weapon, the similarity of the wounds left on the vaults indicates that a weapon of a consistent type and size was used in killing (or mutilating) the victims.

One of the enigmas about Ofnet is the interment of only the heads and attached cervical vertebra. It will probably always be a mystery who conducted the burial(s) and for what reason(s) the heads were severed from the bodies. The circumstances of the burial pits differs from the Talheim massacre, where the whole bodies were simply tossed into a pit without any major funereal processing (Wahl and König 1987). Also, unlike the Maori (Vayda 1960) and some prehistoric and historic groups (Sjøvold 1984; Wright 1988) where skulls were decorated and kept as trophies, charms or reverent objects, the Ofnet heads could not have been displayed for any substantial length of time following the death of the victims. Rather, shortly following the massacre, the mutilated corpses were interred. Since the women and children had necklaces associated with them in the grave, these victims were not even stripped of their personal adornments before burial.

An attempt was made to determine if the skulls were placed in the grave following a particular order. Since the smaller pit contained only six skulls, the analysis was limited to the main pit. Besides the association of skulls which appear to show cranial cutmarks in the northern part, adult males seem to be clustered more towards the front (northwest) section. Adult and adolescent females are essentially aligned in a southwest-northeast direction, generally located in the southern half of the pit. Children occur in the northwest and southeast corners with a line of five skulls separating the four adult males from five adult and young females. To further reconstruct the distribution of sexes in the main pit, an attempt was made to estimate sex for the subadult remains. This was done on the basis of the lengths and breadths of canines and first and second molars for both the deciduous and permanent teeth. While plots of each tooth dimension show a clear lack of bimodality, I made the assumption that those specimens near the bottom or top of the range were likely to be female and male, respectively. A range test was used where dimensions for each specimen were compared to a frequency distribution of each tooth as represented by all individuals from the site. If a length or breadth fell at the bottom or top of the range, a "probable" sex was assigned for the specimen. Specimens close to the mean for a particular dental dimension were left as unsexed. Based on this technique, a number of specimens fell near the top or the bottom of the range, making it possible to assign a "probable" sex of some of the subadults in the main pit. Using this sexing method, subadult specimens seem to cluster by sex with a greater number of males in the northern half and a greater number of females in the southern half of the pit. Other than the possible arrangement of skulls by sex, there appears to be no other, even vague, patterning of the skulls. The specimens in the main pit do not cluster by age and, based on about 20 discrete traits, there were no aggregations of specific nonmetric markers. In sum, if the skulls were placed in the main pit in a predefined pattern, it may have followed a protocol according to sex or some other pattern not discernible from the remains as they now exist.

CONCLUSION

It is one thing to document evidence for this mass killing, but quite another to provide a sociocultural context which accounts for the

event. There is considerable evidence to show that disputes leading
to homicide or warfare are common occurrences in foraging and
horticultural societies (Bamforth 1994; Ember 1978; Knauft 1987),
but little evidence for mass killings. While all the hunter-gatherer
and horticultural groups reviewed by Knauft (1987:464) have extremely high homicide rates, most of these deaths occur as single
murders, related to retribution, retaliation, revenge or other matters. Most homicides in hunter-gatherer and horticultural groups
are randomly directed at single individuals, often a victim who just
happens to be in the wrong place at the wrong time. Thus, homicides tend to be aimed at the first rival encoutered and, as Harner
describes for the Jívaro "[g]reat pains are usually taken to kill only
one person in retaliation for one murder" (1973:172). Yet occasionally, blood feuds escalate into organized raids where the aim
of the offensive foray is to completely decimate a rival population,
including women and children. For example, Vayda reviewing
warfare among the Maori reports:

> Far from sparing women and children, Maori warriors sometimes...
> took the opportunity to massacre them, together with the more de-
> crepit males, while the able-bodied men of the village were away on
> some military or economic expedition." (1960:92).

Young and old were often cannibalized or butchered with the various body parts saved as trophies or for making utilitarian objects
(Vayda 1960:94). Little of this ethnographic example seems to fit
the Ofnet case. There is no evidence for cannibalism and little
evidence for butchering as measured by cutmarks. The skulls were
not kept as trophies, but were buried shortly after the deaths of the
individuals, and there are few "decrepit" males in the two pits.
However, there are high numbers of women and children, which
might indicate that the males were absent from the residential unit
when the massacre occurred. Alternatively, the males may have
escaped or, if captured, were not included in the mass graves.

   In addition to the above case, there are examples where the aim
of raid was group annihilation, whether because retribution could
not be satisfied with a single killing, to acquire a group's land, or
whatever cause. Among the Netsilik

> [p]hysical revenge in traditional times did exist following the mur-
> der of defenseless strangers. ... The revenge party was organised by
> a headman (generally a close relative of the victim) and consisted of
> his kindred, organized as an action group. There was a formalized
> pattern of intergroup fighting,... The objective of the revenge party

was not just to kill the original murderer but members of his kindred as well. In a sense the members of the kindred shared responsibility for the murder (Balikci 1970:184).

In this instance, the main participants in the raid were males and the incident followed organized principles for conducting a feud. Even if the whole kindred was held accountable for the crime, the antagonists were males. While genocide was the intent of the retributive kindred, it bears little resemblance to the situation at Ofnet, where women and children predominate in the mass graves.

In summary, we will probably never be able to unravel the sequence of events and circumstances which led to the murders of these Mesolithic people and culminated in the two skull nests buried in the small cave now called Ofnet. Questions like who buried the heads, why were the heads severed from the body, what happened to the parts of the corpses below the neck, why are there so few adult males, why were no ornaments associated with adult males, why were the majority of the skulls lacking cutmarks, were the two pits filled at the same event, who did the killings, etc. are not possible to reconstruct or answer given current information. What is evident, however, is that these Mesolithic men, women, and children were victims of a massacre and ceremonial burial. Ofnet, along with the much smaller burial pit at Hohlenstein, indicates that multiple homicides, possibly relating to an attempt of one group to annihilate another, were not rare among the hunter-gatherers of Mesolithic Western Europe. Like much more recent hunter-gatherers, the Mesolithic past was not always peaceful.

ACKNOWLEDGEMENTS

Free access to the Ofnet collections in München was provided by Professor G. Ziegelmayer, former curator of the Anthropologische Staatssammlung. While in München I greatly profited from discussions with Dr. Peter Schröter, who provided extremely useful information about the history of the Ofnet collections. I also thank Dr. Alfred Czarnetzki curator of the human skeletal collection in Tübingen for allowing me to study the material under his care. I thank my colleagues Debra Martin (Hampshire College) and Jack Hofman (Kansas) for critically reading the manuscript, Linda Greatorex for Figure 7.4, Cristiana Bauer for her German translations, and Carol Archinal for aid in manuscript preparation. Some of this research was funded by BNS8419057 and the University of

Kansas General Research Fund whose support I acknowledge and appreciate.

REFERENCES

Albrethsen, S. and Brinch Petersen, E. (1976). "Excavation of a Mesolithic Cemetery at Vedbaek, Denmark," *Acta Archaeologica*, **47**:1–28.

Ardrey, R. (1961). *African Genesis*, New York: Atheneum.

Balikci, A. (1970). *The Netsilik Eskimo*, Garden City (NY:) Natural History Press.

Bamforth, D. B. (1994). "Indigenous People, Indigenous Violence: Precontact Warfare on the North American Great Plains." *Man*, **29**:95–115.

Bennike, P. (1985). *Paleopathology of Danish Skeletons*, Copenhagen: Akademisk Forlag.

Bhootra, B. K. (1985), "An Unusual Penetrating Head Wound by a Yard Broom and its Medicolegal Aspects." *Journal of Forensic Sciences*, **30**: 569–571.

Birkner, F. (1915). "Der Eiszeitmensch in Bayern." *Beiträge zur Anthropologie und Urgeschichte Bayerns*, **19**:105–134.

Boule, M. and Vallois, H. V. (1937). "Anthropologie," In *Téviec: Station-Nécropole Mésolithique du Morbihan*, eds. M. and St-J. Péquart, M. Boule, and H. V. Vallois, pp. 111–223. Paris: Archives de l'Institute de Paléontologie Humaine, Volume 18.

_____ (1957). *Fossil Men*. New York: Dryden.

Breuil, H. (1909). "Le Gisement Quaternaire d'Ofnet (Bavière) et la Sépulture Mésolithique." *L'Anthropologie*, **20**:205–214.

Chagnon, N. A. (1988). "Life Histories, Blood Revenge, and Warfare in a Tribal Population." *Science*, **239**:985–992.

Constandse-Westermann, T. S. and Newell, R. R. (1982). "Mesolithic Trauma: Demographical and Chronological Trends in Western Europe." *Proceedings of the Paleopathology Association, Middelburg/Antwerpen*.

Cook, J. (1986). "The Application of Scanning Electron Microscopy to Taphonomic and Archaeological Problems." In *Studies in the Upper Palaeolithic of Britain and Northwest Europe*, eds. D. Roe, pp. 143–163. Oxford: B. A. R. International Series, # 296.

Courville, C. B. (1962). "Forensic Neuropathology." *Journal of Forensic Sciences*, 7:303–322.

Dart, R. (1953). "The Predatory Transition from Ape to Man." *International Anthropological and Linguistic Review*, **1**:201–218.

Ember, C. (1978). "Myths about Hunter-gatherers." *Ethnology*, **18**: 439–448.

Frayer, D. W. (1978). *Evolution of the Dentition in Upper Paleolithic and Mesolithic Europe*. Lawrence: University of Kansas Publications in Anthropology, 10.

Gieseler, W. (1938). "Anthropologischer Bericht über die Kopfbestattung und die Knochentrümmerstätte des Hohlensteins in Lonetal." *Deutsche Gesellschaft für Rassenforchung Verhandlungen*, 27–29:213–228.

_____ (1949). "Uber die Epipaläolithscehn Kopfbestattungen aus Süddeutschland." *Homenaje a Don Luis de Hoyos Santos*, pp. 173–181. Madrid: Graficas Valera.

_____ (1951). "Die Süddeutschen Kopfbestattungen (Ofnet, Kaufertsberg, Hohlestein) und ihre Zeitliche Einreihung." *"Aus die Heimat"*, 59:291–298.

Glowatzki, G. and Protsch, R. (1973). "Das Absolut Alter der Kopfbestattungen in der Grossen Ofnet-Höhle bei Nördlingen in Bayern." *Homo*, 24:1–6.

Gurdjian, E. S. (1973). *Head Injury from Antiquity to the Present with Special Reference to Penetrating Head Wounds*. Springfield (IL): Charles C. Thomas.

Gurdjian, E. S. and Webster, J. E. (1958). *Head Injuries*, Boston: Little, Brown.

Harner, M. J. (1973). The Jivaro. New York: Anchor.

Heberer, G., Kurth and I. Schwidetzky-Rösing (1959). *Das Fischer-Lexicon: Anthropologie*. Frankfurt am Main: Gustav Fischer.

Hedges, R. E. M. Housley, R. A. Law, I. A. and Bronk, C. R. (1989). "Radiocarbon Dates from the Oxford AMS System: Archeometry Datelist 9." *Archaeometry* 31: 207–234.

Howell, N. (1979). *Demography of the Dobe !Kung*. New York: Academic.

Knauft, B. M. (1987). "Reconsidering Violence in Simple Human Societies." *Current Anthropology*, 28:457–498.

Lewin, R. (1988). "New Views Emerge on Hunters and Gatherers." *Science*, 240:1146–1148.

Malez, M. (1985). "Spilja Vindija kao kultno mjesto neandertalaca." *Gradski Muzej Varazdin*, 7:31–47.

Mc Cown, T. D. and Keith, A. (1939). *The Stone Age Men of Mount Carmel*. Oxford: Clarendon.

Merkenschlager, F. and Saller, K. (1934). *Ofnet. Wanderungen zu den Mälern am Weg der deutschen Rasse*. Berlin: K. Wolff.

Mollison, T. (1936). "Zeichen gewaltsamer Verletzungen an den Ofnet-Schädeln." Anthropologischer Anzeiger, 13:79–88.

Naber, F. B. (1974). "Das Ende des Ofnet-Problems?" *Quartär*, 25:73–84.

Newell, R. R. Constandse-Westermann, T. S. and Meiklejohn, C. (1979). "The Skeletal Remains of Mesolithic Man in Western Europe: An Evaluative Catalogue." *Journal of Human Evolution*, 8:1–228.

Ortner, D. J. and Putschar, W. G. J. (1981). *Identification of Pathological Conditions in Human Skeletal Remains*, Washington: Smithsonian Institution Press.

Roper, M. K. (1969). "A Survey of the Evidence for Intrahuman Killing in the Pleistocene." *Current Anthropology* 10:427–439.

Saller, K. (1962). "Die Ofnet-Funde in neuer Zusammensetzung." *Zeitschrift für Morphologie und Anthropologie*, **52**:1–51.

Scheidt, W. (1923). *Die Eiszeitlichen Schädelfunde aus der Grossen Ofnet-Höhle and von Kaufertsberg*. München: J. F. Lehmanns.

Schmidt, R. R. (1913). *Die Altsteinzeitlichen Schädelgräber der Ofnet und der Bestattungsritus der Divialzeit*. Stuttgart: E. Schweizerbartsche.

Schulte im Walde, T. J. C. Freundlich, Schwabedissen, H. and Taute, W. (1986). "Köln Radiocarbon Dates." *Radiocarbon*, **28**:134–140.

Schwabedissen, H. (1983). "Antworten zu Beitrag von R. Protsch: 'Wie alt is der Homo sapiens?'" *Archäologische Informationen*, **5**:55–56.

Schwidetzky, I. (1970). *Rassengeschichte*. Fischer-Lexikon, Volume 15. Frankfurt: Fischer Taschenbuch.

Shipman, P. and Rose, J. (1983). "Early Hominid Hunting, Butchering, and Carcass-producing Behaviors: Approaches to the Fossil Record." *Journal of Anthropological Archaeology*, **2**:57–98.

Sjøvold, T. (1984). "A Report on the Heritability of Some Cranial Measurements and Non-metric Traits." In *Multivariate Statistical Methods in Physical Anthropology*, eds. G. N. Van Vark and W. W. Howells, pp. 223–246. Dordrecht: D. Reidel.

Spitz, W. U. (1973). "Blunt Force Injury." In *Medicolegal Investigation of Death*, eds. W. U. Spitz and R. S. Fischer, pp. 122–150. Springfield IL: Charles C. Thomas.

Takizawa, H., Nakamura, I. Hashimoto, M. Maekawa N. and Yamamura M. (1989). "Toolmarks and Peculiar Blunt Force Injuries Related to an Adjustable Wrench." *Journal of Forensic Sciences*, **34**:258–262.

Trinkaus, E. (1983). *The Shanidar Neandertals*. New York: Academic Press.

Ubelaker, D. H. (1978). *Human Skeletal Remains*. Washington: Taraxacum.

Ullrich, H. and White, T. H. (1988). "Modifications of Fossil Human Bones: Current Status of Facts and Interpretations." Symposium at 12th International Congress of Anthropological and Ethnological Sciences, Zagreb. *Collegium Antropologicum* 12 (Supplement):343–346.

Vayda, A. P. (1960). *Maori Warfare*. Wellington (N. Z.): The Polynesian Society.

Villa, P. (1992). "Cannibalism in Prehistoric Europe." *Evoluntionary Anthropology*, **1**:93–104.

Villa, P. C. Bouville, Courtin, J. Helmer, D. Mahieu, E. Shipman, P. Belluomini, G. and Branca, M. (1986). "Cannibalism in the Neolithic." *Science*, **233**:431–437.

216 DAVID W. FRAYER

Wahl, J. and König, H. G. (1987). "Anthropologisch-Traumatologische Untersuchung der menschlichen Skelettreste aus dem bandekeramischen Massengrab bei Talheim, Kreis Heilbronn." *Fundbericht Aus Baden-Württemberg*, **12**:65–193.

Weidenreich, F. (1939). "The Duration of Life of Fossil Man in China and the Pathological Lesions Found in the Skeleton." *Chinese Medical Journal*, **55**:34–44.

Weidenreich, F. (1943). "The Skull of *Sinanthropus pekinensis*." *Paleontologica Sinica* (D) 10:1–298.

Weiss, K. M. (1973). "On the Systematic Bias in Skeletal Sexing." *American Journal of Physical Anthropology*, 37:239–250.

White, T. D. (1986). "Cut Marks on the Bodo Cranium: A Case of Prehistoric Defleshing." *American Journal of Physical Anthropology*, 69:503–511.

White, T. D. and Toth, N. (1989). "Engis: Preparation Damage, not Cutmarks." *American Journal of Physical Anthropology*, **78**:361–368.

Willey, P. (1990). *Prehistoric Warfare on the Great Plains*. New York: Garland.

Wright, G. R. H. (1988). "The Severed Head in Earliest Neolithic Times." *Journal of Prehistoric Religion*, **2**:51–56.

Chapter
EIGHT

Evidence for Human Sacrifice, Bone Modification and Cannibalism in Ancient México

Carmen Ma. Pijoan Aguadé and
Josefina Mansilla Lory
Instituto Nacional de Antropologia e Historia.
Dirección de Antropología Fisica

When the Spaniards arrived in México, the cultural trait that shocked them most was the widespread practice of human sacrifice. As a consequence of this, we have long descriptions of these ritual practices from the different chroniclers, friars and soldiers (Cortés 1970; Sahagún 1989) who wrote about the history, culture and beliefs of the different populations of ancient México.

A few of them also mention the existence of ritual cannibalism (Duran 1967:278), though this has been disputed (Arens 1981: 63–71). There are also representations of human sacrifices, and in some cases, what appears to to be cannibalism in prehispanic and posthispanic codices, ceramics, murals, and stelae. In this paper, we review evidence preserved in skeletal remains for human sacrifice and cannibalism in periods predating the first European contact and demonstrate that these practices were not absent in the Méxican past.

HUMAN SACRIFICE AND CANNIBALISM

For a long time, archaeologists have recognized that some prehispanic sites exhibited peculiarities in the distribution of bones at localities and in burial practices, as well as marks on the recovered skeletons, that seemed to indicate human sacrifice and/or cannibalism. There are reports of offerings of severed heads or extremities, as well as great heaps of human bones that in some cases showed anatomical relations between the bones. Some of these showed cutmarks and postmortem fractures, which led to the conclusion that these were evidence for the existence of cannibalism. For example, Anderson (1967: 94, 96) reported on burials 2 and 3 from Coxcatlan Cave in the Tehuacan valley, belonging to El Riego Phase (6500–5000 B.C.). Found in preceramic contexts, in these graves the heads of two children, a five year old and a newborn, had been removed and exchanged with each other. Chronologically, this is the earliest evidence of corpse manipulation (perimortem treatment) in México. Later in the Formative period cultures of Tlapacoya-Zohapilco (Estado de México), Niederberger (1987:674) has discussed the practice of cannibalism for sites in the Ayotla, Manantial, and Tetelpan phases (1250–700 B.C.). In addition, Faulhaber (1965:94) discusses evidence for cannibalism in Tlatilco (Estado de México) in sites dating between 1100–600 B.C.

During the Classic Period (100–800 A.D.) there are reports of decapitation, dismemberment and defleshing, principally affecting skulls and long bones. For example, at Alta Vista (Zacatecas) and Cerro del Huistle, Huejuquilla el Alto (Jalisco) evidence exists for the practice of making a small hole on the top of the skulls in order to hang them, along with long bones, from the roofs of temples (Hers 1989:89–93; Holien and Pickering 1978:146–147; Kelley 1978; Pickering 1985). Dismemberment, defleshing and intentional breakage has been documented at Electra (San Luis Potosi) by

Braniff (1992:149) and by Pijoan and Mansilla (1990). In Teotihuacán (Estado de México) skeletal evidence for decapitation and dismemberment have been reported (Serrano and Lagunas 1974; González 1989:143–193; Cabrera *et al.* 1990). All the burials mentioned above were found associated with religious centers.

In the Postclassic (800 A.D. to contact), evidence for cannibalism and sacrifice is common, documented extensively from written references and codex representations. Examples include reports from Tlatelolco (González 1963:5; Matos 1978:143, 1972:112; Noguera 1966:78) and Templo Mayor in México City (Román 1986; López 1993:262-278), Cholula in Puebla (Serrano 1972:369–371; López *et al.* 1976:61–78), Teotenango in Estado de México (Zacarias 1975:392) and Teopanzolco in Morelos (Lagunas and Serrano 1972:430–432). In all of these sites, great heaps of bones were found, many of them with cutmarks, as well as evidence of decapitation and dismemberment, and offerings of feet or heads on dishes. In all of these reports there was no attempt to study the information that could be analyzed from the bones. Conclusions about ceremonial treatment of human victims were based only on the burial practices (e. g., bone heaps) or the presence of cutmarks. In these studies, when cutmarks were found, cannibalism was the general interpretation.

In our research reported here, we are interested in extending this archaeological and textual data, by documenting evidence for human sacrifice and cannibalism left directly on the skeletons. This systematic study allows us to conduct comparative analyses between different populations. The major difficulties we encountered in documenting cannibalism and/or human sacrifice involve recognition of different modes of the phenomena and developing methods for identifying them in different situations. In our approach, we followed the recommendations and observations outlined by Turner (1983), Turner and Turner (1993), and White (1992). According to these studies the minimal amount of bone damage or modification required to accept a judgement of cannibalism included (1) intentional bone breakage, (2) evidence of exposure to heat, (3) anvil or hammerstone abrasions, (4) cutmarks, (5) extensive absence of missing bones such as vertebrae or coxae, and (6) bone polishing. If the sample studied presented only a few of these factors, cannibalism was rejected and ritual behavior associated with human sacrifice was proposed.

SAMPLES

The osteological samples studied form part of the collections under the Direction of Physical Anthropology of the INAH (National Institute of Anthropology and History) and are housed in the National Museum of Anthropology in México City. Analysed collections (Fig. 8.1) have come from the following sites: Tlatelcomila, Tetelpan (México City) dating to upper Preclassic or Formative Period (500–300 B.C.) (Reyna, N.D.); Electra, Villa de Reyes, San Luis Potosí from the late Classic (350–800 A.D.) (Braniff 1992:149–151), and Tlatelolco, México City from the Postclassic (1337–1521 A.D.). The sample from Tlatelcomila, Tetelpan, México City was excavated 22 years ago by Rosa Reyna, when she dug several one square meter stratigraphic pits to determine the chronological cultural sequence at the southern end of the Méxican basin. The osteological remains were found in four of these pits, two of which constitute a unit, as they were made side-by-side. The human bones were found in intrusions, mixed with pot sherds and animal bones. The areas between the four pits were never excavated, so we only have the material obtained from them and not from all the deposits.

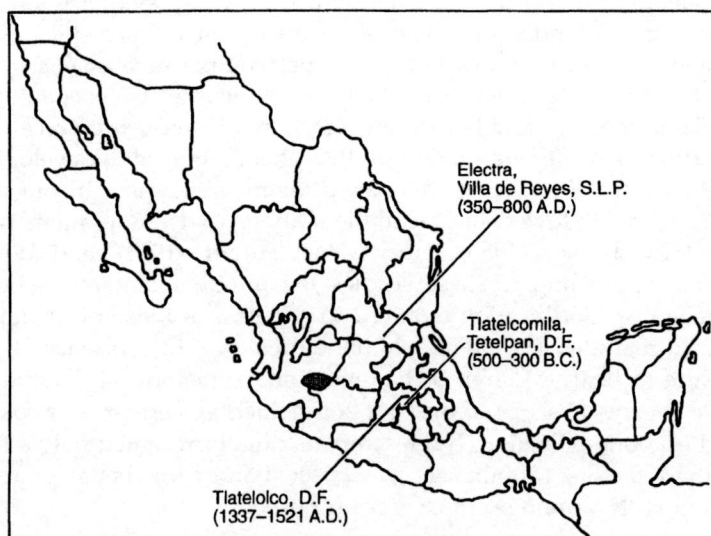

Figure 8.1. Locations of the sites studied.

All the bones appeared to be intentionally broken, some exhibited cutmarks, and there was evidence of them being exposed to fire. We tried to determine the minimum number of persons buried in the different deposits. Using skull fragments, especially the maxilla and temporals, the sample is composed of 18 individuals: one infant less than 2 years, a 2–3 year old, two 4–6 year olds, three 7–12 year olds, one 18–20 year old subadult (possibly female), and ten adults. The adults are comprised of six males, one female, and three whose sex could not be determined. Based on the ceramic analyses made by the archaeologist, the skeletal remains correspond to the late Preclassic or Formative Period between 500–300 B.C.(Reyna, N.D.)

The second sample comes from Electra, Villa de Reyes (San Luis Potosí). Excavated in 1966 by Braniff and Crespo, it is one of the villages which belongs to the region Braniff has named the Tunal Grande archaeological subarea (Braniff 1992:17–19). Time of both principal and more extended occupation was during the San Luis phase that corresponds to the Classic period, between 350–800 A.D. (Braniff 1992:149–151). The osteological materials used in our study were found in a 2-by-2 meter pit in the center of a patio. During the oldest epoch this patio was built with a depression surrounded by stones, with several rooms around it. Later, the level was raised with an artificial filling on which a big fire was made and the remains of several individuals were placed atop the ashes. This ossuary was perfectly sealed by several clay floors which belong to a subsequently constructed square central patio. This second patio had a gallery and four doors which afterwards were walled up when the patio was filled in.

The osteological material consists primarily of broken long bones, none of which were found in anatomical order. A great number possess cutmarks and intentional fractures in addition to showing evidence of exposure to heat or direct fire. As in the case of Tetelpan, we only have materials from the pit and not all the bones that constituted the deposit. Nevertheless, we counted the subjects using the postcranial bones, mainly the scapula since there were very few cranial fragments. We estimate the minimal number was ten individuals comprised of one 0–3 year old, one 4–6 year old, one adolescent (13–17 year old), one female subadult (18–20 year old), and six adults (three males, one female , and two of undeterminable sex).

The third sample derives from the 1961–62 excavations of the prehispanic city of Tlatelolco, México City. Tlatelolco was the twin city of Tenochtitlan, the ancient capital of the Aztec culture. It was founded in 1337, thirteen years after the establishment of Tenochtitlan when the Mexicas divided themselves (Barlow 1987:60). It fell under the Spanish conquerors in 1521. At the site, 140 burials and two ossuaries were found (Noguera 1966:78). In 1962, González (1963) found to the northeast of the Great Pyramid 170 skulls with their mandibles and in some cases the articulated first three cervical vertebrae. The skulls were buried in an orderly fashion and each typically had a large hole in the temporal and parietal region on both sides. The skulls were aligned in groups of five, one next to the other (Matos 1978:143, 1972:112). This grouping, as well as the hole in the temporal region, led the archaeologists to conclude they were part of a *tzompantli* or skull rack, as described by the chroniclers. The skulls and mandibles preserve evidence of cutmarks and blows delivered to the side of the head for making the holes. We studied 100 of them. All were between 18 and 40 years old and consisted of 43 female and 57 males.

METHOD FOR ESTABLISHING INTERHUMAN VIOLENCE AND CORPSE PROCESSING

To undertake this analysis it was necessary to make a systematic study of the cutmarks visible on the surface of the human bones. In addition, it was necessary to establish criteria for recognizing intentional fractures and blows and exposure to heat. Using the results of our analysis we were able to evaluate the patterns of different ritual practices in prehispanic México. We first identified and inventoried the bones and determined age and sex when possible. Then we catalogued the location and frequency of each of the human manipulations (defleshing, dismemberment, intentional breakage, burning), as well as noted the presence of pigment on the bones. In evaluating and analyzing the cutmarks, all surfaces of each bone were examined through a magnifying glass using a tangential light. This information was transferred to graphic registration sheets where the location and angle of inclination of the marks were drawn. We also analyzed some of the cuts through microphotographs, which provided information about the kind of blades used in corpse processing. Using our procedures, we were able to distinguish between cuts on bone and cuts of bone. The former is the indirect result of cutting soft tissue adjacent to the bone and the marks are produced when the bone serves as the underlying support. These marks are usually perpendicular to the direction of muscle and tendon attachment and can take the form of either a number of small parallel cuts or a region of scraping. Some of these only affect the surface of the bone, while others are deeper. We identified "cuts of bone" when bony parts were separated in two by a sharp instrument or blade, used repeatedly in the same place (Pijoan and Pastrana 1989:293). In addition to these considerations, recordings of the distribution of the cutmarks must take into account their anatomical relation, which provides clues for the type of activity, whether skinning, defleshing, dismembering or butchering.

An important consideration when analyzing bone fractures is to establish if they were made by natural causes or human agents and if on dry or fresh bone. The latter has flexibility and ductility and the material is capable of resisting great pressure and deformation before breaking. On the other hand, dry bones are rigid and brittle (Johnson 1985: 160). Breaks on fresh bone produce a characteristic spiral or helical fracture, which takes the form of a radial pattern in a 45° angle with respect to the longitudinal axis of the bone (Johnson 1989:433–434). Techniques to break fresh bone include dynamic loading or a high velocity impact. The minimal technological equipment includes a hammerstone (or hammer) and one or two supports which serve as anvils (Johnson 1985: 192). The hammer produces a circular depression area, as well as bone flakes and negative scars on the wall at the point of impact. Several fracture fronts expand out in a radial pattern from it (Johnson 1985: 194). To establish the patterns of these fractures, we traced them on the same registration sheet where we drew the cutmarks, showing, when evident, the point of impact location.

For determining if bones were exposed to fire or heat, we found visual evidence to be often equivocal and unreliable. Published studies have documented modifications in texture, color, form and size of the bones following exposure to high temperature, usually from cremation (Krogman and Işcan 1986:37–40; Stewart 1976:59–66; Buikstra and Swegle 1989). However, in our Méxican samples the bones were not cremated, but probably roasted or boiled. Thus, we attempted to determine heat exposure by bone histology. In collaboration with the Zentrum Anatomie des Fachbereichs Medizin of the Georg-August-Universität in Göttingen, in particular with Dr. Michael Schultz, we undertook the study of several bones from Tetelpan. These tests have demonstrated that it is possible to determine if a bone has been exposed to direct heat and also the intensity of it (Schultz and Pijoan 1993), but the analysis on the bones which may have been boiled has yet to be done.

SKELETAL EVIDENCE FOR VIOLENCE AND CANNIBALISM

The materials from Tlatelcomila, Tetelpan, have a consistent pattern of cutmarks, mainly on the vault, face, and the mandible (Pijoan and Pastrana 1987). These were produced when the skin, epicranial aponeuroses, and different muscles of the skull, face, and neck were severed. On two parietal fragments, one of a child and the other of an adult, the bone had been cut with a sharp instrument in a semicircular shape (Fig. 8.2). In both cases the intention seems to have been to obtain a circular piece of bone. On a facial fragment, we observed that the inferior border of the zygomatic bone had been removed, probably at the moment the masseter muscle was severed. On several mandibles, part of or the entire condyle had been sliced off during the butchering. Regarding the intentional blows and/or fractures on the skulls, in general,

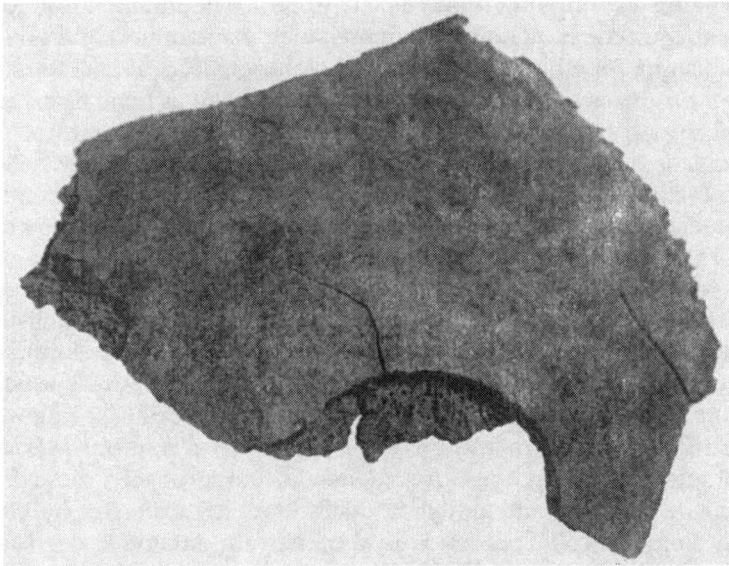

Figure 8.2. Parietal fragment of an adult from Tlatecomila, Tetelpan, Mexico City that shows a semicircular cut. (Photo R. Enríquez. DAF-INAH)

all the temporal bones showed points of impact on the squama or the adjacent bones (parietal or sphenoid), while the parietals had radiating fractures. The face was separated from the vault by means of blows on the zygomatic and the frontal processes of the maxilla (Fig. 8.3). In addition to this corporeal treatment, almost all cranial fragments seem to have been exposed to heat and some were carbonized. On the contrary, the mandibles did not show a constant pattern of intentional fractures. However, all seem to have been placed on top of a fire which caused the inferior border to be burned (Fig. 8.4).

On the postcranial skeleton the cutmarks exhibited a consistent pattern where cutmarks were near muscle or tendon attachments. Cutmarks on the postcranial skeleton were deeper and coarser than those on the skulls, perhaps because it is harder to cut thick muscles, strongly attached to the extremities compared to the skin and the thin muscles of the head and face. Cutmarks on the post-cranial bones exhibited different prevalences depending on the bone studied. For example, cutmarks were much more common on the femur and tibia (Fig. 8.5) than on the bones of the upper limb.

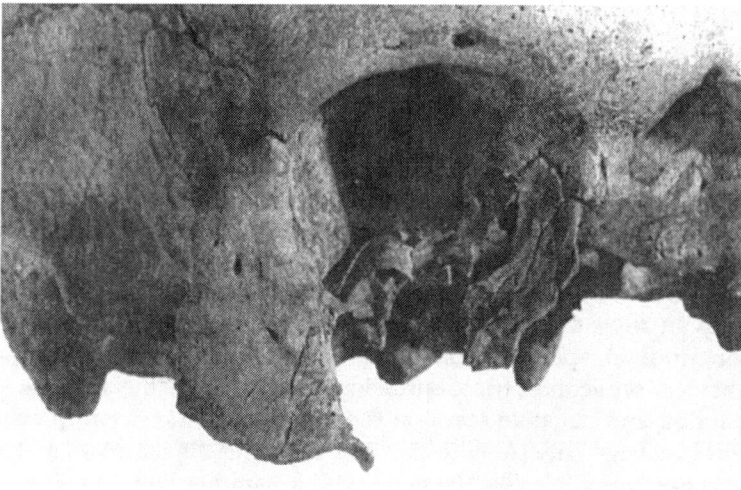

Figure 8.3. Adult skull from Tlatelcomila, Tetelpan, Mexico City. The facial cranium was brokem off by means of blows on the maxilla. (Photo R. Enríquez. DAF-INAH)

Figure 8.4. Adult mandible from Tlatelcomila, Tetelpan, Mexico City, that has the inferior border burned. (Photo R. Enríquez. DAF-INAH)

Considering all postcranial bone fragments in the sample, only 71 (16 %) showed cutmarks.

In contrast to the relatively rare postcranial cutmarks, 98% of the same bones showed intentional breakage. These appear to have been done after the the bodies were butchered since it was clear in several cases that a cutmark continued on the other side of a break. Fractures of long bones showed predominantly a helical pattern, with an angle of break of 45° to the axis of the bone. This produced longitudinal splinters less than 15 cm long. Points of impact showed semiconcentric depressions from which the fracture expanded and negative scars on the bone wall. In order to produce this breakage pattern, with one end exposing the marrow cavity, it was necessary to strike the bone with a hammer with the help of a platform or anvil. Following White's analysis of pot boiling (1992: 120–123), we studied these bone splinters to see if they also presented pot polish on the projecting parts. Since some did we assume this means that meat chunks with bones in them were cooked in a pot, the contents being stirred repeatedly.

Figure 8.5. Tibia epiphyse from a subadult from Tlatelcomila, Tetelpan, Mexico City that shows cut marks and intentional breakage. (Photo I. Borja. DAF-INAH)

Beyond the shaft damage, the epiphyses of some long bones, especially the larger ones (femur, tibia, humerus), appeared crushed and had impacts immediately under their heads. The others (radius, ulna, fibula), as well as long bones of children were fractured in half. Finally, flat bones were smashed and the ribs were broken by flexion. It is important to note that some bones, like the hand and foot bones, vertebrae, scapulae and coxae were mostly missing. Almost all the postcranial bones seemed to have been exposed to heat, either directly or indirectly, and some appear carbonized. Results of histology determined that none were exposed to a temperature above 200°C. (Schultz, Schwartz and Pijoan 1982; Schultz and Pijoan 1993).

At Electra, the skulls were fractured by impacts usually on the parietal and the fragments showed cutmarks on the external surface (Pijoan and Mansilla 1990). On the mandibles we found slight blows on the condyles and cuts on the posterior border of the vertical ramus and on the body. The few vertebrae were all from the cervical region and showed, as well as the three manubria, cutmarks and indications of impacts. The clavicles had cuts on the area of muscle attachments and intentional breaks of the diaphyses. The scapula was the most frequent bone found in this sample, and showed both cutmarks and smashing of the glenoid cavity, the acromion and the coracoid process (Fig. 8.6).

The upper extremity was represented only by the long bones; there were no remains from the hands. All showed cuts in the area of muscle and tendon attachments together with intentional breakage, either of the epiphyses or the medial part of the diaphyses. The few ribs found were snapped by torsion, while the bones of the pelvis were broken by impacts, primarily on the pubis or on the iliac crest. Both exhibited cutmarks. The lower extremity is represented by long bones (but no patellas) and a few foot bones (one calcaneus with impacts on its posterior part, three metatarsals two with impacts and the other with cuts, and one unmodified phalanx). A number of the major bones of the leg were represented only by splinters, while others had their epiphyses removed by blows (Fig. 8.7). These helical fractures indicated impacts on fresh bone and were associated with cutmarks. The cutmarks appeared to be done with different instruments: very fine cuts were probably made by obsidian blades, while in other cases, instruments with more abrupt edges, such as flint, were probably used. A majority of the bones seem to have been exposed to indirect heat, but histological analysis has not yet been performed. We also noted the presence of small quantities of red pigment, as well as some black pigment on the impact points.

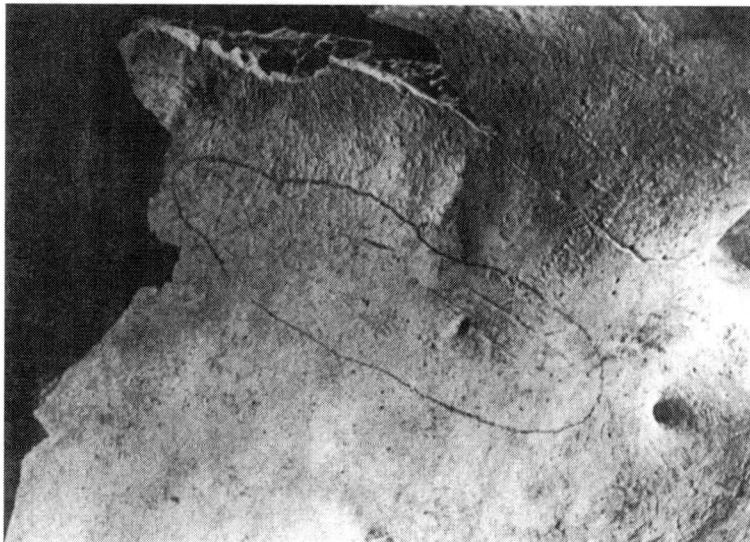

Figure 8.6. Right scapula from Electra, Villa de Reyes, San Luis Potosí, that shows cut marks under the spine. (Photo R. Enríquez. DAF-INAH)

Finally, in the third sample, the skulls from the Tlatelolco skull-rack (Pijoan *et al.* 1989) exhibit a great number of cutmarks as well as consistent perforations of the temporal region. Figures 8.8 and 8.9 review the placement and frequency of the skull treatments, with respect to holes in the cranium and cutmarks on the vault, face, and mandible. Of the 100 skulls studied, only one lacked perforations or cutmarks, 86 had bilateral perforations, and 13 had only unilateral ones (three on the left and 10 on the right side). We suspect the latter represent left and right "row ends" in the rack. All perforations are clearly intentional and have been done with great care. They generally are circular, with a vertical diameter between 5.0–7.5 cm and the horizontal axis between 5.5–8.5 cm. Since all the diameters were greater than 5 cm, this must mean the rod must have been approximately the same size. On the edges of the perforations there were a number of small impact scars made by a hard and pointed chisel or punch. In several cases we found a number of bone flakes inside the skull derived from the missing part. It would appear that the perforation was initiated by a small hole and enlarged by pressure and torsion.

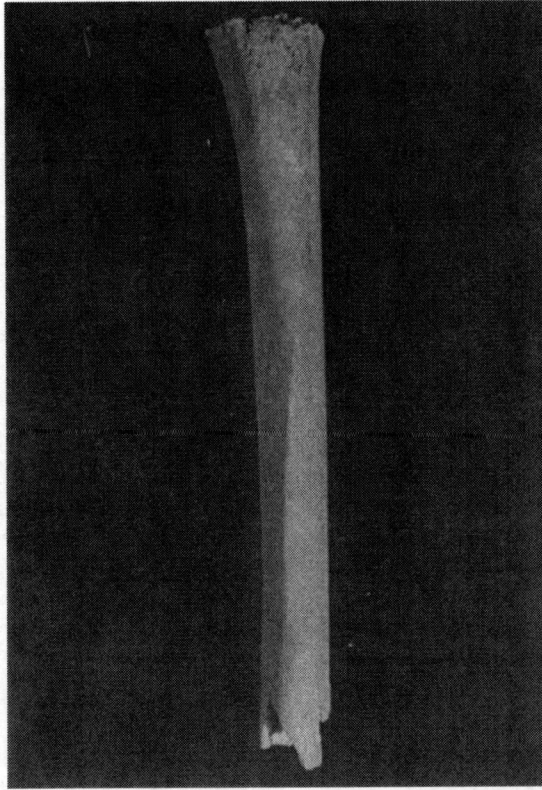

Figure 8.7. Right adult tibia that had its epiphyses removed by small blows. (Photo R. Enríquez. DAF-INAH)

The most visible and most prevalent cutmarks were long cuts beginning at *glabella*, then upward along the frontal midline, continuing along the sagittal suture to the occipital, where they lost continuity due to irregularities of the bone, but clearly ended on the nuchal lines (Fig. 8.10). The cutmark(s) were made by a single cut or multiple, parallel cuts, apparently when the scalp and the epicranial aponeurosis were cut. In 40% of the cases tangential cutmarks of different lengths appeared around the large perforation on the parietal/temporal wall (Fig. 8.8). These cuts were along the origin of the temporal muscle indicating it was probably severed to make the holes. On 50% of the skulls there were small marks on the mastoid process. These are deeper than those on the

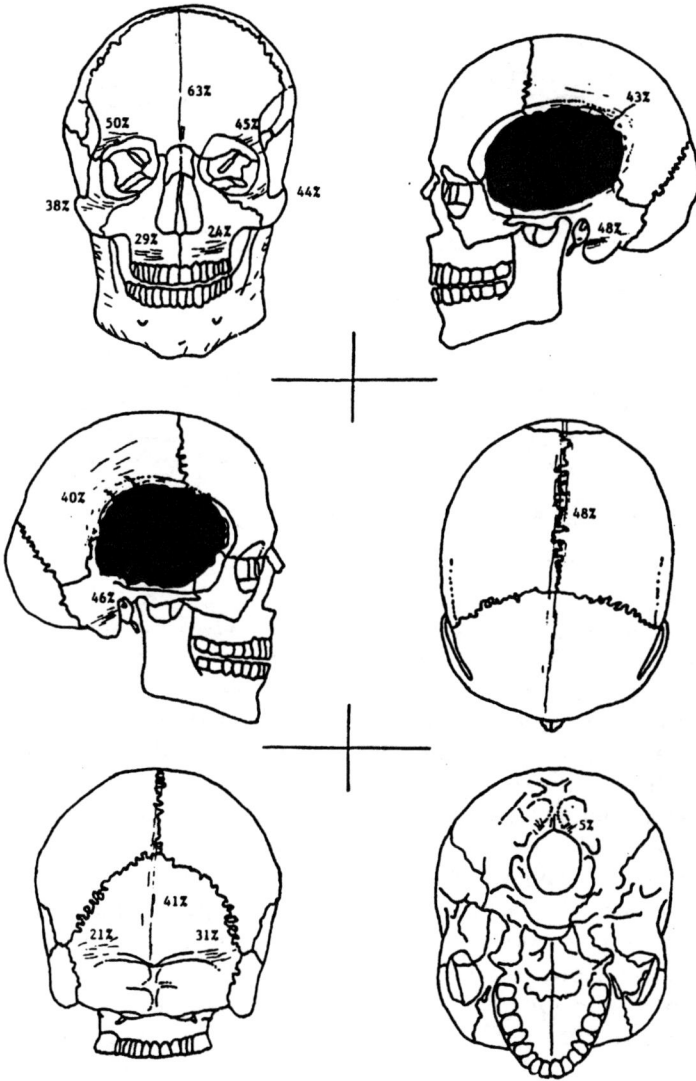

Figure 8.8. Prevalence of cut marks on the skulls from the Tlatelolco Tzompantli.

vault or the face. They appear in the attachment region for the sternocleidomastoid muscle and must be related to severing it (Fig. 8.11). On the lateral edges of the nuchal plane in 30% of the skulls, but lacking a consistent location, were several parallel cuts

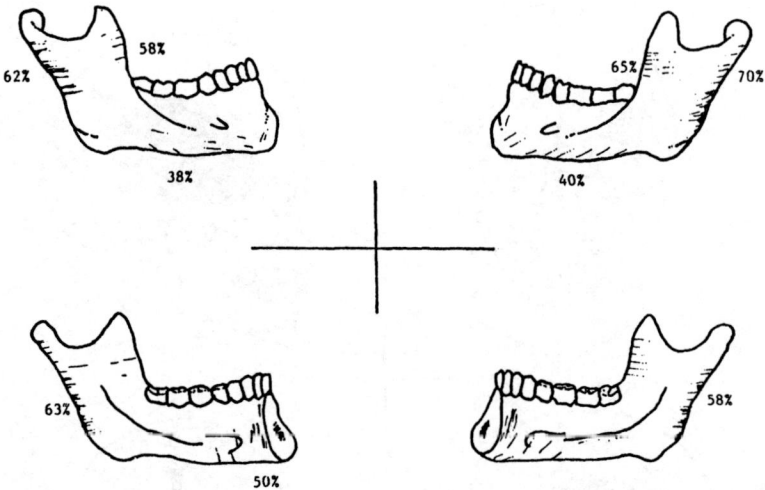

Figure 8.9. Prevalence of cut marks on the mandibles from the Tlatelolco Tzompantli.

(Fig. 8.8). Apparently, these were made when the neck muscles were cut. In a few cases there were cutmarks on the periphery of the foramen magnum, but these were generally minor and isolated. On the supraorbital region as well as the zygomatic bones, semiparallel, slanting small cuts were made, while in one third of the skulls there were several marks on the maxilla above the alveolar border. Finally, nearly all the mandibles had cutmarks, generally around the edge of the vertical ramus, either on the internal or the external view where the masticatory muscles attach. Approximately 40% of them had oblique cuts on the external, lower border of the corpus and half of them also had some on the internal aspect. However, there were no cuts on or under the condyles, or on the zygomatic processes, which indicate that the temporomandibular joint ligaments were not affected, keeping the mandible in its place. In several cases cervical vertebrae, usually the atlas, were associated with the skulls. The vertebrae showed cutmarks above the inferior articular facets, indicating where the head had been separated from the body. Finally, none of the skulls showed any evidence of having been exposed to heat.

From the cutmarks and blows present on these skulls we were able to determine the type of instruments used in the ritual preparation. Impacts around the perforations were made by a hard pointed chisel or punch probably made from obsidian. These

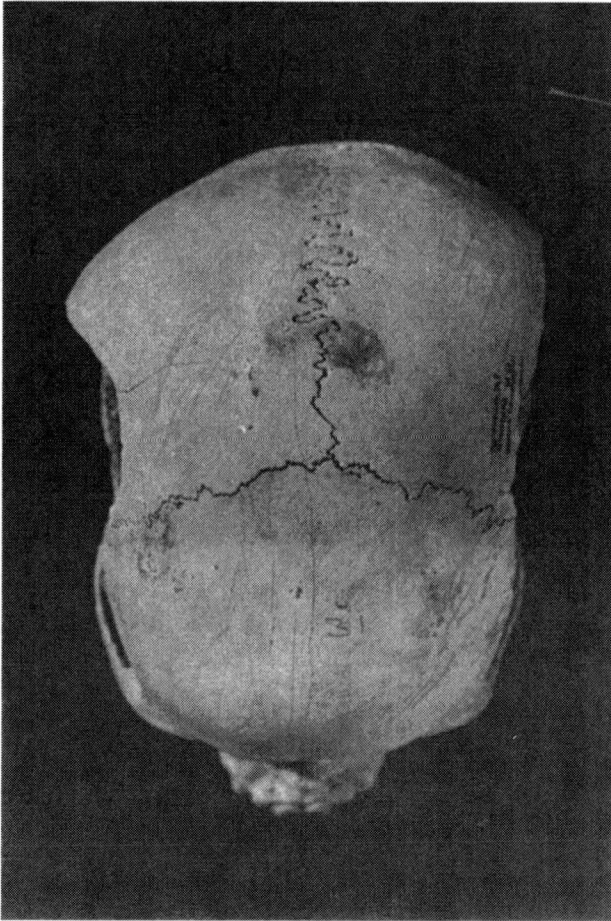

Figure 8.10. Skull from the Tlatelolco Tzompantli, Mexico City that shows cut marks on the vault and perforations on the temporal regions. (Photo R. Enríquez. DAF-INAH)

impacts produced an initial hole that was progressively enlarged by carefully fracturing the edges by pressure (Fig. 8.11). The cutmarks were probably made by obsidian blades, the sharpest instrument known in the prehispanic world (Pijoan and Pastrana 1987:100). However, some coarser cuts, such as those on the borders of the mandibular ramus and on some of the vaults were likely made by an instrument with a "dented" blade. This tool was made by

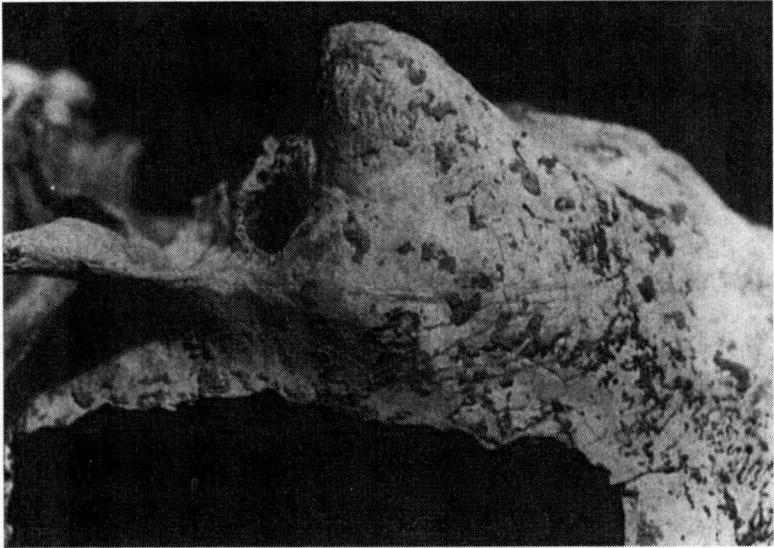

Figure 8.11. Skull from the Tzompantli of Tlateloclo, Mexico City that shows cut marks on the masoid process and the blows used to make the perforation on the temporal. (Photo R. Enríquez. DAF-INAH)

retouching a bifacial artifact, such as a knife or scraper, where the projecting edges are not aligned. In this instance, the cuts generally leave a double or triple mark (Fig. 8.12).

DISCUSSION AND CONCLUSIONS

The bones from Tetelpan are the earliest in our sample, dating prior to 300 B.C. The bones were deposited in what appears to have been a trash deposit. The human bones were mixed with animal bones and pot sherds, and no pigment was detected. Details from the site indicate a pattern of bone modification consistent with an interpretation of perimortem violence and cannibalism. Bone modification is present in individuals of all ages and both sexes, although males have a higher frequency of criteria indicative of violence and cannibalism. Around 16% of the postcranial bones showed cutmarks near muscle and tendon attachments. On the skulls, cuts were consistent with the action of skinning and defleshing. Intentional fractures showed a regular pattern of

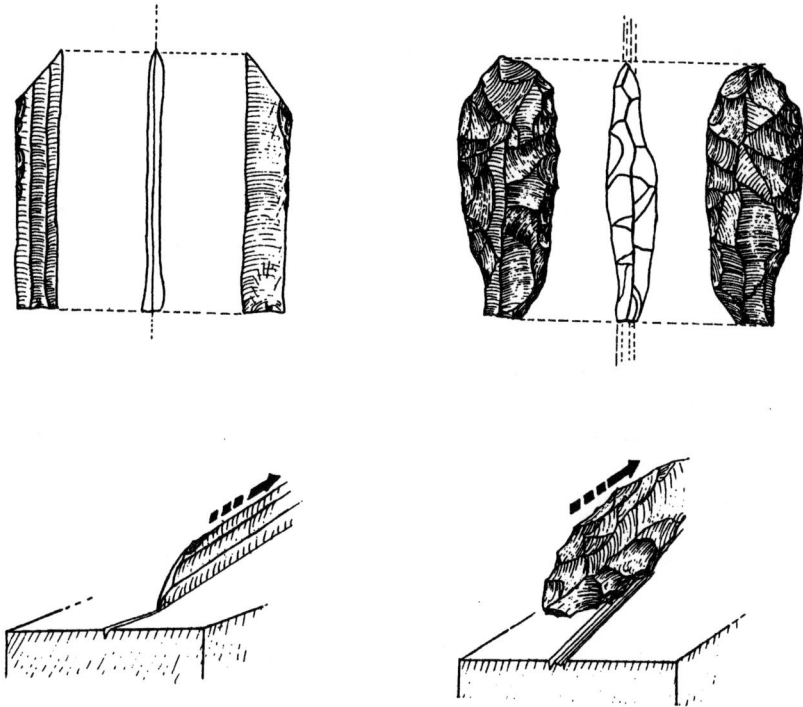

Figure 8.12. Cut marks that are left by different kinds of instrument blades. Prismatic blades leave a single cut, unless its border has chipped, while a dented blade leaves a double or triple mark.

breakage. The skulls were crushed by strong blows to the parietal region, perhaps to remove the brain, although there is the possibility that they were the cause of death or both. The face was separated from the vault by impacts on the zygomatic bone and the frontal processes of the maxilla. Flinn *et al.* (1976:313) proposed that facial mutilation such as we observed at Tetelpan is one of the characteristics of cannibalism in the Southwest US. For the rest of the skeleton, the long bones were broken by a hammerstone and anvil which caused helical fractures exposing the marrow cavity, while the epiphyses and flat bones were crushed. The bones were exposed to long periods of direct heat of less than 200° C and meat portions with bone splinters were put in a ceramic pot and cooked and stirred.

In the case of Electra, while the sample showed the same characteristics as those from Tetelpan, there were several features that differentiated them. The bones were found above an old patio, that had its level raised by an artificial filling, on top of which a big fire had burned. Afterwards, the human remains were placed over the ashes, mixed with animal bones, pot sherds, and some red pigment. Bone modification is present in individuals of all ages and both sexes. On top of these were spread several clay floors, completely sealing the deposit. We believe that the human remains at Electra represent the result of human sacrifice. They were buried in this place after being defleshed, dismembered, butchered and cannibalized, probably as an offering to the construction of a new building.

The skulls from the Tzompantli of Tlatelolco in México City were buried near the Great Pyramid. Individuals are represented by adult males and females and all had a common pattern of cutmarks and impact fractures. Our observations are consistent with an interpretation that the skulls belonged to sacrificed individuals who were afterwards decapitated, skinned, and defleshed. Perforations were made in the temporal region and the skulls placed in a *tzompantli* or skull rack. Because of the different types of cutmarks on the vaults, we think the heads were probably prepared by different persons. However, given the consistency of the cutting and especially the holes in the temporals, it is clear that the people performing the ritual were specialists. Because the mandibles and cervical vertebrae were associated with each cranium, it appears that these skulls were exposed in the *tzompantli* for only a short time before they were buried. It is clear that these skulls show a high ritual context, where cannibalism may or may not have been present, as we only have the skulls and do not know what happened with the rest of the body.

From these three samples, we can propose that human sacrifice and cannibalism were interrelated to each other, both dating to deep antiquity in México. In village communities, like the ones from the Formative Period, they were a community event with a ritual base, where the importance was the act of cannibalism, and afterwards the remains lost all their ritual meaning and were thrown in domestic trash deposits. Through time, with the development of more complex societies and religious rituals, the bones themselves assumed importance as a part of the ritual, and were either buried in special places or exposed in temples as offerings to the gods (Pijoan and Mansilla 1990b). Presumably, these ritual treatments were done by high status individuals. Finally, with the appearance of militaristic societies such as the Aztecs, the number of human sacrifices increased dramatically, related to increased ritualism and the number of war captives.

In summary, we feel these three sites, spread over 2000 years of Mexican prehistory, show a pattern of violence, cannibalism, and sacrifice through time. Based on the archaeological evidence, the distribution of human bones, and the indications of violence left on them, there can be little doubt that that cannibalism and human sacrifice were long prevalent in ancient societies of México.

REFERENCES

Anderson, J. E. (1967). "The Human Skeletons." In *The Prehistory of the Tehuacan Valley. Vol. I: Environment and Subsistence*, ed. R. McNeish, pp. 91–113. Austin: University of Texas Press.

Arens, W. (1981). *El Mito del Canibalismo*. México: Siglo Veintiuno Editores.

Braniff, C. B. (1992). La *Estratigrafa Arqueológica de Villa de Reyes, San L uis Potosí*. México: I.N.A.H.

Barlow, R. H. (1987). *Tlatelolco Rival de T enochtitlan*, eds. Monjarás-Ruiz, J., E. Limón and M. C. Paillés. México: I.N.A.H.-U.D.L.A.

Buikstra, J. E. and Swegle, M. (1989). "Bone Modification due to Burning: Experimental Evidence." In *Bone Modification*, eds. R. Bonnichsen and M. H. Sorg, pp. 247–258. Orono: University of Maine.

Cabrera, C. R., Cowgill, G. L. and Sugiyama, S. (1990). "El Proyecto Templo de Quetzalcoatl y la Práctica a Gran Escala del Sacrificio Humano." In *La Epoca Clásica: Nuevos Hallazgos, Nuevas Ideas*, ed. A. Cardós, pp. 123–146. México: M.N.A.-I.N.A.H.

Cortés, H. (1970). *Cartas de Relación*. México: Editorial Porrúa.

Durán, F. D. (1967). *Historia de las Indias de Nueva España e Islas de la Tierra Firme*. México: Editorial Porrúa.

Faulhaber, J. (1965). "La Población de Tlatilco, México, Caracterizada por sus Entierros." In *Homenaje a Juan Comas en su 65 Aniversario, Volume II*, pp. 83–121. México: Editorial Libros de México.

Flinn, L., Turner, C. G. and Brow, A. (1976). "Additional Evidence for Cannibalism in the Southwest, the Case of LA 4528." *American Antiquity* 41:308–318.

González, R. F. (1963). "Un Tzompantli en Tlatelolco." *Boletín del INAH*: 3–5.

González, M. L. A. (1989). *La Población de Teotihuacán: Un Análisis Bio-Cultural*. México: Tesis Profesional, E.N.A.H.

Hers, M. A. (1989). *Los Toltecas en T ierras Chichimecas*. Cuadernos de Historia del Arte 35, I.I.E. México: U.N.A.M.

Holien, T. and Pickering, R. B. (1978). "Analogues in Classic Period Chalchihuites Culture to Late Mesoamerican Ceremonialism." In *Middle*

Classic Mesoamerica: A.D. 400-700, ed. E. Pasztory, pp. 145–157. New York: Columbia University Press.

Johnson, E. (1985). "Current Developments in Bone Technology." In Advances in Archaeological Method and Theory, Vol. 8, ed. M.B Schiffer, pp. 157–235. Orlando: Academic Press.

_____ (1989). "Human Modified Bones from Early Southern Plains Sites." In Bone Modification, ed. R. Bonnichsen and M. H. Sorg, pp. 431–471. Orono: University of Maine.

Kelley, E. A. (1978). "The Temple of the Skulls at Alta Vista, Chalchihuites." In Across the Chichimec Sea, ed. C. Riley and B. C. Hedrick, pp. 102–126. Carbondale: Illinois University Press.

Krogman, W. M. and Isan, M. Y. (1986). The Human Skeleton in Forensic Medicine. Springfield IL: Charles C. Thomas.

Lagunas, Z. and Serrano, C. (1972). "Decapitación y Desmembramiento Corporal en Teopanzolco, Morelos.' In Religión en Mesoamérica, XII Mesa Redonda, eds. J. Litvak and N. Castillo, pp. 429–433. México: Sociedad Mèxicana de Antropología.

López, A. S., Lagunas Z. and Serrano, C. (1976). Enterramientos Humanos de la Zona Arqueológica de Cholula, Puebla. Colección Científica 44. México: S.E.P.-I.N.A.H.

López, L. L. (1993). Las Ofrendas del Templo Mayor de Tenochtitlan. México: I.N.A.H.

Matos M. E. (1972). "El Tzompantli en Mesoamérica." In Religión en Mesoamérica, XII Mesa Redonda, eds. J. Litvak and N. Castillo, pp. 109–116. México: Sociedad Mexicana de Antropología.

_____ (1978). Muerte a Filo de Obsidiana. L os Nahuas Frente a la Muerte. México: S.E.P.-I.N.A.H.

Niederberger, B. C. (1987). Paleopaysages et Archaeologie Pre-Urbaine du Bassin de México. Tome II. México: Centre d'Etudes Méxicaines et Centroamericaines.

Noguera, E. (1966). "Historia de las Exploraciones en Tlatelolco." In Summa Anthopologica en Homenaje a Roberto J. Weitlaner, pp. 71–78. México: I.N.A.H.-S.E.P.

Pickering, R. B. (1985). "Human Osteological Remains from Alta Vista, Zacatecas: An Analysis of the Isolated Bone." In The Archaeology of West and Northwest Mesoamerica, ed. M.S. Foster and P. C. Weigand, pp. 290–325. New York: Westview Press.

Pijoan, C. M. and Mansilla, J. (1990a). "Prácticas Rituales en el Norte de Mesoamérica. Evidencias en Electra, Villa de Reyes, San Luis Potosí." Arqueología 4: 87–96.

_____ (1990b). "Evidencias Rituales en Restos Humanos del Norte de Mesoamérica." In Mesoamérica y Norte de México. Siglo IX– XII, ed. F. Sodi, pp. 467–478. México: M.N.A.-I.N.A.H.

Pijoan, C. M. and Pastrana A. (1987). "Evidencias de Antropofagia y Sacrificio Humano en Restos Oseos." *Avances en Antropología Física* 4:95–102. México: I.N.A.H.

Pijoan, C. M., Pastrana, A. and Maquivar, C. (1989). "El Tzompantli de Tlatelolco. Una Evidencia de Sacrificio Humano." In *Estudios de Antropologa Biológica*, eds. C. Serrano and M. Salas, pp. 561–583. México:U.N.A.M.-I.N.A.H.

Reyna R. R. M. (N.D.). *Tetelpan: Un Sitio de las Estribaciones del Ajusco.* unpublished manuscript.

Roman, B. J. A. (1986). *El Sacrificio de Niños en Honor a Tlaloc (La Ofrenda No. 48 del Templo Mayor, México)*. Tesis Profesional, E.N.A.H.

Sahagún, F. B. de (1989). *Historia General de las Cosas de Nueva España*. México: C.N.C.A. Alianza Editorial Mexicana.

Schultz, M., Schwartz, P. and Pijoan, C.M. (1982). "Microscopical Investigations on Some Long Bones from Tetelpan, D. F., México." *Proceedings Paleopathology Association*. 4th. European Meeting, pp. 192. Middleburg-Antwerpen.

Schultz, M. and Pijoan, C. M. (1993). "Results of Microscopic Research on Bones from Preclassic Tetelpan, México." Paper presented in 13th International Congress of Anthropological and Ethnological Sciences. México City, México.

Serrano, C. (1972). "Un Sitio de Entierros Ceremoniales en Cholula, Puebla.' In *Religión en Mesoamérica, XII Mesa Redonda*, eds. J. Litvak and N. Castillo, pp. 369–374. México: Sociedad Mexicana de Antropología.

Serrano, C. and Lagunas, Z. (1974). "Sistema de Enterramientos y Notas sobre el Material Osteológico de la Ventilla, Teotihuacán, México." *Anales del INAH*, Epoca 7a 4:105–144.

Stewart, T. D. (1979). *Essentials of Forensic Anthropology*. Springfield IL: Charles C. Thomas.

Turner, C. G. (1983). "Taphonomic Reconstructions of Human Violence and Cannibalism Based on Mass Burials in the American Southwest." In *Carnivores, Human Scavengers and Predators: A Question of Bone Technology*, eds. G. M. Lemoine and A. S. MacEachern, pp. 219–240. Calgary: University of Calgary.

Turner, C. G. and Turner, J. A. (1993). "Taphonomic Analysis of Anasazi Skeletal Remains From Largo-Gallina Sites in Northwestern New Mexico." *Journal of Anthropological Research* 49:83–110.

White, T. D. (1992). *Prehistoric Cannibalism at Mancos 5MT UMR-2346*. Princeton: Princeton University Press.

Zacarías, P. (1975). "Los Enterramientos." In *Teotenango. El Antiguo Lugar en la Muralla (II)*, pp. 365–409. México: Dirección de Turismo, Gobierno del Estado de México.

Chapter
NINE

Osteological Indications of Warfare in the Archaic period of the Western Tennessee Valley

Maria Ostendorf Smith
Department of Anthropology
Northern Illinois University

Osteoarchaeologically derived information about the nature and pattern(s) of American Indian warfare-related perimortem violent trauma (*e.g.*, inflicted projectile points, scalping, decapitation and other dismemberment trophy-taking practices) is essentially confined to the late prehistoric and protohistoric time periods. Much of this paleopathological literature focuses on osteological collections from the North American Plains (*e.g.*, Owsley *et al.* 1977; Williams 1991; Willey 1990) or the Southwest (*e.g.*, Allen *et al.* 1985; Turner and Morris 1970). Information about intergroup violence from earlier archaeological horizons does appear intermittently in the literature (*e.g.*, Milner *et al.* 1991; Owsley and Berryman 1975; Seeman 1988) but, most references are limited to a description of an inflicted projectile point or a presumptive scalping victim (*e.g.*, Morse 1989; Neumann 1940; Ortner and Putschar 1985:93; Owsley and Berryman 1975; St. Hoyme and Bass 1962; Snow 1941; Tiffany *et al.* 1988). At this research juncture, little is known of the patterns or the temporal and spatial distribution of intergroup violence outside of the above-mentioned geographic areas. Certainly little is known about warfare among Archaic period (specifically 6000 to 1000/500 B.C.) hunter-gatherers.

In a much broader sense, this means that there is a shortage of basic information that is potentially germane to hypotheses, perhaps even underlying assumptions, about the origins and maintenance of war. It has been asserted that incipient status differentiation is present in all hunter-gatherer societies (Begler 1978; Cashdan 1980; Leacock and Lee 1982). Certain paradigms (specifically materialist/ecological models) stress the dynamic role of warfare in the genesis of social complexity (see Ferguson 1990). Therefore, information about intergroup violence in prehistoric hunter-gatherer societies would not only provide much needed diachronic information but might impact discussion of the process of cultural evolution.

The Archaic period human osteological sample from the Kentucky Lake Reservoir of western Tennessee is large (seven sites, over 600 individuals) and geographically discrete (Fig. 9.1). Its informative potential for warfare-associated paleopathology can be demonstrated by observing that the cemetery samples yielded the first documented Archaic period occurrences of scalping (Smith 1992, 1993a, 1995), an antiquity corroborated in the Bahm site in the northern Plains (Williams 1994). In the Cordell Hull Reservoir of adjacent middle Tennessee, the earliest example of decapitation and forearm trophy-taking was identified (Smith 1993b). The Kentucky Lake Reservoir human osteological remains are therefore potentially well-suited to providing baseline information about patterns or endemicity of intergroup violence.

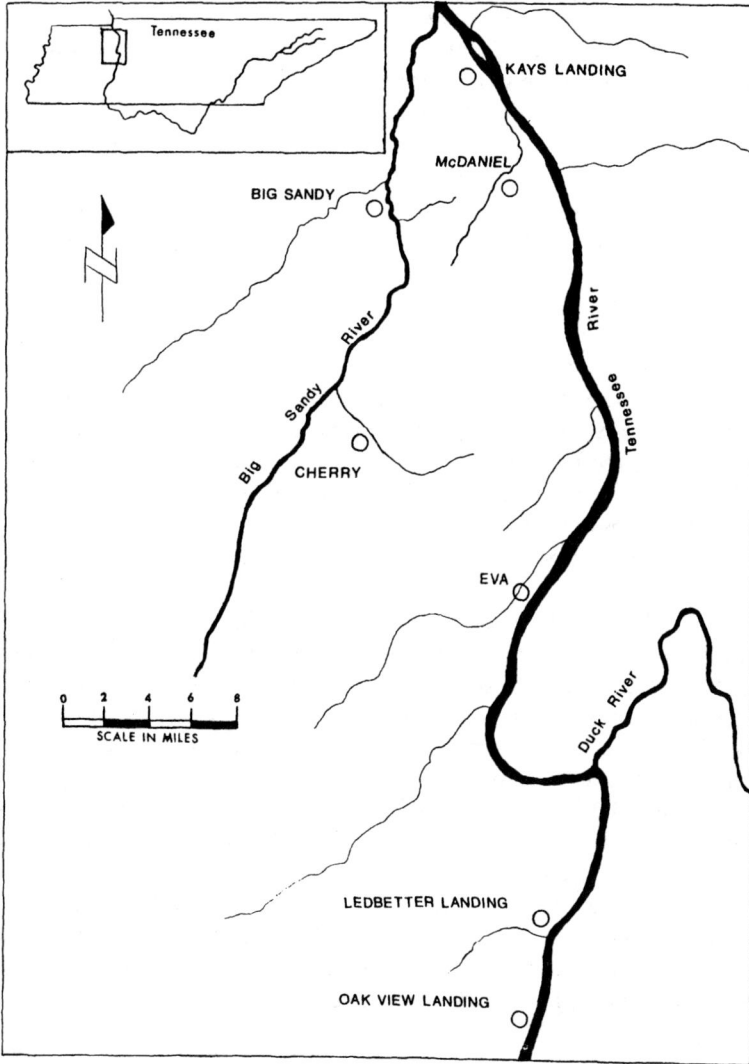

Figure 9.1. Map of the Archaic sites in western Tennessee. The sites and river contours reflect pre-reservoir relationships.

THE KENTUCKY LAKE SAMPLE

The seven sites which yielded the human osteological remains are located in what is now the Kentucky Lake Reservoir of the western

Tennessee River Valley. These sites are dated to the late Archaic period (circa 2500–1000/500 B.C.) with the addition of a middle Archaic (6000–3500 B.C.) component at the Eva site (Bowen 1975; Lewis and Kneberg 1947, 1959; Lewis and Lewis 1961; Magennis 1977). Based on the occurrence of subadult victims of intergroup violence in some late prehistoric sites (*e.g.*, Crow Creek, South Dakota) both adult and subadult individuals were examined. Out of 662 interments, 439 (both primary and secondary) were deemed complete enough for this study, including 90 subadults. Infants under two years of age were not included.

Warfare-associated perimortem violent trauma such as scalping and dismemberment trophy taking are identifiable by a specific pattern of macroscopic cutmarks. Mortuary treatment which includes defleshing or dismemberment may introduce ambiguity and perhaps offer an alternative etiology for cutmarks (Fenton 1991; Olsen and Shipman 1994; Raemsch 1993). Therefore, it is prudent to review the interment practices of late Archaic populations in west Tennessee to assess, if not eliminate, alternative etiologies for macroscopic cutmarks. The various studies of the mortuary treatment of Kentucky Lake Archaic populations indicate that the principle mortuary treatment is the primary interment in a flexed or semi-flexed position (Brown 1982; Higgens 1982; Hofman 1985; Magennis 1977). Secondary burials (cremations and bundle burials) also occur but are infrequent (Hofman 1985). Neither the primary nor the secondary interments have been characterized by segregation (i.e., a cache) or differential retrieval (i.e., *memento mori*, Fenton 1991) of body parts. Although defleshing is not part of the mortuary treatment for the late Archaic population from middle Tennessee (Smith 1993a), there are no complete published data for the Kentucky Lake Archaic sample. The current examination of perimortem violent trauma will therefore include a comprehensive examination of all cutmarks for all seven sites.

SELECTION OF PARAMETERS

For convenience, perimortem trauma associated with intergroup aggression may be segregated into two data cohorts (Tab. 9.1). The first cohort consists of evidence suggesting violent death. This includes inflicted projectile points, blunt force trauma to the cranium (depression or pond fractures) (Merbs 1989:166–168; Ortner and Putschar 1985:71–73; Ubelaker 1989:109) and cutmarks to the trunk which suggest attempted or successful infliction of mortal stab

Table 9.1. Categories of Warfare Related Perimortem Violent Trauma

Violent Death
    Inflicted Projectile Points
    Blunt Force Trauma (depression fractures of the cranial vault)
    Cutmarks on the Trunk (stab wounds)
Trophy Taking
    Scalping
    Decapitation
    Disembodiment and Retrieval of Portable Body Elements (limbs, mandibles)

wounds (Olsen and Shipman 1994:385). Parry fractures, non-lethal trauma to the radius and/or ulna, have also been used to suggest intergroup violence (Angel 1974; Lahren and Berryman 1984; Wood-Jones 1910), but must be regarded as equivocal in the absence or corroborative cranio-facial trauma. Parry fractures in conjunction with cranio-facial data have, however, been associated with interpersonal (female-directed) rather that intergroup violence (Martin *et al.* 1993; Martin and Akins 1994; Shermis 1982/84; Wilkinson and Van Wagenen 1993). Parry fractures are dismissed from the data set in this examination because previous research on interpersonal violence in the Kentucky Lake Archaic sample did not support a non-accidental etiology (Smith 1993c, 1996).

A second suite of warfare-related trauma suggests trophy taking. This form of perimortem mutilation includes scalping and the retrieval of non-torso body components such as mandibles, crania, and distal limb elements (*e.g.*, fingers, hands, forearms, feet, etc.). These have been identified by a particular pattern of cutmarks and the concomitant absence of certain body elements on numerous individuals from sites such as the Crow Creek massacre (Willey 1990; Willey and Emerson 1993), the massacre at Hopi (Turner and Morris 1970), Chavez Pass and Grasshopper Ruin (Arizona) (Allen *et al.* 1985), and the Oneota site of Norris Farm #36 from Illinois (Milner *et al.* 1991). There are also various descriptions of scalping victims from the ethnohistorical (*e.g.*, Adair 1775:387-88; Catlin 1841:328; Timberlake 1927:113) and bioarchaeological literature (*e.g.*, Morse 1989; Neumann 1940; Ortner and Putschar 1985:93; Owsley and Berryman 1975; St. Hoyme and Bass 1962; Snow 1941). In the identification of Kentucky Lake hunter-gatherer conflict-related violent trauma, the criteria for violent trauma have been

complemented by mortuary-related dismemberment and/or defleshing cutmark diagnostics (Fenton 1991; Olsen and Shipman
1994; Raemsch 1993; White 1986, 1992).

DISCRIMINATION AND INTERPRETATION OF CUTMARKS

In the postdepositional environment, bony alterations may occur
which superficially mimic blade induced cutmarks. These alterations include cracking and weathering (Miller 1975), root stains
(Binford 1981), trowel and instrument damage (Blakely and Matthews 1990; White and Toth 1989), small carnivore and rodent
damage which "trench" or "trough" bone often without punctur-
ing the cortex (Milner and Smith 1989; Potts and Shipman 1981;
Snyder and Willey 1989), and vascular channels (Saul and Saul
1993). These may often be readily distinguished from cutmarks
associated with mortuary activity and perimortem violent trauma
by the latter's isomorphy to "green bone" butchering marks identified on faunal samples (e.g., Hill 1976, 1979; Russell 1987; Russell
and LeMort 1986; Shipman and Rose 1983), resemblance to experi-
mentally induced cutmarks (Friederici 1907; Hamperl and Laughlin 1959; Hamperl 1961), and patterned rather than serendipitous
location on the skeleton.

Cutmarks associated with scalping are highly diagnostic and are
identified as a series of cuts made in a somewhat circular path
around the crown of the head. They are most commonly found in
the hairline region of the frontal, on the mid-parietal, and more
inferiorly on the suprameatal crest of the temporal bone and the
nuchal crest of the occipital. The scoring of the cortical bone is
more likely wherever subcutaneous tissues are minimal (Adair
1775:387–88; Catlin 1841:328; Friederici 1907; Knowles 1940; Nadeau 1944; Owsley et al. 1977; Reese 1940; Timberlake 1927:113;
Willey 1990). Decapitation is identified osteoarchaeologically by the
absence of any cranio-facial fragments and/or C1/C2 in an undisturbed context with cutmarks at the site of the most superior surviving cervical vertebra (Merbs 1989:176; Owsley and Berryman
1975; Smith 1993c; Willey 1990).

Dismemberment trophy taking of bones of the appendicular
skeleton may be identified osteoarchaeologically in an undisturbed
primary interment which exhibits circumferential cutmarks restricted to the area proximal to an absent limb. These cutmarks, if
adjacent to the joint, may be accompanied by indications of perimortem snapping or splintering of the longbone shaft (Willey

1990:123–126). Any suggestion of defleshing such as numerous short stroke cutmarks or scraping over a broader surface area (Raemsch 1993; Olsen and Shipman 1994; White 1986) or cutmarks anywhere on the bone irrespective of kind or depth of the subcutaneous structure (Olsen and Shipman 1993:381) would undermine confidence in a warfare etiology for retrieval of particular bones. Rendering or cleaning of an individual, whether perimortem or consequential to extended taphonomic processes, will also enable selective retrieval of body elements. Although previous examinations of the mortuary patterning of the Kentucky Lake sample indicate that dismemberment was not part of the interment process, osteological corroboration is necessary and vital if a warfare etiology is acceptable for any given suite of cutmarks. Therefore, all cutmarks are recorded. Any striations not clearly identifiable as cutmarks were excluded from the data set.

MORTUARY BEHAVIOR

In general, sixteen individuals exhibited discernable cutmarks and six individuals possessed inflicted projectile points. There were no examples of perimortem or healed blunt trauma to the cranial vault. The individuals with observed cutmarks were carefully assessed against the aforementioned criteria as well as the available data on mortuary treatment in the Kentucky Lake Reservoir.

Of the sixteen interments who exhibited perimortem cutmarks, six had marks which are best interpreted as mortuary treatment. With one exception, discussed below, the cutmarks are confined to the areas adjacent to the joints of the hip, knee, and elbow (Fig. 9.2). They are superficial (occasionally just glancing the cortex) and few in number (generally two or three at any given location). They are inconsistent with disarticulation. Therefore, both dismemberment and defleshing are contraindicated in this sample. The mortuary treatment recorded for these individuals may provide an interpretive framework for assessing a motive for the cutmarks. This treatment is flexure in a primary interment. Indeed, several were identified in the field notes as being flexed "knees to chin" or a "tightly flexed ball burial" (suggesting binding). It should be noted that amount of flexure is not offered as a predictor of cutmark occurrence. Apart from flexure dictated by pit dimensions, factors such as body mass or postmortem delay before interment may affect the amount of flexure which may be accomplished.

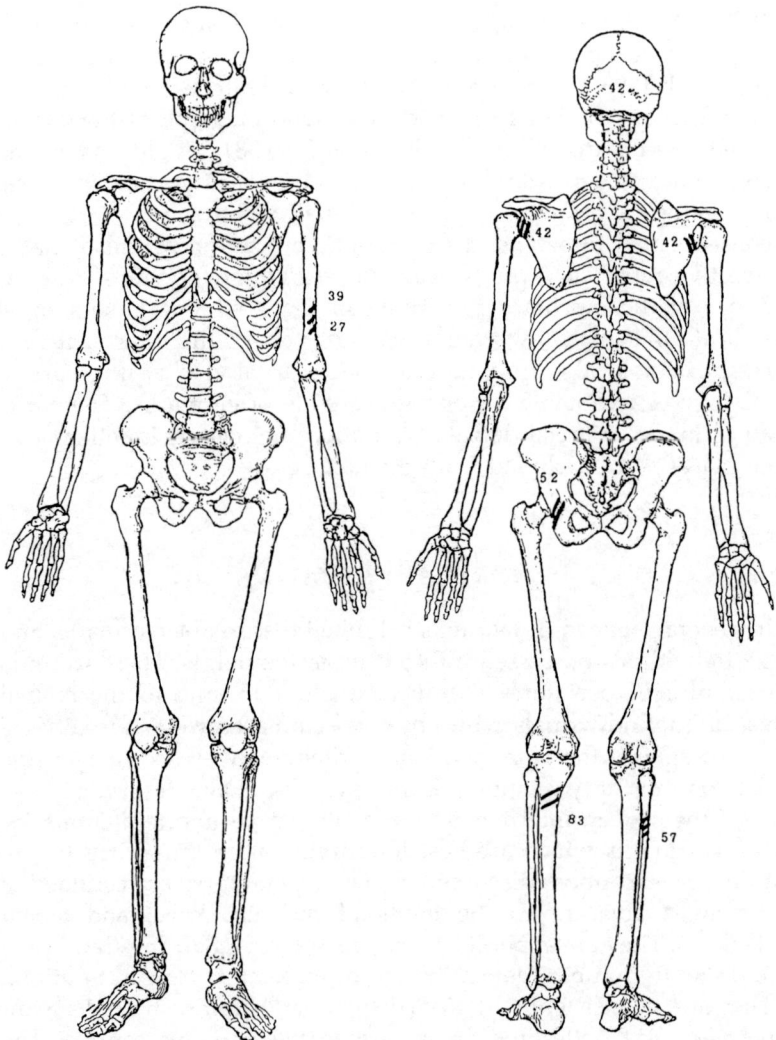

Figure 9.2. Location of the cutmarks associated with mortuary treatment. The numbers reflect the burial numbers.

The cutmarks that are found at the hip occur on a single interment. They are located in the middle of the sciatic notch of the left innominate. Scoring of the innominate at this deep location may be incidental to thorough severing of thigh extensors. It is possible

Table 9.2. Summary Data of Mortuary Related Cutmarks

Site Name	Burial Number	Gender	Location of Cutmarks			
			Elbow	Hip	Knee	Other
Eva	83	?			X	
	39	F	X			
Big Sandy	27	M?	X			
Ledbetter Landing	42	?				X
	52	F?		X		
	57	F			X	
Total Cases	6	2	1	2	1	

that this was accomplished by extreme thigh flexure (knee to chin) which is a frequent burial posture in the Kentucky Lake sample. Joint flexure also seems to be the motive for the cutmarks on two individuals with striae adjacent to the knee. One individual exhibits cutmarks on the proximal dorsal tibia. The second exhibits cutmarks on the lateral surface of the proximal fibula. Cuts in this area would have severed the posterior crural muscles where ligaments of several flexor muscles (e.g., *m. gastrocnemius, m. popliteus*) would have spanned the joint. The cuts are not circumferential and do not suggest disarticulation.

There are two cases of cutmarks on the distal humerus. The few glancing cuts generally straddle the lateral supracondylar ridge. In neither case were the cutmarks bilateral or circumferential. Like the hip and knee joints, there is no evidence to suggest that the purpose of the cuts was disarticulation. It is likely that the scoring of the ridge occurred coincident to severing various tendons (e.g. *m. triceps brachii*) to promote unrestricted flexure at the elbow joint. Therefore, at this time, the cutmarks which occur on these five individuals are best interpreted as facilitating limb flexure which would enable the burial to accommodate the burial pit.

The only "stray" cuts found in the Kentucky Lake sample appeared on a single burial, a partial cremation, from the Ledbetter Landing site. The interment is one of nine *in situ* pit cremations from the site. It is also the only one of the nine with cutmarks. In this complete skeleton, the cutmarks occur internal to the cranium (three or four striations on the occipital) and on the dorsal surfaces of both scapulae (Fig. 9.2). The location of the cutmarks on this articulated skeleton, particularly the ones on the cranium, suggest efforts to facilitate burning. There is no evidence that pit cremations were occasions for defleshing or dismemberment.

Although the mortuary practices of the Kentucky Lake populations included opportunities to engage in defleshing prior to final
interment, there is no evidence to suggest that such postmortem
rendering occurred. This is an important observation. The elimination of defleshing as an etiology for any or all cutmarks irrespective of mortuary treatment strengthens the warfare etiology of
those cutmarks which otherwise conform to the pattern and location of deliberate violent trauma.

VIOLENT TRAUMA

Out of 439 interments, ten individuals, all male, exhibit features
consistent with warfare-related perimortem violent trauma
(Fig. 9.3, Tab. 9.3). Evidence suggesting violent death includes six
individuals, mostly from the Cherry site, who possessed imbedded
projectile points. Although no individual exhibited evidence of
blunt trauma to the cranium, a male from the Ledbetter Landing
site (Burial 49) may have survived cranial injury from a sharp
object, conceivably a projectile point. Since the traumatic origin of
the cranial injury is presumptive, this case cannot be introduced as
evidence for intergroup violence. However, the suggested etiology,
an inflicted projectile point in the cranium, does occur (with lethal
consequences) in Burial 73 from the Cherry site.
      Cutmarks in conjunction with corroborating evidence indicate
violent death in two individuals. A mature male (Eva site, Burial
194) exhibits cutmarks bilaterally on the superior surface of the first
rib and the surviving clavicle (Fig. 9.4). From the field notes, this
undisturbed primary interment was observed *in situ* with a totally
dorsally-facing cranium. The scenario suggests a deeply slit throat
either as the manner of death or an attempted decapitation. The
field notes also indicate that the burial was inexplicably minus both
arms and a leg. The surviving joints did not indicate any antemor-
tem process (*e.g.*, congenital absence, amputation, etc.) to account
for the absence, but without cutmarks, deliberate limb removal
cannot be demonstrated. The second case is a young male (approximately 17 years old) from the Cherry site who exhibits
multiple stabbing injuries to the dorsal and ventral trunk. The
upper chest cavity received at least one deep lance thrust which
resulted in the scoring of the posterior end of two ribs (probably
ribs 4 and 5) (Fig. 9.5). The dorsal trunk injuries corroborate the
violent trauma etiology of the rib cutmarks. The evidence consists
of a point tip lodged in the neural arch of an upper thoracic vertebra

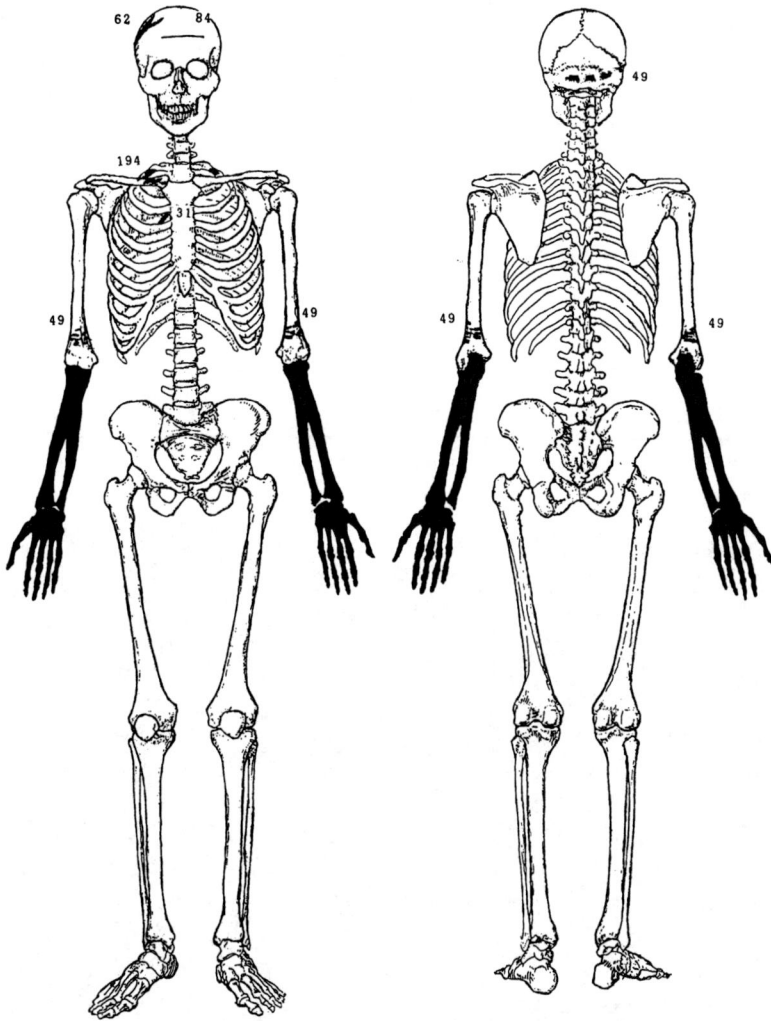

Figure 9.3. Location of the cutmarks associated with warfare. The numbers reflect the burial numbers and the blackened limb elements indicate retrieved trophy items.

(T2) and the imbedded blade sans tip in T8 where it severed the spinal cord.

Although there is no direct evidence for violent death in three other individuals, they do exhibit cutmarks consistent with two forms of perimortem trophy-taking, scalping and forearm retrieval.

Table 9.3. Summary Data of Warfare-Related Violent Trauma

Site Name	Burial Number	Inflicted Projectile	Scalping	Dismemberment Trophy	Stab Wounds
	56	X			
	62		X		
	194			?	X
Big Sandy	49		X	X	
Kays Landing	84		X		
Cherry*	31	X			
	37	X			
	69	X			
	71	X			X
	73	X			
Total Cases	10	6	3	1	2

*not including 'massacre' (6 individuals)

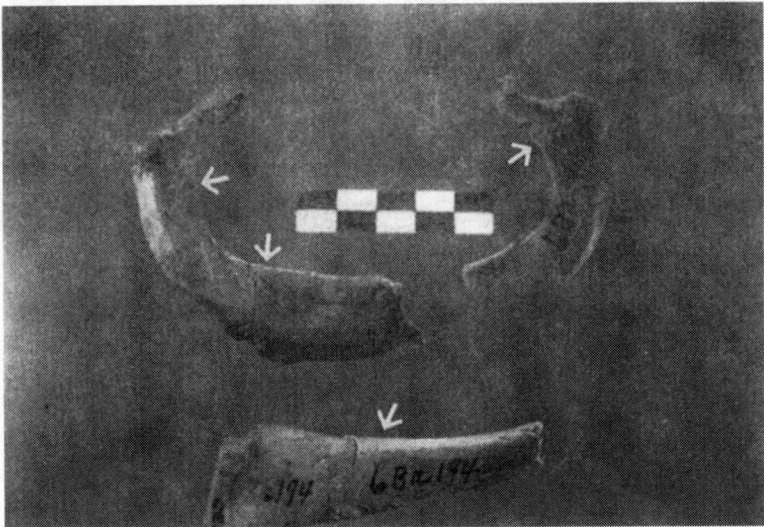

Figure 9.4. Cutmarks on the first rib and surviving clavicle of Burial 194 from the Eva site.

Significantly, these are the earliest occurrences of these forms of trophy-taking in the Southeast. The individuals, all primary interments, are from the Eva (Burial 62), Kays Landing (Burial 84), and Big Sandy (Burial 49) sites (Smith 1992, 1993a, n.d.). In each case,

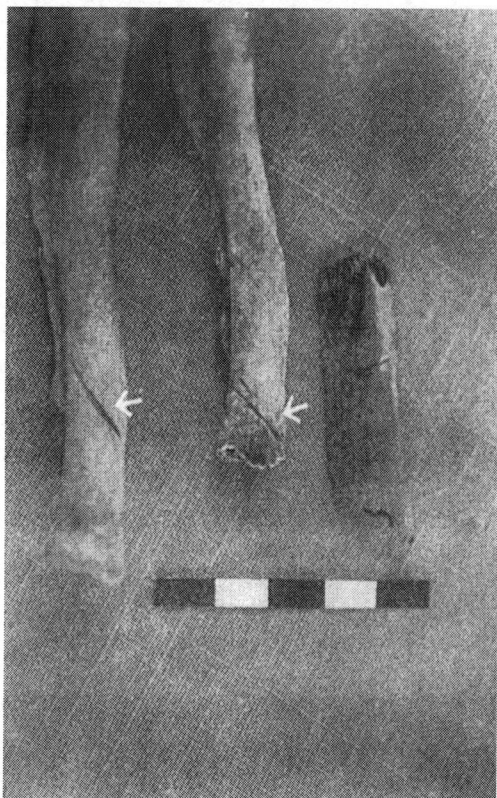

Figure 9.5. Cutmarks on the ribs of Burial 71 from the Cherry site. They are contrasted with a vascular channel (top)

the cutmarks circumnavigate the crown of the head in a pattern and manner totally consistent with the descriptions of scalping derived from the osteoarchaeological literature. In view of the dismissal of defleshing from the mortuary repertoire of the Kentucky Lake sample, no other interpretation is supportable.

Burial 62 from Eva exhibits the most extensive series of cutmarks. They are found on the right side of the calotte from the coronal margin of the frontal bone, across the parietal to its posterior-inferior margin (Fig. 9.6). The cutmarks also extend to the nuchal area of the occipital as a series of short striations. There are no other cutmarks on the cranium and none on the postcrania. The Kays Landing burial exhibits less extensive cranial cutmarks but the single long horizontal cutmark across the frontal (Fig. 9.7) at

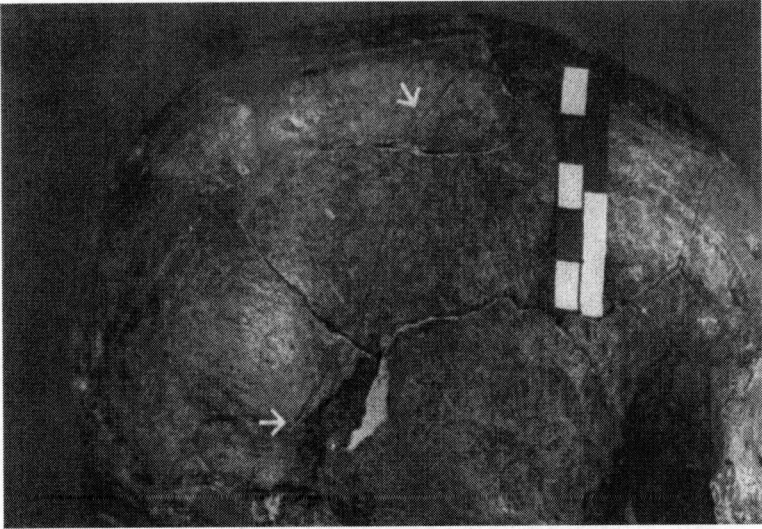

Figure 9.6. Lateral view of Burial 62 from the Eva site illustrating the cutmarks attributed to scalping.

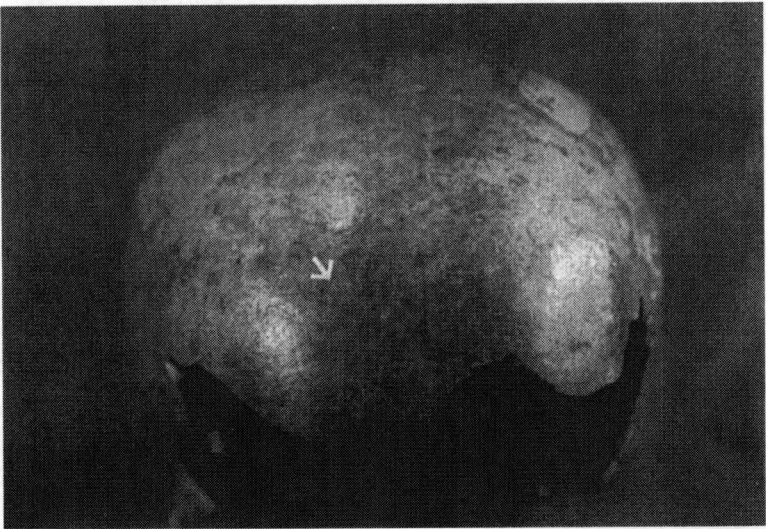

Figure 9.7. Cutmark on the mid frontal bone of Burial 84 from Kays Landing. Two otherlong cutmarks are located perpendicularly on the right parietal.

the level of the hairline and the two long vertical and overlapping cutmarks on the right mid-parietal are still best interpreted as scalping. As with Burial 62 from the Eva site, there are no other cutmarks on either the cranium or the postcrania. The Big Sandy cranium, in contrast to the postcrania, is unfortunately quite fragmentary. The frontals and most of the parietals are either absent or not reconstructible. However, cutmarks are clearly visible on the suprameatal crest of both temporal bones and the surviving posterior right parietal just anterior to the lambdoidal suture. There is also a single short, but distinct, cutmark on the right lateral occipital just inferior to the lambdoidal suture. The burial from Big Sandy also exhibits circumferential cutmarks on the distal shafts of both humeri (Fig. 9.8) in addition to bilaterally missing the forearms in an otherwise complete interment. The cutmarks exhibited by this individual are best interpreted as scalping and forearm trophy taking.

Although scalping has not been identified in the Southeast in an Archaic horizon outside of the Kentucky Lake Reservoir, forearm trophy taking (in conjunction with decapitation) has been reported in middle Tennessee at the Robinson site (Smith 1993b). It is

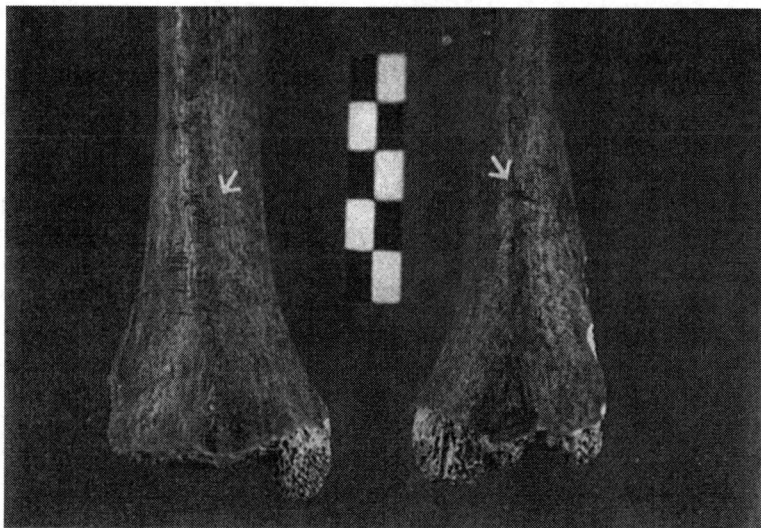

Figure 9.8. Cutmarks on both distal humeri of Burial 49 from the Big Sandy site.

possible that forearm trophy taking may also be indicated at the
40DV35 site in the Cumberland River Valley west of the Robinson
site (Moore *et al.* 1992).

An additional six individuals may be victims of intergroup conflict. A multiple burial at the Cherry site represents one of only two
departures from single interments at the site. The other is a triple
burial with two individuals exhibiting inflicted points. In the
multiple burial, the six individuals (two adults and four juveniles)
were haphazardly deposited in a single mass grave. The upper
bodies of the adults (a young male and an adolescent female) were
unfortunately destroyed by a later intrusive pit but, the male does
possess an inflicted projectile point in the greater trochanter of one
of his femora. It is the only perimortem trauma exhibited. While it
is tempting to interpret this mass grave as the result of a raid,
without more evidence it must remain equivocal.

DISCUSSION

With the exception of massacre episodes or frequencies of perimortem trauma which suggest endemic warfare, intergroup violence is
likely to be identified at any given site in only a small percent of
individuals. Multiple site samples from discrete geographical areas
would predictably generate more cases and hopefully reveal patterns that might be parlayed into testable hypotheses. The present
intersite study has revealed several patterns which provide points
of departure for future investigations.

The first pattern is suggested by the differential site distribution
of perimortem violent trauma (Tab. 9.3). The seven sites are clustered in the vicinity of the confluence of the Tennessee and Big
Sandy rivers. Previous site analysis identified six of the sites
(Fig. 9.1) as main channel sites. The seventh, Cherry, is upstream
along a small tributary of the Big Sandy river. The site has been
characterized as a remote upland site (seasonal fall/winter)
(Bowen 1975). Even without the so-called massacre episode, the
Cherry site accounts for half of the violent trauma in the reservoir
area or 10.2% of the Cherry sample (5/49) died violently. If for
argumentative reasons, the "massacre" event is included, the frequency increases to a dramatic 20.4%. Even using the more conservative 10.2%, this is in marked contrast to the 1.2% (5/416) for the
combined sample from the other six sites. An interpretation for the
differential distribution might be found in materialistic/ecological
models which associate warfare with economic or population

stress (see Bender 1985; Braun and Plog 1982:506–508; Haas 1990; Harris 1974:61–81; Rappaport 1967; Vayda 1969a, 1969b, 1976). It has been observed that in the late Archaic in the Southeast, particularly among the interior riverine populations of the midsouth, there is a dramatic increase in population density resulting in, among other things, restricted range of group territories and sedentism (Bense 1994:105–107; B. Smith 1986; Steponaitis 1986: 372–375). This demographic change and subsistence intensification could conceivably increase the competition for prime resource areas. If warfare is indeed dynamically linked to environmental stress or risk, then remote sites, such as Cherry, which perhaps straddle territorial frontiers, may be disputed in times of ecological stress. Indeed, Price and Brown suggest that intergroup conflict emerged as a likely consequence of boundary maintenance (1985:12). However, equally plausible, remote sites may be smaller and simply more vulnerable to raiding.

The second pattern contributes data which impacts hypotheses promoting a catalytic role for warfare in the genesis of social stratification. Based on the Kentucky Lake results as well as corroborative occurrences in the Cordell Hull Reservoir (Robinson site) and the northern Plains (Bahm site), scalping and forearm trophy-taking occur in Archaic hunter-gatherers. The most prevalent motive for retrieving trophy items is prestige enhancement (Friederici 1907; Knowles 1940; Nadeau 1944; Owsley and Berryman 1975). The occurrence of trophy-taking at such an early archaeological horizon among intensive hunter-gatherers suggests an avenue of prestige enhancement which may prove to be important in documenting incipient social complexity. This may be particularly true if intersite differences in amount of intergroup violence can be linked to intersite patterns of differential mortuary treatment (e.g. grave goods). Considerably more interarea information is needed before materialist/ecological models can adequately be tested synchronically as well as diachronically. An important step to that end might be in applying a trophy-taking motive to certain grave accoutrements found in Archaic contexts.

The appearance of trophy-taking at this early time period offers an interpretive framework for modified human bone grave goods which, although better known from Adena and Hopewell contexts, are not infrequent in Archaic sites of the interior riverine midsouth. The Archaic occurrences are routinely omitted in discussions of the motives for these grave goods. The motives offered for Woodland human bone grave inclusions are that they are as likely to be *mememto mori* (Fenton 1991) as trophy items (Seeman 1988). Clearly, mortuary treatment which includes defleshing and dismemberment complicate the interpretive environment. The absence of defleshing and dismemberment in the Kentucky Lake sample inclines this author to interpret the modified human bone grave inclusions found in the Kentucky Lake sample as trophy items. A polished human femoral shaft was recovered in two Kentucky Lake Archaic interments (Ledbetter Landing). One of the shafts was found cradled in the arms of a mature male skeleton.

Evidence which suggests that trophy-taking is a tenable interpretive alternative comes from applying the paleopathological data on trophy-taking with a review of the reported modified human bone grave inclusions recovered from Archaic sites in the mid-south. In the middle Tennessee River Valley of northern Alabama a skull "cup" and two carved fibulae were recovered from the Mulberry Creek site (Webb and Dejarnette 1942; Webb 1946), a radius awl/pin and four fibulae awl/pins were recovered from Bluff Creek (Webb and Dejarnette 1942), and two skull gorgets were found at the Flint River site (Webb and Dejarnette 1948). From Kentucky, modified remains include tibia shafts from Carlson Annis (Webb 1950) as well as cut shaft sections and tibia/femur pins from Indian Knoll (Webb 1946). Cut femur shafts like the ones from Ledbetter Landing occur at Sloan in Arkansas (Morse 1967) and Indian Knoll (Webb 1946). These human bone grave accompaniments mirror the removed items found in warfare contexts in late prehistoric horizons as well as the presumptive trophy items recovered from the Kentucky Lake and Cordell Hull sites.

However tenable a warfare etiology for human bone grave inclusions may be at this juncture, more baseline information is needed, particularly of mortuary treatment. For example, at Indian Knoll, Webb observed a number of individuals, including at least one with an inflicted projectile point (Burial 537) were "(not) dismembered merely to allow all parts of it to be placed in the grave...(a)lways some parts were missing, usually the extremities (1946:153)." This assessment suggests trophy taking at Indian Knoll. However, Snow interpreted the dismemberment as an alternative mortuary treatment (1948:523). In the absence of data eliminating dismemberment as a mortuary treatment in sites outside of the Kentucky Lake area, a general interpretation of human bone grave inclusions as trophy items is premature.

The absence of defleshing and dismemberment in the Kentucky Lake sample would suggest that there were no opportunities for selective retrieval. However, secondary inhumations provide occasions for retrieval without tell-tale cutmarks. Although no differential retrieval has been observed, without directed examination of postdepositionally undisturbed secondary interments for the patterned absence of possible *memento mori*, the identity of these grave inclusions as trophy items remains tentative. Clearly more research is needed.

A final pattern which emerges is subject to more speculative interpretation. None of the traumatic injuries inflicted on the individuals from the Kentucky Lake Reservoir were the result of blunt trauma. These do occur in late prehistoric horizons in the context of warfare-related trauma (*e.g.*, Norris Farms #36, [Milner *et al.* 1991]). Indeed, at the Crow Creek massacre, 40% of the crania exhibited perimortem depression fractures (Willey 1990:114). It is possible, though highly speculative, that the arsenal of Archaic period warriors did not include clubs or cudgels.

The collective examination of cases of perimortem violent trauma has provided a modest first step to a better understanding of the patterns of intergroup conflict in Archaic period intensive hunter-gatherers from the midsouth. The interpretive potential suggested by intersite differences and prestige-enhancing practices for materialistic/ecological models hopefully will encourage directed examination of perimortem violent trauma in other Archaic sites.

REFERENCES

Adair, J. (1775). *The History of the American Indians*. London: Edward and Charles Dilly.

Allen, W. H. Merbs, C. F. and Birkby, W. (1985). "Evidence for Prehistoric Scalping at Nuvakwewtaqa (Chavez Pass) and Grasshopper Ruin, Arizona." In *Health and Disease in the Prehistoric Southwest*, eds. C. F. Merbs and R. J. Miller, pp. 23–42. Tempe: Anthropological Research Papers No. 34, Arizona State University.

Angel, J. L. (1974). "Patterns of Fractures from Neolithic to Modern Times." *Anthropologiai Kozlemenyek* 18:571–588.

Begler, E. (1978). "Sex, Status, and Authority in Egalitarian Society." *American Anthropologist* 80:571–588.

Bender, B. (1985). "Emergent Tribal Formations in the American Midcontinent." *American Antiquity* 50:52–62.

Binford, L. R. (1981). *Bones: Ancient Men and Modern Myths*. New York: Academic Press.

Blakely, R. L. and Matthews, D. S. (1990). "Bioarchaeological Evidence for a Spanish-Native American Conflict in the Sixteenth Century Southeast." *American Antiquity* 55:718–744.

Bowen, W.R. (1975). *Late Archaic Subsistence and Settlement in the Western Tennessee Valley: A Reevaluation.* Masters Thesis, Department of Anthropology, University of Tennessee, Knoxville.

Brown, T. (1982). *Prehistoric Mortuary Patterning and Change in the Normandy Reservoir, Coffee County, Tennessee.* Masters Thesis, Department of Anthropology, University of Tennessee, Knoxville.

Braun, D. P. and Plog, S. (1982). "Evolution of "Tribal" Social Networks: Theory and Prehistoric North American Evidence." *American Antiquity* 47:504–525.

Cashdan, E. A. (1980). "Egalitarianism Among Hunters and Gatherers." *American Anthropologist* 82:116–120.

Catlin, G. (1841). *Letters and Notes on the Manners, Customs and Conditions of the North American Indians, Volume 1.* London: Tosswill and Myers.

Ferguson, R. B. (1990). "Explaining War." In *The Anthropology of War*, ed. J. Haas, pp. 26–56. Cambridge: Cambridge University Press.

Friederici, G. (1907). "Scalping in America." *Annual Report of the Smithsonian Institution*, **1906**:423–438.

Fenton, J. P. (1991). *The Social Uses of Dead People: Problems and Solutions in the Analysis of Post Mortem Body Processing in the Archaeological Record.* Ph.D. Dissertation, Department of Anthropology, Columbia University, New York.

Haas, J. (1990). "Warfare and the Evolution of Tribal Politics in the Prehistoric Southwest." In *The Anthropology of War*, ed. J. Haas, pp. 171–189. Cambridge: Cambridge University Press.

Hamperl, H. (1967). "The Osteological Consequences of Scalping." In *Diseases in Antiquity*, eds. D.R. Brothwell and A.T. Sandison, pp. 630–634. Springfield IL: Charles C. Thomas.

Hamperl, H. and Laughlin, W. S. (1959) "Osteological Consequences of Scalping." *Human Biology* 31:80–89.

Harris, M. (1974). *Cows, Pigs, Wars and Witches: The Riddle of Culture.* New York: Vantage Press.

Higgins, K. (1982). *The Ledbetter Landing Site: A Study of Late Archaic Mortuary Patterning.* Masters Thesis, Department of Anthropology, University of Tennessee, Knoxville.

Hill, A. P. (1976). "On Carnivore and Weathering Damage to Bone." *Current Anthropology* 17:335–336.

———— (1979). "Butchery and Natural Disarticulation: An Investigatory Technique." *American Antiquity* 44:739–744.

Hofman, J. L. (1985). "Middle Archaic Ritual and Shell Mound Archaeology:Considering the Significance of Cremations." In *Exploring Tennessee*

Prehistory, eds. T. R. Whyte, C. C. Boyd Jr. and B. H. Riggs, pp. 1–21. Knoxville: University of Tennessee Reports of Investigations, No. 42.

Knowles, N. (1940). "The Torture of Captives by the Indians of North America." *Proceedings of the American Philosophical Society* 82(2):151–255.

Lahren, C. H. and Berryman, H. E. (1984). "Fracture patterns and Status at Chucalissa (40SY1): A Biocultural Approach." *Tennessee Anthropologist* 9:15–21.

Leacock, E. and R. Lee (Eds.) (1982). *Politics and History in Band Societies.* Cambridge:Cambridge University Press.

Lewis, T. M. N. and Kneberg, M. (1947). "The Archaic Horizon in Western Tennessee." *Tennessee Papers 2*, Vol. **23**, Number 4.

      (1959). "The Archaic Culture in the Middle South." *American Antiquity* **25**:161–183.

Lewis, T. M. N. and Lewis, M. K. *Eva: An Archaic Site.* Knoxville: University of Tennessee Press.

Magennis, A. L. (1977). *Middle and Late Archaic Mortuary Patterning: An Example from the Western Tennessee Valley.* Masters Thesis, Department of Anthropology, University of Tennessee, Knoxville.

Martin, D. L. Akins, N. J. and Goodman, A. (1993). "Health Profile for the La Plata Highway Project." Paper presented at the Fifth Occasional Anasazi Symposium, Farmington, New Mexico.

Martin, D. L. and Akins, N. J. (1994). "Patterns of Violence Against Women in the Prehistoric Southwest." Paper presented at the Southwest Symposium, Tempe, Arizona.

Merbs, C. (1989). "Trauma." In *Reconstruction of L ife from the Skeleton*, eds. M. Y. Iscan and K. A. R. Kennedy, pp. 161–190. New York: Alan R. Liss.

Miller, G. J. (1975). "A Study of Cuts, Grooves, and Other Marks on Recent and Fossil Bone: II. Weathering Cracks, Fractures, Splinters, and other Similar Natural Phenomenon." In *Lithic Technology: Making and Using Tools*, ed. E. Swanton, pp. 211–226. The Hague: Mouton.

Milner, G. R. Anderson, E. and Smith, V. G. (1991). "Warfare in Late Prehistoric West-Central Illinois." *American Antiquity* 56:581–603.

Milner, G. R. and Smith, V. G. (1989). "Carnivore Alteration of Human Bone from a Late Prehistoric Site in Illinois." *American Journal of Physical Anthropology* 79:43–49.

Moore, M. C. Breitberg, E. Dowd, J. T. Stripling, C. P. and Broster, J. B. (1992). "Archaeological Investigations at 40DV35: A Multicomponent Site in the Cumberland River Valley, Davidson County, Tennessee." *Tennessee Anthropologist* 17:54–78.

Morse, D. (1967). *The Robinson Site and Shell Mound Archaic Culture in the Middle South.* Ph.D. Dissertation, Department of Anthropology, University of Michigan, Ann Arbor.

_____ (1977). "A Human Femur Tube from Arkansas." *Arkansas Archaeologist* **16**–18:42–44.

_____ (1989). "Pathology and Abnormalities of the Hampson Skeletal Collection." In *Nodena: An Account of 90 Years of Archaeological Investigation in Southeast Mississippi County, Arkansas (2nd Edition)*, ed. D. Morse, pp. 41–60. Fayetteville: Arkansas Archaeological Survey Research Series No 30.

Nadeau, G. (1944). "Indian Scalping Techniques in Different Tribes." *Ciba Symposia* **5**:1677–1681.

Neumann, G. (1940). "Evidence for the Antiquity of Scalping from Central Illinois." *American Antiquity* **5**:287–289.

Olsen, S. L. and Shipman, P. (1994). "Cutmarks and Perimortem Treatment of Skeletal Remains on the Northern Plains." In *Skeletal Biology in the Great Plains*, eds. D. W. Owsley and R. L. Jantz, pp. 377–390. Washington D. C.: Smithsonian Institution Press.

Ortner, D. J. and Putschar, W. G. (1985). *Identification of Paleopathological Conditions in Human Skeletal Remains*. Washington D. C.: Smithsonian Institution Press.

Owsley, D. W. and Berryman, H. E. (1975). "Ethnographic and Archaeological Evidence of Scalping in the Southeastern United States." *Tennessee Archaeologist* **31**:41–58.

Owsley, D. W. Berryman, H. E. and Bass, W. M. (1977). "Demographic and Osteological Evidence for Warfare at the Larson Site, South Dakota." *Plains Anthropologist Memoirs* **13**:119–131.

Potts, R. B. and Shipman, P. (1981). "Cutmarks Made by Stone Tools from Olduvai Gorge, Tanzania." *Nature* **291**:577–580.

Price, T. D. and Brown, J. A. (1985). "Aspects of Hunter-Gatherer Complexity." In *Prehistoric Hunter-Gatherers: The Emergence of Complexity*, eds. T. D. Price and J. A. Brown, pp. 3–20. San Diego: Academic Press.

Rappaport, R. (1967). "Ritual Regulation of Environmental Relations Among a New Guinea People." *Ethnology* **6**:17–30.

Raemsch, C. A. (1993). "Mechanical Procedures Involved in Bone Dismemberment and Defleshing in Prehistoric Michigan. *Midcontinental Journal of Archaeology* **18**:217–244.

Reese, H. H. (1940). The History of Scalping in its Clinical Aspects. *Yearbook of Neurology, Psychiatry and Endocrinology*, 1940: 3–19.

Russell, M. D. (1987). "Mortuary Practices at the Krapina Neandertal Site." *American Journal of Physical Anthropology* **72**:381–397.

Russell, M. D. and LeMort, F. (1986). "Cutmarks on the Engis 2 Calvarium?" *American Journal of Physical Anthropology* **69**:317–323.

St. Hoyme, L. E. and Bass, W. M. (1962). "Human Skeletal Remains from the Tolliferro (Ha6) and Clarksville (Mc14) Sites, John H. Kerr Reservoir Basin, Virginia. *Bureau of American Ethnology*, Bulletin **182**:329–399.

Saul, F. P. and Saul, J. M. (1993). "Cutmarks or Vascular Channels? Clues from Paleopathology and Anatomy." Paper presented at the Paleopathology Association Meetings, Toronto, Canada.

Seeman, M. (1988). "Ohio Hopewell Trophy-skull Artifacts as Evidence for Competition in Middle Woodland Societies Circa 50 B.C.–350 A.D." *American Antiquity* **53**:565–577.

Shermis, S. (1982/84). "Domestic Violence in Two skeletal Populations." *Ossa* **9–11**:143–151.

Shipman, P. and Rose, J. (1983). "Early Hominid Hunting, Butchering and Carcass-processing Behaviors: Approaches to the Fossil Record." *Journal of Anthropological Archaeology* **2**:57–98.

Smith, B. D. (1986). "The Archaeology of the Southeastern United States: From Dalton to De Soto, 10, 500–500 B. P." *Advances in World Archaeology* **5**:1–92.

Smith, M. O. (1992). "Osteological Indications of Warfare in the Archaic Period of West Tennessee." Paper presented at the Southeastern Archaeological Conference, Little Rock.

_____ (1993a). "Intergroup Violence Among Prehistoric Hunter-Gatherers from the Kentucky Lake Reservoir." *American Journal of Physical Anthropology* (Supplement) **16**:183–84.

_____ (1993b). "A Probable Case of Decapitation at the Late Archaic Robinson site (40SM4), Smith County, Tennessee." *Tennessee Anthropologist* **18**:131–142.

_____ (1993c). "Forearm Trauma and Status in the Archaic." Paper presented at the Southeastern Archaeological Conference, Raleigh.

_____ (1995). "Scalping in the Archaic Period: Evidence from the Western Tennessee Valley." *Southeastern Archaeology* **14**:60–68.

_____ (1996). "Parry Fractures and Female-directed Interpersonal Violence: Implications from the Late Archaic Period of West Tennessee." *International Journal of Osteoarchaeology* **6**:84–91.

Snow, C. (1941). "Possible Evidence of Scalping at Moundville." In *Anthropological Studies at Moundville*, pp. 53–59. Tuscaloosa: Geological Survey of Alabama, Museum Paper 15.

_____ (1948). "Indian Knoll Skeletons of Site Oh 2, Ohio County, Kentucky." *University of Kentucky Reports in Anthropology*. Vol. IV, Number 3, Part II.

Steponaitis, V. P. (1986). "Prehistoric Archaeology in the Southeastern United States, 1970–1985." *Annual Review of Anthropology* **15**:363–404.

Tiffany, J. A. Schermer, S. J. Thelar, J. L. Owsley, D. W. Anderson, D. C. Bettis III E. A. and Thompson, D. M. (1988). "The Hanging Valley Site: A Stratified Woodland Burial Locale in Western Iowa." *Plains Anthropologist* **33**:219–259.

Timberlake, H. (192). *The Memoirs of Lieutenant Henry Timberlake*, 1756–1765. Johnson City, TN: The Watauga Press.

Turner, C. G. II and Morris, N. T. (1970). "A Massacre at Hopi." *American Antiquity* **35**:320–331.

Ubelaker, D. H. (1989). *Human Skeletal Remains. (2nd Edition)* Washington D.C.:Teraxacum.

Vayda, A. (1969a). "Expansion and Warfare Among Swidden Agriculturalists." In *Environment and Cultural Behavior: Ecological Studies in Cultural Anthropology*, ed. A. Vayda, pp. 202–220. Garden City: Natural History Press.

_____ (1969b). "The Study of the Cause of War, with Special Reference to Headhunting Raids in Borneo." *Ethnohistory* **16**:211–224.

_____ (1976). *War in Ecological Perspective: Persistence, Change, and Adaptive Processes in Three Oceanian Societies*. New York: Plenum Press.

Webb, W. S. (1946). "Indian Knoll." *University of Kentucky Reports in Anthropology* **4(3)**, Part 1.

_____ (1950). "The Carlson Annis Mound, Site 5, Butler County, Kentucky." *University of Kentucky Reports in Anthropology* VII(4).

Webb, W. S. and Dejarnette, D. L. (1942). "An Archaeological Survey of the Pickwick Basin in the Adjacent Portions of the States of Alabama, Mississippi, and Tennessee." *Bureau of American Ethnology*, Bulletin 129.

_____ (1948). *The Flint River Site*, Na 48. Tuscaloosa: Alabama Museum of Natural History, Museum Paper 23.

White, T. D. (1986). "Cutmarks on the Bodo Cranium: A Case of Prehistoric Defleshing." *American Journal of Physical Anthropology* **69**:503–509.

_____ (1992). *Prehistoric Cannibalism at Mancos 5MTUMR-2346*. Princeton: Princeton University Press.

White, T. D. and Toth, N. (1989). "Engis: Preparation Damage, Not Ancient Cutmarks." *American Journal of Physical Anthropology* **78**:361-368.

Wilkinson, R. G. and Van Wagenen, K. M. (1993). "Violence Against Women: Prehistoric Skeletal Evidence from Michigan." *Midcontinental Journal of Archaeology* **18**:190–216.

Willey, P. S. (1989). "Canid Modifications of Human Skeletal Remains: A Comparison of Archaeological Materials from Crow Creek, Modern Forensic Cases and a Controlled Non-Human Sample." Paper presented at the Society for American Archaeology, Atlanta.

_____ (1990). *Prehistoric Warfare on the Great Plains*. New York:Garland.

Willey, P. S. and Emerson, T. E. (1993). "The Osteology and Archaeology of the Crow Creek Massacre." *Plains Anthropologist* Memoir 27:227–269.

Williams, J. A. (1991). "Evidence of Scalping from a Woodland Cemetery on the Northern Plains." *American Journal of Physical Anthropology* (Supplement) **12**:184.

...... (1994). "Disease Profiles of Archaic and Woodland Populations in the Northern Plains." In *Skeletal Biology in the Great Plains*, eds. D. W. Owsley and R. L. Jantz, pp. 91–108. Washington D. C.: Smithsonian Institution Press.

Wood-Jones, F. (1910). "Fractured Bones and Dislocations." In *The Archaeology of Nubia Report for 1907–08, Volume II: Report on the Human Remains*, eds. G. Elliot-Smith and F. Wood-Jones, pp. 293–342. Cairo: National Printing Department.

Chapter
TEN

The Evolution of Northwest Coast Warfare

Herbert D. G. Maschner
Department of Anthropology
University of Wisconsin–Madison

ABSTRACT

Warfare played an important role in the structure of historic Northwest Coast society and recent archaeological research demonstrates that warfare has a long history in the region. The first evidence for conflict on the Northwest Coast occurs by 3000 B.C. and is seen primarily in non-lethal skeletal injuries. By A.D. 200–500 warfare is seen in the construction of defensive sites, the formation of large amalgamation villages, a shift in village settlement to more defensible locales in southeast Alaska and the Queen Charlotte Islands, and a population decline along the British Columbia mainland coast and the Gulf of Georgia. By A.D. 900 another apparent escalation of conflict is seen archaeologically as a proliferation of defensive site construction and a shift in subsistence in some areas. In the early nineteenth century, conflict was prevalent throughout the region despite a population density lower than any in the last 1000 years, casting doubt on materialist explanations for warfare based on the ethnographic data, while supporting a more historical perspective.

INTRODUCTION

In this paper I present an archaeological analysis of the evidence and potential causes of warfare on the Northwest Coast (Fig. 10.1). Using archaeological data collected by the author, as well as skeletal, archaeological, and ethnographic data collected by others, I demonstrate that warfare has a long history in the region. I further draw comparisons with the ethnographic and ethnohistoric records, which, albeit anecdotal (Ferguson 1984), are the only comparative data available. Lastly, I show that warfare was probably much more common prehistorically than historically, and that the ethnographically recorded incidences of warfare were likely a remnant of the prehistoric pattern.

For this presentation, the Northwest Coast consists of the areas between the Pacific Ocean and the coastal ranges of the mountain systems of northwest North America. As a culture area, it stretches from Yakutat Bay in the north to the central Oregon coast on the south. It can be divided, both ethnographically and archaeologically, into three broad areas. The northern Northwest Coast, which includes southeast Alaska and the northern coast of British Columbia, which is the area where I have done most of my research. It includes the homelands of the Tlingit, Haida, and Tsimshian. The central Northwest Coast is composed primarily of the middle part of the British Columbia coast, the traditional territories of the Bella Bella, Bella Coola, southern Tsimshian, and Kwakiutl. The southern Northwest Coast includes most of Vancouver Island, the southern British Columbia coast, Puget Sound, the Washington coast, and coastal Oregon. This region includes territories traditionally occupied by Nootka, Makah, Salish, Chinookan, and many smaller groups.

At European contact, the Northwest Coast of North America supported some of the most socially complex hunters and gatherers ever encountered ethnographically. Characterized by a hereditary nobility (Oberg 1973; Townsand 1978), institutionalized slavery (Donald 1983; Mitchell and Donald 1986), part-time craft specialization (de Laguna 1972), and large, sedentary villages (de

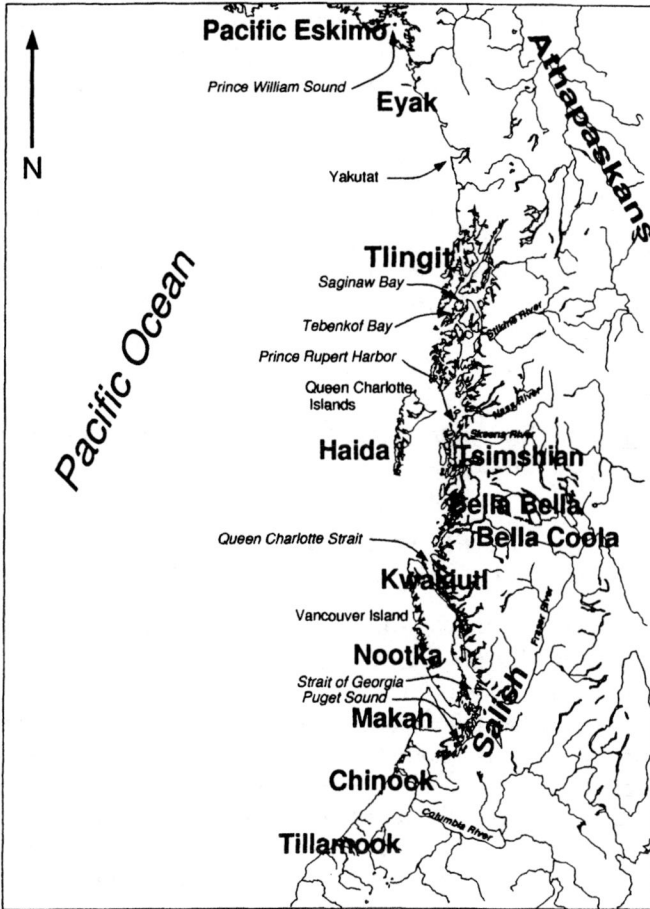

Figure 10.1. The Northwest Coast Showing Some of the Locations and Culture Groups Mentioned in the Text.

Laguna 1983; Drucker 1983; Townsand 1985), these societies were supported primarily by the massive yearly salmon run (Suttles 1968; Schalk 1977, 1981; Langdon 1979). Living in one of the most affluent and richest landscapes on earth, prehistoric populations rose to levels seen only in a handful of non-agricultural societies. The people of the Northwest Coast also had one of the most aggressive systems of organized conflict seen in hunter and gatherer societies (Ferguson 1983, 1984; Kamenskii 1906; Maschner 1992;

Moss and Erlandson 1992). Here among the forests and the salmon, raids were planned and wars were fought over status, prestige, revenge, woman, rare materials, and occasionally, food and territory.

In order to understand the development of warfare on the Northwest Coast, it is important to review the current data on the prehistory of warfare for this region. This will be followed by a summary of eight years of research on Northwest Coast warfare, sedentism, and ranking conducted by the author in Tebenkof and Saginaw Bays on Kuiu Island in southeast Alaska. I then present ethnographic and ethnohistoric descriptions of Northwest Coast warfare and a brief review of how anthropologists have interpreted these data. I conclude with an attempt to reconcile differences between the ethnohistoric record of warfare and the archaeological data.

THE PREHISTORY OF WARFARE
ON THE NORTHWEST COAST

The prehistory of the Northwest Coast can be divided into two broad periods, the latter being further divided into three phases. The first period, the Lithic Stage, Lithic Period (Fladmark 1982, 1986) or simply the Early Period, extends from approximately 9000 to 3500 B.C. and is characterized by small, mobile groups that practiced a diversified subsistence strategy consisting of both terrestrial and marine resources (Ackerman et al. 1985; Cressman et. al. 1960). The Developmental Stage (Fladmark 1982) or the Pacific Period (Ames and Maschner, in preparation), the time period we are most concerned with here, extends from approximately 3500 B.C. to European contact. The Pacific Period is divided into three phases that have a diverse array of regional names but for this discussion will be referred to as the Early Pacific (3500 to 1500 B.C.), the Middle Pacific (1500 B.C. to A.D. 200–500), and the Late Pacific (A.D. 200–500 to European contact). During the Pacific Period the first large villages appear, status differences become apparent, a heavy emphasis on marine subsistence develops, and warfare becomes visible in the archaeological record.

Evidence for prehistoric warfare on the Northwest Coast comes in three forms. The first, and most obvious, is skeletal evidence of violent injury or death, as indicated by broken bones from club wounds or by projectiles embedded in bone. Although there are only a few skeletal samples known from the Northwest Coast, there are sufficient numbers of individuals to provide useful information (Cybulski 1990, 1992, 1994). The second is the presence of defensive sites and fortifications. These are identified archaeologically by bluff-top habitations, palisaded enclosures, or trench-embankment features around sites. A limited number of excavations have occurred at defensive locations and the only data we have about them are the approximate dates of occupations, and that the activities performed and the foods eaten in them were approximately the same as those in other villages (de Laguna 1960; Mitchell 1981; Moss 1989; Maschner 1992, in preparation). The final type of evidence is problematic and includes the presence of tools and weapons that are considered by archaeologists to have been used for attacking other humans. This line of evidence is troublesome since very few artifacts are found in Northwest Coast sites and the chances of finding weapons of war are low. Nevertheless, there are sufficient data available to present a broad archaeological overview of the development of warfare on the Northwest Coast.

The Lithic Period and the Early Pacific: 9000 B.C. to 1500 B.C.

There is no archaeological evidence for warfare or conflict on the Northwest Coast during the Early Period. This does not mean that warfare did not exist, it merely indicates two things. First, populations during these times were small and groups were mobile. We know from modern ethnographic data that some violent acts do occur in small scale foraging societies (Lambert 1994; Lee 1979), but it is unlikely that such infrequent events would be recognized archaeologically.

During the Early Pacific, when the earliest shell middens appear in the archaeological record (see for example Okada *et al.* 1989, 1992), the first evidence for violent interactions is found (Cybulski 1994). In an analysis of 77 burials from two cemeteries on the British Columbia coast dating to this time period, Cybulski noted that 21% had evidence of trauma resulting from interpersonal violence. It appears from Cybulski's descriptions that most of these are from the Namu skeletal series on the central mainland coast (1994). The skeletal series from Blue Jacket's Creek on the Queen Charlotte Islands shows little evidence for violence (Cybulski 1990:58; Murray 1981). In southeast Alaska there are several bluff-top shell midden sites that have base deposits dating to approximately 2200 B.C. that, given the evidence for violence on the British Columbia coast, may be indicative of the early use of these landforms for defensive purposes.

The Middle Pacific: 1500 B.C. to A.D. 200–500

The Middle Pacific is critical to Northwest Coast prehistory because it is during this phase that large villages formed for the first time. In the Gulf of Georgia, Prince Rupert Harbor, southeast Alaska, and elsewhere along the north Pacific Coast, extremely large accumulations of shell midden are found, often with associated house floors and occasional house depressions. In the Middle Pacific many categories of artifacts and behaviors began to take a more typical Northwest Coast ethnographic appearance. These include artistic styles, fishing systems, village organization, both utilitarian and non-utilitarian artifacts, and economic practices (Carlson 1994). It is significant that Middle Pacific villages do not seem to have the permanence that we see in the Late Pacific, and that the size of the houses, and thus the corporate groups, are much smaller than in the Late Pacific (Coupland 1988; Maschner 1992; Ames, personal communication).

It is during the Middle Pacific that the first evidence for a region-wide proliferation of violent conflict appears (Cybulski 1990, 1992, 1994; Fladmark, Ames, and Sutherland 1990). Cybulski has studied 584 burials dating to the Middle Pacific phase from several areas of the British Columbia coast. He has reported that 32% of the burials from the northern and central coasts (mostly from Prince Rupert Harbor and Namu) have evidence for interpersonal violence while only 6% of the individuals from the south coast (Gulf of Georgia) show evidence for violent trauma (Cybulski 1994:83, Tab. 1; 1990:58). Cybulski (1990:58) notes that these injuries include depressed skull fractures from club blows, facial and anterior tooth fractures, defensive forearm "parry" fractures, defensive fractures of the outer hand, disarming fractures of the forearm and hand, and instances of decapitation.

In discussing the Middle Pacific materials from Prince Rupert Harbor, Fladmark, Ames, and Sutherland (1990) argue that a high rate of conflict is supported by three different lines of evidence. First, there is a disproportionately high ratio of men to women in the skeletal sample. Second, males show unusually high levels of trauma including parry fractures of the forearm and depressed skull fractures. Third, there are clearly weapons such as bone and stone clubs, bipointed ground stone objects, and ground slate daggers in the Prince Rupert Harbor archaeological sites (1990:234). At this time there is little direct evidence for conflict on the adjacent Queen Charlotte Islands, but the presence of several Prince Rupert "style" effigy stone war clubs in non-village contexts is evidence that contacts between the islands and the mainland were not always peaceful.

The Late Pacific: A.D. 200–500 to A.D. 1800

During the Late Pacific, most of the cultural characteristics seen ethnographically first become visible archaeologically, including, most significantly, the evidence for large-scale warfare. In the Late Pacific, the first large, Northwest Coast style villages formed in southeast Alaska and on the Queen Charlotte Islands (Acheson 1991; Maschner 1991, 1992), and defensive sites began to be constructed throughout the region (Emmons 1991; MacDonald 1989; Moss 1989; Moss and Erlandson 1992; Maschner 1992). It is also in the Late Pacific that the bow and arrow appears to have arrived on the Northwest Coast (Blitz 1988; Maschner 1992). Based on the presence of much larger houses and corporate groups than are present in the earlier phases (Coupland 1985, 1988; Maschner 1992), this is also the time when many believe social ranking developed, at least on the northern Northwest Coast.

Cybulski analyzed 84 individuals dating to the Late Pacific. In small samples from both the north and south coasts, he found that approximately 27% of the individuals had evidence for violent trauma. Thus, while the south coast had much less skeletal evidence for violent conflict in the Middle Pacific, the region matches the north coast during the Late Pacific. Overall though, skeletal data for conflict in the Late Pacific are generally rare. This is because many of the peoples of the Northwest Coast switched from subsurface burials in shell midden deposits to inhumations in above-ground boxes or in trees during the cultural transition from the Middle to the Late Pacific. Thus, there are few preserved skeletons from any Late Pacific deposits from which to collect such data.

Defensive sites provide the single-most important Late Pacific evidence for conflict on the Northwest Coast. For the southern Northwest Coast, Mitchell notes that refuges formed by walls and ditches enclosing temporary shelters were often located near villages in the Late Pacific (1990:348; see also 1981:114,117). He states that for the Queen Charlotte Strait Culture type, "conflict is suggested by the presence of fortified sites..." (1990:355). He also points out that in the Strait of Georgia Culture type, there is a widespread distribution of sites with trench embankment features (1990). He argues that this is evidence for intergroup warfare of sufficient intensity, severity, and frequency to justify a considerable labor investment in construction and maintenance (Mitchell 1990:348). While many trench-embankment sites are known for both the southern British Columbia Coast and Washington State (Bryan 1963; Wessen 1986), few of these sites have been excavated or dated. Keddie (personal communication in Moss and Erlandson 1992) reports a few trench-embankment sites in the Victoria area of the Gulf of Georgia. These include the Peddler Bay site (DcRv 1) that dates to A.D. 370 ± 100, Finlayson Point (DcRu 23) dating to approximately A.D. 800, and the Lime Bay Peninsula Defensive Site (DcRu 123), which dates to approximately A.D. 800. The Flemming Beach site, near Esquimail (DcRu 20 and DcRu 21) is a large shell midden bounded by two defensive locations. The main shell midden has a basal date of over 4000 years ago, but the trenched-off defensive sections of the site date to around A.D. 800 to A.D. 1000 (Moss and Erlandson 1992:84). Moss and Erlandson point out that a number of researchers have noticed that these defensive sites are often situated on the edges of historically known territorial boundaries, especially in the Straits Salish area (1992:84).

On the northern Northwest Coast the presence of numerous defensive sites suggests that warfare was common and widespread. Historically, these defensive fortifications were impressive. Large palisades which might have contained several houses were built on headlands or rocky bluffs with difficult access. In 1779 De la Boca y Quadra described a Tlingit fortification west of Prince of Wales Island as "situated on the summit of a high hill, so precipitous in its sides that they used wooden ladders to get up to it..." (cited in Wooley 1984:4). Captain Cook described a similar Haida hilltop fortification on Graham Island in 1778 and Newcombe recorded several dozen similar Haida defensive locales. In August 1779 Vancouver described a number of defensive locations near the Keku Straits in central southeast Alaska as:

> ...the remains of no less than eight deserted villages... all uniformly situated on the summit of some precipice, or steep insular rock, rendered by nature almost inaccessible, and by art and great labor made a strong defense... These fortified places were well constructed with a strong platform of wood, laid on the most elevated part of the rock, and projecting so far from its sides as to overspread the decliv-

ity. The edge of the platform was surrounded by a barricade of raised logs of wood placed on each other (Vancouver 1984:1386).

On the central Northwest Coast, historic sites were less often palisaded but many villages were placed in defensive locations. In June 1793 Bell described a Bella Coola village as "situated on a bare rock about fifty yards from the mainland ...not more than three or four hundred yards in circumference" (in Vancouver 1984:934). On several occasions Vancouver actually camped on what appear to have been abandoned defensive sites.

Defensive sites were being constructed throughout southeast Alaska (Moss 1989, Moss *et.al.* 1989; Moss and Erlandson 1992), and the Queen Charlotte Islands (Acheson 1991) in the Late Pacific. Over 30 defensive sites have been securely dated and many more have been identified but not dated (Moss 1989; Moss and Erlandson 1992; Maschner 1992, in preparation). Both Moss (1989; Moss *et. al.* 1989) and Maschner (1990, 1991, 1992) have stressed the significance of the fact that a majority of the dated defensive sites occur near the beginnings of the Little Ice Age. Maschner has further argued that this deterioration of climate might have had a deleterious effect on fish and sea mammal populations, creating region-wide economic problems (1990). However, it is becoming more clear that the majority of defensive sites in southeast Alaska were being built between A.D. 800 and A.D. 1300, long before any radical climatic changes occurred (Fig. 10.2).

Artifactual data for warfare are rare. Ethnographically, war paraphernalia included armor, helmets, bows and arrows, spears, clubs, and daggers (Emmons 1991). In 1792 Khlebnikov (1973:8–9), a Russian naval officer, described a battle between the Yakutat Tlingit (who were hunting for Chugach [Pacific Eskimo or Alutiiq]), and Aleuts and Russians, where 12 on each side were killed:

> The Kolosh [Tlingit] were wearing war dress consisting of wooden armor tightly wound about with whale-gut. Their faces were covered with masks made to resemble the faces of bears, seals, and other mammals striking for their fearsome appearance. On their heads they had tall, thick wooden hats joined to their outer clothing with straps. Their weapons consisted of spears, arrows, and two-ended daggers.

Niblack (1970), an American army officer who visited the northern coast in the 1870s, also described Tlingit war paraphernalia. He observed that Tlingit armor consisted of up to three layers of hide

NUMBER OF CALIBRATED DATES

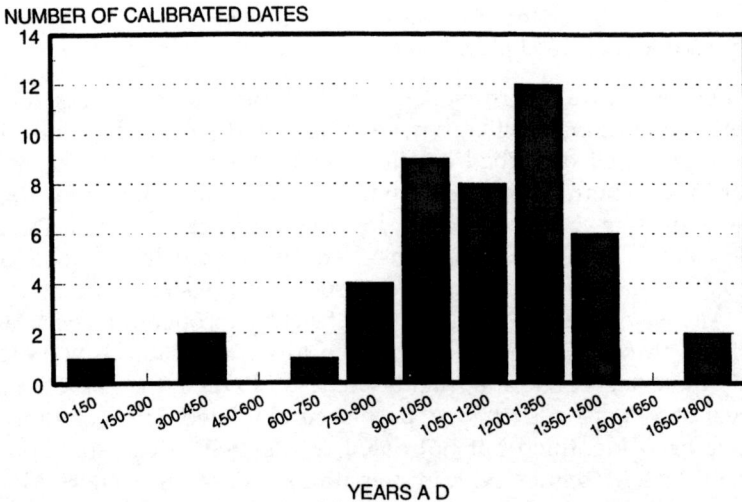

YEARS A D

Figure 10.2. Histogram of the distribution of radiocarbon dates for Southeast Alaska defensive sites.

re-enforced with wood slats and provided protection against spears, arrows and knives. Russian America Company Director, Alexander Baranof, found, much to his dismay, that Tlingit armor was also adequate protection against musket balls (Khlebnikov 1973).

Unfortunately, few of the material aspects of conflict would be likely to preserve in the archaeological record, the exceptions being bone, polished or chipped stone arrow and spear points, bone or polished slate daggers, and bone and ground stone clubs. There has been some debate among Northwest Coast archaeologists as to the nature of archaeological finds of these types and as to whether or not they demonstrate conflict as opposed to hunting or ceremony. Although the function of daggers and clubs is somewhat problematic, recent research on Northwest Coast projectile points has proven enlightening.

An experimental study of Northwest Coast armor and projectiles conducted by Lowrey (1994) has provided important insights into the function of certain projectile types. From ethnographic reports and collections, Lowrey replicated armor in all of the styles represented on the Northwest Coast, as well as bows and arrows with points of ground slate, chipped stone, and bone. He found that while bone points had a devastating impact on Northwest Coast armor, slate and chipped-stone points fractured before fully penetrating most styles of armor. It is important to note that although stone projectile forms and styles are highly variable on the Northwest Coast, every group has a similar bone projectile. These projectiles are occasionally found on the outside of the palisades of defensive fortifications (Maschner, in preparation), and proliferate with the postulated introduction of the bow and arrow in the region after A.D. 200 to A.D. 500 (Maschner 1991, 1992).[1]

I have stated previously that the bow and arrow probably altered inter-village politics in the region, and may have been responsible for both the abandonment of small, single lineage villages for large, multilineage villages and an increase in warfare (Maschner 1991, 1992). The fact that the bow and arrow radically changed strategies of warfare is seen in the apparent change from hand to hand combat to bow and arrow wars. The most obvious attribute of this change is the construction of cliff-top, palisaded, or embankment/trench surrounded defensive forts, villages, and refuges.

INVESTIGATING NORTHWEST COAST WARFARE: THE KUIU ISLAND PROJECT

My own research on Northwest Coast warfare has involved four archaeological field seasons and eight years of laboratory research. The goal of this research has been to develop a model of the relationship between warfare and the rise of sedentary villages and ranked societies on the northern Northwest Coast (Maschner 1990, 1991, 1992, 1996). To address this problem, I have investigated the structure and organization of early villages, shifts in settlement, changes is regional subsistence strategies, and population dynamics. Each of these components are described in detail below.

In total, I have discovered and investigated over 200 prehistoric sites in Tebenkof and Saginaw Bays on Kuiu Island, southeast Alaska (Fig. 10.1). Of these, over 20 Middle and Late Pacific village sites and eight defensive sites have been studied. The following data are primarily based on my research in Tebenkof Bay, but I will also make reference to a number of recently discovered fortification sites in Saginaw Bay (Maschner, in preparation). The goal of the following sections is to describe the types of data that can be collected for Northwest Coast warfare in the absence of skeletal remains, and to describe the inferences that can be drawn from these data.

The Sites

Both defensive sites and village sites are important to our understanding of the rise and maintenance of Northwest Coast warfare. The majority of defensive sites in southeast Alaska date between A.D. 800 and A.D. 1300 but a few date between A.D. 400 and A.D. 900 as well (Fig. 10.2). These sites are common throughout the region and both historic and prehistoric versions share many characteristics. Villages are common as well although actual house depressions are not visible in all areas. Both kinds of sites are visible in the Kuiu Island archaeological record and are described below.

One of the earliest defensive sites is XPA-138 in Tebenkof Bay, Kuiu Island, which is dated to about A.D. 500 (Fig. 10.3) (Maschner 1992). This site is located on the edge of a four meter terrace and had a number of leveled areas. The associated beach consists of large boulders and bedrock, making it impossible to land canoes except at extreme high-tide. Another site in Tebenkof Bay with a clearly defensive function, XPA-188, is located near the most important salmon stream in the local area. Dated to between A.D. 1160 and 1285, this site is an isolated island in the only channel leading to this stream. The island has vertical rock walls on all sides, making it nearly impossible to safely land a boat. The top has been leveled, and the entire island is covered in shell midden (Maschner 1992). This site also has the highest density of salmon bone of any location in Tebenkof Bay, indicating that it was probably a salmon storage area as well.

Four recently investigated defensive sites in Saginaw Bay on the north end of Kuiu Island are similar in appearance to those in Tebenkof Bay. One of these, XPA-061, has been known for many years but remained uninvestigated because of the impassibility of its vertical rock walls (Fig. 10.4). When we managed to reach the summit, we found dense shell midden deposits covering the surface. Many areas seem to have been leveled, and some areas appear to have stone-fronted terraces. The site dates to between A.D. 1440 and 1650, but the presence of dense second-growth berries indicates that it was utilized historically as well. A long span of use can also be inferred for XPA-289, another defensive site identified in Saginaw Bay (Fig. 10.5). This site dates to A.D. 500 to 800 and also to A.D. 1250 to 1600. It was probably not used in the recent past as there are spruce and hemlock trees in excess of 1.5 meters in diameter covering the site. The presence of over two meters of highly stratified shell midden deposits indicates that this site was also

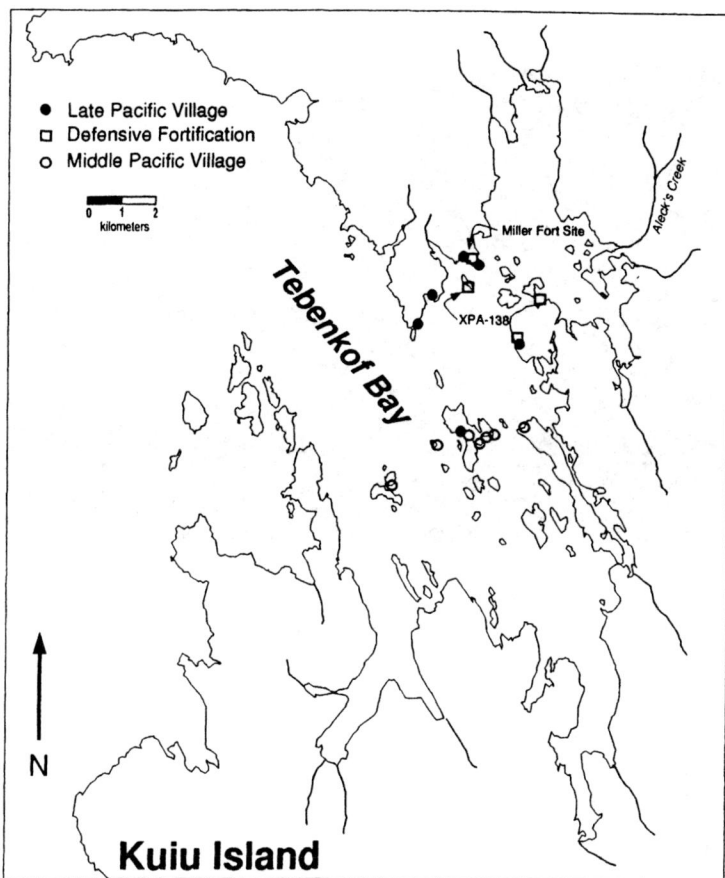

Figure 10.3. Tebenkof Bay, Kuiu Island, Southeast Alaska, showing the spatial distribution of Late Pacific and Middle Pacific Villages, and defensive sites.

occupied for a long period. The distribution of the midden deposits is a good indicator of the location of the palisade as garbage was often dumped along the walls. At XPA-289 these deposits also follow the contours of the hill and there is even some evidence for a second fortification on the center hill top because of the midden deposits located there. The islet itself is surrounded by either rocky beaches or natural vertical rock walls. Given the geological history of the region, which has the land rising at a faster rate than the sea level, the low area on the west end of the islet was probably

Figure 10.4. Photograph of XPA-061, a defensive site and fortification in Saginaw Bay, Kuiu Island, Southeast Alaska.

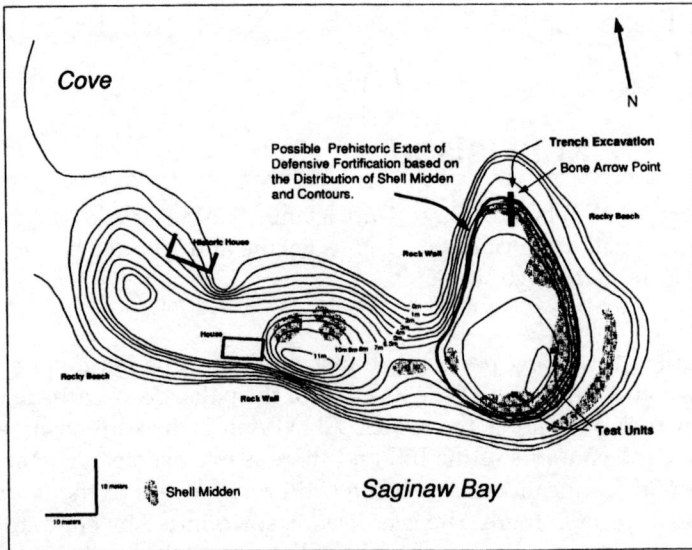

Figure 10.5. Map of XPA-289, a prehistoric defensive site in Saginaw Bay, Kuiu Island, Southeast Alaska.

submerged at the time of occupation as it is less than one meter above sea level at present. Interestingly, an armor-piercing bone point was found in an excavation on the outside of what is considered to have been the palisaded area at this site. Both XPA-061 and XPA-289 are defensive sites typical of those found throughout southeast Alaska.

Defensive sites in southeast Alaska, like those on the southern Northwest Coast, were often located near villages, or sometimes constituted the village itself. But this was not always the case, as many sites were suitable for village location but were not defensible, and vice versa. An example of the relationship between villages and defensive sites is seen in Tebenkof Bay. The Miller Fort Site (XPA-114) is a small point of land with vertical rock walls and steep slopes on three sides, and a small ridge leading to higher ground on the fourth (Maschner 1992). The entire top of the small point has been leveled where structures may have been placed. Across the ridge leading away from the site is a one meter wide mound of shell midden spanning the breadth of the causeway (14 meters long by one meter high), which probably outlines a former wall or palisade. The midden remains on this site are over 1.5 meters deep, indicating that the site may have been used for habitation. Up the ridge 60 meters from the site are several cache depressions confirming many ethnographic accounts of foodstuffs hidden in the forest. This site has large house-depression village sites (XPA-112 and XPA-116) within 100 meters on either side and was probably the refuge for both villages.

Village sites are also important for investigating warfare in this region. The very structure of historic Northwest Coast houses with thick plank walls and roofs made them defensible. These types of houses are visible in the Late Pacific archaeological record by the presence of large, rectangular house depressions with 70 to 300 square meters of floor area. The first large, typically Northwest Coast villages occur in Tebenkof Bay between A.D. 300 and A.D. 500. This is approximately the date they appear in the Queen Charlotte Islands (Acheson 1991) and shortly after they first occur in Prince Rupert Harbor (Archer 1992). They are often in defensible locations or have a defensive refuge in close proximity.

Settlement

Changes in settlement patterns can also be good indicators of conflict. As can be seen in Figure 10.3, the Middle Pacific villages are located in the central part of Tebenkof Bay, whereas Late Pacific villages (as well as defensive sites) are located primarily in the northern part of the bay (see also Maschner 1992, 1996; Maschner and Stein 1995). In attempting to understand this settlement shift, I discovered that Middle Pacific villages are located on extremely convoluted shorelines with excellent intertidal resources but low visibility out from the village. Further, they are located in the middle of the bay, which allows for easy access to all of the required resources such as salmon streams, cod banks, herring spawning areas, and seal haul-outs. Late Pacific villages, on the other hand, are closer to Aleck's Creek, the primary salmon stream. They are also located on long, straight shorelines with limited intertidal resources and at a greater distance to open-water resources.

Since all Northwest Coast raids are conducted over water, defensive considerations can be measured by the quality of the visibility out from a village. In order to better understand what cultural considerations were responsible for these different settlement strategies, I used a geographic information system to model and compute the amount of open water visible (viewshed) from each Middle and Late Pacific village (Maschner 1992, 1996). I found that Late Pacific villages have over three times the amount of visible surface water than those of the Middle Pacific ($t = 2.86$, $df = 11.7$, $p = 0.01$). Thus, sometime between A.D. 300 and A.D. 500, villages moved from highly convoluted shorelines in the middle of the bay to long, straight shorelines in the northern part of the bay. This transition included a reduction in the accessibility of intertidal resources and open-water resources, and made the sites more vulnerable to seasonal storms. But this appears to have been a trade-off in favor of sites that were much more defensible.

I also found that the Middle Pacific villages were about the size that would be expected for a single lineage occupation. The much larger size of the Late Pacific villages suggests the amalgamation of a number of lineages, as was recorded ethnographically. This can be seen by the average size of the Middle Pacific villages, which I found to be almost exactly the same as the average area inhabited by a single lineage house in the Late Pacific villages – between 2200 and 2300 square meters ($t = 0.277$, $df = 10.4$, $p = 0.787$). Thus, Late Pacific amalgamation villages appear to be the result of a number of independent lineage-based Middle Pacific villages coming together to form a single Late Pacific village. This process of amalgamation, as well as the shift from village locations emphasizing subsistence maximization to locations better suited to defense, and the beginning of defensive site construction, occurred at the same time as the introduction of the bow and arrow.

Subsistence

The shift in settlement locations suggested that subsistence may have also been affected. But subsistence in Tebenkof Bay from the Early Pacific through the Middle Pacific and half-way into the Late Pacific is fairly homogeneous. Cod, herring, and sea mammals make up the primary constituents, with salmon and other species much less common (Figs. 10.6 and 10.7). Moss (1989) has noticed that salmon seem to become more important in the latter half of the Late Pacific in the Angoon area. In Tebenkof Bay this is seen as a radical shift in subsistence about A.D. 1200. This shift is seen in the transition from an economy based on open-water fishing and sea mammals to one grounded in salmon and terrestrial mammals (Figures 10.6 and 10.7).

To explain this change, I originally evaluated hypotheses involving over-exploitation of the Tebenkof Bay resource base and population pressure. But after evaluating historic fishing records for the

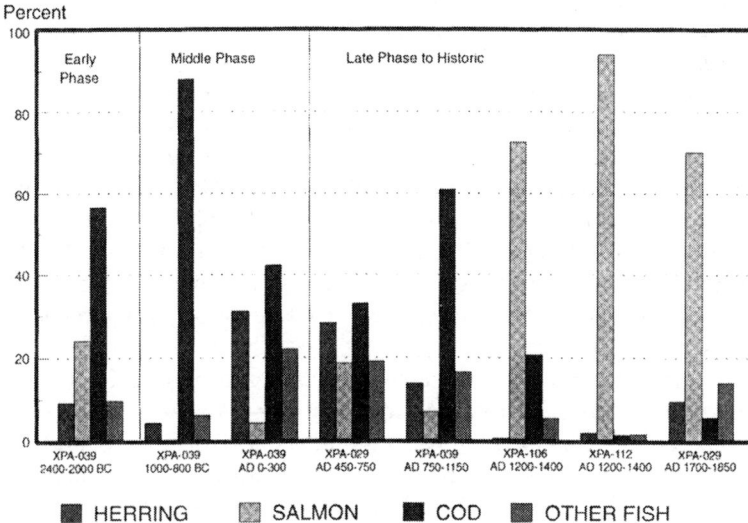

Figure 10.6. Chart of the temporal variation in subsistence fishing in Tebenkof Bay, Kuiu Island, Southeast Alaska. "Phase" in this figure corresponds to "Pacific" in the text.

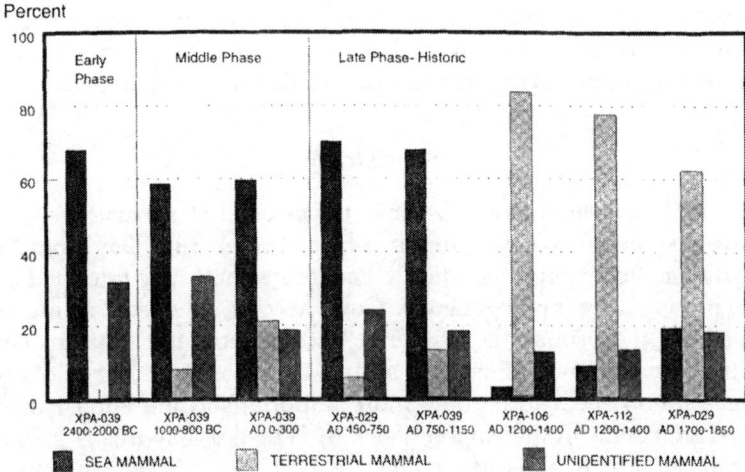

Figure 10.7. Chart of the temporal variation in subsistence hunting in Tebenkof Bay, Kuiu Island, Southeast Alaska. "Phase" in this figure corresponds to "Pacific" in the text.

region, I came to the conclusion that it was unlikely there was ever pressure on the primary resource base and there is no evidence that harvesting pressure could ever have occurred with an aboriginal technology (see also Hayden 1981). This is because the primary salmon stream in the bay, Aleck's Creek, which is only four meters wide and one-half meter deep, had an early twentieth century salmon catchment of over 500,000 fish, with over 1,000,000 salmon spawning in the bay as a whole. Herring, as little as 20 years ago, spawned in Tebenkof Bay in volumes measured in thousands of tons. Further, at Russian contact, the bay was dense with otter and seal. After studying the archaeological data for shellfish growth and age, cod length, and species diversity, I found that I had no archaeological evidence whatsoever of any resource stress (Maschner 1992).

It was not until I investigated harvesting strategies for the two different subsistence regimes that a more likely explanation became evident. Historically, open water fishing for herring and cod, as well as sea mammal hunting, was performed by small task groups. Salmon, on the other hand, were harvested by entire villages moving to a major salmon stream for a short time and returning with the catch, while deer were hunted around the village. When looked at from this perspective, the significance of these two strategies is apparent. Small task groups are more vulnerable to attack than whole villages. So it is not surprising that this transition occurs at the point in time when we have a peak in the construction of defensive fortifications. Thus, it would appear that this shift was a product of decreased access due to political pressure rather than resource stress.

Population

I have just argued above that there is no evidence of subsistence stress during the Late Pacific on the northern Northwest Coast, but there is evidence for dense populations during this time. In fact, it appears that the period between A.D. 900 to A.D. 1300 was the most populous of any on the Northwest Coast. Maschner and Ames (1992) argue, from the numbers of radiocarbon dated habitation sites, that the Northwest Coast reached its highest population level long before historic contact and that the population was actually in decline for several hundred years before European contact. This is a conclusion reached independently by Cybulski for the British Columbia coast (1992:39, Fig. 10.11).

I estimated village populations in Tebenkof Bay based on house floor area of the houses (under the assumption, possibly unjustified, that the house floors were contemporaneous) using Coupland's (1988:254) linear relationship of one individual/4m^2 which appears to reflect the historic Northwest Coast pattern. When applied to the Tebenkof Bay villages, a general population increase can be seen from slightly over 100 people around A.D. 400, to 200 between A.D. 750 and 1150, to nearly 300 occupants between A.D. 1150 and 1350 (Fig. 10.8). After A.D. 1350, the population in Tebenkof Bay crashes, only to rise again just before historic contact.

Although there does appear to be a correlation between the construction of defensive sites, the change in subsistence, and the peak population level, this peak population in Tebenkof Bay was only about 300 people. Regardless of the prehistoric inhabitants' subsistence strategy, it is difficult to imagine that this number of people could not have subsisted using a resource base that, even today, could feed several thousand.

Prehistoric Overview

To summarize the archaeological data, there is no evidence of warfare or other violent conflict in the Early Period. In the Early and

Numbers of Individuals

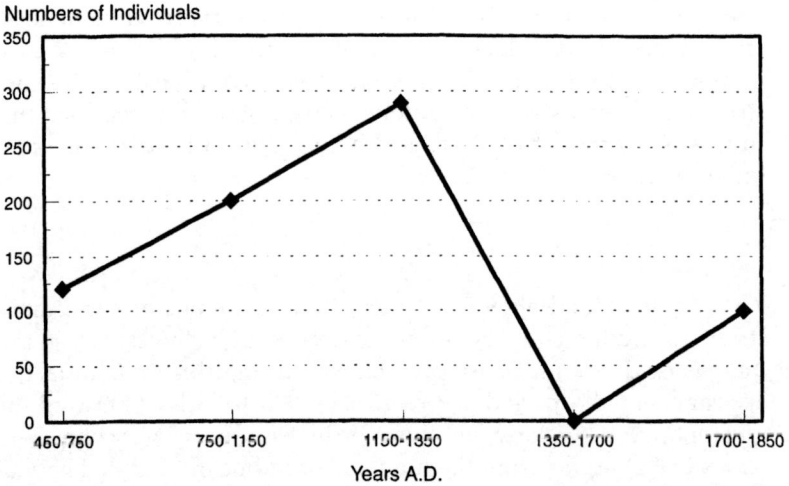

Figure 10.8. Population growth curve for Tebenkof Bay, Kuiu Island, Southeast Alaska.

Middle Pacific the data are more substantial. Conflict is seen in numerous skeletal injuries and the presence of weapons best suited to hand-to-hand combat. Sometime between A.D. 200 and 500 the bow and arrow as a tool and weapon entered the technology of the Northwest Coast peoples, as seen in the regional proliferation of armor-piercing bone points and other small points in the Late Pacific. It is less than coincidental that every regional cultural chronology on the Northwest Coast has a break at approximately this same point in time. This can be seen in the Middle to Late Phase transition in southeast Alaska (Maschner 1992), the first large villages of the Graham Tradition of the Queen Charlotte Islands (Acheson 1991), the Prince Rupert Harbor Phase II to Phase I transition (Fladmark, Ames, and Sutherland 1990), and the decline of Marpole and the rise of the Coast Salish cultures in the Gulf of Georgia (Mitchell 1990), to name a few.

Escalating conflicts with the introduction of the bow and arrow resulted in large villages composed of multiple lineages on the north coast and the construction of villages in defensible locations, earthen embankments, and palisades on the south coast. On the northern Northwest coast this transition began with the construction of large villages and was followed by a proliferation in defensive site construction a few hundred years later. Moreover, since most of the defensive villages on the southern Northwest Coast date to after A.D. 800, the boom in the construction of these defensive sites may have occurred at the same time as the peak in construction of defensive sites on the northern coast – sometime between A.D. 900 and A.D. 1300. On Kuiu Island this escalation of warfare eventually led to a complete shift is subsistence from open-water fishing and sea mammal hunting to salmon and terrestrial mammals. This time period was also an apparent peak in population throughout the region.

THE CAUSES OF NORTHWEST COAST WARFARE

Ferguson has been the most prolific writer in discussing and analyzing the causes and consequences of Northwest Coast warfare. He recognizes (1984:269, see also 1983) that there have been two prevailing views on the ultimate cause of Northwest Coast conflicts. The first, presented by Swadesh (1948), states that Nootka warfare was for territory and for slaves. The second, stated by Codere (1950), argues that Southern Kwakiutl warfare was highly ceremonial, involving few casualties, with wars fought to regain lost prestige rather than for material gain. Ferguson (1984:269) seems surprised that Rosman and Rubel (1986:139), in their synthesis on the Northwest Coast potlatch, endorse both views of warfare and argue instead that "the long coexistence of these two views testifies to anthropology's general disinterest in the topic of war" (1984:269). He goes on to side with Swadesh, maintaining that the underlying cause of all Northwest Coast warfare was conflict over critical resources (1984:270). He justifies a disinterest in symbolic and social explanations for warfare by reasoning that, given the hazards of war, life-threatening circumstances such as food shortages must have been more important than social considerations. He believes that emphasizing economic goals does not imply that a variety of other reasons did not enter into decisions to go to war, but concludes that motivations such as the quest for status, prestige, or acquisition of ceremonial titles are constant cultural norms whereas warfare is not. He further implies that cultural norms, although present in other social institutions, have no place in warfare. So, although he acknowledges that some peoples may occasionally fight to maintain status (1984:271), Ferguson believes that scarce resources are the only practical reason to fight.

I take a somewhat more generous view of the data. I believe that the long coexistence of Codere's and Swadesh's views is not a product of anthropology's general disinterest in warfare but rather, a product of the fact that people will fight over anything that they consider important to their social, economic, and political well being. This does not detract from the fact that the original cause of Northwest Coast warfare may have been related to a scarcity of food or land. However, according to observations made by explorers and traders, and statements made by informants, the causes of warfare along the Northwest Coast were extremely variable. All ethnographic data indicate that there were many reasons for conflict, reasons tempered by group size, kinship, and history, and these cannot be ignored.

THE ETHNOGRAPHIC AND ETHNOHISTORIC DATA ON NORTHWEST COAST WARFARE

The primary causes of Northwest Coast warfare cited in the both the ethnographic and ethnohistoric literature include revenge wars, wars to capture slaves, fights over women and infidelities, and wars for either access to desirable foods or territory. These will each be described below.

Revenge is often cited as a primary cause of Northwest Coast warfare. This type of conflict was best expressed by the Russian Orthodox Priest Ivan Veniaminov, who lived in southeast Alaska in the 1820s. He maintained that "a Kolosha [Tlingit] does not seek out blood: he only exacts blood for blood" (1984:432), a characteristic that describes much of Northwest Coast revenge warfare. Nearly every explorer, missionary, and ethnographer has expressed the importance of revenge and revenge wars among the Tlingit and elsewhere on the Northwest Coast (Holmberg 1985 [1855–1863]:22; Krause 1970:169; L.F. Jones 1914:112; Niblack 1970:340; Swanton 1970:449). Blackman (1990) states that revenge was one of the primary motivations for Haida warfare, and there are a number of examples of Tsimshian revenge wars (Barbeau and Beynon 1987). Revenge wars were also fought among the Bella Bella (Hilton 1990:314) and Kwakiutl intratribal revenge wars were well known (Codere 1990). Among the Kwakiutl, whenever someone was killed, a person of equal rank to the deceased from the offending group had to be killed in order to satisfy revenge. This inspired head-hunting raids that sought to kill either a high-ranking member of the offending group or a number of low-ranking individuals (Codere 1990:359; Boas 1921:1375, 1966:109). The Northern Coast Salish also participated in revenge wars, particularly against the invading Lekwiltok Kwakiutl (Kennedy and Bouchard 1990:443). Among the Central Coast Salish, raids were less common but when they did occur, revenge was a common motivation (Suttles 1990:465). This was also the case among the Quileute (Powell 1990:431). Further south, revenge wars could more often end in payment or enslavement of the offenders. The victors usually took payment from the losers, but there appears to have been no change in territory (Silverstein 1990:542). This system was common among the Chinookan-speaking groups of the lower Columbia, as well as the Tillamook, Lower Chihalis, Lower Cowlitz, and Tualatin (Franchere in Thwaites 1904–1907, 6:330–331; Henry in Coues 1897:2:855, 867, 879–880, 905, 908; Scouler 1905: 279; Minto 1900:311).

Capturing slaves was another important motive for conflict (Mitchell 1984, 1985; Donald 1983, 1984; Mitchell and Donald 1986). Slaves were a measure of wealth (de Laguna 1983:75), as well as a source of labor (Mitchell and Donald 1986). Kamenskii stated that warfare provided the Tlingit with booty, mainly in the form of slaves and argued that "the Tlingit himself considered it demeaning to perform dirty work... this was the duty of slaves or at least women" (1985:29–30). Jones (1914:116) wrote that chiefs and those of high rank were the sole slave holders among the Tlingit, and Holmberg stated that captured enemies were enslaved (1985 [1855–63]:22). In speaking of the Tsimshian, Garfield (1939:267) noted that "raiding parties were organized for the capture of slaves or to avenge a wrong or injury inflicted by another group," and that "raiding for captives, either to be returned to their relatives for ransom or kept as slaves, was profitable." Slave raiding was also common among the Haida (Blackman 1990), who slaved throughout the northern Northwest Coast against the Tlingit, Tsimshian, Bella Bella, Kwakiutl, and other Haida. The Lekwiltok Kwakiutl were avid slavers preying against Northern, Central, and Southern Coast Salish groups; Salish slaves often ended up being traded to the Haida or Tlingit, nearly 1000 kilometers from their home. Several Southern Coast Salish revenge wars were mounted against the Lekwiltok in retaliation for the taking of their people (Suttles and Lane 1990:488; Brown 1873–1876, 1:70–72; Curtis 1907–1930, 9:14–16).

The most southern groups do not appear to have been active slave raiders; rather, they were more often being raided or enslaved. If slaves were present in a village, they were usually acquired through trade. The Chinook of the Lower Columbia were well known historically as being slave traders, most of whom came down the Columbia and its tributaries from groups on the Plateau. On the Oregon coast the Tillamook may have been involved in slave raiding (Seaburg and Miller 1990:560); early battles between the Tillamook and the Chinook (Franchere 1967:117) and the Tillamook and the Tualatin (Mallery 1886:26) have been recorded.

Women are also mentioned as a cause of war. De Laguna (1983:77) mentions that quarrels over women are traditionally cited as a cause of group fissioning and emigration. Among the Eyak, the northern neighbors of the Tlingit, it was found that most Eyak conflicts were with the Chugach Eskimo, who used to steal Eyak women when they were caught performing tasks such as berrying away from the village. The Eyak sometimes fought with the Tlingit, and many had Tlingit wives, which were "always (frequently?) stolen..." (Birket-Smith and de Laguna 1938:149). Garfield (1939:267), on the Tsimshian, states that "in the myths illicit love affairs are also related to the cause of trouble between groups." She argued that female slaves were often made wives, especially if they were Tlingit, Haida, or Tsimshian (1939:272–273). Veniaminov (1984:418) claimed that many conflicts occurred over adultery. Wars fought over infidelities, theft of women, or incest appear to be much more rare on the southern Northwest Coast than in the northern areas (see Arndt 1988:2,11–12; Veniaminov 1984; Golovnin 1983:89; and Tihkmenev 1979:352, for examples).

During the historic era there was intense competition for access to trade and trade routes and there are numerous accounts of conflicts over historic trade (Ferguson 1984). Wooley has argued that many of the early historic conflicts over trade were products of depopulation and the stresses that result from unrelated groups amalgamating in areas where contacts with traders could be made (1984; Wooley and Haggerty 1989). The Chilkat and many other groups on the north coast prohibited trade between the interior Athapaskans and the Europeans on the coast, effectively monopolizing the flow of goods to and from these regions. In 1852, on hearing that the Hudson Bay Company had built Fort Selkirk in the interior to promote trade, Chief Chartrich (Shotridge) of the Chilkat Tlingit led a war party over 300 miles into the interior, destroyed the fort, and effectively ended competition (de Laguna 1990:209; Davidson 1901).

A number of intense wars were fought over the Nass River. Candlefish oil was prized because it was excellent for the long-term storage of fish and also as a commodity in trade, especially with the interior. It was a renowned source of fat, and was often consumed with dried fish. The mouth of the Nass River is the location of the largest candlefish spawning area on the Northwest Coast and Boas (1916) recorded a number of stories about exterminanitive raids between the Tlingit and Tsimshian over this region. The Tsimshian eventually prevailed and the Tlingit were pushed northward. The Bella Bella also participated in warfare during times of food shortages (Hilton 1990:314), and many of the Nootkan wars may have been for food as well (Drucker 1951). An analysis of Tlingit and Tsimshian myths suggests that there were a series of territorial shifts just prior to historic contact (Wooley and Haggerty 1989; Barbeau and Beynon 1987). These include the Kaigani Haida expansion into Tlingit territory (southern Prince of Wales Island), and the Tlingit expansion northward into Eyak territory. There is also evidence that the Tlingit once resided in Prince Rupert Harbor and were later pushed out by the Tsimshian expanding down the Nass and Skeena Rivers.

OTHER CONSIDERATIONS IN NORTHWEST COAST WARFARE

Wars were fought over great distances. Blackman (1990:246) states that the Haida not only fought their closest neighbors, the Tsimshian, southern Tlingit, and Bella Bella, but also raided Kwakiutl, Coast Salish, and Nootka villages over 600 kilometers away. The Tlingit raided northward against Chugach Eskimo and Eyak, eastward against some Athapaskans, and regularly against the Tsimshian and Haida. These wars were not limited to the northern coast, as there are examples of Tlingit war parties going as far south as the Strait of Georgia for revenge and slaves and the Kwakiutl regularly raided the Southern Coast Salish groups on the south end of Puget Sound for slaves.

Boyd (1990:136) suggests that many Northwest Coast wars probably affected the demographic histories of the groups who participated. He states that traditional tales of the Haida (Swanton 1905:364–447), the Tsimshian (Boas 1916:124–145), and the Nootka (Sapir and Swadesh 1955:336–457) speak of territorial wars with a high mortality rate, some leading to the extermination of whole villages. It was rather common for one Nootka group to attack and annihilate a neighboring Nootka group in order to take their lands and primary fishing locales (Drucker 1951:333). The

Lekwiltok Kwakiutl waged wars against the Northern Coast Salish, eventually driving them out of their traditional territories and villages between the Salmon River and Cape Mudge (Taylor and Duff 1956).

There is evidence that these early conflicts were not a product of resource scarcity. Lambert (1993, 1994, this volume) and Lambert and Walker (1991) have clearly shown that there is a correlation between levels of conflict and poor health among coastal hunters and gatherers along the Santa Barbara Channel. This does not appear to be the case on the Northwest Coast. Cybulski found that in the 5000 years spanning the Early, Middle, and Late Pacific Periods there was no decrease in stature, no change through time in the amount of cribra orbitalia (14%), and only scattered evidence for treponematosis in the Middle Pacific (1994).

Two final points are critical in explaining Northwest Coast warfare. First, wars were never fought for a single reason. Arguments over insults or infidelities often escalated into revenge wars that lasted for decades (Arndt *et al.* 1987). These long-term wars might ultimately end up in the annihilation of one or more participants, but almost never resulted in a shift in the location of the participants or a change in territory (de Laguna 1983; Golovnin 1983). The wars that did result in changes in territory, at least in every recorded case, were a result of expansionist activities by the most populous and strongest group in a region, and the group that had the greatest amount of subsistence resources in their own territory (Langdon 1977; Boas 1921, 1966; de Laguna 1990; Garfield 1939). This is another point, that wars were most often instigated by those who had the numbers, wealth, and resources to be successful combatants. Those in the greatest need had neither the wealth nor the numbers to launch raids against those who could have alleviated their poverty.

DISCUSSION AND CONCLUSION

Historically, the natives of the Northwest Coast had a number of reasons why, and situations where, they chose violent conflict and warfare over other means of resolution. Although conflicts between villages with close kin ties were usually appeased with trade and gifts, conflicts with distant peoples usually resulted in violence. There are three important conclusions to be drawn from these examples.

The first is that in simply trying to explain warfare as a response to competition over scarce foodstuffs, we ignore the great range of variability in how the historically known peoples actually behaved. Although there are a number of examples of territorial and food-based conflicts, Northwest Coast scholars have no evidence that these foods were a necessary resource critical to the survival of those who wanted its control. Whether the Northwest Coast peoples ever regularly fought over food as a scarce commodity is still unknown. But in the 19th century, when the original population had been reduced by as much as two-thirds and many of the Northwest Coast groups were at their lowest population density in the last several thousand years, conflicts continued.

The second point is that wars were never fought for a single reason. A war fought over territory, insults at potlatches, or infidelities, could result in a prolonged revenge war lasting several centuries. Yet all of these kinds of conflicts were intimately related. Many of the conflicts witnessed in the 19th century were wars that probably had more to do with historical precedence than with any verifiable ultimate cause.

The third point is that the most actively aggressive groups were the strongest, wealthiest, and most populous – not those in the greatest economic need. The Tlingit, Haida, Tsimshian, and Kwakiutl were the most prolific raiders and these were the groups with the most numbers of individuals, the greatest resource bases, and ultimately, the groups that could economically launch a raid. The societies and villages with the greatest need, and those that might have most benefitted from raids on other villages, were the groups most often in a defensive posture. Such were the circumstances of the Eyak, the Bella Bella, the southern Tsimshian, the Central and Southern Coast Salish, the interior Athapaskans, the outer coastal groups of Washington and Oregon, and the southern interior groups.

In applying these examples to the archaeological data we are struck by a number of issues. First, none of the cultural processes that were the causes of violent conflict in the recent past are visible archaeologically. Thus, when we recognize the first conflicts as hand-to-hand combats with evidence of club blows from skeletal data, we can only argue from the ethnographic literature that humans will be combative over anything they consider important at the time and that stresses inherent in all village-based societies often lead to interpersonal violence. The fact that there are few examples of lethal injuries in the Early and Middle Pacific skeletal data does indicate that conflict may have been more symbolic than not.

The escalation of warfare with the introduction of the bow and arrow after A.D. 200–500 is probably responsible for the shifts in the settlement system, changes in village organization, and in the increasing investment in defensive fortifications. Despite the shift in settlement and in the size of both houses and villages, I found no change in economy whatsoever. But warfare escalates after A.D. 900. Perhaps due to the change in village patterns that began 500 years before, populations seem to be rising and there is a substantial shift in subsistence and a peak in the construction of defensive fortifications, all occurring between A.D. 900 and A.D. 1300. Yet it appears that the change in economy was mandated by the escalation of conflict, and not the opposite. During this time, warfare was probably a response to the tensions that arise when there are simply too many unrelated groups living in the same area.

Whether prehistoric Northwest Coast peoples ever fought over food or territory as a scarce commodity is still unproven, and will probably remain so. However, in the 19th century conflict was still very much a part of Northwest Coast society. These conflicts often resulted in the deaths of hundreds of warriors in a single battle, yet these conflicts occurred at a time when the population sizes of Northwest Coast groups were so low that there was absolutely no possibility of resource stress or population pressure. Thus, these conflicts must have been integral to the maintenance of Northwest Coast culture, a culture founded in the protection of status and prestige for noble leaders and their kinsmen.

ACKNOWLEDGEMENTS

Funding for the Tebenkof Bay Archaeological Project was provided to Maschner through a Wenner-Gren Foundation for Anthropological Research Predoctoral Grant, a National Science Foundation Doctoral Improvement Grant, the Stikine Area of the Tongass National Forest-Petersburg, the University of California-Santa Barbara, the Alaska State Historic Preservation Office, and Sigma-Xi Grants-in-Aid of Research. Funding for the North Kuiu Archaeological Project was provided by the Stikine Area of the Tongass National Forest-Petersburg and the Graduate School of the University of Wisconsin-Madison. I would like to thank Madonna Moss for instigating much of the modern research on the archaeology of Northwest Coast warfare and Mark McCallum of the Tongass

National Forest (USDA) for making my research possible. Thanks to Debra Martin and David Frayer for organizing the original AAA session and putting this volume together. Thanks to Caroline Funk and Kate Reedy who assisted in editing this paper and in preparing the bibliography, and to Andrew Lydecker who drafted the base map for Figure 1. My close association with Napoleon Chagnon helped to formulate many of the ideas presented in this paper and I will always be appreciative of his encouragement. I will be forever grateful to Patricia Lambert, whose own research on warfare stimulated much of this research and whose helpful comments, editing, and support made it a better paper. All errors are my own.

NOTES

[1] Ken Ames notes that in Prince Rupert Harbor, there are many bone points dating to the Middle Pacific. He also notes that among the numerous varieties, there seem to be some types similar to those under discussion (Ames 1993). Ames also notes that the Prince Rupert Harbor materials seem to be somewhat out of sequence with the regional trends (personal communication), the regional trend being toward a proliferation of bone projectiles in the Late Pacific.

REFERENCES

Acheson, S. R. (1991). *In the Wake of the ya'aats' xaatgaay ['IRON PEOPLE']: A Study of Changing Settlement Strategies Among the Kunghit Haida.* Ph.D. Dissertation. Oxford: University of Oxford.

Ackerman, R. E. Reid, K. C. Gallison, J. D. and Roe, M. E. (1985). "Archaeology of Heceta Island: A Survey of 16 Timber Harvest Units in the Tongass National Forest, Southeastern Alaska." Pullman: Washington State University. *Center for Northwest Anthropology.* Project Reports 3.

Ames, K. M. (1993). *The Archaeology of the Northern Northwest Coast: The North Coast Prehistory Project Excavations in Prince Rupert Harbor, British Columbia.* Report on file at the Archaeological Survey of Canada, Ottawa.

Ames, K. M. and Maschner, H. D. G. (in preparation). *The Northwest Coast.* London: Thames and Hudson.

Archer, D. J. W. (1992). "Results of the Prince Rupert Harbour Radiocarbon Dating Project." Report prepared for the British Columbia Heritage Trust. Manuscript. pp. 17.

Arndt, K. L. Sackett, R. and Ketz, J. A. (1987). *A Cultural Resources Overview of the Tongass National Forest, Alaska.* Report submitted to the U.S. Forest Service, Tongass National Forest.

Barbeau, M. and Beynon, W. (1987). "Tsimshian Narratives 2: Trade and Warfare." G. F. MacDonald and J. J. Cove (eds.). Ottawa: *Canadian Museum of Civilization. Mercury Series Directorate Paper 3.*

Birket-Smith, K. and de Laguna, F. (1938). *The Eyak Indians of the Copper River Delta, Alaska.* Copenhagen: Levin and Munksgaard.

Blackman, M. B. (1990). "Haida: Traditional Culture." In *Handbook of North American Indians, Vol. 7: Northwest Coast*, W. Suttles, vol. ed. pp. 240–260. Washington D. C.: Smithsonian Press.

Blitz, J. H. (1988). "Adoption of the Bow in Prehistoric North America." *North American Archaeologist* **9**(2):123–145.

Boas, F. (1916). "Tsimshian Mythology." Based on Texts Recorded by Henry W. Tate. Washington: *31st Annual Report of the Bureau of American Ethnology for the Years 1909–1910*, pp. 29–1037.

_____ (1921). "Ethnology of the Kwakiutl" (Based on data collected by George Hunt). 2 Pts. Pp. 43–1481 in *35th Annual Report of the Bureau of American Ethnology for the Years 1913–1914*. Washington.

_____ (1966). *Kwakiutl Ethnography.* Helene Codere, ed. Chicago: University of Chicago Press.

Boyd, R. T. (1990). "Demographic History: 1774–1874." In *Handbook of North American Indians, Vol. 7: Northwest Coast*, W. Suttles, vol. ed. pp. 135–148. Washington D.C.: Smithsonian Press.

Brown, R. (1873–1876). *The Races of Mankind: Being a Popular Description of the Characteristics, Manners and Customs of the Principle Varieties of the Human Family.* 4 vols. London: Cassell, Petter, and Galpin.

Bryan, A. L. (1963). "An Archaeological Survey of Northern Puget Sound." *Occasional Papers of the Idaho State Museum 11.* Pocatello.

Carlson, R. (1994), "Trade and Exchange in Prehistoric British Columbia." In *Prehistoric Exchange Systems in North America.* Timothy G. Baugh and Jonathon E. Ericson, eds. New York: Plenum Press.

Codere, H. (1950). *Fighting With Property: A Study of Kwakiutl Potlatching and Warfare 1792–1930.* Seattle: University of Washington Press.

_____ (1990). "Kwakiutl: Traditional Culture." In *Handbook of North American Indians, Vol. 7: Northwest Coast*, W. Suttles, vol. ed. pp. 359–377. Washington D.C.: Smithsonian Press.

Coues, E. (editor) (1897). *New Light on the Early History of the Greater Northwest: The Manuscript Journals of Alexander Henry, Fur Trader of the Northwest Company, and of David Thompson... 1799-1814...* 3 vols. New York: Francis P. Harper. (Reprinted: Ross and Haines, Minneapolis, 1965).

Coupland, G. (1985). "Household Variability and Status Differentiation at Kitselas Canyon." *Canadian Journal of Archaeology* **9**:39–56.

_____ (1988). *Prehistoric Cultural Change at Kitselas Canyon.* Ottawa: Canadian Museum of Civilization, National Museums of Canada.

Cressman, L. S. Cole, D. L. Davis, W. A. Newman, T. M. and Scheans, D. J. (1960). "Cultural Sequences at The Dalles, Oregon: A Contribution to Pacific Northwest Prehistory." *Transactions of the American Philosophical Society* **50(10)**. Philadelphia.

Curtis, E. S. (1907–1930). *The North American Indian: Being a Series of Volumes Picturing and Describing the Indians of the United States, the Dominion of Canada, and Alaska.* Fredrick W. Hodge, editor. 20 volumes. Norwood, Mass.: Plimpton Press (reprinted Johnson Reprint, New York, 1970).

Cybulski, J. S. (1990). "Human Biology." In W. Suttles, vol. ed., *Handbook of North American Indians, Vol. 7: Northwest Coast*, pp. 52–59, Washington D.C.: Smithsonian Press.

_____ (1992). *A Greenville Burial Ground, Human Remains and Mortuary Elements in British Columbia Coast Prehistory.* Mercury Series Paper No. 146, Archaeological Survey of Canada, Canadian Museum of Civilization. Hill, Quebec.

_____ (1994). "Culture Change, Demographic History, and Health and Disease on the Northwest Coast," In *In the Wake of Contact: Biological Responses to Conquest*, pp. 75–85. Clark Spenser Larsen and George R. Milner, editors. New York: Wiley-Liss, Inc.

Davidson, G. (1901). "Explanation of an Indian Map of the Rivers, Lakes, Trails and Mountains from the Chilkaht to the Yukon Drawn by the Chilkaht Chief Kohklux in 1869." *Mazama* 2(2):75–82.

de Laguna, F. (1960). "The Story of a Tlingit Community: A Problem in the Relationship Between Archaeological, Ethnological, and Historical Methods," *Bulletin, No. 172, Bureau of American Ethnology*, Smithsonian Institution.

_____ (1972). "Under Mount Saint Elias: The History and Culture of the Yakutat Tlingit," *Smithsonian Contributions to Anthropology*, Vol. 7, parts I–III.

_____ (1983). "Aboriginal Tlingit Sociopolitical Organization," In *The Development of Political Organization in Native North America*, Elizabeth Tooker, ed., Morton Fried, organizer. The American Ethnological Society, Washington D. C., pp 71–85.

_____ (1990). "Tlingit." In W. Suttles, vol. ed., *Handbook of North American Indians,* **Vol.** 7: *Northwest Coast*, pp. 203–228. Washington D. C.: Smithsonian Press.

Donald, L. (1983). "Was Nuu-chah-nulth-aht (Nootka) Society Based on Slave Labor?" In E. Tooker, ed., *The Development of Political Organization in Native North America*, pp. 108–119. Washington D. C.: Proceedings of the American Ethnological Society, 1979.

_____ (1984). "Slave Trade on the Northwest Coast of North America." *Research in Economic Anthropology* 6:121–158.

Drucker, P. (1951). "The Northern and Central Nootkin Tribes." *Bureau of American Ethnology Bulletin 144.* Washington.

_____ (1983) "Ecology and Political Organization on the Northwest Coast of America," in Elizabeth Tooker, ed., Morton Fried, organizer, *The Development of Political Organization in Native North America*. The American Ethnological Society, Washington D. C., pp 86–96.

Emmons, G. (1991). *The Tlingit Indians*. Seattle: University of Washington Press.

Ferguson, B. (1983). "Warfare and Redistributive Exchange on the Northwest Coast," In *The Development of Political Organization in Native North America*. Elizabeth Tooker, ed., Morton Fried, organizer. The American Ethnological Society, Washington D. C., pp. 131–147.

_____ (1984). "A Re-Examination of the Causes of Northwest Coast Warfare." In *Cultures at War: Essays on the Economy and Ecology of Warfare*. Brian Ferguson (ed). New York, Academic Press.

Fladmark, K. (1982). "An Introduction to the Prehistory of British Columbia." *Canadian Journal of Archaeology* **6**:95–156.

_____ (1986) *British Columbia Prehistory*. Ottawa: Archaeological Survey of Canada, National Museum of Man, National Museums of Canada.

Fladmark, K. R. Ames, K. M. and Sutherland, P. D. (1990). "Prehistory of the Northern Coast of British Columbia." In *Handbook of North American Indians, Vol. 7: Northwest Coast*. W. Suttles, vol. ed., pp. 229–239. Washington D. C.: Smithsonian Press.

Franchere, G. (1967). *Adventures in Astoria, 1810–1814*. Hoyt C. Franchere, ed. and trans. Norman: University of Oklahoma Press.

Garfield, V. E. (1939). *Tsimshian Clan and Society*. University of Washington Publications in Anthropology, Vol. 7, No. 3, pp 167–340. Seattle: University of Washington.

Golovnin. P. N. (1983). *Civil and Savage Encounters*. B. Dmytryshyn and E. A. P. Crownhart-Vaughan, trans. Portland: The Press of the Oregon Historical Society.

Hayden, B. (1981). "The Carrying Capacity Dilemma." *American Antiquity* **40(2)**, Part 2:11–21.

Hilton, S. F. (1990). "Haihais, Bella Bella, and Oowekeeno." In *Handbook of North American Indians, Vol. 7: Northwest Coast*. W. Suttles, vol. ed. pp. 312–322. Washington D. C.: Smithsonian Press.

Holmberg, H. J. (1985). *Holmberg's Ethnographic Sketches*, originally published 1855–63, English translation by Fritz Jaensch, Edited by Marvin Falk, The Rasmuson Library Historical Translation Series, vol. 1. Fairbanks: The University of Alaska Press.

Jones, L. F. (1914). *A Study of the Thlingets of Alaska*. Fleming H. Revell Company, New York.

Kamenskii, Fr. Anatolii (1906). *Tlingit Indians of Alaska*. Translated and Supplemented by Sergei Kan, The Rasmuson Library Historical Translation Series, Volume II, Marvin W. Falk, ed. Fairbanks: The University of Alaska Press.

Kennedy, D. I. D. and Bouchard, R. T. (1990). "Bella Coola." In *Handbook of North American Indians, Vol. 7: Northwest Coast*. W. Suttles, vol. ed. pp. 323–339. Washington D. C.: Smithsonian Press.

Khlebnikov, K. T. (1973). *Baranov, Chief Manager of the Russian Colonies in America*. Translated from the Russian edition (St. Petersburg, 1835) by Colin Bearne. Ontario: The Limestone Press.

Krause, A. (1970). *The Tlingit Indians*. Seattle: University of Washington Press.

Lambert, P.M. (1994). *War and Peace on the Western Front: A Study of Violent Conflict and its Correlates in Hunter-Gatherer Societies of Coastal Southern California*. Unpublished Ph.D. Dissertation. University of California – Santa Barbara.

(1993) "Health in prehistoric populations of the Santa Barbara Channel Islands." *American Antiquity* 58:509–521.

Lambert, P. M. and Walker, P. L. (1991). "Physical anthropological evidence for the evolution of social complexity in coastal southern California." *Antiquity* 65:963–973.

Langdon, S. (1977). *Technology, Ecology, and Economy: Fishing Systems in Southeastern Alaska*. Ph.D. dissertation. Palo Alto: Department of Anthropology, Stanford University. Ann Arbor: University Microfilms.

(1979). "Comparative Tlingit and Haida Adaptation to the West Coast of the Prince of Wales Archipelago." *Ethnology* 18(1):101–119.

Lee, R. (1979). *The !Kung San: Men, Women and Work in a Foraging Society*. New York: Cambridge University Press.

Lowrey, N. S. (1994). "An Ethnoarchaeological Inquiry into the Interactive Relationship Between Northwest Coast Projectile Point and Armor Variants." Unpublished manuscript on file at the University of Wisconsin, Madison.

MacDonald, G. F. (1989). *Kitwanga Fort Report*. Canadian Museum of Civilization, Quebec.

Mallery, G. (1886). "Pictographs of the North American Indians: A Preliminary Paper." pp. 3–256 in *4th Annual Report of the Bureau of American Ethnology for the Years 1882-1883*. Washington.

Maschner, H. D. G. (1990). "Resource Distributions, Circumscription, Climatic Change, and Social Inequality on the Northern Northwest Coast." Fairbanks: Paper presented at the 6th International Conference on Hunting and Gathering Societies, May 26-June 1, 1990.

(1991). "The Emergence of Cultural Complexity on the Northern Northwest Coast." *Antiquity* 65:924–934.

(1992). *The Origins of Hunter and Gatherer Sedentism and Political Complexity: A Case Study from the Northern Northwest Coast*. Unpublished Ph.D. Dissertation, University of California, Santa Barbara.

(in preparation). "Report of the 1994 North Kuiu Archaeological Project." Manuscript in possession of the author. University of Wisconsin, Madison.

_____ (1996). "The Politics of Settlement Choice on the Prehistoric Northwest Coast: Cognition, GIS, and Coastal Landscapes." In *Anthropology Through Geographic Information and Analysis*. H. Maschner and M. Aldenderfer, eds. pp. 185–200. Oxford: Oxford University Press.

Maschner, H. D. G. and Ames, K. M. (1992). "Prehistoric Population Dynamics on the Northwest Coast of North America." Paper presented at the Annual Meeting of the *Northwest Anthropological Association*, Burnaby, British Columbia.

Maschner, H. D. G. and Stein, J. (1995). "Multivariate Approaches to Site Location on the Northwest Coast." *Antiquity*, **69**:61–73.

Minto, J. (1900). "The Number and Condition of the Native Race in Oregon When First Seen by the White Man." *Oregon Historical Quarterly* 1(3):296–315.

Mitchell, D. (1981). "Test Excavations at Randomly Selected Sites in Eastern Queen Charlotte Straits." In *Fragments of the Past: British Columbia Archaeology in the 1970s*. K. R. Fladmark, ed. pp. 103–123. B.C. Studies 48 (Winter). Vancouver.

_____ (1984). "Predatory Warfare, Social Status, and the North Pacific Slave Trade." *Ethnology* **23**(1) 39–48.

_____ (1985). "A Demographic Profile of Northwest Coast Slavery." In *Status, Structure and Stratification: Current Archaeological Reconstructions*. M. Thompson, M. T. Garcia, and F. J. Kense, eds., pp. 217–226. Calgary, Alta: Archaeological Association of Calgary.

_____ (1990). "Prehistory of the Coasts of Southern British Columbia and Northern Washington." In *Handbook of North American Indians*, Vol. 7: Northwest Coast, W. Suttles, vol. ed., pp. 340–358, Washington D.C.: Smithsonian Press.

Mitchell, D. and Donald, L. (1986). "Some Economic Aspects of Tlingit, Haida, and Tsimshian Slavery." In *Research of Economic Anthropology*. B. L. Isaac, ed., 7:19–35. Greenwich, Conn.

Moss, M. (1989). *Archaeology and Cultural Ecology of the Prehistoric Angoon Tlingit*. Ph.D. dissertation. Santa Barbara: Department of Anthropology, University of California.

Moss, M. and Erlandson, J. (1992). "Forts, Refuge Rocks, and Defensive Sites: The Antiquity of Warfare Along the North Pacific Coast of North America.' *Arctic Anthropology* **29**(2):73–90.

Moss, M. Erlandson, J. and Stuckenrath, R. (1989). "The Antiquity of Tlingit Settlement on Admiralty Island, Southeast Alaska." *American Antiquity* **54**(3):534–543.

Murray, J. S. (1981). "Prehistoric Skeletons from Blue Jackets Creek (FlUa 4), Queen Charlotte Islands, British Columbia." In J. Cybulski, ed., *Contributions to Physical Anthropology 1978–1980*. National Museum of Man, Mercury Series **106**:127–175.

Niblack, A. (1970). *The Coast Indians of Southern Alaska and Northern British Columbia. Reprinted from the Annual Report of the United States National Museum for 1888*, pp. 225–386 by the Johnson Reprint Company.

Oberg, K. (1973). *The Social Economy of the Tlingit Indians*. Seattle: University of Washington Press.

Okada, H. Okada, A. Kotani, Y. Yajima, K. Olson, W. Nishimoto, T. Okino, S. (1989). *Hecata Island, Southeastern Alaska: Anthropological Survey in 1987*. Sapporo, Hokkaido, Japan: Hokkaido-tosho-kikaku.

Okada, H. Okada, A. Yajima, K. Olson, W. Sugita, M. Shionosaki, N. Okino, S. Yoshida, K. Kaneko, H. (1992). *Hecata Island, Southeastern Alaska: Anthropological Survey in 1989 & 1990*. Sapporo, Hokkaido, Japan: Hokkaido-tosho-kikaku.

Powell, J. V. (1990). "Quileute." In *Handbook of North American Indians, Vol. 7: Northwest Coast*. W. Suttles, Vol. ed., pp. 431–437, Washington D. C.: Smithsonian Press.

Rosman, A. and Rubel, P. G. (1986). *Feasting With Mine Enemy*, Waveland Press, Prospect Heights, IL.

Sapir, E. and Swadesh, M. (1955). "Native Accounts of Nootka Ethnography." *Indiana Research Center in Anthropology, Folklore, and Linguistics Publications* **1**:1–457. Bloomington. (Reprinted: AMS Press, New York, 1978).

Schalk, R. (1977). "The Structure of an Anadromous Fish Resource." In *For Theory Building in Archaeology*, L. R. Binford, ed., pp. 207–249. New York: Academic Press.

_____ (1981). "Land Use and Organization Complexity among Foragers of Northwestern North America," In *Affluent Foragers: Pacific Coasts East and West*. S. Koyama and D. H. Thomas, eds., Senri Ethnological Series, National Museum of Ethnology, Osaka.

Scouler, J. (1905). "Dr. John Scouler's Journal of a Voyage to N.W. America [1824]." F. G. Young, ed. *Oregon Historical Quarterly*. **6**(1):54–75, (2):159–205, **(3)**:276–287.

Seaburg, and W. R. Miller, J. (1990). "Tillamook." In *Handbook of North American Indians, Vol. 7: Northwest Coast*, W. Suttles, vol. ed., pp. 560–567. Washington D. C.: Smithsonian Press.

Silverstein, M. (1990). "Chinookans of the Lower Columbia." In *Handbook of North American Indians, Vol. 7: Northwest Coast*, W. Suttles, vol. ed., pp. 533–546. Washington D. C.: Smithsonian Press.

Suttles, W. (Ed.) (1990). *Handbook of North American Indians, Vol. 7: Northwest Coast*. Washington D.C.: Smithsonian Press.

(1968). "Coping with Abundance: Subsistence on the Northwest Coast." In *Man the Hunter*, R. Lee and I. DeVore, eds., pp. 56–68. Chicago: Aldine.

Suttles, W. and Lane, B. (1990). "Southern Coast Salish." In *Handbook of North American Indians, Vol. 7: Northwest Coast*, W. Suttles, vol. ed., pp. 485–502, Washington D. C.: Smithsonian Press.

Swadesh, M. (1948). "Motivations in Nootka Warfare." *Southwestern Journal of Anthropology* 4:76–93.

Swanton, J. R. (1905). "Contributions to the Ethnology of the Haida." New York: *Publications of the Jesup North Pacific Expedition 5: Memoirs of the American Museum of Natural History* **8(1)**:1–300.

(1970). *The Social Conditions, Beliefs, and Linguistic Relationship of the Tlingit Indians*. Johnson Reprint Corporation, New York, New York.

Taylor, H. C. Jr. and Duff, W. (1956). "A Post-contact Southward Movement of the Kwakiutl." *Washington State College Research Studies* **24(1)**: 55–66. Pullman.

Tihkmenev, P. A. (1979). *A History of the Russian America Company, Volume 2, Documents*. D. Krenov (trans.), R. Pierce and A. Donnelly (eds.). Kingston, Ontario: Limestone Press.

Thwaites, R. G., (Ed.) (1904–1905). *Original Journals of the Lewis and Clark Expedition, 1804–1806*, 8 Vols. New York: Dodd, Mead.

Townsand, J.B. (1978). "Ranked Societies of the Alaskan Pacific Rim." In *Alaska Native Culture and History*. Y. Kotani and W. Workman, eds., pp. 123–156. Osaka: National Museum of Ethnology, Senri Ethnological Series 4.

(1985). "The Autonomous Village and the Development of Chiefdoms." In *Decline and Development: The Evolution of Sociopolitical Complexity*, H. J. Classen, et. al. eds, pp. 141–155. Mass.: Bergin and Garvey.

Vancouver, G. (1984). *A Voyage of Discovery to the North Pacific Ocean and Round the World*. London: T. Gillet (original 1801).

Veniaminov, I. (1984). "Notes on the Islands of the Unalaska District [1840]." L. Black and R. H. Goeghegan, trans., R. A. Pierce, ed. (*Alaska History* 27). Kingston, Ont.: The Limestone Press.

Wessen, G. (1986). *Prehistoric Cultural Resources of San Juan County, Washington*. Report Prepared for the Washington State Office of Archaeology and Historic Preservation, Olympia.

Wooley, C. B. (1984). "Isla de la Empalizada: Defensive Sites and Early Culture Change in Southeast Alaska." Fairbanks: Paper presented at the 13th Annual Meeting of the Alaska Anthropological Association.

Wooley, C. B. and Haggerty, J. C. (1989). "Tlingit-Tsimshian Interaction in the Southern Alexander Archipelago." Anchorage: Paper presented at the 16th Annual Meeting of the Alaska Anthropological Association.

Chapter
ELEVEN

Frontier Warfare in the Early Neolithic

Lawrence H. Keeley
University of Illinois at Chicago
Department of Anthropology

Agricultural economies and farming settlements first appeared in Central and Northwestern Europe as a result of a colonization by farmers bearing the Linear Pottery or Linienband-keramik (LBK) Culture. The huge area colonized by LBK farmers stretched from northern France in the west to the western Ukraine in the east. These settlers exclusively settled the loess soils charac-teristic of the southern part of the North European Plain. This large scale colonization occurred around 7000 (calibrated) years ago and, judging from radiocarbon dates, took no more than a few hundred years to reach from Czechoslavakia to Belgium and N. France. The regions colonized were, however, already occupied by Late Me-solithic hunter-gatherers. Contrary to some recent 'farmer-forager interaction' theories and traditional views on this encounter between LBK farmers and Mesolithic foragers, relations between them were not peaceful.

LBK AND MESOLITHIC IN NORTHWESTERN EUROPE

LBK culture shows a remarkable homogeneity in material culture, subsistence economy and settlement pattern despite the extent of the area colonized. LBK farmers built a very distinctive type of longhouse. The post-patterns, dimensions and even the NW-SE orientations of these houses show no discernible regional variations. LBK takes its name from an easily-recognizable pottery. Regional stylistic variations in decoration are very slight and only discernable in the very late stages. LBK stone tools include large blades, sickles, a special projectile point, groundstone axes and adzes, and a distinctive type of saddle quern. LBK lithic technology and typology were very different from those of the local Mesolithic industries that precede LBK's appearance. In general and in detail, LBK material culture is very distinctive, especially from that of the Final Mesolithic that preceded it. The LBK subsistence economy was based almost exclusively on simple mixed-farming. Einkorn and emmer wheat were the staple crops, complemented by legumes, flax and few other domesticated plants. Their livestock was dominated by cattle and sheep/goat. The LBK diet was almost entirely agricultural since wild plants and animals are rarely found in their food remains (Bogucki 1988:53–61). Pollen analysis indicates that they cleared the Atlantic deciduous forest to open fields and pastures for their domesticated crops and livestock. The current consensus among Western European archaeologists is that LBK famers were not slash- and-burn extensive horticulturalists. Given their diverse and complementary crops, the potential for manuring and crop rotation, they could have maintained soil fertility over long periods. Palynology indicates that deforestion was sustained around some villages over several generations. Some LBK settlements appear to have been permanent with occupations lasting several house generations (i.e. for more than a century). At least on a local scale, LBK farmers were transforming the ecology of the loess lands by substituting their domesticated plants and livestock for the native flora and fauna. Certainly their land-use pattern was radically different from that of Mesolithic foragers and would have had a negative impact on the fish, wild mammals and plants that were the mainstays of the foraging economy. The LBK expansion represents perhaps the clearest and most unequivocal example of colonization in the prehistoric record. Although the acid soils of this region seldom preserve human skeletons, the human physical type found in LBK cemeteries is a gracile "Mediterraneanoid" while that associated with the Late Mesolithic is a robust "Cromagnonoid" (i.e., the type found in this region throughout Upper Paleolithic and Mesolithic). Apparently, LBK farmers were newcomers to the regions they colonized (e.g., Riquet 1976; Telehin and Potehkina 1987; Wahl and König 1987; Bach and Bach 1989).[1] In every area of life visible to archaeology, LBK traits were complete novelties relative to comparable Late Mesolithic traits. There is nothing in Mesolithic material culture or economy that can be regarded as a precursor or ancestral to any comparable feature of LBK culture. Nor is there any feature of LBK material culture or economy that can be regarded as a "survival" of any comparable feature of Mesolithic lifeways. Many archaeologists have noted the remarkable coincidence of the final radiocarbon dates for Mesolithic and the earliest dates for LBK in any area colonized by LBK (Dennell 1985, Ammerman and Cavalli-Sforza 1984:58–60). This implies that the change from Mesolithic foraging to LBK farming was very rapid and that Mesolithic lifeways did not long survive the first settlement of any region by LBK farmers. This change in loess lands of Northwest Europe can be bluntly summarized: farmers of a (putatively) novel physical type bearing a wholly new way of life arrived and the indigenous foragers and their way of life quickly and completely disappeared. Despite the "violence" of this transformation, until very recently, LBK colonization and LBK lifeways were regarded as being exceptionally peaceful. This interpretation was based on the judgement that there were no obvious weapons of war in LBK material culture and that LBK settlements were not fortified. The few LBK burials that survived in the acid soils of this region supposedly showed no signs of violent death, nor did the equally rare skeletons of Late Mesolithic folk. More recently a number of archaeological theorists have proposed that farmer-forager interactions should be overwhelmingly peaceful (see Moore 1985; Bogucki 1988; Gregg 1988; Dennell 1985). Indeed, it is difficult to find another area of archaeological theory that is more optimistic about social relations or more innocent of cynicism than farmer-forager interaction theory. And, if the traditional view of LBK-Mesolithic relations is accepted, it would be hard to find a better prehistoric exemplar for these hopeful theories.

EVIDENCE FOR FRONTIER VIOLENCE

Unfortunately for both the theoretical and traditional views, during the last few years, a growing body of evidence indicates that neither Late Mesolithic nor LBK life' was especially peaceful. Contrary to theory, the available data indicates that exchange between Mesolithic foragers and LBK farmers was very limited or nonexistent. Other data imply that any interactions between them were at least occasionally hostile or expected to be so. Evidence for the violence of this Early Neolithic frontier include: 1) finds of homicide victims in both Late Mesolithic and LBK burial populations, 2) fortified LBK border settlements, 3) no-man's-lands between LBK and Final Mesolithic settlements, and 4) war weapons in LBK material culture.

There are also other aspects of LBK behavior that are inexplicable unless violent hostilities were a significant part of their social life. Despite the very small skeletal samples available, homicide victims are not rare in those that have been preserved and recovered from the Late Mesolithic and the LBK of northwestern Europe. David Frayer (this volume) discusses the Ofnet "trophy" skulls dating to the Late Mesolithic. This gruesome find implies that some Late Mesolithic foragers may have practiced head-hunting and that their relatively rare axes were, on occasion, used as weapons. Many other other Late Mesolithic human skeletons, admittedly mostly from outside the LBK settlement zone show evidence of violent deaths. Indeed, so common are homicide victims in Mesolithic burial samples, that Vencl (1991) regards the Mesolithic as the period in European prehistory when true warfare first appears. In the few LBK cemeteries where skeletons are well-preserved (e.g. Stuttgart), some individuals do bear weapons traumas (D. Frayer, personal communication). One of the most dramatic finds was a mass grave at Talheim in Germany which contained the bodies of 34 men women and chidren. All had been killed by blows to the head, usually multiple, delivered by the distinctive LBK adzes and axes (Wahl and König 1987). One skull also retained the imprint of an arrow wound. There are as yet no finds of LBK colonists killed by Mesolithic arrows or Mesolithic foragers killed by LBK weapons. But if both groups warred among themselves, can we expect them to have been uniformly peaceable with each other?

Contrary to traditional opinion, many LBK settlements are enclosed by defenses, especially in the western part of the LBK distribution (Höckman 1990). Many of these "enclosures" were clearly fortifications, that is, defenses against other humans, consisting of 2 to 3 meter deep, V-shaped ditches backed by sometimes multiple palisades (Bosquet 1992). Most of the more completely excavated examples display other features typical of fortifications up until the age of gunpowder such as "baffled" gates and, in the case of Darion, a "battlement" or gate tower (Fig. 11.1).[2]

A glance at the distribution map of LBK "enclosures" indicates they were clustered along the limits of the LBK settlement zone (Fig. 11.2). Clearly, the threat they were erected against came from beyond the frontier and, given these locations, the only possible adversaries were Mesolithic foragers living beyond the limits of agricultural colonization. There is, in Belgium, additional support for the inference of LBK-Mesolithic hostilities in the no-man's-land apparent between LBK settlements and Final Mesolithic sites where no geographic barrier exists (Fig. 11.3). Rather than attracting each other for symbiotic "interaction", Late Mesolithic and LBK settlements seem to have repelled one another.

At one site in Belgium, it appears that the first houses built were all destroyed by fire (Keeley and Cahen 1989). After this conflagration, the site was fortified with a ditch and palisade, and any newer houses were built inside the defenses. At another site a few kilometers distant, pollen in bottom of ditch indicates that before forest clearance, apparently before any houses were built, the fortifications were constructed. It appears that LBK farmers, in Northeast Belgium at least, were pioneering a hostile territory.

In Belgium, there is also no evidence for the theoretically expected farmer-forager exchange (see Keeley 1992 for more details and sources). The only items that were apparently "exchanged" between the LBK farmers and Mesolithic foragers were projectile points. Also, a few LBK adze/axes have been found at a handful of Mesolithic sites. But, as the axe/adze traumas on the skulls of the Talheim victims indicates, these LBK "tools" were weapons. There is certainly no reason to presume that these arrows or axes were exchanged peacefully.

All the evidence we currently possess from the northwestern portion of the LBK colonization zone, suggests that, in the case of the LBK and Mesolithic, "farmer-forager interaction" has much bleaker meaning than some Panglossian theorists have predicted. LBK frontier settlements were often protected by defensive ditches and palisades, in a few cases the defenses were constructed before fields and pastures were cleared. Moreover, violent death was not

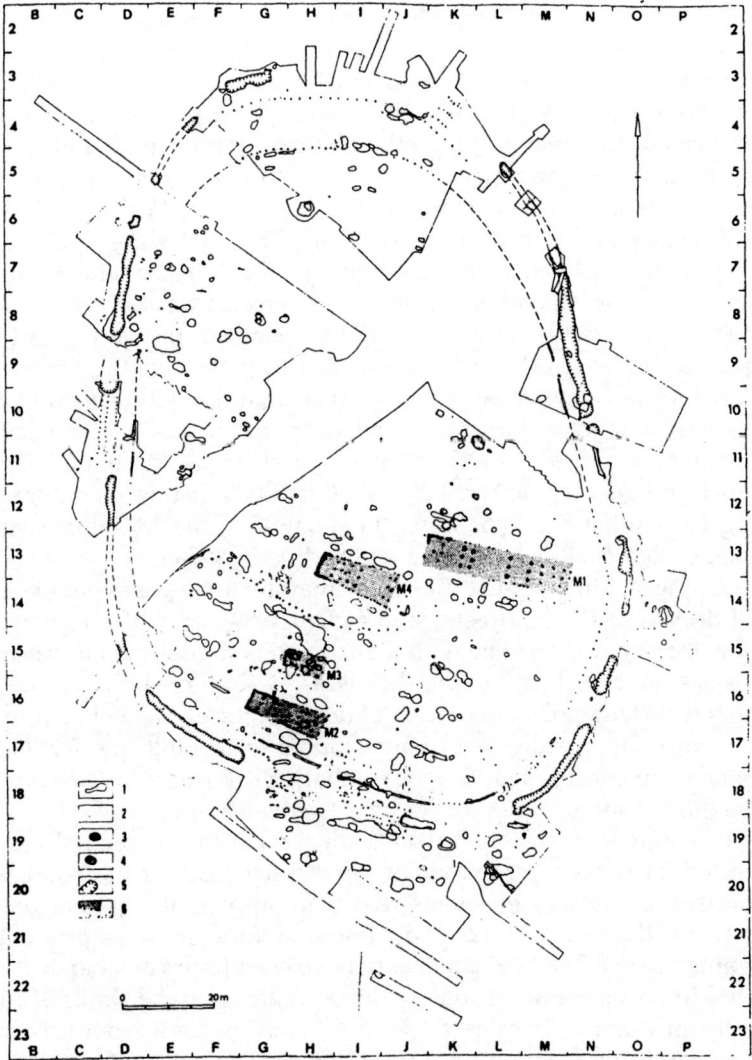

Figure 11.1. Plan of the fortified LBK site of Darion, Lige Province, Belgium (from Cahen, et al. 1987).

uncommon among either the LBK farmers or Late Mesolithic foragers. LBK axes and adzes, whatever their other prosaic uses, certainly served as weapons of war. Where no geographic barriers existed, a no-man's-land developed between the LBK and

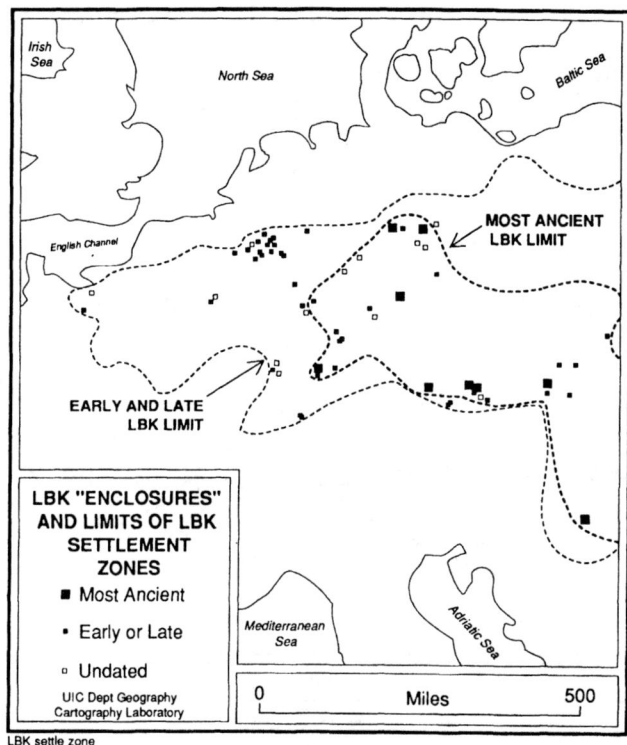

Figure 11.2. Map showing the association between LBK fortifications and the limits of LBK settlement.

Mesolithic settlement zones. The only demonstrable exchanges between the farmers and foragers involve weapons. The fortifications imply that the colonizers either expected or experienced hostilities, other evidence implies that, whatever interactions there were between these two groups, they were at best chilly and at worst violent.

In addition, there are several aspects of LBK archaeology that cannot be explained or understood without writing warfare back into our interpretations. Milasauskas (1978) noted many years ago that in the western LBK zone, the same area in which fortifications have been found, projectile points are very common in LBK lithic assemblages. Yet, as noted above, wild fauna are extremely rare in LBK faunal assemblages. If LBK farmers were not hunting, why

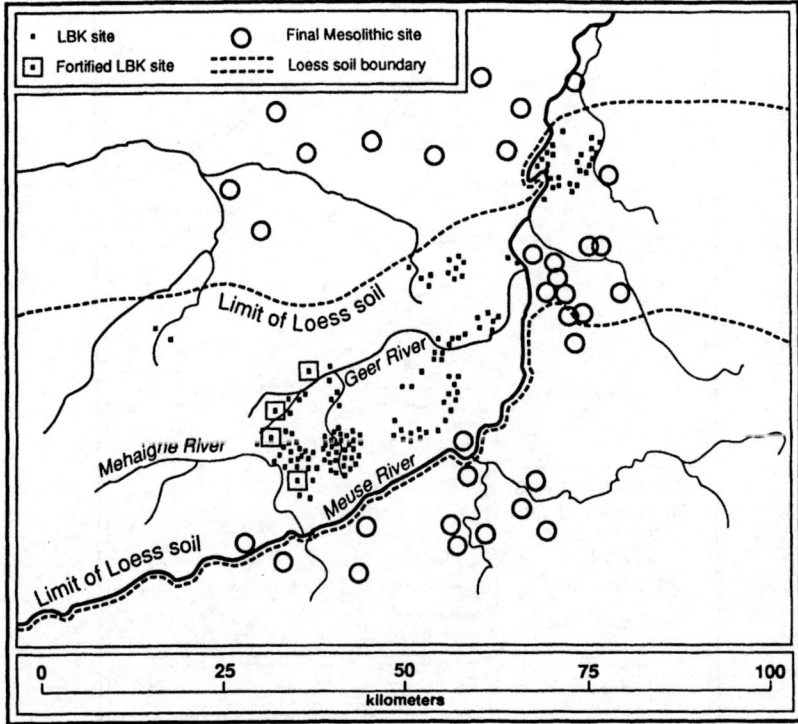

Figure 11.3. Map of Final Mesolithic and Early Neolithic (LBK) sites. Note the separation to the north between the nearest Mesolithic and Neolithic settlements; such settlements only are in close proximity where the 'trench' of the Meuse/Maas intervenes.

did they need so many arrow points? Of course, the most reasonable alternative is that the arrows were needed as weapons of war.

LBK axes and adzes have been traditionally assumed to be purely wood-working tools. Given the forest clearance, house building and the belatedly-recognized palisade construction that are characteristic of LBK settlements, this assumption is certainly reasonable. But these artifacts do have some peculiar features and associations that fit poorly with the wood-working model. At some LBK cemeteries, adzes and axes are only found in older male burials (e.g., Champion, *et al.* 1984:143). This implies that they were also symbols of achieved status for men since if they merely symbolized masculinity we would expect them in all male graves. If the standard interpretation of the function of the axes is accepted, these finds would imply that wood-working skill was a primary component of male status. This conclusion, while not impossible, would at least be unusual judging from the ethnographic record where achieved male statuses usually depend on wealth, oratorical talent and, most commonly, skill in hunting or warfare. At the Belgian LBK sites that my Belgian colleagues and I excavated, a few of these adze/axes were made of raw materials that were too friable or otherwise unsuitable for wood-working. What is even more peculiar is that these unsuitable raw materials were "exotic", that is, obtained from distant sources and presumably at some cost. These puzzles become soluble when we recall that Talheim indicates that axes and adzes were also weapons of war.

The role of these artifacts in LBK social and economic life was probably very similar to that documented ethnographically among many tribes in highland New Guinea. Among the Enga, for example, men were never without an axe/adze in their belt (until the practice was outlawed, for obvious reasons, by local ordinances) and "felt naked" without one (Meggitt 1977:57–58). Enga men did not constantly carry one of these axes because they were subject to sudden impulses to clear forest or work wood, but because they never knew when they might need to bust someone's skull. Indeed, they were the only weapon carried by Enga emissaries to peace negotiations, an unlikely setting for woodworking but not, alas, for violence. Of course, most of these Enga axes were indeed used for woodworking as were, presumably, the LBK adzes and axes. But the fact remains that, while this prosaic function of LBK axes must be inferred, their only documented use was for cracking heads.

The work of Daniel Cahen, several Belgian colleagues and myself at several LBK villages in close proximity to one another has uncovered evidence that some of them had part-time craft specializations (Keeley and Cahen 1989, 1990; Sliva and Keeley 1994). One village clearly specialized in producing flint blades, while another six km distant did not manufacture its own blades but must have received them by exchange. The blade producing village also specialized in the production of some form of leather while the 'non-knapping' village, unlike any of the others in the vicinity, yielded considerable evidence of ceramic production. In another case, the village specialization involved the manufacture of adzes from an imported raw material. None of these specializations can be explained by geographic proximity to raw materials. Flint, clay and

hides were equally available to all and the source of the axe material was equally distant. There is also no evidence that these
part-time village specializations developed gradually over time;
they were apparently already established when these various villages were first settled. At least in Amazonia, such 'arbitrary' village specializations in prosaic and essential craft products were
directly associated with the maintenance of military alliances
(Chagnon 1983:149–150; Gregor 1990:111–112). Again, only when
we accept warfare as a significant feature of LBK life can we
account for many of its otherwise inexplicable features.

DISCUSSION

While there are now ample reasons to infer that LBK lifeways and
the LBK colonization were often bellicose, it is also important to
recognize that this pattern may have been variable. It is worth
repeating that all of the clearest evidences of warfare – fortifications, over-abundant arrowheads, homicide victims – are, as yet,
almost exclusively known from the western half of the LBK distribution. A glance at Figure 11.2 indicates that while LBK enclosures have been found in Czechoslovakia and Hungary, they are
much rarer in the east and unknown in the northeast area, particularly Poland. One can always claim that these geographical patterns, which I will over-simplify by the term 'east-west,' are merely
a consequence of inadequate surveillance and limited excavations.
While differences in 'coverage' surely explain some of this variability, there are also arguments against such special pleading. There is
positive evidence that the LBK frontier in the Poland was not as
'hard- and-fast' as that in the northwest. In the west, LBK material
culture, except the afore-mentioned arrow points and adze/axes, is
never found beyond the limits of Loess soils (or Loess-derived
soils). This is not the case in eastern Germany or Poland (Bogucki
1988:77) where variously LBK ceramics, lithics and domestic livestock (but not houses or villages) are commonly found in the
'Cover Sand' and Till soils north of the Loess. Whether these di-
luted extensions of LBK culture beyond the limits of unequivocal
LBK settlement represent an acculturation of the local Mesolithic
foragers or some more pastoral and simplified variant of the LBK is
unclear. Whatever may have been the case, these finds are evidence
that the LBK-Mesolithic frontier in this region was more permeable
than that in the northwest.

Explanation of the apparently more peaceful character of LBK settlement in the east, in the current climate of opinion, requires first a recognition of the violent nature of the LBK-Mesolithic frontier in other areas. While speculation is all that is possible at this juncture, the primary possibilities are a geographical difference in LBK societies or economies, a similar variation in Mesolithic lifeways, or both. Other than the warfare-related western features and the simplified LBK found beyond the Loess in Poland, the material culture inventory, settlement pattern and subsistence economy of the LBK show no consistent differences from east to west. In general, it would difficult to argue that somehow eastern LBK societies were very different from those to the west.

However, there is one east-west difference that is usually glossed over as an interpretative disagreement between most Western and some Eastern European LBK archaeologists. This debate concerns the intensity of LBK agriculture and settlement permanence (see the summary in Bogucki 1988:79–82). East European specialists have tended to interpret LBK farming as more or less 'shifting' and LBK villages as being periodically moved when local soils became exhausted. This interpretation is supported by apparent stylistic 'saltations' in pottery styles at some sites, implying lengthy interruptions in occupation, and microstratigraphic analysis of pit fills implying occupations no longer than a human generation. As noted above, Western European prehistorians are now unanimous in inferring that LBK farming was more intensive and capable of sustaining more continuous occupation at some sites. The 'western' position is based on a lack of ceramic stylistic evidence of interrupted occupations, the size and density of houses at some large sites and, primarily, hypothetical arguments based on the diversity and potential complementarity of LBK crops and livestock. However, it is worth considering whether both sides in this dispute might be right but only about their respective regions.

The more continental climate of Central and Eastern Europe, with its colder and drier winters, thus, relatively wetter summers, slightly lower annual precipitation and greater long-term variability may have affected (even in the warmer Atlantic period) both annual yields and the intensity with which the Loess soils could be farmed. If eastern LBK settlements were less permanent and their agriculture system less intensive, both the demographic and ecological impact of their colonization would have been less severe and, thus, less antagonizing to the forgers. The lower population densities that more extensive agriculture implies would have made the colonists militarily more vulnerable and perhaps more inclined to accomodate their foraging neighbors. Even where hostilities existed, ethnographic groups with more mobile settlement systems were less likely to construct labor-intensive fortifications that could only be used for a few months or years (Keeley, 1996). All of these points, however, remain mere speculations until geographical variations (or their absence) in LBK agricultural and settlement systems are more clearly demonstrated.

In my estimation, the more likely east-west difference involves the Mesolithic foragers rather than the relatively homogeneous LBK. Inspection of Figure 11.2 shows a very high concentration of LBK 'enclosures' in the Rhine-Meuse area which is certainly partially explained by the extensive excavations and intensive surveys of German, Dutch and Belgian archaeologists in this region. But it is also worth noting that the Final Mesolithic groups to the north and west of this 'enclosure' cluster give evidence of being more sedentary, more socio-economically 'complex' and perhaps more densely settled than foraging groups deeper in the interior of the continent. The Late Mesolithic evidence recovered at De Leien-Wartena, Swifterbant, and Ellerbek settlements in the Netherlands and Northwest Germany indicates longer-term occupations, more intensive exploitation of aquatic resources and the occasional manufacture of crude ceramics very different from those of the LBK (Barker 1985:165-166). There is also evidence from the Middle Danube region, where a number of oldest and later LBK enclosures are known, that the final Mesolithic groups there were more sedentary and economically complex (Barker 1985:89; Whittle 1985:22). Judging from ethnographic surveys, there are theoretical reasons for believing that the density, social complexity and sedentism of hunter-gatherers will vary according to the continentality of the climate, forest closure and availability of aquatic resources (Keeley 1988, 1991). Accordingly, the conditions favoring denser, more complex foragers would have been much more common in mid-Holocene Northwest Europe than in Central or Eastern Europe. Such high-density, sedentary foragers would have been more sensitive to ecological disturbance, less able to yield territory to newcomers and more formidible adversaries once antagonized. Thus, one explanation for the apparent geographical variation in evidence for LBK warfare may be that, for demographic, economic and social reasons, the 'touchiness' and 'toughness' of the Mesolithic 'natives' varied.

This raises a much larger issue: warfare is a variable feature of social life, not a constant. Many cross-cultural researchers have found that warfare was an extremely common but by no means universal feature of pre-civilized life (see Ember and Ember, this volume, as well as Otterbein 1980; Ross 1985; Jorgensen 1980). These cross-cultural surveys have found that the frequency of armed conflict is high at all levels of social organization, in all types of subsistence economies, and at all levels of population density. Frustrated ethnographer Thomas Gregor (1990:106) laments that the woeful 'scarcity of peace' visible in the ethnographic record hinders ethnologists from isolating the variables that may encourage or help maintain peace. The key points raised by these studies are that violent conflict is an extremely common feature of social life but not an invariable one. Relying on implicit ethnographic analogies, archaeologists typically devote a considerable amount of attention to prehistoric exchange and trade. This cross-cultural research on warfare indicates that prehistoric warfare deserves a comparable level of expectation and investigation.

Another possible reason for archaeologists disregard for warfare is the popular idea that 'primitive warfare' is more ritualized, more desultory, less destructive and less dangerous (i.e., less effective) than the 'true' or 'real' warfare conducted by civilized states. If this were true, then prehistoric warfare, when it did occur, would be a relative weightless and trivial activity, no more deserving of archaeological attention than games and sports. However, this prevasive idea about 'primitive war' is simply false (Keeley, 1996). Pre-state warfare is at least as brutal, deadly, destructive and as effective as modern civilized warfare. The damage and deaths inflicted, the spoils won or lost, proportional to the size and economies of 'small-scale' societies, equal or exceed those inflicted or sustained by modern civilized states. In short, war is hell whether it is fought with wooden spears or napalm. Thus, prehistorians should not only expect prehistoric warfare, they should also anticipate that it had dramatic effects.

Nevertheless, however common and terrible, warfare is not a constant of social life or human existence. However rare, some ethnographic and historical civilized societies were especially peaceful. The incidence of warfare and its intensity varies in time and space even for a specific culture or society (Keeley, 1996). Relations between neighboring social groups can turn from brutally violent to amiably peaceful within a single generation. Consider that for a thousand years Scandinavia was home to some of the most violent and militarily aggressive societies on earth, yet their descendents over the last two centuries have earned a reputation for non-violence and pacifism. The Embers' (this volume) have noted that ethnographically the frequency of warfare was correlated with the 'riskiness' of a group's environment. There are also other circumstances that seem to be correlated with more frequent and bitter armed conflicts, such as frequent economic exchange (Ember and Ember 1990:256), intermarriage, moving frontiers between major cultural types and the proximity of an aggressive neighbor (Keeley, 1996). Archaeologists cannot contribute to the analysis of the factors that affect war and peace until they recognize that prehistoric warfare is not an oxymoron. What is especially frustrating about archaeologists' 'see no evil' prejudice regarding ancient warfare is that there apparently were some periods and regions of the prehistoric world that were remarkably peaceful. For example, despite undergoing dramatic demographic and economic changes, there is no evidence of warfare from the final foraging and first agricultural societies in the historically blood-soaked Near East (O. Bar-Yosef, personal communication). The peaceful nature of this period, or any other such periods and places, can only be understood, indeed, can only be recognized as such, by contrasting them with regions and eras that were more violent. Archaeologists of my generation accept that the analysis of variation lies at the heart of archaeological method and theory. But how can we analyse significant variables that we avert our eyes from or special plead away? Warfare is certainly a variable and, as ethnography and history attest, worthy of our attention.

CONCLUSIONS

It is now becoming clear that collective violence, war, was part of LBK life. Relations between pioneer LBK farmers and indigenous Mesolithic foragers appear in some regions to have been at best chilly and at worst bellicose. Indeed, the archaeological record of this crucial period in the European past is much less mysterious if we accept this fact. Most archaeologists concede that prehistoric peoples adapted to their social as well as their physical environment, but they seem quite reluctant to acknowledge that that some social environments could include frequent armed conflicts. In the case discussed here, LBK farmers were foreign colonists, literally invaders, intruding into territory already occupied by Mesolithic foragers. The very nature of the LBK economy required that they disrupt the native ecology, replacing indigenous flora and fauna with their imported crops and livestock. Given these circumstances, it is amazing that archaeologists took so long to realize that the spread of LBK farmers might have provoked hostilities with the indigenous foragers and that the colonists might have developed institutional ways of coping with, or at least anticipating, such conflict. This blindspot concerning warfare is not just peculiar to LBK specialists or European prehistorians, it may be found in many other regions of the world. I have tried to show here that such Neo-Rousseauian attitudes may hide much from us and unnecessarily complicate our understanding of prehistoric life. I also judge that there is a moral point: when we attribute to prehistoric humans (or to recent tribal peoples) only our virtues and none of our vices, we dehumanize them as much as ourselves.

NOTES

[1] This Meso-Neolithic difference in human "physical type' may indeed be more apparent than real. The small number of surviving LBK and late Mesolithic human skeletons and their variability make it difficult to accept any blithe assertions on this issue. David Frayer (personal communication), a physical anthropologist who has studied relevant Mesolithic and Early Neolithic human remains in western Germany, is very skeptical about such claims. While I must defer to more expert opinion on this issue, I will only note that claims of physical differences between Mesolithic and Early Neolithic populations are both widespread and persisent among European physical anthropologists.

[2] It is fair to note that there is one rare form of LBK enclosure that may not be defensive in function. These are circular in plan with usually several concentric ditches, un-baffled or otherwise undefended gates, do not enclose houses, and are found away from habitations (e.g., Langweiler 8 or Ergolding-West; see Höckmann 1990:75). The similarity of this type of enclosure to Later Neolithic and Bronze Age 'henge' ritual enclosures may be indicative of its function. Much pointless argument and confusion might have been created by a failure to distinguish this circular-concentric type from the more common defensive type. It is very difficult to imagine that such labor-intensive constructions with so many defensive characteristics were merely status symbols, ritual enclosures or, the most popular 'peaceful' interpretation, livestock enclosures. If such elaborate defenses were meant to protect LBK householders and their livestock from predators, the 'predators' were probably of the two-legged variety.

REFERENCES

Ammerman, A. and Cavalli-Sforza, L. (1971). "Measuring the rate of spread of early farming in Europe." *Man* (N.S.) **6**:674–688.

_____ (1984). *The Neolithic Transition and the Genetics of Populations in Europe*. Princeton, NJ: Princeton University Press.

Bach, H. and Bach, A. (1989). Paläanthropologie im Mittelelbe-Saale-Werra-Gebiet. *Weimarer Monographien zur Ur- und Frhgeschichte* **23**:7–65.

Barker, G. (1985). *Prehistoric Farming in Europe*. Cambridge: Cambridge University Press.

Bogucki, P. (1988). *Forest Farmers and Stockherders*. Cambridge: Cambridge University Press.

Bosquet, D. (1992). *Les Dispositifs d'Entree des Enceintes du Rubane de Belgique*. Unpublished Mémoire de Licence, Université Libre de Bruxelles.

Cahen, D., Caspar, J.-P., Gosselin, F. and Hauzeur, A. (1987). Le village rubané de Darion. *Archäologisches Korrespondenzblatt* **17**:59–69.

Cahen, D. and Otte, M. (Eds.) (1990). *Rubané et Cardial*. Liége: E.R.A.U.L.

Chagnon, N. (1983). Yanomamo: *The Fierce People*. New York: Holt, Rinehart & Winston.

Champion, T., Gamble, C., Shennan, S. and Whittle, A. (1984). *Prehistoric Europe*. Orlando, FL: Academic Press.

Dennell, R. (1985). "The Hunter-Gatherer/Agricultural Frontier in Prehistoric Temperate Europe." In *The Archaeology of Frontiers and Boundaries*, edited by S. Green and S. Perlman, pp. 113–139. New York: Academic Press.

Donahue, R. (1992). "Desperately Seeking Ceres." In *Transitions to Agriculture in Prehistory*, edited by A. Gebrauer and T. D. Price, pp. 73–80. Madison, WI: Prehistory Press.

Ember, C. and Ember, M. (1990). *Cultural Anthropology*. Englewood Cliffs, NJ: Prentice Hall.

Gregg, S. (1988). *Foragers and Farmers*. Chicago: University of Chicago.

Gregor, T. (1990). "Uneasy Peace: Tribal relations in Brazil's Upper Xingu." In *The Anthropology of War*, J. Haas (Ed.), pp. 105–24, Cambridge: Cambridge University Press.

Höckmann, O. (1990). "Frneolithische Einhegungen in Europa." *Jahresschrift fr Mittleduetsche Vorgeschichte* **73**:57–88.

Jorgensen, J. (1980) *Western Indians*. San Francisco: W. H. Freeman.

Keeley, L. (1988). 'Hunter–Gatherer economic complexity and "population pressure". *Journal of Anthropological Archaeology* **7**:373–411.

_____ (1991). "Ethnographic Models for Late Glacial Hunter-Gatherers." In *The Late Glacial in North-West Europe*, edited by N. Barton, A. Roberts and D. Roe, pp. 179–190, London: Council for British Archaeology.

(1992). "The Introduction of Agriculture to the Western North European Plain." In *Transitions to Agriculture in Prehistory*, edited by A. Gebrauer and T. D. Price, pp. 81–95. Madison, WI: Prehistory Press.

(1996). *War Before Civilization*. New York: Oxford University Press.

Keeley, L. and Cahen, D. (1989). "Early Neolithic Forts and Villages in NE Belgium: a Preliminary Report." *Journal of Field Archaeology* 16: 157–176.

(1990). "Village specialization in the early Neolithic of NW Europe." Paper read at Annual Meeting of Society for American Archaeology, Las Vegas, NV.

Meggitt, M. (1977). *Blood is Their Argument*. Palo Alto, CA: Mayfield.

Milisauskas, S. (1978) *European Prehistory*. New York: Academic Press.

Moore, J. (1985). "Forager/Farmer Interactions: Information, Social Organization, and the Frontier." In The Archaeology of Frontiers and Boundaries, edited by S. Green and S. Perlman, pp. 93–112. New York: Academic Press.

Otterbein, K. (1980). *Evolution of War*. New Haven, CT: HRAF Press.

Price, T. D. and Gebrauer, A. (1992). "The Final Frontier: Foragers to Farmers in Southern Scandinavia." In *Transitions to Agriculture in Prehistory*, edited by A. Gebauer and T. D. Price, pp. 97–116, Madison, WI: Prehistory Press.

Riquet, R. (1976). "L'Anthropologie protohistorique française. In *La Préhistoire Française II*, edited by J. Guilane, pp. 135–152. Paris: Editions de CNRS.

Ross, M. (1985). Internal and External Conflict and Violence. *Journal of Conflict Resolution* **29**:547–79.

Sliva, R. and Keeley, L. (1994). "'Frits' and Specialized Hide Preparation in the Belgian Early Neolithic." *Journal of Archaeological Science* 21: 91–99.

Telehin, D. and Potehkina, I. (1987). *Neolithic Cemeteries and Populations in the Dniepr Basin* B.A.R. International Series No. 383.

Vencl, S. (1991). "Interpertation des Blessures Causé par les Armes au Mésolithique." *L'Anthropologie* **95**:219–228.

Wahl, J. and H. König (1987). "Anthropologische-Traumologische undersuchen der Menlichen Skelettrest aus dem Bandkeramiken Massengrabe bei Talhiem." *Fundberichte aus Baden-Wurttemberg* **12**:65–193.

Whittle, A. (1987). "Neolithic Settlement Patterns in Temperate Europe: Progress and Problems." *Journal of World Prehistory* **1**:5–52.

Chapter TWELVE

Violence and War in Prehistory

R. Brian Ferguson
Dept. of Sociology and Anthropology
Rutgers University, Newark

If there are people out there who believe that violence and war did not exist until after the advent of Western colonialism, or of the state, or of agriculture, this volume proves them wrong. Equally, if there are people who believe that all human societies have been plagued by violence and war, that they were always present in human evolutionary history, this volume proves *them* wrong.

For far too long, efforts to understand of the role of violence in our deep past has been pulled off course by the gravity of these polar ideologies – humans as angels or as devils. On one hand is the uncritical, even enthusiastic acceptance of dubious evidence of injury, as brought to a huge audience by Robert Ardrey (1961; Neuman 1987). On the other is a tendency in some archaeological circles to disregard or minimize evidence of violence. The wars of the Maya, for instance, were long considered to be limited and "ceremonial", despite abundant evidence to the contrary (Webster 1993).

This volume looks at evidence, mostly human skeletal remains from many places and periods, and asks what we can learn about ancient violence, both individual and collective. The editors invited me to comment and extrapolate upon these findings, an invitation that is especially gracious as they know some of my views differ from theirs. The first of two sections in this chapter deals with evidence for violence in general and war in particular, asking first what sorts of evidence exist, looking next at the findings of this volume, and finally comparing them to other research and discussing some theoretical implications. The second section of the chapter focuses on early war specifically, asking what are the preconditions for war, and then outlining spatial and temporal patterns expectably involved in war's actual occurrence.

EVIDENCE AND IMPLICATIONS

Identifying Violence and War

Perhaps the most significant general finding of this volume is that violence and war leave recoverable traces. Not surprising, perhaps, but influential theories rise on the premise that "absence of evidence is not evidence of absence". While still true for particular cases, that axiom must be reconsidered as a generalization. On the other hand, where archaeological evidence of violence exists, it should not be resisted. This volume shows humans have done injury to others for a very long time. Huge ambiguities remain – whether violence is individual or collective (i.e. war), and how to explain/interpret it in either case – but identification of the existence of physical violence and violent group conflict is very possible. As this book shows, they are archaeologically visible behaviors. The following section surveys types of evidence presented in this volume and elsewhere.

To start with osteology, the main concern of this volume, the best evidence for interpersonal violence is a bone-embedded point, from a lance, dart, or arrow. The possibility of this being accidental is remote, especially when injuries appear in numbers and are patterned by age and sex. In one case noted by Lambert, over 20%

of 128 males had these wounds, and as she further notes, it may be only one in four penetrating projectiles that actually lodges in bone and remains there. Although some instances could be from internal clashes, if ethnographic analogy has any value, the presence of many projectile wounds virtually confirms war. Plausible claims for individual projectile woundings extend back as far as 50,000 B.P. (Roper 1969:439–441; Wendorf and Schild 1986:73–74). The earliest evidence (I know) of multiple projectile killings are the Natufian Jebel Sahaba skeletons, of 12,000–14,000 B.P. (Wendorf 1968:993).

Other kinds of postcranial trauma are far more ambiguous. Physical combat produces a wide range of fractures, but so do accidents and sports. The "classic" combat related injury is a parry fracture–a forearm broken as if warding off a blow – but this too could happen in many ways. A high frequency of cranial compression fractures shaped like a blunt instrument seems a solid basis for inferring interpersonal violence. Several studies in this volume discuss such injuries, many non-lethal with clear signs of healing. (They also show how much care must be taken to distinguish perimortem fractures from later breakage, care not always taken by earlier writers.) Taken independently, these fractures could be the result of spousal abuse, sports, or non-lethal conflict resolution, possibilities which Walker explores.

Scalp marks stand out as particularly clear evidence of war, (with the exception of rare pathological mimics [Hamperl 1967]). As Ostendorf Smith demonstrates, scalping was practiced in North America from ancient times, although much less extensively than after Europeans began paying bounties for them (Neumann 1940; Owsley and Berryman 1975). Absent heads or limbs, especially if accompanied by signs of violent removal, or their presence without any other remains, suggests the taking of war trophies. But these could also result from secondary burial and the vagaries of preservation on one side, or an ancestor cult on the other. Interpretation may be in the details, as in Seeman's (1988) argument that several disarticulated skulls found in Hopewell, Ohio, c. 50 B.C. – 350 A.D., seem to be from younger men, and thus are more likely trophies than mementos of revered seniors.

Burial provides other clues. Casual disposal may indicate that the dead were from a different group. Multiple burials are suggestive of war killings, as Frayer notes. A relative absence of male remains, noted by Wilkinson, is consistent with warriors dying and "remaining" elsewhere. The latter is the most plausible scenario in

which war could exist but not leave traces in substantial osteological remains. But of course any of these patterns alone could have
other explanations.

Cannibalism does not necessarily indicate killing. Reacting to
past errors in interpretation and to a greater awareness of the
ideological loading of the label "cannibal" (see Arens 1979; Whitehead 1988:172-180), high standards of evidence have been developed to distinguish it from consumption by animals and the
defleshing and breakage that may accompany secondary burials.
These criteria also aim to distinguish gustatory cannibalism from
ritualized consumption of one's own dead. The latter is evidence of
war, the former is not. Pijoan and Mansilla Lory provide specifics.
Other recent work makes strong arguments for gustatory cannibalism among the Anasazi, 900–1300 A.D. (White 1992) and in Neolithic Provence, c. 3930 B.C. (Villa et al 1986), although there are
challenges to those interpretations (see Villa 1992a; 1992b).

Pijoan and Mansilla Lory also consider evidence for the overlapping practice of human sacrifice. A few "sacrificees" might be vol-
unteers, but large numbers are most probably war captives.
Human sacrifice may also overlap with executions for "crimes" – a
slippery category even within criminology, but one with which the
archaeology of violence must deal – and executions overlap with
simple murder. European bog bodies provide rich data and soft
tissues for mulling these puzzles (Brothwell 1986:24-44; and see
Burkert et al 1987).

Skeletal trauma may come from sources as diverse as subsistence
activities, spousal abuse, sports (see Poliakoff 1987), internal coercion, individual altercations, punishment for crimes, ritual sacrifice – and of course war. Ember and Ember suggest that multiple
forms of violence in society correlate with war (and see Sipes 1973).
But variations are certainly known, such as the internally pacifistic
and externally bellicose Mundurucu (Murphy 1960), and the linkage or separation of these traumatic experiences to war is one of
the intriguing problems highlighted in this book.

This volume focuses primarily on osteological evidence of violence, much of which may be generated within the group. Other
evidence available to archaeology indicates war more specifically.
Fortifications are most important, although as Keeley notes,
whether a structure is defensive in purpose is often debatable (e.g.
Topic and Topic 1987). No less than the original walls of Jericho,
long standing as the earliest *proof* of warfare (Roper 1975:304, 322),
may instead be for flood protection (Bar-Josef 1986). The presence

of true fortifications does not necessarily indicate actual warfare, as strong defenses may dissuade potential attackers, but they do mean that the war is a social reality sufficient to influence behavior. Fortifications often go along with defensible site locations, as Maschner describes.

Violent destruction and abandonment of a settlement is strong evidence of war, especially if found with unburied skeletons (e.g. Mackey and Green 1979). Aspects of settlement patterns may also reveal the influence of war. War leads to both nucleation and dispersal of populations, and empty no-man's-lands between settlements (see Ferguson 1989a). (Ember and Ember suggest settlement permeability as another possible indicator, but it is applicable mainly to developed political centers, such as Cahokia [Peregrine 1993]).

Weapons constitute another set of evidence. The presence or potential of war is obvious with the development of specialized swords and maces – though as Robb cautions, elaboration of a weapons culture may not be an accurate gauge of levels of violence. Pacific Northwest Coast archaeology recovers unusually clear war technology for a non-state society, with armor, specialized war clubs and what may be armor-piercing bone points, as Maschner describes. But few or no specialized war weapons will exist in many simpler societies, where cutting or bashing is done with the tools of everyday life – although an unusual concentration of arrowheads may reinforce other evidence of war, as Keeley argues. Hunters only have to change their targets to become warriors, so better hunting technology may mean better war technology. Maschner's argument that the introduction of the bow and arrow led to changes in warfare and settlement could be tested widely across prehistoric North America (see Blitz 1988).

A final category of evidence is art (see Feest 1980). Although it is not a major consideration in this volume, what may be depictions of interpersonal violence date back to the European Upper Paleolithic (Roper 1969:1969). Recent research in northern Australia (Tacon and Chippendale 1994), documents what appear to be both individual (earlier) and group (later) arrow duels among hunters and gatherers, the earliest dating back about 10,000 years. These graphic representations cannot be taken literally. They may portray shamanic confrontations, among other things (see Campbell 1986; and discussion in Tacon and Chippendale 1994). Whatever is represented, however, it is difficult to believe that such detailed depictions of interpersonal violence could be portrayed if the artists were not familiar with violence as practice.[1]

Obviously, the existence, intensity, and character of warfare can be better established with multiple kinds of evidence, as Maschner outstandingly demonstrates. It would be an important step toward broader comparisons if archaeologists who focus on one type of evidence routinely would summarize the status of other kinds of evidence, even if only to clarify that none is available. That would also allow exploration of Robb's point about non-congruence--that a developed military culture may not mean correspondingly high casualties.

Of course desirable information often is absent, not preserved or not recovered. Yanomami, for instance, cremate their dead and consume what is left, so no future archaeologist will find osteological evidence of their war. But where skeletal, settlement and other remains are abundant, the presence or at least possibility of war should be archaeologically visible – if archaeologists look for it. The maxim that absence of evidence is not evidence of absence remains valid for any particular dig, and for those areas with limited data. But where a cultural tradition is known from many sites and skeletons, absence of any sort of evidence suggesting war can indeed be taken as reasonable evidence of war's absence.

If violence within a society attains the level of a pattern of bone damage, it too should be detectable. A substantial problem remains in distinguishing osteological evidence of war from the physical traces of other violent practices which may exist along with or in the absence of war. Caution is needed both to avoid 'false positives' – seeing war where it is not – and because identification and understanding of internal violence is such an important, neglected topic.

Down to Cases

What evidence of violence and war appears in the situations discussed here? Taking the European cases first, the Ofnet skulls discussed by Frayer offer up a real mystery. Although other indications of homicide exist from the Mesolithic, these two caches of seven-millennium-old, heavily ochered skulls are in a class by themselves. Most of the 37 individuals are children or young people, two thirds of the adults are women, and about half the skulls have evidence of perimortem bludgeoning. Frayer concludes the Ofnet skulls are evidence of a massacre, possibly an attempt by one group to eliminate another, although he also notes that the odd demographics are unlike most massacres. Perhaps this was a local group caught while most of the men were away. On the other hand, the highly unusual character of this find leaves open other avenues of explanation.

Ofnet is exceptional. Typically European sites lack any reported indication of violence, much less war, until well into the time of agriculture. Whittle's (1985) survey of the Neolithic contains no discussion of warfare, and investigation of the interaction of established foragers and expanding farmers has stressed cooperation and mixing (Dennell 1985). Keeley punctures the idea that this period and interaction were entirely peaceable. He identifies what appear to be four fortified agricultural villages within modern Belgium, in sites also unusual for containing a large number of arrowheads.

This conflicted western extension of the far-flung LBK cultural tradition also is exceptional, however, and as Keeley and Cahen note in another article (1989:170), the fortifications may have been maintained for as little as fifteen years, (c. 6300 B.P.). Keeley suggests that this anomalous situation may be related to the fact that both the farmers and the foragers in this particular area were unusually sedentary and intensive in local resource use, and this combination may have produced an unusually negative impact on the foragers, leading to war.

Robb takes us more than thirty-five hundred years forward, to the western coast of Italy from the 7th through 3rd centuries B.C. – long after intensive warfare developed in many parts of Europe (see Ferrill 1985; Schutz 1983). This temporal sequence shows that war changes over time. Early sites are nucleated and surrounded by what Robb interprets as defensive ditches, which are absent in more dispersed sites later. Later times in contrast have greater elaboration of weaponry, in what seems to be a militarization of culture.

Osteological evidence indicates violence throughout. The presence of traumatic lesions for men increases from 25% in the early remains to 51.9% in the later, although cranial trauma is higher per capita in the earlier sample. However, the limited number of individuals (2) in that sample suggests caution before concluding that, contrary to established opinion, war was more intense in the earlier Neolithic than later metal ages. The absence of local fortifications in later times is not unusual, expectably accompanying a shift to wars of external expansion.

Leaving Europe for Mesoamerica, Pijoan and Mansilla Lory describe evidence for cannibalism and human sacrifice from central Mexico, from 500 B.C. – at least a thousand years after the develop-

ment of serious militarism (Hassig 1992) – to the time of the con-
quistadors. The effort is to distinguish cannibalism, identified by
six criteria, from postmortem dismemberment accompanying ritual
sacrifice, lacking the signature characteristics of cannibalism. The
conclusion is that both had deep histories in the area.

Turning to North America, Ostendorf Smith compares osteological remains from a number of sites from the Tennessee River Valley from 2500 to 1000/500 B.C. Ten of 439 individuals appear to
have died from violent trauma, six of those from one site. Smith
notes that while most of the sites with trauma are along a main
river channel, the location with the six cases is up a small tributary,
highlighting the spatial distribution of injury. She hypothesizes
that the six were from an exposed border group during a time of
increasing population density and sedentism, with constricting
group ranges. In this environment, she surmises, war became an
aspect of incipient social differentiation, as some men took to war
as a way to advance their status. Trophies were dramatic symbols
of their deeds.

On the Pacific Northwest Coast, Maschner describes evidence of
interpersonal violence is absent in the earliest remains dating back
to 9000 B.C. War is suggested by bones and technology--from some
locations but not others--around 1500 B.C., contemporaneous with
the development of large villages and reliance on marine resources. Maschner sees war intensifying between 200-500 A.D.,
along with village consolidation, development of defensive locations, and apparent adoption of the bow and arrow. Defensive site
occupation peaked between 900 and 1200 A.D.

Maschner here discounts his earlier idea that the later peak in
war is related to climatic deterioration (which he now believes as
occurring too late in the process), and instead sees war itself as the
force driving economic intensification. That intensification is evident in a pronounced shift to reliance on salmon c. 1150 A.D.,
which was followed by a population crash c. 1350. The intensive
war witnessed later by European observers even with reduced
populations, he argues, was merely a continuation of an established pattern, and was waged for a great variety of reasons. He
takes issue with my own study of Northwest Coast warfare (Ferguson 1983; 1984a). I too see war as dating back to the second
millennium B.C., but posit a major transformation and intensification in the contact period, a point to which I will return.

Further south on the Pacific coast, around the Santa Barbara
channel, Lambert also finds a long history of violence among

hunter-gatherers, especially on the islands. Healed cranial injuries are found in all times periods in a sequence dating back to 3000 B.C. (Walker 1989:318). Lambert suggests this reveals non-lethal violence, perhaps club fights among men and spousal abuse to explain the less frequent injuries of women. These injuries increased in the Middle period, when projectile points begin to appear frequently in skeletal remains. Lethal violence, she argues, became relatively constant then, but small in scale.

The Middle period was a time of increasing sedentism, population growth, and intensifying use of maritime resources. These people were increasingly susceptible to climatic variations, especially those affecting the always limited availability of fresh water. This, Lambert argues, fueled low level warfare, in a competitive situation which eventually gave rise to chiefdoms. Although Lambert warns against placing too much emphasis on European contact as a generator of war in this region, "the level of intergroup conflict appears to have increased significantly... among tribes who came in contact with the early Spanish explorers" (Walker, Lambert, and De Niro 1989:359)

Wilkinson offers another study of cranial trauma, this one from Late Woodland Michigan, c. 1000–1300 A.D. While there is no direct evidence of war, there is a remarkably high level of cranial damage among females, most with signs of healing, suggesting they were assaulted with blunt weapons. There are many possible explanations for this trauma, including violence by other women. But noting that in the Crow Creek massacre site in South Dakota c. 1325 (Willey 1990) – where some 486 people were butchered in the worst pre-contact slaughter known--young females seem to be missing, Wilkinson suggests the traumatized Michigan women may have been war captives (although indications of war are absent in other nearby sites). In this case, the relative absence of male trauma may be a result of the relative absence of male skeletons, warriors who died elsewhere.

In the late prehistoric Southwest, there are many sites with signs of violence, and many without. Martin compares two places, at two times, again highlighting spatial and temporal variation. On Black Mesa 800–1150 A.D., where ecological marginality is manifest in signs of nutritional stress, she sees extensive networks of cooperation, minimal long distance trade, and few signs of interpersonal violence. Along the La Plata River from 1000 to 1300 A.D., an area rich for subsistence and central in trade, there is again healed cranial damage among women, again in the absence of

direct evidence of warfare. Other burial distinctions suggest these
women formed a subordinate group, perhaps captives, perhaps
migrants. Another possibility is suggested by the Yanomami. More
peripheral Yanomami groups cede wives to connect with powerful
trade controllers, and these political brides are commonly mis-
treated (Ferguson 1992:221).

Martin, Wilkinson, Lambert, and Maschner call attention to variation in a time – 500 to 1350 A.D. – when violence and war appear
to be on a generally upward curve across broad swaths of the
continent (see Milner et al 1991:595). It is tempting to infer that
violence against women is in some way related to broader and
more deadly conflicts, as both male supremacist (Divale and Harris
1976) and fraternal interest group (Otterbein 1994) theories would
expect. But that is precisely the sort of question – the relationship
between internal and external violence – that this volume raises for
future researchers.

The two remaining papers are comparative studies, one of osteological evidence of (mostly) non-lethal injuries, the other of statistically coded ethnographic evidence of war. Violence against
women is once again a topic in Walker, although in general men
show more signs of trauma. His wide ranging study illustrates the
need to get beyond an exclusive concern with diagnosing war, as
well as the many difficulties that remain in divining behavior from
bones. A major focus is boxing, and his idea that this violent sport
is associated with other kinds of assault supports a point argued
by Ember and Ember – that different sorts of violence go together
(though not always – see Wolf 1987:129–130). A shorter discussion
indicates that physical injury increased with increasing Russian
penetration of Yakuts society, suggesting that state encroachment
can lead to not only more war, but to other interpersonal violence
as well.

Ember and Ember provide the only study dealing with war using ethnographic data. I must begin by disagreeing with their assessment of the prevalence of war. If one gets beyond the casual
and often highly inaccurate characterizations of war in general
ethnographies, and into historical description of actual wars, it is
unusual to find any non-state local population that is involved in
war on an average once every two years, and even more so to find
one where war is "almost constant."[3]

Take the Yanomami. If one were to read only Chagnon (e.g.
1983), any coder would place them at the peak of warlike behavior.
But if one examines the reported incidence of actual warfare

among all Yanomami over time, as well as the more frequent periods of peace, on average any Yanomami community would be involved in war less than once a decade (see Ferguson 1995)--the lowest of the Embers' categories. The great majority of war incidents can be linked to specific changes in local contact situations. More generally, the practice of reducing the warfare of a 'culture' to one frequency eliminates the temporal and spatial variation demonstrated in the studies collected here and elsewhere. History is removed from consideration.

I must also disagree with the Ember and Ember's suggestion that the ethnographic record would be even more violent if it were not for "pacification". The old imperialist rationale that state expansion stops local fighting is contradicted by a great number of detailed ethnohistoric studies (e.g. Ferguson and Whitehead 1992a; Ferguson with Farragher 1988:242–254) which document the opposite effect. Initially, state encroachment is far more likely to intensify conflict than suppress it. Pacification – if that term is intended to mean military suppression of local conflict – is usually a late development in the process, and one that can be documented if it occurred. It simply cannot be assumed that such areas are peaceable because wars were stopped by government agents – as the Embers suggest here in regard to the !Kung San.

The data assembled by Ember and Ember nevertheless are extremely significant. If war and other violence in the distant past was anything even approaching the extent and intensity they claim for their more recent sample, it should be visible in the archaeological record. The cases collected in this volume, even if read with the most sanguinary interpretation, cannot be viewed as supporting an extension of the Embers' picture into ancient times. How could such intense levels of violence exist in the great majority of cases without leaving recoverable traces? For me this contrast demonstrates quite clearly that the recent ethnographic universe is a much more violent place than the ancient world.

The main explanatory thesis in this and other recent work by Ember and Ember is that it is the threat of natural disaster that best predicts the intensity of warfare. An association between war and ecological crisis is established in ethnology (Ferguson 1990:33) and is born out by numerous archaeological investigations. I will argue below that this connection will be better understood if the whole question is put in more systemic and historical perspective.

PRESENCE AND ABSENCE

What does this evidence tell us? Paradoxically, by documenting violence and warfare and showing variations over space and time, these chapters highlight their absence in much of human prehistory. And this research is gathered together specifically to demonstrate the existence of violence. Another wide-ranging collection on "paleopathology at the dawn of agriculture" (Cohen and Armelagos 1984), is striking for the relative absence of the sort of evidence presented here. Partly, that may be neglect. But where trauma is specifically discussed, in many cases there is little or nothing to suggest any social pattern of violence. (Curiously, much of the evidence of trauma in Cohen and Armelagos comes from sites within the Mississippi drainage, also the focus of papers in this volume).

Other works similarly indicate a late emergence of violence and war. A survey of south Asian sites (Kennedy 1984:178, 183) finds limited skeletal evidence of trauma. Most of that appears in Harappan contexts, and even there earlier reports of massacres have been seriously questioned. In the Levant from the late Paleolithic well into the Neolithic, indications of violence and war are conspicuously absent from the abundant skeletal and settlement remains (Rathburn 1984; Roper 1974; Smith, Bar Yosef, and Sillen 1984).

A dedicated search for archaeological signs of war in South America (Redmond 1994) produces little that is convincing and early. On the pre-ceramic Peruvian coast, any indication of violent conflict is late and limited to a few locations (Quilter 1989:65, 78, 85), except for the highly problematic findings at Ostra (Topic 1989).[4] On the plains of western Venezuela, evidence of war only appears along with agricultural intensification and the rise of chiefdoms, post 500 A.D. (Spencer and Redmond 1992:153).

Europe in the Mesolithic and early Neolithic does produce some indications of personal violence (Meiklejohn et. al 1984; Whittle 1985), as discussed previously, but these are exceptional. The situation in China is similar: a very few signs of interpersonal violence (two skeletons with embedded points) gives way to widespread evidence of war – fortifications, specialized weapons, and multiple osteological signs – only in the final Neolithic, along with the development of economic inequality, not long before the rise of states (Underhill 1989). A similar change occurred in prehistoric Japan, where evidence of violent death goes from about .002% of approximately 5,000 skeletons from pre-agricultural Jomon times, to over

10% of all deaths in the subsequent, agricultural Yayoi epoch (Farris n.d.). In all these areas, war ultimately becomes entrenched and widespread, leaving unmistakable indicators. Again, it is difficult to understand how war could have been common earlier in each area and remain so invisible.

Homicide may be as old as Cain, even antedating our species. Certainly the Gombe chimpanzees can kill (Goodall 1988) in a manner I would call war. On the other hand, this was a situation heavily impacted by *human* encroachment (Goodall 1986:49-59; Power 1995), in a manner much like a "tribal zone" (below), and thus not representative of natural conditions. The violence of these apes suggests that our most distant ancestors were capable of killing even as groups, but not that they often did.

Roper (1969:448) calls into question some alleged instances of killing in the Paleolithic, but others remain convincing. The Australian rock art noted earlier (Tacon and Chippendale 1994) indicates an early pattern of lethal violence, individual and then collective, but it stands as an exception that highlights the rule: individual killings seem rare and organized killing nearly absent throughout most of our collective past.

This conclusion carries heavy theoretical weight. It differs from the position taken by Knauft (1987a; 1991), who accepts the relatively recent development of war, but argues that individual homicide is and has been common in the simplest societies. Based on observations of recently observed peoples, this proposition is woven through a complex and wide ranging theory. The recent findings on Australian rock art (Tacon and Chippendale 1994) clearly support his position. But osteological evidence generally does not. If our ancestors were killing each other at the posited rates, if a quarter or more of adult men were dying after being stabbed, clubbed, or shot, we would see it in their remains. Perhaps some of recently noted homicide rates in simple societies stem from disruptions attendant on Western encroachment (Marshall 1994).[5] At any rate, caution is advised before generalizing about homicide from a few modern cases.

The evident absence of *warfare* during most of our evolutionary past sinks a boat load of theories. Van der Dennen (1990:149–168, 182–186) summarizes and critiques (and see Meyer 1990) a range of approaches which assume that war has always been with us, from old racial conquest theories, 19th century evolutionism, and 20th century instinct theories, through hunting hypotheses and territorial imperatives, brain evolution, cultural pseudospeciation, and kin selection. Recently, sociobiological theories, put forward as explaining much violence in the contemporary world, rise upon the claim that for hundreds of thousands or even millions of years, humans typically lived in tightly knit and mutually belligerent groups (Alexander 1979:222–228; Daly and Wilson 1988:221–224; Reynolds et al 1987; Shaw and Wong 1989:14–17). Alexander, who provides the theoretical foundation for other work, deals with the lack of evidence for ancient war by arguing we could not see it even if it had been present – i.e. absence of evidence is not evidence of absence.[6] After this volume, that position is very difficult to maintain.

To understand the importance of the findings of this volume, it must be clearly understood that what these widely broadcast theories *require* to be plausible, is not merely that war *sometimes* happened in humanity's distant past, but that it was ubiquitous and intensive throughout human prehistory. Seen in that light, the chapters compiled here provide a decisive falsification.

THEORIZING ANCIENT WAR

Preconditions

While the inclusive orientation of this volume highlights unasked questions about a variety of violence, the kind of violence that has acquired the most theoretical encrustation is war. This section examines a question: if it is true that we come from a sporadically violent past, why did war eventually become common? What happened?

Some think war came only with agriculture (e.g. Leakey and Lewin 1977:221-223; Carneiro 1994:12). That was when all hunters and gatherers were thought to be scattered and mobile, with the settled, complex fishers of the Pacific Northwest Coast a virtually unique exception. Now we know "complex hunter-gatherers" settled in many areas, intensively exploiting concentrated natural resources (Hayden 1992; Price and Brown 1985). What may be unique about the Northwest Coast is that the environment prevented agriculture from ever emerging. Several cases in this volume concern such non-agricultural peoples, who are shown to be quite capable of both individual and collective violence.[7] Vencl's (1984:121) assertion that warfare in Europe began during the Mesolithic rather than the Neolithic may have broader application.

Sedentism, more than agriculture, makes the difference. The emergence of war is associated with people who are notably more settled than their predecessors. The relative peaceablility of some mobile groups, in the present and in the ancient past, has been attributed to their need to maintain wide, cooperative networks to cope with scattered and fluctuating resources (Martin this volume, Knauft 1994:460–47; Wolf 1987:132). But perhaps more important is simply their ability to move away from conflict. In Amazonia (Ferguson 1989b:195–196), semi-sedentary "hunters and gardeners" quickly move away from actual or potential enemies. Situations building toward violence are regularly resolved by exit ("almost wars"). Sedentism removes this peaceable alternative.[8]

But since archaeology provides many examples of sedentary living with no indications of war, that condition alone cannot explain the development of war. What else might? I contend (Ferguson 1984a:308–310; 1984b:37–38; 1990a:28–31; 1995:9–13) that wars occur when it is in the material self-interest of decision makers to fight.[9] This directs theoretical attention to both the possibility of interests to be gained, and to those aspects of political organization which structure public decisions.

When and how did war become gainful? What are objectives of war which might be archaeologically visible? Sedentism makes territorial gain a possible objective, especially with concentrated resources, or the investment of labor in land (see Wolf 1987:136–140). Conquest leaves traces. But conquest is always uncertain and difficult to attempt, and so would seem an unlikely goal until people already had some proficiency in war.[10]

Raiding to capture movable valuables is far less ambitious, as is punitive retaliation, and the two may precede wars over territory. Domesticated livestock, of course, can be run off. Stored food can be plundered, although that possibility may be limited with foot transportation (see Hassig 1977).[11] Capturing people may be underappreciated as a goal of war (see Starna and Watkins 1991), but it too would seem to be a relatively advanced form of predation, an option only for accomplished raiders.

Looting manufactures or precious materials takes little sophistication, although concentration of these goods was probably unusual before the rise of extensive trade. The first conclusive evidence of widespread and enduring wafare (excepting Jebel Sahaba, below) is from the mid sixth millenium Near East, in association with major trade routes (Roper 1975:317–330). In my estimate, plunder of trading parties and efforts to forcibly improve position in trading networks were probably the most common incentives for the earliest wars.

But like sedentism, concentrated material value is found without war. Still more is involved, and that more involves the political evolution of contending parties. Although Ember and Ember's statistics may not support an association, I still believe there is a relationship between increasing hierarchy and centralization and the intensification of war. (This relationship may be masked in statistics by the unappreciated 'warrification' of contact.) War is an expression of a political structure, and the characteristics of that structure shape the character of war.

In the more egalitarian societies, every man ultimately decides on war for himself.[12] The only man a Yanomami leader can order into combat is a subservient son-in-law. In the absence of political control and coercion, every death may require extensive discussion to hammer out a new consensus for action (see Morren 1984:200–201). To pursue war, interests must be very clear and general.

With developing hierarchy and centralization, dynamics of decision-making change in a way that increases the likelihood of war. Such polities become more capable of concerted action, in general. Moreover, leaders develop distinctive interests, matched by a disproportionate say in group policy (see Sillitoe 1978). In areas familiar with war, "military entrepreneurs" (Ferguson 1994:94) may arise, seeking to raise their position in society by initiating violence. That may be what Ostendorf Smith detects in ancient Tennessee. With increasing development of more complex social arrangements, and more concentrated leadership,[13] military policy increasingly tilts toward the interests of a few, and critical among those interests are external relations which support the internal structure of inequality (Ferguson 1984b:39).

Hierarchy is one thing, group boundedness another. A break or boundary may be a line of conflict. Fraternal interest groups – solidary local groups of male blood kin – are prone to various kinds of local violence. Bounding of larger tribal networks is associated with war (Ferguson n.d.b). It has long been known that conflict and boundedness are mutually reinforcing (Coser 1956; Simmel 1964). What is often at issue, as reflected here by Ember and Ember, is whether more causal weight is assigned to the underlying conflict or to the existing organizational structure. Here I go along with the Embers – the boundary is derivative and may change in short order. Yet, boundaries can be very important as visible clues to past antagonisms.

Increasing sedentism, concentration of material value, hierarchy, and boundedness, all make war an evolving possibility. Not that war is impossible without them, but all four together set the stage, making war increasingly likely.[14] In my view (Ferguson 1994), entirely peaceful political structures may develop even up to the level of a chiefdom, but they become increasingly rare.

I do not think that any search for one or several general characteristics will answer the riddle of war's occurrence. To understand why a real war really happened, it must be situated within a pattern of conditions and relationships, as they vary over time. The analytic challenges are to bring in both system and process, and to simultaneously recognize the causal roles of localized interactions with the natural environment, and of participation in a larger and constantly changing social universe. The remaining two sections of this chapter outline some of those considerations, derived from my own theory, as they might be approached by archaeologists and paleoanthropologists.

Across Space...

War is a relationship *between* groups. If the fight is over food or resources, it will arise not in the circumstance of one group, but in the relative circumstances of different groups. There must be both a local need and a militarily achievable solution. Two groups suffering equally from drought may have no reason to fight, but give one a well... This means looking at comparative subsistence situations across a region, and *mapping* war patterns against ecologies. Which locations are the source of attacks, which are the targets?

I take issue with Maschner's assertion, that on the ancient Northwest Coast subsistence was assured by the area's over-all productivity. This de-emphasizes well-documented spatial and temporal variations in resources. Some local groups which usually had enough, sometimes had famine. Until post-contact depopulation, groups on exposed coasts, in lands without salmon streams, and up productive streams but away from the coast, raided groups with more assured resources (often near estuaries), and/or tried to drive them away and replace them (Ferguson 1983; 1984a; and see Cannon 1992).

Population characteristics should be added to ecological variables. Number of fighters is a major concern in combat. Combat manpower may be a crucial element in regional demographic systems. In prehistoric Amazonia and highland New Guinea warfare may have powered a flow of people outward from growing population centers towards peripheral demographic sinks (Ferguson 1989a:255–258). In urbanized areas of the ancient world, where

338 R. BRIAN FERGUSON

power centers were also areas of accelerated mortality (Knauft 1987b), the opposite directionality might be expected, with peripheral peoples frequently invading and taking over.

These infrastructural conditions of ecology and demography are most important, but they are still only part of the story. No local group is an island, and an "isolated tribe" is an oxymoron. Connections come in many forms. Local bands must interpenetrate to constitute a viable breeding population (Wobst 1974). At the other end of the scale, prehistoric trade can knit together entire continents (Wood 1980), though as Martin notes, different locales can be heavily involved in trade or hardly at all. Prehistoric boundaries are spanned by a wide variety of ties (Green and Perlman 1985). Ancient regions appear structurally integrated by tribal networks (Bender 1985; Braun and Plog 1982; Friedman and Rowlands 1982; Kristiansen 1982). In the many "world systems" before the current one, local social situations were strongly affected by position within the whole (Champion 1989; Peregrine 1993; Rowlands et al 1987; Schneider 1977).[15] "Tribal zones"--spaces not directly administered by a state but feeling the destabilizing effects of state proximity-- existed through much of the ancient world (Ferguson and Whitehead 1992b:4–8).[16]

One complex social universe of the 16th century was located across and beyond the Guyana region, integrated in peace and war by trade, marriage, alliance, and ritual (all of which was reshaped and then destroyed by Western intrusion) (Arvelo Jimenez and Biord 1989; Spencer and Redmond 1992; Whitehead 1995). The Yanomami, survivors of that holocaust, reveal the microsociology of this integration. Relationships between groups are complex, multidimensional, and any aspect can stand for the whole. But the key ordering principle is trade, and the value of trade can be tapped in various ways via the application of force (Ferguson 1995; and see 1984a). As noted above, development of rich trade networks, and of trade-good haves and have nots, may provide sufficient bases for early war. But answers to where? when? and who? must be sought in the structure of social relationships.

Trade, and the whole gamut of social relationships that rise upon and reinforce trade ties, can have a profound effect on the life circumstances of everyone in a local group. But their significance will be magnified for leaders, even those constrained by requirements of consensus. Leaders getting no respect at home may rise in importance as representatives in intergroup relations. Sumptuary goods are tangible symbols of those distinctive interests. Northwest Coast potlatches, for example, were linchpins of systems of war and exchange, in which nobles often acted for themselves as well as their kin (Ferguson 1983). Thus, leaders have distinctive interests in military policy, which become more pronounced with increasing hierarchy and centralization. Pursuing these interests, they can move society toward war.

The potlatch brings up another point. I argue (1983:138) that redistributive exchange gained allies and reduced enemies, and so was selected for since war became endemic on the Northwest Coast, which following MacDonald (1979) I put before 1000 B.C. War as a mechanism of group selection is part of my general model (Ferguson 1990:28–29). Recently (1994:101–105) I suggested that war may select for itself: non-militaristic social formations might be made untenable when some competitors opt for war. There may be alternative system states and evolutionary trajectories, peaceable and warlike.

The cases in this volume and other readings, however, lead me to a qualification. Once introduced, war does not automatically become the rule. On the Northwest Coast, yes, war seems to spread widely and stay. But elsewhere war is scattered and sporadic. It came, but it went. Contra Schmookler's simplistic 'parable of the tribes' (1984:21), the appearance of one war making group does not force all others to turn to war in perpetuity. Since chronic warfare is more theoretically interesting than an occasional outburst, archaeologists should ask not just when war first appeared in an area, but when it became general and persistent.

When more people within a regional system live in conditions of sedentism, concentrated material values, pronounced political hierarchies and boundaries, sharp ecological and demographic inequalities, and developed but unequally beneficial trade networks, it is more likely that some people, especially some leaders, will find themselves in situations where it appears reasonable to be violent. The more groups use violence regularly, the more readily will others do the same, or face physical or social elimination. Thus as a systemic process, war may become an established way of dealing with problems, and an entire region restructured for war.

Summarizing spatial considerations, war is a relationship within an extensive social system, where people with varying ecologies, populations, trade positions, and political organizations are joined in multidimensional networks which have their own systemic tendencies toward war or peace. But a systemic perspective is still not enough. Anthropological theorizing about war has been distorted by the absence of historical perspective (Ferguson 1990b). Warfare we know varies by historical circumstance. There is no reason to believe that ancient societies, in contrast to recently known ones, were static or "cold". Historical variation certainly is indicated in the studies collected in this volume. Indeed, it can be argued that regional systems of the sort just discussed experienced major intensifications of warfare (and perhaps other violence) in response to ecological and social *changes*, which are identifiable archaeologically.

...and Time

Can there be a historical perspective on prehistory? Although the detail provided by written accounts can never be matched, outlines of historical process may be developed in at least two ways. One way is to adopt a more dynamic conceptualization of human interaction with the physical world. Recent work in "historical ecology" (Balee n.d.; Crumley 1994) stresses the impact of climatic change, human modification of the landscape, demographic shifts, and the transformations brought on by external introductions.

Climatic change, for instance, affects not only the subsistence situation of every local group, but the relative position and interrelationships of different groups. As McGovern (1987) reconstructs the well-studied area of Transjordan at the end of the Bronze Age (1250–1150 B.C.), declining precipitation led to intra-regional population shifts, aggravated by the arrival of new people (including the Philistines) by sea. These changes shattered existing trade routes, upset farmer-pastoralist relations, and led to the collapse of some cities. A situation of apparent peace broke down into widespread and destructive war, creating a more insular and impoverished social world in the Iron Age.

Such detailed regional reconstructions would be beyond most present archaeological knowledge. But the conflict-generating impact of climatic deterioration does seem visible. Major benchmarks in human military-political history are linked to climatic change. What may be the earliest evidence of war anywhere in the world – projectile points associated with numerous skeletons at the Natufian Jebel Sahaba Site 117, perhaps from 10,000 B.C. – come from an exceptional fishing site in a time of ecological deterioration (Hoffman 1979: 97–99; Wendorf 1968:993). In Mesopotamia, the emergence of warring city-states c. 2,800–2,350 B.C. followed climatic changes that altered river channels, accompanied by salinization of farmlands caused by irrigation (Nissen 1988:129–135).

Weiss (1996) advances the provocative assertion that the recorded collapse of civilizations from the Indus to the Aegian was caused by a three-century drought starting around 2200 B.C. Civilizations do not die peacefully.

Deteriorating climatic conditions are strongly implicated in several studies of war in North America from about 500 to 1300 A.D. (Eddy 1974; Moss and Erlandson 1992). In parts of the southwest, Haas and Creamer (1993) discuss a long term process culminating in pervasive warfare in the dry century bracketing 1300 A.D. An even more sanguinary portrait characterizes dessicating areas of the Great Plains at about the same time (Bamforth 1994; Milner et al 1991; Willey 1990).

Current international security studies focus on decaying environments and the future of global warfare (ECSP 1995), so it is vital that archaeologists address possible connections in this area. A great start would be a survey of evidence regarding climatic change, population growth, ecological degradation, and war in North America in the millennium before Columbus. But sociopolitical transformations should also be included.

Along with attention to changes in societal infrastructures, history can be approached by looking for changes in regional sociopolitical patterns. The rise or fall of hierarchical, centralized polities will strongly affect the character of intergroup violence far beyond their borders, as appears common over time in the Mississippi drainage. Expanding states destabilize political and military relations among non-state peoples in their peripheries (Ferguson and Whitehead 1992a). Recent world events provide tragic evidence of the destabilizing impact of retracting or collapsing governments (Ferguson n.d.c).

One genera of state expansionism encompasses most of the known ethnographic universe. European colonialism since the late 15th century is more disruptive and violence-provoking than prior state-system expansions, for several reasons (Ferguson 1993). The vast geographical and social distances traversed meant that contact involved transfers of system-transforming infrastructural elements. New diseases, plants, animals, populations, and technologies, especially iron or steel tools (Ferguson n.d.d), are archaeologically visible. European contact provides dramatic examples of the historically changing character of ecological relations.

Europeans, like many earlier expansionists, used local peoples to fight each other, but Europe is in a class by itself in the immensity of its demand for land and coerced labor. All this combined to produce massive changes in both society and warfare in the New World and elsewhere. Transformations ran far ahead of direct control by colonialists, and often far ahead of any direct contact at all. These spaces of transformation Neil Whitehead and I call "tribal zones" (Ferguson and Whitehead 1992b).

Some authors misunderstand our position, asserting we claim there was no serious war until the rise of states (Knauft 1993:1186), or until the arrival of Europeans (Marcus 1994). In a book which arrived during final revision of this chapter, Keeley (1996:20, 22) misrepresents our position, claiming we make "a Rousseauian declaration of universal prehistoric peace". Hardly. Our position, clearly stated in several publications and a fundamental premise of many others, is that European contact regularly transformed the local practice of war, frequently led to intensification of fighting, and sometimes generated war where none had been occurring. All of this had been documented by many authors before us (Ferguson with Farragher 1988:242–254).

North American archaeology already provides evidence of the transformation and intensification of war in the early phases of contact (Blakely 1988; Dye 1990:212-213; Owsley et al 1977:51; Pfeiffer and Fairgreave 1994:54; Solecki 1993; Stodder 19194:104; Turner and Morris 1970; cf. Pietrusewsky and Douglas 1994:155). Regarding the Northwest Coast, Moss and Erlandson (1992:74) make an argument similar in many ways to that of Maschner, yet acknowledge that Western contact brought changes in war similar to those I have stressed. Even Bamforth (1994:111), in a paper arguing for indigenous sources of violence in North America, acknowledges that near the Missouri indeed "fortified sites were more common during post-contact than precontact times, and this may reflect more frequent attacks following the Western intrusion". Regarding the Santa Barbara Chumash, he notes "increased conflict between Europeans and natives and among native groups themselves" (Bamforth 1993:49).

Archaeologists can provide crucial evidence on the impact of European contact (see Rogers and Wilson 1993), and would set their sights far too low if the only question asked was simply whether war existed before the arrival of new, expanding states. The issue is what happened to war in protohistoric times. How and why did it change? In what ways are war patterns of the ethnographic literature truly indigenous, and in what ways are they responses to European expansionism? What does all this tell us about causes of war in general? Archaeology can even investigate war in tribal zones of ancient state systems, something which at present seems beyond the capabilities of ethnohistory.

CONCLUSION

This volume looks back to the early history of interpersonal violence and war. It represents a major advance in a topic long dominated by conjecture and projection rather than evidence. Much more work must be done before we have a firm understanding of how and why violence and war ultimately became commonplace. As archaeological research progresses, it should articulate with theory in cultural anthropology – which at present is far more developed regarding war specifically than other kinds of violence. But even that theory comes in many different constructions.

I have offered my own take on where explanations may lie, and what sort of variables should be considered. These include preconditions which make local groups candidates to develop war: degree of sedentism, concentration of material value, political centralization and hierarchy, and boundedness. They include key spatial arrangements which give structure to regional political arenas: inequality in subsistence situations and population size, trade and other social ties, the influence of nearby states on tribal peoples, and the presence of war itself. Over time, ecological crises and changes associated with state impingement, especially that of European states, are both responsible for major increases in war in such regional systems, although certainly not the only reasons why wars occur.

This is a lengthy and mixed set of factors, probably unsatisfactory to those who favor monocausal theories. I favor a more inclusive concept of explanation (Ferguson 1990a), which treats different hypotheses as potentially complementary within a larger theoretical structure. There is no reason to assume that ecological explanations of war are necessarily at variance with trade or political explanations. In my view, these and many more explanations can be combined and applied to the holistic process that is war. Nevertheless, there is uniting all these variable one central proposition, which I offer for archaeological evaluation: generally speaking, war is the outgrowth of the material self-interest of those who decide military policy.

Evaluating whether this or any other perspective holds true in prehistoric war will depend on building a robust and accessible evidentiary base. Along with basic empirical research of the sort highlighted in this volume, archaeologists will need to generalize and compare. The identification of war and other violence is a step toward explanation. Any explanation will involve relating signs of violence to other recoverable features. Just what kind of data we really need will only become apparent as theory develops.

Situations with signs of violence should be contrasted to those without, for as the anthropology of peace has shown, peace is a positive condition, not just the absence of war (Sponsel and Gregor 1994). Patterns of violence should be mapped, both in micro and macro, and plotted over time. Studies focused on any one part of the puzzle should routinely summarize other relevant evidence regarding violence and the basic variables such as those outlined in this chapter. Comparative studies, of regions or larger areas, and of different time periods, are especially useful, making archaeological findings available to non-archaeological theorists.

This volume also has implications for cultural anthropology. It highlights the paucity of ethnographic data and theory about practices of non-lethal violence, much of which is summarized here by Walker. Demographic patterns and the physical patterning of trauma are rarely reported. Knauft (1987a; 1991) and Otterbein (1994) have begun to raise theoretical issues (and see Riches 1986), and my own work is currently examining the role of force in policing. But in general cultural anthropology has not theoretically problematized the kind of violence that archaeologists are now turning up. Until we know more about non-lethal violence in living societies, prospects for understanding its practice in ancient times will remain limited. If studies in this volume are any indication, cultural anthropology may be neglecting a very significant, if ugly, side of social life.

NOTES

[1] Redmond (1994) should be consulted for an innovative effort to identify other archaeological indicators of war. See Vencl (1984) for discussion of aspects of war that are *not* recoverable.

[2] My attempt to understand why Yanomami men of the Venezuelan Orinoco-Mavaca area (Chagnon 1983) are so unusually brutal to women, compared to other Amazonians (Ferguson 1988:148-152) and even to other Yanomami (1992:220–221; 1995:357–358), identifies several contributing factors: an unusually limited basis for female cooperation in an economy reliant on plantains rather than bitter manioc; the existence of strong fraternal interests groups; the ideological reinforce-

ment of intensive warfare; the atypical number of women from other villages married in to trade centers, living without protecting brothers; the large numbers of families shattered by disease and war, leading to more instrumental violence in establishing domestic relations; and the use of women as political pawns and symbols in larger political relationships. Only some of these are potentially applicable to cases in this volume, but the total list of variables implicated in the Yanomami case suggests how complex the question can be.

[3] One of the most influential articles in the anthropology of war is Carol Ember's expose of myths about hunter-gatherers, which provides statistics indicating a high frequency of warfare. The data utilized in that study are very difficult to check. After working through the codes in old issues of Ethnology, one is referred to general sources without specific page citations. But one group coded as having war "more than once every two years" is the Bella Coola (Ember 1978:444), whose war I have studied. To be sure, the Bella Coola lived in an area of endemic warfare, worsened with contact to an awful intensity (Ferguson 1984a:282–284). Even so, the estimate of war 'more than once every two years' seemed well beyond what I found in the ethnohistorical record. Moreover, the sole source noted in Ethnology is McIlwraith (1948). But McIlwraith's (1948 II:338) own assessment of the frequency of war is as follows: 'it appears probable that at least several villages of the Bella Coola were embroiled every few years'. The discrepancy between that assessment and the statistical coding raises questions about that data base.

[4] Lines of small piles of stones, suitable as sling stones, have been offered as the earliest (c. 5400-5200 B.P.) evidence of warfare in the New World (Topic 1989). But any number of explanations are possible–it might have been a sport–and the dating of these surface remains is conjectural.

[5] I suggest (Ferguson and Whitehead 1992b:30 n.19) that high levels of individual killings in feuds are, in part, results of changes associated with living on the fringes of state control.

[6] Alexander (1979:227) dismisses the lack of evidence for the pervasive violence he posits by raising several objections which seem rather off the point. He asks, for instance, if mass slaughters of the 20th century 'will be properly interpreted, say, a million years from now'. Leaving aside the capabilities of archaeology in 1,000,1979 A.D., modern war certainly will be identifiable for millennia (see Wood 1994). Instead of dealing with the archaeological record, Alexander advocates the 'evidence' of 'extrapolating backward in time' from recent history.

[7] It may even be that violence decreased in the earliest phases of agriculture, perhaps linked in some way to what seems to be a general though short-lived improvement in diet and health (Roosevelt 1987:576).

[8] This could be seen as an extension of Carneiro's (1970) idea of circumscription.

⁹ I (Ferguson 1990:29–30; 1995:9–13) argue for pan-human interest in maintaining the material resources at one's disposal, the standards of effort needed to obtain them, and safety–but not reproductive success. These always must be conceptualized in terms appropriate to a particular culture, just as a concept must always be stated in a particular language. Moreover, material interest is regularly converted into moral terms for public discourse and even self evaluation. Needs become rights. Human diversity notwithstanding, few collectivities willingly opt to do with less of what they consume, for more effort, and at greater hazard. And while it is certainly true that individuals will kill for any number of non-materially-beneficial reasons, it is material interests that effectively structure collective decisions regarding war and peace.

¹⁰ Early conquest would probably occur as in highland New Guinea (Sillitoe 1977): one group drives out another and then gradually absorbs their territory, rather than immediately occupying it all. But archaeologically, the two would amount to the same thing.

¹¹ The development of canoe and other forms of transport may be as important as bows or guns in the development of war.

¹² Gender and generational structuring aspects of military decision-making are unquestionably significant (Ferguson n.d.a), but hardly explored.

¹³ This general discussion raises the broader issue of the relationship between war and political evolution. There are actually two sets of issues, one dealing with how the character of collective violence changes with increasing complexity and political centralization; the other with what role war plays in the evolution of the same. I have discussed the latter elsewhere (1994), where I conclude that war is not a prime mover, but one kind of factor in a broader field of change. War itself is a situation, one which fosters an increase in central decision making. If a state of war persists over time, this situation may allow for the development of social structures which act to reinforce this elevated influence or power. Thus proceeding in small steps, hand in glove with other changes in political economy, war acts as an evolutionary ratchet.

¹⁴ To emphasize that exceptions are expected, here is one. In west central New York State around 2500 B.C., the Lamoka people lived alone. Hunters and fishers, they favored sites with concentrated resources, but remained mobile. Then pioneers of the spreading Laurentian tradition arrived, with similar subsistence practices, oriented to the same rich spots. Strong indications of war are found in a few sites in one area where contact was occurring, but these signs soon disappear. Later and elsewhere, everything indicates gradual amalgamation, without traces of war. It still would be a few millennia before war became endemic in this region (Ritchie 1980:43, 77–79, 104, 105, 120, 294). The arrival of strangers competing for the same crucial resources led to warfare among peoples who theoretically should be peaceful. But the shock passed, and politics returned to the norm.

[15] Lambert (this volume) raises the point that peacefulness may be related somehow to contact with states, and raises the case of the Semai. Probably so. Gibson (1990) shows that the Semai are one of several, scattered peaceful groups in similar positions in a regional system--targets of highly effective slave raiders feeding the Sulu sultanate of the Philippines.

[16] In the end, Mann's (1986:1-14) argument may prove both true and helpful: societies as discrete units are largely illusory. Social integration is a function of different kinds of networks, with distinctive qualities and differential reach.

REFERENCE

Alexander, R. (1979). *Darwinism and Human Affairs*. Seattle: University of Washington Press.

Adrey, R. (1961). *African Genesis*. New York: Dell.

Arens, W. (1979). *The Man-Eating Myth*. New York: Oxford University Press

Arvelo-Jimenez, N. and Castillo, H. B. (1989) "Introduccion." In *Exploracion Oficial*, F. Michelena y Rojas, eds. N. Arvelo- Jimenez and H.B. Castillo, pp. 11–26. Iquitos, Peru: IIAP- CETA.

Balee, W. (Ed.) n.d. *Advances in Historical Ecology*. New York: Columbia University Press, in press.

Bamforth, D. (1993) "Stone Tools, Steel Tools: Contact Period Household Technology at Helo'." In *Ethnohistory and Archaeology: Approaches to Postcontact Change in the Americas*. eds. J. Daniel Rogers and S. Wilson. pp. 49–72. New York: Plenum Press.

_____ (1994). "Indigenous People, Indigenous Violence: Precontact Warfare on the North American Great Plains". *Man* **29**:95–115.

Bar Yosef, O. (1986) "The Walls of Jericho: An Alternative Interpretation." *Current Anthropology* **27**:157–162.

Bender, B. (1985). "Emergent Tribal Formations in the American Midcontinent". *American Antiquity* **50**:52–62.

Blakely, R. (1988). *The King Site: Continuity and Contact in Sixteenth-Century Georgia*. Athens, GA: University of Georgia Press.

Blitz, J. (1988). "Adoption of the Bow in Prehistoric North America". *North American Archaeologist* **9**(2):123–145.

Braun, D. and Plog, S. (1982) "Evolution of 'Tribal' Social Networks: Theory and Prehistoric North American Evidence." *American Antiquity* **47**:504–525.

Brothwell, D. (1986) *The Bog Man and the Archaeology of People*. London: British Museum Publications.

Campbell, C. (1986) "Images of War: A Problem in San Rock Art Research." *World Archaeology* **18**:255–268.

Cannon, A. (1992). "Conflict and Salmon on the Interior British Columbia." In *A Complex Culture of the British Columbia Plateau*. ed. Brian Hayden, pp. 506–524. Vancouver: University of British Columbia Press.

Carneiro, R. (1970). "A Theory of the Origin of the State." *Science*
169:733–738.

Carneiro, R. (1994). "War and Peace: Alternating Realities in Human History". In *Studying War Anthropological Perspectives* S. P. Reyna and R. E.
Downs, eds. pp. 3–27. Langhorne, PA: Gordon and Breach.

Chagnon, N. (1983). Yanomamo: *The Fierce People*, 3rd ed. New York: Holt,
Rinehart and Winston.

Champion, T. C. (Ed.) (1989) *Centre and Periphery: Comparative Studies in
Archaeology*. London: Unwin Hyman.

Coser, L. (1956) *The Functions of Social Conflict*. New York: The Free Press.

Crumley, C. (Ed.) (1994) *Historical Ecology: Cultural Knowledge and Changing
Landscapes*. Santa Fe: School of American Research Press.

Daly, M. and Wilson, M. (1988). *Homicide*. New York: Aldine de Gruyter.

Dennell, R. (1985). "The Hunter-Gatherer/Agricultural Frontier in Prehistoric Temperate Europe." In *The Archaeology of Frontiers and Boundaries*,
eds. S. Green and S. Perlman, pp. 113-139. Orlando: Academic Press.

Divale, W. and Harris, M. (1976). "Population, Warfare, and the Male
Supremacist Complex." *American Anthropologist* **78**:521–538.

Dye, D. (1990). "Warfare in the Sixteenth-Century Southeast: The de Soto
Expedition in the Interior." In *Columbian Consequences* Vol. 2: Archaeological and Historical Perspectives on the Spanish Borderlands East,
ed. D. H. Thomas, pp. 211–222. Washington: Smithsonian Institution
Press.

ECSP (Environmental Change and Security Project) (1995) Environment
and Security Debates: An Introduction. ECSP Report 1. Washington, DC:
The Woodrow Wilson Center.

Eddy, F. (1974). "Population Dislocation in the Navaho Reservoir District,
New Mexico and Colorado." *American Antiquity* **39**:75–84.

Ember, C. (1978). "Myths about Hunter-Gatherers." *Ethnology* **17**:439–448.

Ethnology (1963). "Ethnographic Atlas." *Ethnology* (The Editors).

Farris, W. n.d. *Sacred Texts and Buried Treausres: Eassays in the Historical
Archaeology of Japan*. Manuscript.

Feest, C. (1980). *The Art of War*. London: Thames and Hudson.

Ferguson, R. B. (1983). "Warfare and Redistributive Exchange on the
Northwest Coast." In *The Development of Political Organizaton in Native
North America: 1979 Proceedings of the American Ethnological Society*, ed. E.
Tooker, pp. 133–147. Washington D.C.: American Ethnological Society.

———— (1984a). "A Re-Examination of the Causes of Northwest Coast Warfare." In *Warfare, Culture, and Environment*, ed. R. Brian Ferguson, pp.
267–328. Orlando: Academic Press.

_____ (1984b). "Introduction: Studying War." In *Warfare, Culture, and Environment,* ed. R. Brian Ferguson, pp. 1–81. Orlando: Academic Press.

_____ (1988). "War and the Sexes in Amazonia". In *Dialectics and Gender: Anthropological Approaches,* eds. R. Randolph, D. Schneider, and M. Diaz, pp. 136–154. Boulder: Westview Press.

_____ (1989a). "Ecological Consequences of Amazonian Warfare." *Ethnology* **28**(3):249–264.

_____ (1989b). "Game Wars? Ecology and Conflict in Amazonia." *Journal of Anthropological Research* **45**(2): 179–206.

_____ (1990a), "Explaining War." In *The Anthropology of War,* ed. J. Haas, pp. 22–50. Santa Fe: School of American Research Press.

_____ (1990b). "Blood of the Leviathan." *American Ethnologist* **17**(2):237–257.

_____ (1992). "A Savage Encounter: Western Contact and the Yanomami War Complex." In *War in the Tribal Zone: Expanding States and Indigenous Warfare,* eds. R. B.Ferguson and N. Whitehead, pp. 197–227. Santa Fe: School of American Research Press.

_____ (1993). "When Worlds Collide: The Columbian Encounter in Global Perspective." *Human Peace* **10**(1):8–12.

_____ (1994). "The General Consequences of War: An Amazonian Perspective." In *Studying War,* eds. S. Reyna and R.E. Downs, pp. 85–111. New York: Gordon and Breach.

_____ (1995a). *Yanomami Warfare: A Political History.* Santa Fe: School of American Research Press.

_____ (1995b). "(Mis)Understanding Resource Scarcity and Cultural Difference in Contemporary Conflicts." *Anthropology Newsletter,* November, pg. 37.

_____ (n.d.a). "Relations of Production, Politics, and War in Amazonia: Working Paper." Manuscript

_____ (n.d.b). "Tribal Organization." In *Blackwell Dictionary of Anthropology.* Oxford: Blackwell, in press.

_____ (n.d.c). "Dangerous Intersections: The Local and the Larger in African Violence." In *Paths of Violence: Destruction and Deconstruction in African States.* eds. G. Bond and J. Vincent. Langhorne, PA: Gordon and Breach, in press.

_____ (n.d.d). "Whatever Happened to the Stone Age? Steel Tools and Yanomami Historical Ecology." In *Advances in Historical Ecology,* ed. W. Balee, New York: Columbia University Press, in press.

Ferguson, R. B. with Farragher, L. (1988). *The Anthropology of War: A Bibliography.* New York: Harry Frank Guggenheim Foundation.

Ferguson, R. B. and Whitehead N. (Eds.) (1992a). *War in the Tribal Zone: Expanding States and Indigenous Warfare.* Santa Fe: School of American Research Press.

(1992b). "The Violent Edge of Empire." In *War in the Tribal Zone: Expanding States and Indigenous Warfare*, eds R. B. Ferguson and N. Whitehead, pp. 1–30. Santa Fe: School of American Research Press.

Ferrill, A. (1985). *The Origins of War: From the Stone Age to Alexander the Great*. New York: Thames and Hudson.

Friedman, J. and M.J. Rowlands (1982). "Notes Towards and Epigenetic Model of the Evolution of 'Civilisation'." In *The Evolution of Social Systems*, eds. J. Friedman and M.J. Rowlands, pp. 201–276. London: Duckwater.

Gibson, T. (1990). "Raiding, Trading, and Tribal Autonomy in Insular Southeast Asia." In *The Anthropology of War*, ed. J. Haas, pp. 125–145. Santa Fe: School of American Research Press.

Goodall, J. (1986). *The Chimpanzees of Gombe: Patterns of Behavior*. Cambridge: Harvard University Press.

_____ (1988). *In the Shadow of Man*. San Diego: San Diego State Press.

Green, S. and S. Perlmann (Eds.) (1985). *The Archaeology of Frontiers and Boundaries*. Orlando: Academic Press.

Haas, J. and Creamer, W. (1993) *Stress and Warfare among the Kayenta Anasazi of the Thirteenth Century A.D.* Fieldiana, Anthropology, new series no. 21. Chicago: Field Museum of Natural History.

Hamerton-Kelly, R. (Ed.) (1987). *Violent Origins: Ritual Killing and Cultural Formation*. Stanford: Stanford University Press.

Hamperl, H. (1967). "The Osteological Consequences of Scalping." In *Diseases in Antiquity: A Survey of the Diseases, Injuries and Surgery of Early Populations*, eds. D. Brothwell and A.T. Sandison, pp. 630–634. Springfield: Charles Thomas.

Hassig, R. (1985) *Trade, Tribute, and Transportation: The Sixteenth Century Political Economy of the Valley of Mexico*. Norman: University of Oklahoma Press.

_____ (1992). *War and Society in Ancient Mexico*. Berkeley: University of California Press.

Hayden, B. (Ed.) (1992). *A Complex Culture of the British Columbia Plateau*. Vancouver: University of British Columbia Press.

Hoffman, M. (1979). *Egypt Before the Pharoahs: The Prehistoric Foundations of Egyptian Civilization*. New York: Alfred A. Knopf.

Keeley, L. (1996). *War Before Civilization*. New York: Oxford.

Keeley, L. and Cahen, D. (1989). "Early Neolithic Forts and Villages in NE Belgium: A Preliminary Report." *Journal of Field Archaeology* 16:157–176.

Kennedy, K. A. R. (1984). "Growth, Nutrition, and Pathology in Changing Demographic Settings in South Asia." In *Paleopathology at the Origins of Agriculture*, eds. M. N. Cohen and G. Armelagos, pp.169–192. Orlando: Academic Press.

Knauft, B. (1987a). "Reconsidering Violence in Simple Human Societies." Current Anthropology 28:457–499.

(1987b). "Divergence between Cultural Success and Reproductive Fitness in Preindustrial Cities." Cultural Anthropology 2:94–114.

(1991). "Violence and Sociality in Human Evolution." Current Anthropology 32:391–428.

(1993). "Review of War in the Tribal Zone." Science 260:1184–1186.

(1994). "Culture and Cooperation in Human Evolution." In The Anthropology of Peace and Nonviolence, eds. L. Sponsel and T. Gregor, pp. 37–67. Boulder, CO: Lynne Rienner.

Kristiansen, K. (1982). "The Formation of Tribal Systems in Later European Prehistory: Northern Europe, 4000-500 B.C." In Theory and Explanation In Archaeology, eds. C. Renfrew, M. Rowlands, B. A. Seagraves, pp. 241–280. New York: Academic Press.

Leakey, R. and Lewin, R. (1977). Origins. New York: E.P. Dutton.

MacDonald, G. (1979). Kitwanga Fort National Historic Site, Skeena River, British Columbia: Historical Research and Analysis of Structural Remains. Ottawa: National Museum of Man.

Mackey, J. and Green, R. C. (1979). "Largo-Gallina Towers: An Explanation." American Antiquity 44:144–154.

Mann, M. (1986). The Sources of Social Power: Vol. I: A History of Power from the Beginning to A.D. 1760. Cambridge: Cambridge University Press.

Marcus, J. (1994). "Introduction to Volume V." In Tribal and Chiefly Warfare in South America, ed. E. Redman, pp. v-vi. Ann Arbor: Memoirs of the Museum of Anthropology University of Michigan.

Marshall Thomas, E. (1994). "Management of Violence among the Ju/wasi of Nyae Nyae: The Old Way and a New Way." In Studying War: Anthropological Perspectives, eds. S.P. Reyna and R.E. Downs, pp. 69–84. Langhorne, PA: Gordon and Breach.

McGovern, P. (1987). "Central Transjordan in the Late Bronze and Early Iron Ages: An Alternative Hypothesis of Socio-Economic Transformation and Collapse." In Studies in the History and Archaeology of Jordan III, ed. A Hadidi, pp. 267–273. Amman, Jordan: Dept. of Antiquities.

McIlwraith, T.F. (1948). The Bella Coola Indians, 2 Vol. Toronto: University of Toronto Press.

Meikeljohn, C. Schentag, C. Venema, A. and Key, P. (1984) "Socioeconomic Change and Patterns of Pathology and Variation in the Mesolithic and Neolithic of Western Europe: Some Suggestions." In Paleopathology at the Origins of Agriculture, eds. M. N. Cohen and G. Armelagos, pp. 75–100. Orlando: Academic Press.

Meyer, P. (1990). "Human Nature and the Function of War in Social Evolution. A Critical Review of a Recent Form of the Naturalistic Fallacy." In

Sociobiology and Conflict: Evolutionary Perspectives on Competition, Cooperation, Violence and Warfare, eds. J. Van der Dennen and V. Falger, pp. 227–240. New York: Chapman and Hall.

Milner, G. Anderson, E. and Smith, V. (1991). "Warfare in Late Prehistoric West-Central Illinois." *American Antiquity* **56**:581–603.

Moore, J. (1985). "Forager/Farmer Interactions: Information, Social Organization, and the Frontier. In *The Archaeology of Frontiers and Boundaries,* eds. S. Green and S. Perlman, pp. 93–112. Orlando: Academic Press.

Moss, M. and J. Erlandson (1992). "Forts, Refuge Rocks, and Defensive Sites: The Antiquity of Warfare along the North Pacific Coast of North America." *Arctic Anthropology* **29**:73–90.

Neumann, G. (1940). "Evidence of the Antiquity of Scalping from Central Illinois." *American Antiquity* **4**:287–289.

Neuman, G. (1987). "How We Became (In)Human." In *Origins of Human Aggression: Dynamics and Etiology,* ed. Gerard Neuman, pp. 78–104. New York: Human Sciences Press.

Otterbein, K. (1994). "A Cross-Cultural Study of Rape." In *Feuding and Warfare: Selected Works of Keith Otterbein,* pp. 119–132. Gordon and Breach:Langhorne, PA.

Owsley, D. and Berryman, H. (1975). "Ethnographic and Archaeological Evidence of Scalping in the Southeastern United States." *Tennessee Archaeologist* **31**:41–60.

Peregrine, P. (1993). "An Archeological Correlate of War." *North American Archaeologist* **14**:139–151.

Pfeiffer, S. and S. Fairgrieve (1994) "Evidence from Ossuaries: The Effect of Contact on the Health of Iroquoians." In *the Wake of Contact: Biological Responses to Conquest,* eds. C. Larsen and G. Milner, pp. 47–62. New York: John Wiley and Sons.

Pietrusewsky, M. and Douglas, M. (1994). "An Osteological Assessment of Health and Disease in Precontact and Historic (1778) Hawai'i." In *In the Wake of Contact: Biological Responses to Conquest,* eds. C. Larsen and G. Milner, pp. 179–195. New York: John Wiley and Sons.

Poliakoff, M. (1987). *Combat Sports in the Ancient World: Competition, Violence, and Culture.* New Haven: Yale University Press.

Power, M. (1995). "Gombe Revisited: Are Chimpanzees Violent and Hierarchical in the 'Free' State." *General Anthropology* **2**(1): 5–9.

Price, T. D. and Brown J. A. (Eds.) (1985). *Prehistoric Hunter -Gatherers: The Emergence of Cultural Complexity.* Orlando: Academic Press.

Quilter, J. (1989). *Life and Death at Paloma: Society and Mortuary Practices in a Preceramic Peruvian Village.* Iowa City: University of Iowa Press.

Rathbun, T. (1984). "Sekeletal Pathology from the Paleolithic through the Metal Ages in Iran and Iraq." In *Paleopathology at the Origins of Agricul-*

ture, eds. M. N. Cohen and G. Armelagos, pp. 137–167. Orlando: Academic Press.

Redmond, E. (1994). *Tribal and Chiefly Warfare in South America*. Ann Arbor: Memoirs of the Museum of Anthropology University of Michigan.

Reynolds, V. Falger, V. and Vine, I. (Eds.) (1987). *The Sociobiology of Ethnocentrism: Evolutionary Dimensions of Xenophobia, Discrimination, Racism and Nationalism*. London: Croom Helm.

Riches, D. (Ed.) (1986). *The Anthropology of Violence*. New York: Basil Blackwell.

Ritchie, W. (1980). *The Archaeology of New York State*. Harrison, NY: Harbor Hill Books.

Rogers, J. D. and Wilson, S. (Eds.) (1993). *Ethnohistory and Archaeology: Approaches to Postcontact Change in the Americas*. New York: Plenum Press.

Roosevelt, A. (1987). "Chiefdoms in the Amazon and Orinoco." In *Chiefdoms in the Americas*. eds. R. Drennen and C. Uribe, pp. 153–184. Lanham, MD: University Press of America.

Roper, M. K. (1969). "A Survey of the Evidence for Intrahuman Killing in the Pleistocene." *Current Anthropology* **10**:427–459.

_____ (1975). "Evidence of Warfare in the Near East from 10,000-4,300 B.C." In *War: Its Causes and Correlates*, eds. M. Nettleship, R. D. Givens, and A. Nettleship, pp.299–340. The Hague: Mouton.

Rowlands, M. Larsen, M. and Kristiansen, K. (1987). *Centre and Periphery in the Ancient World*. Cambridge: Cambridge University Press.

Schneider, J. (1977). "Was There a Pre-Capitalist World System?" *Peasant Studies* **6**:20–29.

Schutz, H. (1983). *The Prehistory of Germanic Europe*. New Haven: Yale University Press.

Seeman, M. (1988). "Ohio Hopewell Trophy-Skull Artifacts as Evidence for Competition in Middle Woodland Societies Circa 50 B.C.–A.D. 350." *American Antiquity* **53**:565–577.

Shaw, R. P. and Wong, Y. (1989). *Genetic Seeds of Warfare: Evolution, Nationalism, and Patriotism*. Boston: Unwin Hyman.

Sillitoe, P. (1977). "Land Shortage and War in New Guinea." *Ethnology* **16**:71–81.

_____ (1978). "Big Men and War in New Guinea." *Man* **13**:252–271

Simmel, G. (1964). *"Conflict" and "The Web of Group-Affiliations"*. New York: The Free Press.

Sipes, R. (1973). "War, Sports, and Aggression: An Empirical Test of Two Rival Theories." *American Anthropologist* **75**:64–82.

Schmookler, A. (1984). *The Parable of the Tribes: The Problem of Power in Social Evolution*. Boston: Houghton Mifflin.

Smith, P. Bar-Yosef, O. and Sillen, A. (1984). "Archaeological and Skeletal Evidence for Dietary Change during the Late Pleistocene/Early Holocene in the Levant." In *Paleopathology at the Origins of Agriculture*, eds. M. N. Cohen and G. Armelagos, pp. 101–136. Orlando: Academic Press.

Spencer, C. and Redmond, E. (1992). "Prehispanic Chiefdoms of the Western Venezuelan *Llanos*." *World Archaeology* **24**:134–157.

Sponsel, L. and Gregor, T. (Eds.) (1994). *The Anthropology of Peace and Nonviolence*. Boulder, CO: Lynne Reiner.

Starna, W. and Watkins, R. (1991). "Northern Iroquoian Slavery." *Ethnohistory* **38**:34–57.

Stodder, A. (1994). "Bioarchaeological Investigations of Protohistoric Pueblo Health and Demography." In *In the Wake of Contact: Biological Responses to Conquest*, eds. C. Larsen and G. Milner, pp. 97–108. New York: John Wiley and Sons.

Tacon, P. and Chippindale, C. (1994). "Australia's Ancient Warriors: Changing Depictions of Fighting in the Rock Art of Arnhem Land, N.T." *Cambridge Archaeological Journal* **4**:211–248.

Topic, J. (1989). "The Ostra Site: The Earliest Fortified Site in the New World." In *Cultures in Conflict: Current Archaeological Perspectives*, eds. D. C. Tkaczuk and B. Vivian, pp. 215–228. Calgary: University of Calgary Archaeological Association.

Turner, C. and Morris, N. (1970). "A Massacre at Hopi." *American Antiquity* **35**:320–331.

Underhill, A. (1989). "Warfare During the Chinese Neolithic Period: A Review of the Evidence." In *Cultures in Conflict: Current Archaeological Perspectives*, eds. D. C. Tkaczuk and B. Vivian, pp. 229–240. Calgary: University of Calgary Archaeological Association.

Van der Dennen, J. M. G. (1990). "Origin and Evolution of 'Primitive' Warfare." In *Sociobiology and Conflict: Evolutionary Perspectives on Competition, Cooperation, Violence and Warfare*, eds. J. van der Denner and V. Falger, pp. 149–188. New York: Chapman and Hall.

Vencl, S. (1984). "War and Warfare in Archaeology." *Journal of Anthropological Archaeology* **3**:116–132.

Villa, P. (1992a). "Cannibalism in Prehistoric Europe." *Evolutionary Anthropology: Issues, News, and Reviews* **1**:93–104.

(1992b). "Light on Dark Matters." *Science* **257**:1420–1421.

Villa, P. Bouville, C. Courtin, J. Helmer, D. Mahieu, E. Shipman, P. Belluomini, G. and Branca, M. (1986). "Cannibalism in the Neolithic," *Science* **233**:431–437.

Walker, P. (1989). "Cranial Injuries as Evidence of Violence in Prehistoric Southern California." *American Journal of Physical Anthropology* **80**:313–323.

Walker, P. Lambert, P. and DeNiro, M. (1989). "The Effects of European Contact on the Health of Alta California Indians." In *Columbian Conse-*

quences Vol. 1: Archaeological and Historical Perspectives on the Spanish Borderlands West, ed. D. Hurst Thomas, pp. 349–364. Washington: Smithsonian Institution Press.

Webster, D. (1993). "The Study of Maya Warfare: What It Tells Us about the Maya and about Maya Archaeology." In Lowland Maya Civilization in the Eighth Century A.D., eds. J. Sabloff and J. Anderson, pp 415–444. Washington, DC: Dumbarton Oaks.

Wendorf, F. (1968). "Site 117: A Nubian Final Paleolithic Graveyard Near Jebel Sahaba, Sudan." In The Prehistory of Nubia Vol. II, ed. F. Wendorf pp. 954–995. Dallas: Fort Burgwin Research Center and Southern Methodist University Press.

Wendorf, F. and R. Schild (1986). The Wadi Kubbaniya Skeleton: A Late Paleolithic Burial from Southern Egypt. Dallas: Southern Methodist University Press.

White, T. (1992). Prehistoric Cannibalism: At Mancos 5MTUMR 2346. Princeton: Princeton University Press.

Whitehead, N. (1988). Lords of the Tiger Spirit: A History of Caribs in Colonial Venezuela and Guyana 1498–1820. Royal Institute of Linguistics and Anthropology, Caribbean Studies Series 10. Dordrecht/Leiden: Foris/KITLV Press.

(1995). "The Ancient Amerindian Polities of the Lower Orinoco, Amazon, and Guyana Coast. A Preliminary Analysis of the Passage from Antiquity to Extinction." In Amazonian Indians: From Prehistory to the Present. Anthropological Perspectives, ed. A. Roosevelt, pp. 33–54. Tucson: University of Arizona Press.

Whittle, A. (1985). Neolithic Europe: A Survey. Cambridge: Cambridge University Press.

Willey, P. (1990). Prehistoric Warfare on the Great Plains: Skeletal Analysis of the Crow Creek Massacre Victims. New York: Garland Publishing.

Wobst, H. M. (1974). "Boundary Conditions for Paleolithic Social Systems: A Simulation Approach." American Antiquity 39:147–178.

Wolf, E. (1987). "Cycles of Violence: The Anthropology of War and Peace." In Waymarks: The Notre Dame Inaugural Lectures in Anthropology, ed. K. Moore, pp. 127–150. Notre Dame, IN: University of Notre Dame Press.

Wood, W. R. (1980). "Plains Trade in Prehistoric and Protohistoric Intertribal Relations." In Anthropology of the Great Plains, eds. W. R. Wood and M. Liberty, pp. 98–109. Lincoln: University of Nebraska.

(1994). "The Archaeology of Recent Warfare." The Review of Archaeology 15(2):14–21.

Index

A

Abduction
and physical violence, 38
in prehistoric Michigan,
21–43
of women, 21–43, 68

Abrasions
anvil, 219
hammerstone, 219

Abuse, spousal, 36, 37, 69, 329

Accidental injuries, 163, 164;
See also Injuries, accidental

Accidents, 123, 127
motor vehicle, 82, 161–163,
work-related, 123

Adzes
as weapons of war, 311
LBK 306–308, 310–312

Age-injuries relationship,
156–159

Aggression, 7
and violence, 15
gender-based, 36
human, 146
in modern human societies,
78
individual, 3
intergroup, resource stress
as a cause of, 98
socialization for, 15, 16

Aging of subadults, method of
185, 186

Agricultural economies, in
Central and Northwestern
Europe, 303

American Indian wars, 92

Ames, Ken, 295

Amputation, 173

Anderson, J. E., 218

Anemia, 59, 64, 68

Archer, D., 14

Ardrey, Robert, 321

Armor, Tlingit, 275–277, 325

Arrow points, 310, 312

Arrow(s), 275, 286, 322, 328
appearance on Northwest
Coast of, 273
as weapons of war, 310
bone, 276
chipped stone, 276
polished stone, 276
result of introduction of,
286, 325
with points of ground slate,
276

Arrowheads, 312

Art, as evidence of war, 325

Assailants, cultural factors and
the use of weapons by, 161

Assault(s), 3, 14, 15, 33, 161, 162
definition of, 4
frequencies of, 13
nonfatal, 162
of non-spouses, 160
physical, among women, 36
violent, age-sex relationship,
162
with blunt object or fist, 161

Axes
    as weapons of war, 311
    LBK, 306–308, 310–312

B

Backswords, 170, 171

Bamforth, Even, 342

Baranof, Alexander, 276

Barker Arroyo site(s), 58, 59, 63

Battering, 37, 69

Battles, over material resources,
    99

Behavior
    aggressive, 146
    nonviolent 145
    violent, 145, 146

Bella Bella 288, 291

Bennett's fracture, 120

Birkner, F., 186

Black eyes, 160

Black Mesa, 63–65, 69
    burials, 63
    health profile of, 64, 65
    lifestyle, 70

Black Mesa trauma, inventory
    of, 63

Blood feuds, 211; See also Raids,
    organized

Bludgeon wounds, 188–192
    evidence of, 192
    frequencies at Ofnet, 192, 193
    location and orientation
        of, 195–197
    sex/age distribution of,
        192–195

Bludgeoning, perimortem, 326

Bone(s)
    animal/human, 181, 220
    cutmarks on, 222
    cuts of, 222–223
    cuts on, 222–223
    damage, 222, 226, 270, 326
    exposure to heat of, 223, 228,
        235
    histology of, 223
    intentional breakage of,
        218, 219
    polishing, 219
    preservations, 131
    projectile, 277, 295
    scars, 189
    techniques to break fresh, 223

Bone modification, 234, 236, 257
    evidence in Ancient Mexico
        for, 217–237

Bone points, 277, 286, 295
    armor-piercing, 325

Bone scraps, isolated, 131

Boule, M., 186

Bow(s), 275, 277, 286, 325, 328
    appearance on Northwest
        Coast of, 273
    with points of ground slate,
        276

Boxer's fracture, 120–123

Boxing, 163, 168, 170–173, 330
    and cultural patterning of
        violence, 145–179
    in Olympic Games, 170
    See also Violence, patterns, of

Brain herniation, 52

Braniff, C. B., 219, 221

Breuil, H., 186

Broken noses 172; *See also* Violence, cultural patterning of

Bronze Age, 131, 134, 135, 139

Burial(s), 23, 28, 51, 113, 115, 120, 323
  Black Mesa, 63
  bundle, 244
  casual disposal, 323
  group, 38
  location, 53
  multiple, 98, 323
  multiple-individual, primary, 39
  of Big Sandy, 255
  of Kays Landing, 253
  of Santa Barbara Channel Area, 81, 93
  of Wetherill Mesa, 47
  ossuary-type, 38
  partial, 39
  practices, 131, 219
  preparation in ancient populations for, 181
  records, 93, 94
  rites, 38
  secondary, 38, 244, 323, 324
  sex ratio of, 115
  single primary, 131
  subsurface, 273
  treatment for males, 62

Burial remains, as evidence for interpersonal conflict, 81

Burning, 49, 222

Butchering, 211, 223, 224

C

Cannibalism, 47, 181, 182, 211, 218, 324, 327, 328
  codex representations of, 219
  criteria for proposal of, 219
  difficulties in documenting, 219
  gustatory, 324
  in Southwest US, 235
  perimortem, 234
  sites in Ancient Mexico indicating, 213–237
  skeletal evidence for, 224–234
  written references of, 219

Cemeteries, 208, 271
  Mesolithic, 207

Cemetery samples, 242

Chagnon, N., 330

Chiefdoms, 102, 329

Club fights, 89, 329

Clubs, 84, 171, 275

Codex representations, of cannibalism, 219

Colles', fracture 116, 120, 123, 134

Colonization, in North European plains, 303

Combat, 337
  physical, 323
  sports, 171

Conflict, 273, 276, 286, 335, 336
  evidence in Middle Pacific, 272
  first evidence on Northwest Coast, 267
  identification of processes indicating, 81
  in hunter and gatherer societies, 269
  intergroup, 256, 329
  inter-village, 47
  local, 331
  patterns of, 81
  violent, 285, 292, 315

violent group, 322
Wooley's view on early
    historic, 290
Conservation procedure, for
    material from sites at Ofnet,
    188
Consumption, ritualized, 324
Copper Age, 137, 138
Corporeal treatment, 225
Corpse
    manipulation, earliest
        evidence in Mexico of, 218
    processing, 222–224
Coupland's linear relationship,
    285
Cranial depressions, 24, 25
    basic diagnostic criteria of, 83
    variation in size and
        dimension of, 62
Cranial injuries, 65, 84, 163, 165,
    166, 170, 171
    and age, 159
    at San Cristobal, 49
    descriptive data on, 29, 30
    due to automobile accidents,
        164
    female prepondernce of, 33
    frequency estimates in males
        of, 28
    frequency in populations and
        distribution on the skull,
        164
    frequency of, 166
    healed, 157
    in Santa Barbara Channel
        Area, 167
    nonlethal, 146, 147
    sub-lethal, in Aborigine
        societies, 89

Cranial sample, distribution of
    age at death of, 25, 26
Cranial trauma, 55, 57–59, 62,
    65, 68, 128, 132, 134, 137–139
    146, 159, 162, 166, 327, 329
    due to interpersonal violence,
        134
    healed, 115, 117
    high frequency of, 68
    in Yakuts, 173
    inventory by sex, 48
    nonlethal, 151, 154
    observations, 24
    rate of, 134
    violence as main cause of, 163
Cranial vault, blunt trauma to, 153
Cranial vault fractures
    distribution of healed, 158
    frequency of, 90
    perimortem, 89
    sub-lethal, 89, 90
Cranial vault injuries, 149, 153,
    156
    in females, 89
Cranial wound, identification of
    weapon producing, 191
Cremations, 38, 244
    pit 249
Cribra orbitalia, 100, 101, 115,
    125, 126
Crime(s)
    punishment for, 15
    statistics on, 13
Cross-cultural research, 10, 16
Cross-national studies, 10, 14
Crow Creek, 97
    massacre, 245, 329
    intergroup violence in, 37

Cudgels, 170, 171

Cutmarks, 170, 188, 189, 218, 219, 221, 233, 234, 244, 245, 249–251, 253, 255, 259
associated with mortuary activity, 246
associated with perimortem violent trauma, 246
associated with scalping, 246
at hip, 248
blade induced, 246
circumferential, 246
cranial, 197–202, 253
disrimination of, 246
interpretation of, 246, 247
macroscopic, 244
oblique, 232
on Bodo cranium, 181
on bones, 222
on cervical vertebrae, 202–205
on external surface, 228
on face, 224
on mandibles, 222, 224, 232
on postcranial skeleton, 225, 226
on skull, 224, 225
on temporal region, 229
on vault, 224
perimortem, 201, 205, 247
prevalent, 230
reasons for, 230, 232
regions of, 230, 232, 234
shallow, 206
short stroke, 247
tangential, 230

D

Daggers, 275
Dart, 322

Death, 153
due to blunt instruments, 171
due to hitting and kicking, 171, 172
skeletal evidence of, 270
violent; *See* Violent death

Decapitation, 209, 218, 219, 236, 241, 250, 255, 272
earliest example of, 242
osteoarchaeological identification of, 246

Defensible locations, 286, 325

Defensive architecture, 47, 112, 135, 136

Defensive ditches, 307

Defensive site(s), 267, 268, 278–281, 286, 287
construction, 283, 286
earliest, 278
in south east Alaska, 281
in southern Northwest Coast, 281
on north end of Kuiu Island, 278
palisaded enclosures, 271
relationship between village and, 281

Defleshing, 218, 222, 223, 234, 236, 244, 247, 249, 253, 258, 324
cutmark diagnostic of, 245, 246

Developmental Stage; *See* Pacific Period

Digging sticks, 63

Disarticulation, 247, 248

Dismemberment, 218, 219, 222, 223, 244, 247, 249, 258

individual, 49
mortuary-related, 245, 246
postmortem, 328
ritualized, 47
trophy-taking, 244, 246
Duels, 89

E

Early (Lithic) Period, 270–272,
Early Neolithic, frontier warfare
in, 303–317
Early Pacific Period, 270–272,
283
El Riego Phase, 218
Embankments, earthen, 286
Ember, Carol R. 3, 6, 8, 324, 330,
331, 336, 345
Ember, Melvin, 3, 6, 8, 324, 330,
331, 336, 345
Enamel hypoplasia, 115, 125,
126
Eneolithic (Copper Age), 130,
135, 137
Ethnographic record,
implications for prehistory,
16, 17

F

Falls, 83, 161–163
in children and the elderly,
163
in the elderly, 168
Farmer-forager interaction, 304,
307
Farming,
LBK 313

settlements, first
appearance of, 303
Faulhaber, J., 218
Fear, 71
of unpredictable disasters, 8
Ferguson, R. Brian, 22, 40, 78, 80,
81, 98, 105, 106, 242, 260, 268,
269, 287, 290, 298, 321, 325,
328, 330, 331, 335–339,
341–346, 348–350
Feuds, 15, 21, 91
Fist fighting, 172
Foragers (hunters-gatherers;
prehistoric food collectors), 2,
3, 5, 6, 8, 12, 17, 113, 327
Late Mesolothic, 306, 308
nonpacified, 10, 11
versus food-producers, 11
Foraging
and prevalence of
war, 10–13
societies, 2, 6
versus food-production, 17
Formative (Preclassic) Period,
220, 221
Fortification(s), 234, 271, 307,
309, 312, 325, 327, 332
defensive, 274, 277
second, 279
Tlingit, 274
Fracture(s), 24, 25, 33, 128, 223,
323
accidental, 83
Bennett's, 120
Boxer's, 120, 121, 123
clavicle, 48
Colles', 116, 120, 123, 134
compression, 190

cranial, 23, 25, 35, 53, 99, 123, 162
cranial vault, 78, 89, 90, 158, 164; *See also* Healed cranial vault fractures
defensive, 272
defensive forearm "parry", 272
depressed cranial vault, 81, 82–90, 95
depressed skull, 48, 190, 272
depression, 48, 52, 55, 83, 151, 190
dry bone, 223
due to assault, 162
due to stress, 126
evidence for cranial, 33
facial, 116
factors for analyzing, 223
female skull, 28
femur, 48, 123
frequencies of, 31
frequency in Mississipian populations, 35
fresh bone, 223
frontal, 31
head, 62
healed, 86–88, 90, 120, 121; *See also* Healed fractures
healed nasal bones, 155, 156
helical, 223, 228, 235
hinge, 190
humerus, 48
intentional, 221, 225, 234
linear, 117, 153
linear cranial vault, 83
mandibular, 162–164
multiple, 55, 64, 123
nasal, 154, 171, 173; *See also* Nasal fractures
occipital depression, 58
of dry bone, 223

of fresh bone, 223
of long bones, 134, 226
of radius, 48
on skull, 224, 225
parry, 33, 134, 245, 272, 323
patterns of, 223
pond, 33
postcranial, 33, 48, 55
postmortem, 24, 85, 218
prehistoric, 31
radiating, 225
reasons for, 323
rib, 120
spiral, 223
vehicular, 31
zygomatic, 158, 162, 163
Fracture(s), perimortem, 25, 53, 84, 86, 117, 323
compound, 85
depressed, 116
Frayer, David, 306, 317, 323, 326
Frontier violence, evidence in Early Neolithic of, 306–312

G
Gladiators, 123
Grave goods, 53, 59, 64, 69, 113, 134–136, 257
"Green bone", 246
Gunshot wounds, 161

H
Haida warfare, 288
Haillak, 174
Hand-to-hand combat, 49
Hatchets, 209
Head injury, 51, 52

Head trauma, 83, 162

Head-hunting, 306

Healed cranial trauma, 62

Healed cranial vault
fractures, 86–88, 90, 120,
121
frequency of, 86–88
temporal variation of, 90

Healed fractures, 27, 53, 56,
57, 84
age-related changes in, 159
of nasal bones, 155, 156

Healed trauma, frequency in
La Plata, 53, 57

Helmets, 275

Hides, 311–312

Hitting, 161

Holes, 190

Homicide, 3, 181–183,
211, 326, 333
definition of, 4
due to blunt
instruments, 172
evidence in skeletons
indicating, 183
frequenies of, 13, 14
in pre-state groups, 182
individual, 333
victims of, 306, 312

Homicide and assault, 16
as consequence of
socialization, 15
by legitimizing violence
in war, 16

Homicide rates, 136
following a war, 15

"Honor and shame"
ideology, 127

Human manipulations, 222

Human sacrifice 324, 327
criteria for, 219
difficulties in documenting,
219
evidence in Ancient Mexico,
217–237

Human victims, ceremonial
treatment of, 219

Humerus varus, 115

Hunters-gatherers (foragers)
79, 242
burial objects of, 78

Hunters, equestrian, 182

Hunting, 276, 284, 287

Hyperostosis frontalis interna
115

Hypoplasias, 64

Hypoplastic defects, 58

I

Infant mortality, 114

Infection, 24, 64, 65, 68
and skull surface
irregularities, 154
systemic, 59, 126

Inflicted projectile point(s), 241,
242, 244, 247, 250

Inhumations
Iron Age, 131
multiple, 131
primary, 38

Injured women, 27, 28

Injuries, 78, 81
absolute frequency of, 154
accidental, 33, 34, 163, 164,
168, 169

and trauma, 47
Black Mesa, 64
blunt weapon, 190
bodily, 94
boxing, 170
cranial, 31, 32, 329
craniofacial, 163
distribution by age and sex, 25
facial, 161
frontal bone, 32, 154, 156
healed, 84
healed traumatic, 165
identification of nonlethal, 151–154
intentional, 49
limb, 94
location and severity of, 28–34
multiple, 36
non-lethal, 146, 147, 267, 330
non-penetrating, 83
parietal, 32, 156
perimortem, 190, 205, 206
postcranial traumatic, 120
rates, 97
ratio of assault to accidental, 163
relation to sex, 158
severity of, 33
spatial distribution of, 328
sports, 169
to the head, 162
trauma responsible for, 182
traumatic healing, 64
victims of physical, 36
violence and fear of, 65
See also Cranial injuries
See also Cranial vault injuries
See also Nasal injuries
See also Projectile injuries
See also Traumatic injuries

Intentional blows, on skull, 224, 225
Intentional breakage, of bones, 222, 226
Intentional breaks, of diaphyses, 228
Intentional violence, 70, 71, 162
    osteological evidence of, 53–65
Intergroup aggression, resource stress as a cause of, 98
Intergroup conflict, 256, 329
Intergroup relations, 338
Intergroup violence, 22, 36, 242, 250
    ethnographic descriptions of, 36
    methods for establishing 222–224
    occurrence of subadult victims of, 244
Interpersonal violence, 14, 22, 33, 37, 123, 138, 145, 160–163, 167, 168, 182, 245, 271, 272, 322, 323, 325, 328, 332, 343
    cranial trauma as evidence of, 22
    cross-cultural studies of, 13
    data on patterns of, 145
    evidence for, 322
    example in prehistory of, 184
    frequency of, 166
    in an Australian Aborigine population, 36
    injuries to head and neck, 160
Inter-village conflict, 47
Intra-group politics, 136

Intra-sex competition, 37

Iron Age, Italy, 128, 129, 131, 135, 138

K

Keeley, L., 324, 327, 342

Kentucky Lake Sample, 242–244

Kicking, 161, 168

Killings, 35
multiple projectile, 323
organized, 333

Knives, 162

Kolosha [Tlingit], 288

Kuiu Island Project, 277–287

L

La Plata Valley, 53–63, 69
burials 53, 59
enamel defects in females of, 58
infection in females of, 58
frequency of trauma and disease at, 65
pattern of violence in, 67, 70
population of, 67

Lacerations of the forehead and eyebrow, 163

Lambert, P. M., 82, 112, 292, 322, 328–330

Late Mesolithic foragers, 306, 308

Late Pacific Period, 270, 272, 273–277, 283, 295,

villages on Northwest Coast, 282, 283

Lesions, 84
ante-mortem cranial, 84
lytic, 56
nontraumatic origin of, 154
osseous, 151
traumatic, 116

Limestone maces, 209

Lithic (Early) Period, 270–272

Lithic Stage, 270

Little Ice Age, 275

LBK (Linienband-keramik), 327
adzes, 306–308, 310–312
axes, 306–308, 310–312
cemeteries, 304, 306, 310
ceramics, 312
collective violence, 316
colonization, 304, 312
culture, 312
enclosure, 307, 314, 317
farmers, 304, 308, 313, 316, 317
faunal assemblages, 309
in Northwestern Europe, 304, 305
livestock of, 304
settlements, 306, 307, 310, 312, 313
staple crops of, 304
stone tools, 304
subsistence economy, 304
villages, 311, 313
warfare, 314
weapons, 306

Locations, defensible, 286

Locations, defensive, 274, 275

Looting, 335

M

Maasyuk (popular Yakuts game), 173

Maces, 325

Male
  gender ideology, in the Neolithic/Eneolithic transition, 131
  hexis, 127
  honor, 127
  status heirarchies, 136
  violent behavior with reference to cultural structures, 138

Mandibles, blows on, 228

Mansilla Lory, J., 219

Martin, D. L., 52, 330, 338

Maschner, H. D. G., 275, 285, 325, 326, 328, 330, 337, 342

Mass graves, 183, 184, 211

Mass killings, 49, 184, 210, 211

Massacre
  at Hopi, 245
  Crow Creek, 245, 259, 329
  evidence of, 326
  Talheim, 209

Maya, wars of, 322

Mesolithic
  burial samples, 306
  cemeteries, 207
  massacre, 181–212
  See also Northwestern Europe

Middle Pacific Period, 270, 272, 273, 283, 295
  villages on Northwest Coast, 282, 283

Mission Period, life in early, 80

Mollison, T., 186, 188, 89, 193, 205, 209

Mortuary
  behavior, 247–250
  configuration, diagrammatic representation, 60, 61
  flexure, 247, 249
  practices, 250
  remains, 81
  treatment, 244, 247, 257, 258

Muscle insertion markings, 115

Musket balls, 276

Mutilation, 181
  facial, 235
  perimortem, 245

Myositis ossificans, post-traumatic, 128

N

Nasal bones, 154, 162

Nasal fractures, 48, 154, 160, 162, 163, 168, 169
  analysis of, 149
  due to falls, 164
  in 16th–18th century Spanish crania I, 171
  in early 20th century Americans, 172
  in Yakuts, 173
  sports as common cause of, 169

Nasal injuries 156, 165, 170
  frequency in late nineteenth century burials, 169
  in Yakuts, 173

Neolithic, 130, 134, 135, 139
   cases, of peninsular Italy, 128
   societies, 137
   villages, 136

Nonforagers, 5, 8, 11

Non-lethal blows, 51, 68

Nonpacified cases, 14

Nootka warfare, 287

Nootkan wars, 291

Northwest Coast
   archaeological division of,
      268
   ethnographic division of, 268
   evidence for prehistoric
      warfare in, 270
   potential causes of warfare in,
      268
   potlatches, 338
   projectile points on, 276
   raids, 282
   revenge warfare, 288

Northwest Coast warfare
   causes of, 268,
      287–288
   ethnographic data on,
      288–291
   evolution of, 267–297
   prehistory of, 270–277
   result of long-term, 292

Northwestern Europe, 304, 305

O

Occupational specializations,
   in early Italy, 123

Occupational stress, 66

Ofnet, 327
   conservation procedure at,
      188

dating of material, 187
demographic aspects of,
   207–210
evidence for a Mesolithic
   Massacre, 181–212
Mollison's interpretations,
   189
pits, 208
skulls, 198, 326
specimens, cutmarks on, 201
"trophy" skulls, 306

Ossification of tendons, 120

Ossuary, 221, 222

Osteological collections, from
   North American Plains, 242

Osteomyelitis, 56, 115

Osteophytes, 59, 66

P

Pacification, 2, 43, 331

Palaeopathology Association,
   130

Paleopathology,
   warfare-associated, 242

Palisades, 274, 279, 286, 307

Palynology, 304

Parry fractures, 33, 134, 245, 323

Pathological lesions, 53

Perimortem
   bludgeoning, 326
   cutmarks, 201, 205
   damage, 24
   fractures; See Fracture(s),
      perimortem
   holes, 190
   snapping, 246
   trauma, 183, 187, 189, 205, 256

treatment, earliest evidence in Mexico, 218
trophy-taking, 251
violence, 188–192
violent trauma, warfare-associated, 241, 244
wounds, 192, 195, 196

Perimortem injuries, 190, 205
earliest recorded case of, 183
evidence for, 205–206

Period
Early Pacific, 270–272
Early (Lithic), 270–272
Late Pacific, 270, 272, 273–277, 295,
Middle Pacific, 270, 272, 273, 283, 295
Pacific, 270
Postclassic, 219
Preclassic, 220, 221
Mission, 80

Physical repression, 112

Pijoan Aguadé, C. M., 219, 324

Pit cremations, 249

Pits, stratigraphic, 220

Point(s)
armor-piercing bone, 286, 325
arrow 310, 312
bone, 277, 295
bone-embedded, 322
chipped-stone, 277
projectile, 182, 309, 329, 340
slate, 277

Police assaults, 160

Pontecagnano (Picentia) 113–115, 121, 123–127, 130

Post-burial preservation, 131

Postcranial trauma, 138, 55, 57, 59, 65, 128, 134, 138, 323
at Pontecagnano, 121
Eneolithic, 138
Neolithic, 138

Postmortem damage, 83

Postmortem holes, 190

Pot boiling, White's analysis of, 226

Potlatches, 338, 339

Prehistoric skeletal material, 22

Prehistoric societies, 146

Prehistoric violence, 112, 182, 321–344

Prizefighting, 171, 172

Projectile
bone, 277, 295
patterns of violence, 93
penetrating, 323
points, 182, 309, 329, 340
See also Killings
See also Northwest Coast

Projectile injuries, 82, 90–98
age and sex classes of, 95
depressed cranial vault fractures, 98
frequency by age and sex group, 95, 96
lethal, 99
temporal variation in, 97
types of, 91

Pseudarthrosis, 123

Pseudospeciation, cultural, 333, 334

Pueblo culture, 46, 65, 69

Punching, 161

Punishments, in Yakuts, 173

R

Raids, 68, 91, 289, 335
  aim of, 211
  in prehistoric
    Michigan, 21–43
  on Northwest Coast, 282, 293
  organized, 211
  reasons for, 270

Rape of Lucretia, 127

Refuges; See Site(s), defensive

Resource stress model, 99, 102

Revenge warfare; See Northwest
  Coast warfare

Revenge wars, 288, 289
  Kwakiutl intratribal, 288
  result of, 289
  Southern Coast Salish, 289
  Tsimshian, 288

Riviere aux Vase, 22, 23, 34, 38
  injured women from, 34, 38
  palaeodemographic
    reconstructions of, 24
  prehistoric intergroup
    violence in, 37
  severe injuries in females 34
  skeletal remains 24, 25–28

Robb, John, 111, 115, 124, 128,
  131, 134, 136, 137, 139, 143,
  325–327

S

Sacrifice
  human, 217–237, 324, 327
  ritual, 324, 328

Samnite wars, 124

San bands 2, 3

San Luis phase, 221

Santa Barbara Channel Area,
  79, 80–82, 89, 97, 98
  archeological sites 79, 81
  burials 81, 93
  mortuary remains from 82
  paleoclimatic conditions in
    100
  prehistoric hunter-gatherer
    (foraging) societies of 78
  skeletal series of, 84

Scalping 49, 241, 242, 244, 245,
  251, 253, 255, 257, 323
  at Grasshopper Ruin, 49
  at Navakwewtaqa, 49
  cutmarks associated with, 246
  occurrence of, 242

Scars, 84
  in bone surfaces, 91
  on bone, 94

Schmorl's nodes, 124–126

Secondary burials; See Burials,
  secondary

Sedentism, 270, 329, 334–336,
  339, 343

Settlement, LBK, 313

Settlement patterns, 112, 325
  as indicators of conflict, 281

Shell middens, 273, 278
  appearance of earliest, 271
  sites of, 271, 272
  stratified deposits of, 278

Site(s)
  defensive 267, 268, 271,
    273–275, 278, 286, 287, 325
  fortification 277

fortified, 273
Miller Fort, 281
trench-embankment, 274
village, 278

Skeletal assemblages, 47

Skeletal collections, 163

Skeletal evidence for human
health, 100

Skeletal injuries, 162
and violent behavior, 146

Skeletal lesions, due to
childhood iron-deficiency
anemia, 101

Skeletal remains, 93, 112, 187,
218, 277
analysis of, 51, 52
as evidence of war, 322
human, 146, 147
of fourteenth century Indians,
35
of Riviere aux vase, 24, 25–28

Skeletal trauma 112, 324
at Pontecagnano (Picentia),
113–115, 123–127

Skeleton(s), 120, 132, 146
age and sex determination of
149, 150
analyses of, 113
completeness of, 149
determination of age-trauma
relationship from, 124
differential preservation
problems, 149
Shanidar Neanderthal, 182

Skhul IX, 183

Skinning, 223, 234, 236

Skull(s), 153
cutmarks on 224, 225

disarticulated 323
fractures on 224, 225
fragments, 221
intentional blows on, 224, 225
isolated, 38
marks on, 146
nests, 184, 188
Ofnet, 198
perforations of, 229
rack, 222, 229, 236
stages of depressed fractures
of, 83
trophy, 25
Zhoukoudian, 182

Slave, 289, 291
raiders 289, 290
traders 290

Slavery 38
institutionalized, 268

Smith, Maria Ostendorf,
323, 328, 336

Social stratification, 138, 257

Societies
"foragers", 6
matrilocal, 9
"mixed", 6
nonpacified, 5, 7, 15
nonstate, 8, 16
pacified, 5, 7
"pastoral" 6,
polygamous, 36
pre-capitalist, 9
traditional subsistence, 67

Spears, 275, 276

Specialized war clubs, 325

Sports, 160
injuries, 163
warlike, 15

Stelae, 218

Stickfighting, 171

Stone points; 91

Stone tools, LBK, 304

Stratification, social, 257

Stratigraphic pits, 220

Subsistence, 329
  farming, 68
  in Tebenkof Bay, 283
  on Northwest Coast, 283–285
  open-water fishing, 283, 284,
    287

Swords, 325

T

Talheim massacre, 209

Traffic accidents, 168

Trauma, 48, 51, 125, 127, 174,
  330, 332
  "accidental" 182
  and lifestyle, 124
  and post-cranial pathology,
    53
  and violence in the Southeast,
    46–53
  at Black Mesa, 50
  at Pontecagnano, 115–123,
    125, 137
  blunt, 250, 259
  blunt force, 244
  blunt impact, 117
  blunt instument, 84
  causes of modern, 159, 160
  common loci for, 120
  cranio-facial, 245
  cultural causes of, 127, 128
  due to occupational hazard,
    55

  evidence of recovery from, 51
  gender distribution of, 127, 128
  healed blunt, 247
  in Italian prehistory, 128–137
  in La Plata River Valley 50, 54
  in the Copper Age, 128
  in the female subpopulation,
    68
  incidence, 134, 162
  infection or complications of,
    123
  "inflicted", 182
  injuries, 24, 53, 123, 182
  lesions, 56, 124, 131, 133, 139,
    205
  localized to soft tissues, 120
  measure of, 132
  methods of assessment and
    analysis of, 52
  multiple patterns of, 127
  non-lethal, 245
  osteological evidence of, 45
  perimortem, 183, 187, 189,
    205, 247, 256
  probability in complete
    specimens, 133, 134
  rate, 131, 138
  regions of, 131, 132
  repeated low-grade, 126
  resulting from interpersonal
    violence, 271
  severe, 154
  skeletal, 112, 135, 332
  studies of ancient, 149
  to lower limbs, 120
  urban craniofacial, 162
  See also Black Mesa trauma
  See also Cranial trauma
  See also Healed cranial trauma
  See also Healed trauma
  See also Postcranial trauma
  See also Violent trauma

See also Warfare-related trauma

Trauma, patterns of
and culture, 127, 128
and weapon technolgy, 166
in Italian prehistory,
    ethnograpey, 137
in skeletal collections,
    154–159
in the American Southwest,
    46

Tribal zones, 338

Trophy, 209, 258, 328

Trophy-taking, 244, 245, 252,
    257, 258
dismemberment, 246
forearm, 242, 255, 257
in Archaic hunter-gatherers,
    257
perimortem, 251

Tzompantli, 222, 236

V

Village(s)
consolidation of 328
LBK 311, 313
"non-knapping" 311
on Northwest Coast 282–283
sedentary, 268
sites, 281

Violence 13, 49, 137, 139, 181,
    322, 332
among Australian Aborigines
    38
among non-Western peoples
    22
and aggression, 21
and gender, in early Italy
    111–117

and hierarchical structures,
    138
and political symbolization,
    138
and warfare in non-industrial
    societies, 81
archaeological signs in
    prehistoric and early
    historic Italy, 135
as form of social control, 112
blunt weapon, 33
collective, 322
direct, 127
direct skeletal evidence of, 35
domestic, 37, 69
ethnographic record of, 120
family, 36
frequency of, 15
gender segregationo in, 137
iconography of, 135
identificaion of, 322–326, 344
in comtemporary society, 71
in foraging societies, 271
in horticultural groups, 182
in hunter-gatherer groups,
    182
in modern Americans,
    167–169
in prehistory, 181, 321–344
in pre-state groups, 182
in the early Mission Period,
    103
indigenous sources of, 342
individual, 322
intergroup, 242, 244, 245, 250
interhuman, 222–224
intra-group, 36
legitimized
    during wartime, 15
lethal, 90, 97–100, 102, 329,
    333
level of, 139, 165

Marxist views on, 112
modern projectile versus
    prehistoric, 94
non-lethal, 329, 344
organized practice of, 128
osteological record, 51, 327
perceived threat of 136
perimortem, 188–192, 234
personal, 332
prehistoric, 112, 182, 183
quantitative approach in
    Italian prehistory, 128–137
ritualization of, 166
role in society, 138
semantics of, 111
skeletal evidence for,
    145–179, 224–234
skeletal indicators of, 81
social and cultural context in
    early Italy, 112, 113
sporadic, 39
sub-lethal, 100
temporal and spatial
    variations of, 166
unorganized (spontaneous
    fighting), 128
urban, 166
variations in, 138
victims of, 39
warfare-related, 127
within society, 25
See also Intentional violence
See also Intergroup violence
See also Interpersonal violence
See also Projectile violence
Violence against women, 46, 69,
    70, 136, 329, 330
degree of, 68
in La Plata River valley,
    45–75
in prehistoric Michigan,
    21–43

Violence, patterns of, 134, 139,
    145, 170–173
collections studied indicating,
    147–149
cultural differences in, 146
cultural-historical factors
    determining, 165
in Coastal Southern
    California, 77–109
in modern groups, 78
in prehistoric hunter-gatherer
    (foraging) societies, 77–109
research methods used for
    studying, 147–149
systemic analysis of skeletal
    evidence for, 174, 175

Violent assaults, 83

Violent combat sports, 170

Violent conflict, 82, 98, 315
archaeological studies of, 80
domestic, 172
evidence in skeletal remains
    for, 78
in modern groups, 80
in prehistoric societies, 78
mortuary evidence for, 82–98
on Northwest Coast in Early
    Pacific, 285
resource stress as a cause of,
    99

Violent death, 251, 307, 308

Violent injury, skeletal evidence
    of, 270

Violent sports, 170

Violent trauma, 245, 246,
    250–256, 272
at or before death, 120
criteria for, 245, 246
deliberate, 250
hunter-gatherer,

conflict-related, 245
perimortem, 244, 246, 250, 259

W

Walker, P. 36, 52, 68, 84, 101,
    112, 292, 323, 330
War(s)
adultery as a cause of, 290
American Indian, 92
and aggression, 1–20
and violence, 15
as a relationship between
    groups, 337
captives, 324, 329
causes of, 2
climatic change as a reason of
    340
cross-cultural studies of, 1–20
definition of, 3
evidence of, 323–325, 330,
    332
external, 3
for economic reasons, 9
frequency of, 5, 6, 11, 16
goal of, 335
identification of, 322–326, 344
in prehistory, 321–344
influence of, 325
internal 3, 9, 10, 12, 13
interpersonal, 343
maintenance of, 242
Nootkan, 291
of the Maya, 322
origin of, 242
paraphernalia in Late Pacific,
    275
predicting variation in
    frequency of, 6–10
prevalence of, 2, 5, 10, 16
reasons for, 270, 336

Samnite, 124
territorial, 291
trophies, 323
Tsimshian, 288
weapons, specialized, 325
women as cause of, 290

Warfare 45, 113, 127, 211, 267,
    274, 292, 331, 333, 337, 339
ancient, 334–337
Blackman's views on, 288, 291
Boyd's views on, 291
chronic, 47
Codere's views on, 287
cross-cultural results of, 9, 10
direct violence in, 138
economic consequences of, 9
endemic, 256
ethnographic record of, 4
evidence of, 312, 330, 335
external, 9
Ferguson's views on, 287
frequency of, 3–5, 7, 11, 12, 17
global, 341
Haida, 288
Holmberg's views on, 289
in Early Neolithic, 303–317
in Native American groups,
    35
in Western Tennessee Valley,
    osteological indications,
    241–259
intergroup, 91, 139, 274
internal 9, 11
Kamenskii's views on, 289
LBK, 314
low-level, 329
modern tribal, 94
Nootka, 287
on Kuiu Island, 287
on Northwest Coast, 267–294
pervasive, 341
prehistoric, 315

pre-state, 315
primitive, 315
reasons for, 257, 293
Southern Kwakiutl, 287
Swadesh's views on, 287
Veniaminov's views on, 288
See also Northwest Coast
    warfare

Warfare-related trauma, 241,
245, 250, 259

Weapons, 49, 83, 84, 112, 134,
136, 325
and Iron Age. 136
blunt, 209, 329
differences in use of, 162
in Middle Pacific, 272
sharp, 162
specialized, 332
symbolism of, 137, 138

Weathering, 246
in situ, 119, 120
White's "fracture antiquity"
    criteria, 119

Wife beating, 15, 160, 172
and cultural patterning of
    violence, 145–179
patterns of soft tissue injury,
    161

Wilkinson, R. G., 46, 112, 323,
329, 330

Witchcraft, 47

Women
conflict among, 36
See also Societies, polygamous

Wound(s)
bludgeon, 192
cranial, 191, 62
gunshot, 161
head, 206
healed, 182
multiple, 94
non-lethal, 94
perimortem, 183, 192, 195, 196
post-cranial, 62
postmortem factors resulting
    in, 196
premortem, 206
projectile 78, 81, 93
stab, 244, 245

Written references of
cannibalism; *See* Cannibalism

Y

Yakuts, 173, 174
Yanomami, 330, 338

Lightning Source UK Ltd.
Milton Keynes UK
UKOW022134131011

180237UK00003B/14/P